MW00857062

MODERN ODYSSEYS

CLASSICAL MEMORIES/MODERN IDENTITIES

Paul Allen Miller and Richard H. Armstrong, Series Editors

MODERN ODYSSEYS

*Cavafy, Woolf, Césaire, and a
Poetics of Indirection*

∼

MICHELLE ZERBA

THE OHIO STATE UNIVERSITY PRESS
COLUMBUS

Copyright © 2021 by The Ohio State University.
All rights reserved.

Library of Congress Cataloging-in-Publication Data
Names: Zerba, Michelle, 1953– author.
Title: Modern odysseys : Cavafy, Woolf, Césaire, and a poetics of indirection / Michelle Zerba.
Other titles: Classical memories/modern identities.
Description: Columbus : The Ohio State University Press, [2021] | Series: Classical memories/ modern identities | Includes bibliographical references and index. | Summary: "Explores the relationships between antiquity and modernity through C. P. Cavafy, Virginia Woolf, and Aimé Césaire's engagement with Odyssean tropes"—Provided by publisher.
Identifiers: LCCN 2020036595 | ISBN 9780814214640 (cloth) | ISBN 0814214649 (cloth) | ISBN 9780814280980 (ebook) | ISBN 0814280986 (ebook)
Subjects: LCSH: Homer. Odyssey—Influence. | Cavafy, Constantine, 1863–1933—Criticism and interpretation. | Woolf, Virginia, 1882–1941—Criticism and interpretation. | Césaire, Aimé—Criticism and interpretation. | Modernism (Literature) | Literature, Modern— History and criticism. | Classical literature—Influence.
Classification: LCC PN56.M54 Z46 2021 | DDC 883/.01—dc23
LC record available at https://lccn.loc.gov/2020036595

Cover design by Laurence J. Nozik
Text design by Juliet Williams
Type set in Adobe Minion Pro

♾ The paper used in this publication meets the minimum requirements of the American National Standard for Information Sciences—Permanence of Paper for Printed Library Materials. ANSI Z39.48-1992.

For my father

As a woman, I have no country. As a woman, I want no country. As a woman, my country is the whole world.

—Virginia Woolf, *Three Guineas*

Master of the three paths, you have before you a man who has walked a lot . . . who has walked on his hands walked on his feet walked on his belly walked on his ass. From Elam. From Akkad. From Sumer.

Maître des trois chemins, tu as en face de toi un homme qui a beaucoup marché . . . qui a marché sur les mains marché sur les pieds marché sur le ventre marché sur le cul. Depuis Elam. Depuis Akkad. Depuis Sumer.

—Aimé Césaire, "From Akkad from Elam from Sumer" ("*Depuis Akkad depuis Elam depuis Sumer*")

And now what's to become of us without barbarians. Those people were a sort of solution.

Καὶ τώρα τί θὰ γένουμε χωρὶς βαρβάρους. Οἱ ἄνθρωποι αὐτοὶ ἦσαν μιὰ κάποια λύσις.

—C. P. Cavafy, "Waiting for the Barbarians" ("Περιμένοντας τοὺς βαρβάρους)

CONTENTS

～

Acknowledgments ix

INTRODUCTION A Poetics of Indirection and Telling It Slant 1

CHAPTER 1 Diffusion and Mixture 27
Homer: The *Odyssey* in a Sea of Difference
Cavafy: Diaspora, Oblique Encounters, and Homoerotic Desire
Césaire: The Colonial Antilles and a Map of One's Own Spilled Blood
Woolf: Tilting at Pagans' Heads in a House That Is a Town

CHAPTER 2 Islands and Isolation 75
Homer: From Calypso to the Therapy of the Word
Cavafy: Cosmopolitan Isolation and Sexual Shaming
Woolf: Domestic *Katabasis* and Moments of Being
Césaire: Peléan Eruptions and Portraits of Blood

CHAPTER 3 Passage and Detour 115
Homer: Odysseus's Wound and Narrative Detours
Césaire: Lagoons of Blood and Literary Cannibalism
Woolf: Constantinople and Exile as Carnival
Cavafy: Mediterranean Routes and Ephebic Visions

CHAPTER 4 Return and Split Endings 161
Homer: Murder in the Home and Split Endings
Woolf: Time Warps and Wild Goose Chases
Césaire: The Incised Tree, the Slave Ship, and the Pirogue
Cavafy: Hedonic Ships on Policed Waters

EPILOGUE Toward an End 209

Bibliography 213

Index 233

ACKNOWLEDGMENTS

~

THERE ARE MANY who have helped make this book possible. The project began when I was a visiting scholar at Columbia University in 2014 under the auspices of the Institute for Comparative Literature and Society and with the sponsorship of my colleague Akeel Bilgrami. Early conversations with Suleymane Bachir Diagne oriented me in my work on Césaire. A grant from the National Endowment of the Humanities held at the American School of Classical Studies at Athens in 2016 and early 2017 gave me access to excellent research libraries where my work was supported by James Wright, Maria Georgopoulou, Irini Solomonidi, Maria Tourna, and Eleftheria Daleziou, among many others. During my time in Athens, I profited from the generosity and guidance of Diana Haas and Agis Marinis and from my conversations with Martin McKinsey. Thanks to Thodoris Chiotis and Dimitris Papanikolaou for facilitating access to the Cavafy Archive at the Onassis Foundation. My work on Cavafy has been enriched by Gregory Jusdanis, who has been generous in sharing his ongoing research on the Greek poet, and by the professional encouragement of Donald Mastronarde.

In 2017 and early 2018, a grant from the Partnership University Fund of the French government under the auspices of the Center of French and Francophone Studies at Louisiana State University enabled me to pursue a research and teaching collaboration with the University of the Antilles, Martinique, where my work was supported by Alexandre Leupin, Franck Collin, Dominique Aurelia, Liliane Fardin, and Florence Menez. During my residency on Martinique, I learned a great deal about Aimé Césaire from Alfred Alexandre. I also gained valuable knowledge about the cultural life of Martinique from speakers who presented their work at an international colloquium on Édouard Glissant held at the University of the Antilles, Martinique, in 2018.

Two Regents' Research Grants from Louisiana State University in 2014 and 2018 gave me valuable time off from teaching to pursue writing, and two travel grants from the Office of Research and Economic Development and the College of Humanities and Social Sciences in 2014 and 2017, respectively, enabled trips to Martinique and international conferences. At LSU, my work has been inspired and guided by Suzanne Marchand, James Stoner, Sharon Weltman, Alkis Tsolakis, and by a grant from the Center for Collaborative Knowledge. In the final stages of the manuscript, Casey Dué Hackney offered valuable comments on Homer and The Homer Multitext Project for which I am grateful. As always, my daughters, Claire and Rachel, have been my most devoted supporters, and to them I owe a great deal more than thanks. My father led me on my earliest journeys across the globe and opened my eyes to the need for telling it slant. To him I dedicate this book.

~

A Poetics of Indirection and Telling It Slant

QUESTIONS OF THEORY AND METHOD

The concept of "odyssey" has passed into common parlance in many places around the world. Evoking a journey of discovery that encompasses both physical and psychic challenges, it opens a vision of life that involves departure from home, travel to foreign lands, contact with ways of life beyond one's ken, and a return that may never let one settle back into the ordinary or domestic again. While odysseys may be trials that exercise us at the limits of our abilities, high jeopardy endeavors that arouse a thrill about new frontiers, or nightmarish ordeals of forced exile and wandering, they also hold out a promise that with endurance and survival comes enlightenment or at least enrichment. Even the odyssean descent to the underworld—the *katabasis*—typically involves a comeback, and after long years of waiting, those left behind, who have their own struggles, often meet up again with the wanderer, the exile, or the emigré, for better or worse.

Not surprisingly, the concept of odyssey has been widely marketed. These days, it provides a name for travel agencies, car models, publishing houses, drug rehabilitation facilities, recording companies, and NASA exploration programs. It has inspired road flicks, science fiction tales, adventure stories, westerns, comic book series, and pop songs. Metamorphic and resonant, the concept is equally at ease in high, middle, and lowbrow contexts, and this is only to mention its range in modern America and Europe. Over the two and a half millennia since Homer's *Odyssey*, it has shaped great pieces of literature, including Virgil's *Aeneid*, Dante's *Divine Comedy*, Cervantes's *Don Quixote*, Joyce's *Ulysses*, and Walcott's *Omeros*. It has also spun off a number of genres including romance, the picaresque novel, the travelogue, and the biography, to name a few. In the visual arts and music, the richness of its history is stunning. It has inspired works from Monteverdi's *Il Ritorno d'Ulisse in Patria* and Fauré's three-act opera *Pénélope* to Geoffrey Oryema's Ugandan-inspired album · *The African Odysseus*. Already in antiquity Odysseus's wanderings were a popular subject in vase painting,[1] and in the fifteenth and sixteenth centuries, they appeared on expensive Italian wedding chests and in monumental fresco cycles such as the one in the palace at Fontainebleau, which has not survived.[2] This was before the Pre-Raphaelites dipped deeply into the well centuries later, creating sumptuous visual representations of its female figures,[3] and artists of the Harlem Renaissance explored its contemporary resonances.[4] Homer's version has been translated into about seventy languages and dialects, a quarter of them dating from the mid-twentieth century, and it has stimulated interaction with non-Western cultures that have living oral traditions of poetry.[5]

Homer's epic of wandering is quite obviously in the world, and its avatars are identifiable. Recent work on the *Odyssey* in cultural history has demonstrated its remarkable resilience and currency across very different places and times.[6] Yet it is also a famously crafty story that prefers to approach its subject circuitously and often keeps us wondering. Its plot, characters, and forms of storytelling are sly. Odysseus is so well known for his "many turns" that Homer has an epithet for that quality—*polytropos*—and associates it with

1. Anthony Snodgrass, *Homer and the Artists: Text and Picture in Early Greek Art* (New York: Cambridge University Press, 1998); Steven Lowenstam, "The Uses of Vase-Descriptions in Homeric Studies," *Transactions of the American Philological Association* 122 (1992): 165–98; and "Talking Vases: The Relationship between the Homeric Poems and Archaic Representations of Epic Myth," *Transactions of the American Philological Association* 127 (1997): 21–76.

2. Michelle Zerba, "Renaissance Homer and Wedding Chests: The *Odyssey* at the Crossroads of Humanist Learning, the Visual Vernacular, and the Socialization of Bodies," *Renaissance Quarterly* 70.3 (2017): 831–61.

3. Michael Robinson, *The Lives and Works of the Pre-Raphaelites* (London: Hermes House, 2012).

4. Robert O'Meally, *Romare Bearden: A Black Odyssey* (New York: Moore Gallery, 2007).

5. Philip Young, *The Printed Homer: A 3000-Year Publishing History of the* Iliad *and the* Odyssey (Jefferson, NC: McFarland, 2008), 84–158.

6. Edith Hall, *The Return of Ulysses: A Cultural History of Homer's* Odyssey (Baltimore: Johns Hopkins University Press, 2008); and Piero Boitani, *The Shadow of Ulysses: Figures of a Myth*, trans. Anita Weston (Oxford: Clarendon, 1994). For an influential earlier work, see W. B. Stanford, *The Ulysses Theme: A Study in the Adaptability of a Traditional Hero*, 2nd ed. (Oxford: Blackwell, 1968).

metis, a kind of mental dexterity revealed in the manipulation of multiple identities, the weaving of tales, and the capacity to act effectively in treacherous conditions.[7] The stories within the epic include cleverly confabulated lies, and the bard identifies them this way, raising questions about the reliability of his own narration. Ingenious detours abound in Homer's poem, from the delay of the hero's appearance until Book 5 and the enigmas of his name to the motives of Penelope and the conundrum of slaughtering the suitors. The audience first meets Odysseus through report—disseminated forms of speech whose truth value is questionable. If the third-person narrator is devious, his central character is no less so.[8] The epic is part of an oral-formulaic tradition, but it is also a tale of trickery told in large part by a trickster. In short, the *Odyssey* invites us to consider not only the story it tells, but the stories it does not tell or tells obliquely. By doing so, it draws us into reflections about lateral forms of storytelling—narratives that move at an angle and through deferrals, covering their tracks, dissimulating sources, and escaping genealogical ties. The techniques associated with such narratives invite an exploration of why tales of wandering are sometimes wandering tales—stories that wind deviously around other stories rather than adapting them or receiving them in direct ways. By calling attention to how the skew in a return voyage is linked with skews in storytelling, Homer presses us to reexamine common assumptions embedded in studies of literary influence and reception, which depend upon notions of how we receive, assimilate, and adapt texts.

This book found its shape in curiosity about journeys that tell it slant. As is often the case with a piece of literature that becomes a companion, I found bearings in works I read alongside it, particularly texts that were coming to the fore in the study of global modernisms. Journey-related motifs emerged as vital in some of these texts, especially those exploring late nineteenth- and early twentieth-century subjectivities taking shape around what we now call homoeroticism, transsexuality, and racial consciousness. That wasn't surprising since literary journeys are frequently bound up with passage through strange territory and extreme experiences, but the works toward which I was gravitating were handling this material through roundabout, cunning, and oblique strategies that enabled the writers to speak of forbidden and half-

---

7. On *metis,* see Marcel Detienne and Jean-Pierre Vernant, *Cunning Intelligence in Greek Culture and Society,* trans. Janet Lloyd (Atlantic Highlands, NJ: Harvester, 1978), especially 27–53; and Ann Bergren, *Weaving Truth: Essays on Language and the Female in Greek Thought* (Washington, DC: Center for Hellenic Studies, 2008).

8. On the distinction between the *aoide,* or song of the epic narrator, and the speech, or *epos,* of Odysseus as narrator, see Egbert Bakker, *The Meaning of Meat in the* Odyssey (New York: Cambridge University Press, 2013), 1–12.

hidden things in poetic forms that were themselves evasive and elusive. In different ways, these were pioneering texts. They did not espouse an ancient heritage or situate themselves in a tradition, as did many modernist writings, but they began to cluster in my readings of them around the *Odyssey,* loosely linked by a certain isomorphism of form and content. I began thinking of them as modern odysseys—works that traveled through outlying lands and seas, practicing a poetics of indirection and weak links.[9]

Three geographical regions merged in my research: the Anglo-European world that was most familiar to me through the study of antiquity in which I was trained; the modern Mediterranean where I traveled often, sometimes directing study abroad programs; and the Caribbean, especially the franco-phone plantation culture of the Antilles, which shares a history with southern Louisiana, where I live. Facilitating this merger were three writers who had led me to the basic building blocks with which I was working. The Greek-Alexandrian poet C. P. Cavafy (1863–1933), well known in the Mediterranean, was garnering a broader international reputation because of how he positioned homoerotic desire in the contexts of diaspora, and he had lived on the shores of a Homeric sea. More famous but still at the edges of the canon, the British novelist and essayist Virginia Woolf (1882–1941) was being reimagined as a feminist whose interests in Greek, Russian, and French literature were integral to her creative life and, particularly, her revisioning of sexuality. The ancient Hellenic world enticed her and wound its way through her writing. Regionally famous but known best in francophone cultures, the Martiniquan poet-politician Aimé Césaire (1913–2008), was being increasingly acknowledged as the first Caribbean writer to chart the subjectivities of race, and he had a deep training in Greek and Latin literature through his studies in Paris as a young man. At the edges of metropolitan centers or in metropolitan centers where they worked at the margins by virtue of gender or race, these writers began to unfold in dialogue with the *Odyssey,* bringing new insight not only into the ancient epic but into the cultures that shaped their own artistic endeavors.

Other factors were at play in the evolution of this project. The emergence of geomodernisms and World Literature was bringing ancient Greece and Rome into contact with worlds beyond Europe, particularly, Asia and Africa, whose continental rims bound the Mediterranean Sea.[10] Classical reception,

---

9. For a similar set of concepts generated from the work of Borges, see Laura Jansen, "Borges and the Disclosure of Antiquity," in *Deep Classics: Rethinking Classical Reception,* ed. Shane Butler (London: Bloomsbury, 2016), 291–307.

10. See Laura Doyle and Laura Winkiel, eds., *Geomodernisms: Race, Modernism, Modernity* (Bloomington: University of Indiana Press, 2005; Susan Stanford Friedman, "World Modern-

which emphasizes the historically mediated character of texts and the ever-shifting nature of interpretive horizons, was adapting these broadening perspectives to its own disciplinary areas.[11] Homer was at the forefront of these pioneering discussions, his epics a fulcrum for moving beyond Greek antiquity and into other epic traditions,[12] but so was classical tragedy in studies of the black Aegean, which continue to illuminate African receptions of ancient drama.[13] The field was being broadened by black classicism, a predominantly American inquiry into how Africa and the African diaspora have contributed to the making of classical literature.[14] As the book took shape, I found these reconfigurations of race in cross-continental frameworks illuminating but

---

isms, World Literature, and Comparativity," in *The Oxford Handbook of Global Modernisms*, ed. Mark Wollaeger and Matt Eatough (New York: Oxford University Press, 2012), 499–525; David Damrosch, *What Is World Literature?* (Princeton: Princeton University Press, 2003); and the essays in Haun Saussy, ed., *Comparative Literature in an Age of Globalization*, (Baltimore: Johns Hopkins University Press, 2006). For another articulation of world literature, see Susan Stanford Friedman, *Planetary Modernisms: Provocations on Modernity across Time* (New York: Columbia University Press, 2015). For a critique of the field, see Emily Apter, *Against World Literature: On the Politics of Untranslatability* (New York: Verso, 2013).

11. The *Classical Receptions Journal* published its first volume in 2009. See also Charles Martindale and Richard Thomas, eds., *Classics and the Uses of Reception* (Oxford: Blackwell, 2006); and Lorna Hardwick and Christopher Stray, eds., *A Companion to Classical Receptions* (Oxford: Blackwell, 2008). Hans-Georg Gadamer developed the concept of "horizon of expectation" in *Truth and Method*, trans. Joel Weinsheimer and Donald Marshall, 2nd ed. (New York: Crossroad, 1992), 302–7 and 576–77; German edition, *Wahrheit und Methode* (Tübingen: Mohr Siebeck, 1960).

12. See James Porter, "Homer: The History of an Idea," in *The Cambridge Companion to Homer*, ed. Robert Fowler (New York: Cambridge University Press, 2004), 324–43; Barbara Graziosi and Emily Greenwood, eds., *Homer in the Twentieth Century: Between World Literature and the Western Canon* (New York: Oxford University Press, 2007); Daniel Orrells, et al, eds., *African Athena: New Agendas* (New York: Oxford University Press, 2011); Justine McConnell, *Black Odysseys: The Homeric Odyssey in the African Diaspora since 1939* (Oxford University Press, 2013); Sheila Murnaghan and Hunter Gardner, eds., *Odyssean Identities in Modern Cultures* (Columbus: The Ohio State University Press, 2014); and Leah Flack, *Modernism and Homer: The Odysseys of H. D., James Joyce, Osip Mandelstam, and Ezra Pound* (New York: Cambridge University Press, 2015).

13. See Barbara Goff and Michael Simpson, *Crossroads in the Black Aegean: Oedipus, Antigone, and Dramas of the African Diaspora* (Oxford: Oxford University Press, 2007), 8 and 38–42, who coined the term "black Aegean"; and Barbara Goff, ed., *Classics and Colonialism* (London: Duckworth, 2005).

14. *Classica Africana* is a term that Michele Valerie Ronnick coined; see *The Autobiography of William Sander Scarborough: An American Journey from Slavery to Scholarship* (Detroit, MI: Wayne State University Press, 2004). For other works focused on African American receptions of classics, see Patrice Rankine, *Ulysses in Black: Ralph Ellison, Classicism, and African American Literature* (Madison: University of Wisconsin Press, 2006); Tracy Walters, *African American Literature and the Classicist Tradition: Black Women Writers from Wheatley to Morrison* (New York: Palgrave Macmillan, 2007); and John Levi, *Empire of Ruin: Black Classicism and American Imperial Culture* (New York: Oxford University Press, 2017).

also dependent upon notions of literary beginnings, adaptation, and influence that overdetermined the kinds of reading my project was generating. Tools of the discipline were not well suited to interpreting the body of more loosely concatenated modern odysseys that began to cohere in my thinking, chiefly because the errant itineraries they charted in their narratives moved in ways that eluded an engagement with origins and canonical texts.

Work emanating from the French Caribbean provided ways of navigating these challenges because it brought me into contact with thinkers such as Édouard Glissant who were reorienting twentieth-century philosophies of *Antillanité* and *négritude*. As a concept, *négritude* emanated from an activist group of black intellectuals in 1930's Paris who were involved with ethnographic inquiries into civilization by such German thinkers as Oswald Spengler in *The Decline of the West* (*Der Untergang des Abendlandes*, 1918) and Leo Frobenius in *A Cultural History of Africa* (*Kulturgeschichte Afrikas*, 1933).[15] Spengler argued that civilizations evolve through stages that are akin to those of human organisms, who are born, decay, and die, and that Western civilization had been on the decline since the end of the eighteenth century. Frobenius advanced a theory about African Atlantis and called the idea of "the barbarous Negro" an invention of Europe. Scholarly reassessments of this modern formulation of Caribbean identity were reshaping conceptualizations of *Antillanité*, and Glissant was at the forefront of a new poetics of relation, which sought to update what he considered an essentialist *négritude*, first through a theory of creolization and later a poetics of relation.[16] Using a rhizomatic model for understanding the complexity of cultural exchange, Glissant was emphasizing unpredictability, openness to the unknown, and the impossibility of systematizing paths of often hyperactive, multilateral change. These views were mixing with scholarship on black internationalism and theo-

---

15. On Frobenius, see Suzanne Marchand, "Leo Frobenius and the Revolt Against the West," *Journal of Contemporary History* 32.2 (1997): 153–70. On Césaire, Senghor, Frobenius, and Spengler, see Robin Kelley, "A Poetics of Anticolonialism," *Monthly Review* 51.6 (1999), accessed 5 May 2019, http://monthlyreview.org/1999/11/01/a-poetics-of-anticolonialism; János Riesz, "Senghor and the Germans," *Research in African Literatures* 33.4 (2002): 25–37; and Gary Wilder, *Freedom Time: Negritude, Decolonization, and the Future of the World* (Durham, NC: Duke University Press, 2015), 1–73.

16. Édouard Glissant, *Poétique de la relation* (Paris: Gallimard, 1990); *Poetics of Relation*, trans. Betsy Wing (Ann Arbor: University of Michigan Press, 1997); and *Le Discours Antillais* (Paris: Seuil, 1981; Paris: Gallimard, 1997). For similar theories, such as *mestizaje*, see Antonio Benítez-Rojo, *The Repeating Island: The Caribbean and the Postmodern Perspective*, trans. James Maraniss, 2nd ed. (Durham, NC: Duke University Press, 1996). For an anthology of critical readings, see Françoise Lionnet and Shu-Mei Shi, eds., *The Creolization of Theory* (Durham, NC: Duke University Press, 2011).

ries of the Black Atlantic,[17] but they also gathered impetus from theoretical work in cosmopolitanism, which was moving across expansive geographies and generating dialogue about how to approach the incommensurability of cultural values.[18]

Working on a wide scale and breaking from Eurocentric models, the comparative study of modernities was developing a variety of sideways concepts, which enabled an appreciation of how the interactions between peoples in former colonial empires, whether European or Ottoman, operate more laterally than hierarchically, more reciprocally than unidirectionally, and more through movements of displacement or mixing than through linear traditions and formal networks. Complementing these concepts, the field of trans* studies was exploring the valence in such terms as transnational, transgender, and transsexual, focusing on how the development of nations relies upon social norms of embodiment, gender, and sexuality.[19] Woolf was finding new relevance in these contexts, especially since her fictional biography, *Orlando,* includes a sex change whose consequences she traced in the phenomenology of erotic desire. So was Cavafy, at least in part, because of his attention to forbidden encounters he situated in places ranging from Byzantine imperial courts and remote Greek colonies to run-down Near Eastern towns where sensuality stirs

---

17. On black internationalism, see Brent Hayes Edwards, *The Practice of Diaspora: Literature, Transnationalism, and the Rise of Black Internationalism* (Cambridge, MA: Harvard University Press, 2003); and Ifeoma Nwankwo, *Black Cosmopolitanism: Racial Consciousness and Transnational Identity in the Nineteenth-Century Americas* (Philadelphia: University of Pennsylvania Press, 2005). For one of the texts that paved the way, see James Clifford, *The Predicament of Culture: Twentieth-Century Ethnography, Literature, and Art* (Cambridge, MA: Harvard University Press, 1988). On the Black Atlantic, see Paul Gilroy, *The Black Atlantic: Modernity and Double Consciousness* (Cambridge, MA: Harvard University Press, 1993).

18. See Dieter Haller, "The Cosmopolitan Mediterranean: Myth and Reality," *Zeitschrift für Ethnologie* 129 (2004): 29–47; Iain Chambers, *Mediterranean Crossings: The Politics of an Interrupted Modernity* (Durham, NC: Duke University Press, 2008); Natalie Melas, *All the Difference in the World: Postcoloniality and the Ends of Comparison* (Redwood City, CA: Stanford University Press, 2007); and Rita Felski and Susan Stanford Friedman, "Comparison," *New Literary History* 40.3 (2009): v–ix.

19. Trans with an asterisk (trans*) is a shorthand way of conveying a wildcard term open to connectors, additions, and mixing. See Paul Jay, *Global Matters: The Transnational Turn in Literary Studies* (Ithaca, NY: Cornell University Press, 2010); Jessica Berman, *Modernist Commitments: Ethics, Politics, and Transnational Modernism* (New York: Columbia University Press, 2012), and "Is the Trans in Transnational the Trans in Transgender," *Modernism/Modernity* 2.2 (2017), accessed 5 May 2019, https://modernismmodernity.org/articles/trans-transnational; Matthew Hart, *Nations of Nothing but Poetry: Modernism, Transnationalism, and Synthetic Vernacular Poetry* (New York: Oxford University Press, 2012); and Peter Morgan, "Literary Transnationalism: A Europeanist's Perspective," *Journal of European Studies* 47.1 (2017): 3–20.

in passing engagements with strangers.[20] Sexuality and migration were linked in his writing.

As Cavafy, Woolf, and Césaire came into soft focus through oblique ways of imagining relation, a particular area of Homeric studies offered new theoretical enlightenment. The Homer Multitext Project at Harvard University's Center for Hellenic Studies, which has been creating a digital library of papyri, manuscripts, and ancient quotations that allows us to appreciate the different stages of historical development in the Homeric poems, invites us to reimagine what a text is when a millennium-long oral history has produced it.[21] By radically altering notions of authorship and source, and by emphasizing the concept of multiformity and local versions of the return tale, the Homer Multitext Project has enabled a way of thinking about the *Odyssey* as a composition in performance that competed with and marginalized other tales. Telling it slant was, in one sense, a poetic way of acknowledging a wider context of alternative retellings. Second odysseys were already circulating in the system of oral transmission, and Homer gave them sometimes more than passing glances.

During two extended periods of research, one in the Mediterranean at the American School of Classical Studies at Athens and the other in the Caribbean at the University of the Antilles on Martinique, the construction of Cavafy, Woolf, and Césaire as a viable threesome with oblique links to Homer became easier to imagine. As one of seventeen foreign archaeological schools in Athens, the American School has not only a large noncirculating collection of works on classical antiquity, held in the Blegen Library but also extensive holdings in the work of Cavafy, which are housed in the Gennadius Library across the street. This made it possible for me to put Homer and one of the most famous modern Greek poets into closer dialogue. Moreover, the archaeological work so vital to the identity of the American School was opening new perspectives in modernist studies, offering a materialist dimension to the notion of stratigraphic time, which was being theorized in literary concepts of sedimentation and multiple mediated pasts.[22]

---

20. See Gregory Jusdanis, "Why Cavafy Is So Popular," *Studies in the Literary Imagination* 48.2 (2015): 111–21.

21. See Casey Dué and Mary Ebbott, introduction to the Homer Multitext Project, accessed 8 September 2019, https://chs.harvard.edu/CHS/article/display/1169.

22. See the essays in the special edition of *Modernism/Modernity* 11.1 (2004), notably, Jeffrey Schnapp, Michael Shanks, and Matthew Tiews, "Archaeology, Modernism, Modernity," 1–16; and Gregory Jusdanis, "Farewell to the Classical: Excavations in Modernism," 37–53. See also Shane Butler, "On the Origin of 'Deep Classics,'" in *Deep Classics: Rethinking Classical Reception*, ed. Butler (London: Bloomsbury, 2016), 1–19.

Enriching this environment was the work of the Onassis Foundation in Athens, which now owns the Cavafy archive and was in the process of digitalizing it during the period of my residency, often in an atmosphere of heated debate about transmission of the archive and the accessibility of its holdings. What was obvious above the fray is that Cavafy has become not only a prominent figure in the international arena but a poet of the Greek people, and fragments of his verse may be found around Athens in bright urban frescoes, shop windows, and civic buildings. His capacity to bridge cultures, however loosely and provisionally, was apparent in a lively exhibition held at the National Archaeological Museum in Athens entitled "Odysseys" (2017–18). The curators imaginatively wove verses of Cavafy's poetry in electronically projected waves of sea-blue on the walls of rooms that held a wide range of visual art loosely linked with Homer's epic.[23]

Among the sculptures, the most prominent was the Odysseus statue from the Antikythera shipwreck, gnarled by fossil shells, lacking two hands and a leg, and every bit the image of the scrapper from Homer's epic. The links between the artifacts and the poetic verses in the exhibition were evocative rather than explicitly Homeric. Spectators were drawn into an experience of floating odyssean tonalities and inflections rather than into a Cavafy who adapted the ancient *Odyssey*. The style of presentation echoed E. M. Forster's characterization of Cavafy as "a Greek gentleman in a straw hat, standing absolutely motionless at a slight angle to the world."[24] By creating a relaxed collage of associations, the exhibition encouraged visitors to think along the lines of weak links and oblique relations between works that did not directly "receive" notional source texts. The Antikythera Odysseus, barnacled and battered, visually encoded the accidents of survival through deep time. Its random discovery alongside the more famous Antikythera mechanism, an ancient analogue computer used to predict astronomical positions, was an uncanny signifier of how an estranged past can sit so close to modernity, in a relation of contiguity rather than causality. Odysseus rises from the depths by accident with objects that have little to do with him, one a striking harbinger of twentieth-century technology. His image became a visual metaphor for the kind of indirect and contingent relations my project was forging between antiquity and modernity.

Surprisingly, Virginia Woolf (1882–1941) was also very much present in Greece at the time of the "Odysseys" exhibition. Increasingly, she was being

---

23. See https://www.namuseum.gr/en/periodic_exhibition/odysseies/. Passages by other Greek poets, including George Seferis, Odysseas Elytis, and Iannis Ritsos, were also exhibited, and music was incorporated in the presentation.

24. E. M. Forster, *Pharos and Pharillon,* 2nd ed. (London: Hogarth, 1923), 91.

studied "out of bounds" and in international contexts, with attention to her
critique of respectable womanhood in late nineteenth-century England and
how it upheld structures of empire.[25] She seemed part of the Athens cityscape,
her reputation attested in bookstores that sold her work in both English and
Greek translation, in advertisements that announced performances adapted
from her fiction, and in literary journals where her Hellenism, now a topic of
wider study, was being discussed. This attention was and is, at least in part, a
consequence of her own interest in Greece, perhaps most familiar to audiences
from her essay "On Not Knowing Greek." Woolf could be bluntly colonialist in
her attitudes toward modern Greeks, as a reading of the autobiographical "A
Dialogue on Mount Pentelicus" bears out. But in her essay on ancient Greek,
and in her diaries and letters, she waxes large upon a mysterious and enticing language whose sound we cannot hear and whose works come down to
us without a context that would help us know "where precisely we ought to
laugh or how the actors acted."[26] As with Cavafy, her instincts were to come at
her subject matter sideways or through essayistic strikes, and this is especially
apparent in *Orlando*.

If a Mediterranean poet and an Anglo-European fiction writer developed
into a more viable pair during my residency at the American School, Césaire
came more clearly into view shortly afterward during my time at the University of the Antilles in an exchange supported by the Center for French
and Francophone Studies at LSU and the Partnership University Fund of the
French government. Having graduated from the École Normale Supérieure
where he studied Greek and Latin, Césaire's first job after returning from
Europe to Martinique was as a teacher of classics at the lycée in Fort-de-
France. Like Cavafy and Woolf in Athens, Césaire had become part of the
landscape of his country, his poetry appearing ubiquitously on civic buildings,
sea walls, nature walks, and posters in local shops. *Cahier d'un retour au pays
natal (Journal of a Return to the Native Land)* was already being approached
as a Black odyssey when I began my work in earnest on the poem, but critics were not always sensitive to the oblique treatment of Homer and the uses
of detour that are characteristic of the poem's coming-into-consciousness.[27]

---

25. See Jessica Berman and Jane Goldman, eds., *Virginia Woolf Out of Bounds* (New York:
Pace University Press, 2001); Urmila Seshagiri, *Race and the Modernist Imagination* (Ithaca,
NY: Cornell University Press, 2010), 140–91; and Sonita Sarker, "Woolf and Theories of Post-
colonialism," in *Virginia Woolf in Context*, ed. Bryony Randall and Jane Goldman (New York:
Cambridge University Press, 2012), 110–28.

26. Virginia Woof, "On Not Knowing Greek," in *The Essays of Virginia Woolf, 1925–1928*,
edited by Andrew McNellie. Vol. 4 (London: Hogarth Press, 1994), 38.

27. For a notable exception, see Emily Greenwood, *Afro-Greeks: Dialogues Between Anglophone Caribbean Literature and Classics in the Twentieth Century* (New York: Oxford University
Press, 2010), 1.

These detours are linked in the poem with the psychic injuries of slavery and colonial abuse, which blight memory and form blockages through which the poem struggles to arrive at clarity, largely by attempting to bring up from the depths the horrors of the Black Atlantic. If the *Odyssey* gives us insight into posttraumatic stress disorder and the psychic hazards of war,[28] *Cahier* in tandem with the *Odyssey* enables an appreciation of storytelling and dramatized reenactment as forms of self-healing.[29]

How indirection and modes of telling it slant became instrumental in framing this book may now be more apparent, though it will take the balance of the book to work out the details. Still, the question can be brought into sharper focus. While such works as Joyce's *Ulysses,* Pound's *Cantos,* H. D.'s *Helen in Egypt,* and Walcott's *Omeros* invite frontal encounters with the *Odyssey,* Cavafy, Woolf, and Césaire avoid them. Joyce uses the authority of Homer to defend himself against the censors of *Ulysses* and to point a way for bewildered readers who were encountering a work that baffled meaning.[30] In one of his famous critical pronouncements, T. S. Eliot explains that the mythic method deriving from such ancient works as the *Odyssey* is "simply a way of controlling, of ordering, of giving a shape and a significance to the immense panorama of futility and anarchy which is contemporary history."[31] Similarly, H. D. adopts Homer as an explicit point of reference for retelling the story of Helen, turning to the account of the Greek poet Stesichorus, who tells us that Helen was in Egypt during the Trojan War. It was a phantom that appeared on the walls of Troy, which means the war was fought for an illusion. The variant myth provided a potent way of commenting, among other things, upon the vast human waste of the two World Wars. These works are inspired by Homer, declare a filial bond through their titles, and deserve the kind of careful critical attention they have recently been given in reception studies as modernist works with a classicizing bent.

The writing of Cavafy, Woolf, and Césaire can sometimes orient itself in the way these works do, through allusion, citation, adaptation, and reframing, as we will see. But by thinking in terms of a poetics of indirection and weak

---

28. Jonathan Shay, *Odysseus in America: Combat Trauma and the Trials of Homecoming* (New York: Scribner, 2003).

29. Elizabeth Minchin, *Homer and the Resources of Memory: Some Applications of Cognitive Theory to the* Iliad *and the* Odyssey (New York: Oxford University Press, 2001); William Race, "Phaeacian Therapy in Homer's *Odyssey,*" in *Combat Trauma and the Ancient Greeks,* ed. Peter Meineck and David Konstan (New York: Palgrave Macmillan, 2014), 47–66; and Joel Christensen, "The Clinical Odyssey: Odysseus' *Apologoi* and Narrative Therapy," *Arethusa* 51.1 (2018): 1–31. On Freud and the classical world, see Richard Armstrong, *A Compulsion for Antiquity: Freud and the Ancient World* (Ithaca, NY: Cornell University Press, 2005).

30. For a fuller discussion, see Flack, *Modernism and Homer,* 1–22.

31. T. S. Eliot, "Ulysses, Order, and Myth," *Dial* 75 (1923): 483.

links, I wanted to bring other perspectives to bear on the literary inventiveness of these writers. Indirection, as already seen, can take on different forms. It can be an artful way for a poet to shape an encounter with a person or a group as a bearer of multiple identities that are in tension, merely virtual, or unable to cohere and thus do not have a solid ontological status; it can also create a critical orientation toward reading such texts with an appreciation for this indirection. Cavafy's explorations of diasporic consciousness often work in this way, opening up scenarios of hybrid identities that enrich an appreciation of deviant sexuality, lived at the social margins and outside mainstream channels of exchange, including literary exchange. Woolf's treatment of the "phantasmagoria of the mind" in *Orlando* offers another example. Her book illuminates how lateral approaches to subjectivity can more effectively represent the polymorphous selves that constitute sex and gender than narrative forms like biography can (the book is parodically subtitled *A Biography*). On the other hand, indirection can come into play when a poet is confronting an existential or epistemological gap of the sort brought on by the near eradication of a people's history through violent displacement. Césaire struggles to conjure up through the imagination what has been swallowed into the abyss of the African slave trade, which is often experienced as a zone of opacity. Essayistic modes of approach function as strategies for piecing together the memory of an experience that exists only in fragments and must be poetically constructed.

In the case of both multiple identities and a paucity of identities, home and the homeland can become riddling notions that require slant approaches and evasive maneuvers. The *pays natal* for an Antillean is a conundrum, to say the least, and it is shaped by at least three continents; home for the female transsexual returning from abroad means dispossession of property, since ownership is held in a patriarchal line; the fatherland for a diasporic Greek is complicated by its inclusion over time in the Roman, Byzantine, and Ottoman empires. If personal and national identity is problematic for the writers in this study, so is its extension into the idea of a literary tradition since that is a manifestation of exclusionary choices that can provoke dissent toward the canon. To the degree that tradition monitors subject matter, coding, ellipsis, and circumlocution can become hide-and-seek ways of interacting with the censor or the gatekeeper and keeping a wide berth from the forefathers.

Although the poetics of indirection explored in this book arises from comparative readings of Homer, Cavafy, Woolf, and Césaire, it could be extended to such strong odysseys as *Ulysses* and the *Cantos,* which are polysemous and experimental in their own complex and demanding ways. The concept, however, is particularly insightful for the texts featured in this book because it allows us to appreciate how emergent subjectivities in the late nineteenth and early twentieth centuries came to be formulated in conditions of repression, marginality, and linguistic impoverishment. The forms of indirection examined here are not meant to be taxonomically exhaustive. Rather they provide rough and ready ways to approach texts whose odyssean qualities reside in roundabout and nonfrontal ways of representing experience and the relation to literary tradition. What is important to bear in mind overall is that the works under discussion do not want to receive or be received with breaches and ruptures made over by a critical need for wholeness, transparency, and the need to identify sources. Keeping the interpretive space open—not closing prematurely on questions of influence and reception—becomes an act in which the reader is asked to be complicit because sex, gender, sexuality, and race are themselves conceived as open.

HOMER: APPROACHES TO A POETICS OF INDIRECTION

Before describing the organization of this book, I want to return briefly to the question of how current Homeric studies enable what I call a poetics of indirection. While it is generally known that the *Iliad* and the *Odyssey* are the product of a living oral tradition, it is less commonly understood that the widespread influences that fed them and the millennium-long duration of their composition challenge the very notion of a text.[32] Building upon the groundbreaking work of Albert Lord and Milman Parry in Serbo-Croatian epic,[33] scholars have shown that the orality of the poems implicates them in performance culture, and performance is predicated not on repetition but

---

32. For approaches to Homer, the Homeric Question, and problems of dating, see Richard Janko, *Homer, Hesiod, and the Hymns*. Cambridge, MA: Cambridge University Press, 1982; and Franco Montanari, et al, eds., *Homeric Contexts: Neoanalysis and the Interpretation of Oral Poetry* (Berlin: de Gruyter, 2012). For a view of Homer as the name of a collective of singers that extended back a millennium into the bronze age, see Gregory Nagy, The Homer Multitext Project, http://nrs.harvard.edu/urn-3:hlnc.essay:Nagy.The_Homer_Multitext_Project.2010; Gregory Nagy, *Homer: The Preclassic* (Berkeley: University of California Press, 2017); Dué and Ebbott, introduction to the Homer Multitext Project; and Casey Dué, *Achilles Unbound: Multiformity and Tradition in the Homeric Epics* (Washington, DC: Center for Hellenic Studies, 2018), ch. 1, http://nrs.harvard.edu/urn-3:hul.ebook:CHS_Due.Achilles_Unbound.2018. For a reading of Homer premised on the idea of a single poet who created a masterpiece in the last third of the seventh century BCE, see Martin West, *The Making of the* Odyssey (New York: Oxford University Press, 2014), 1–23. For a discussion of competing editorial principles and practices in the modern editing of Homer's poems, see Barbara Graziosi and Johannes Haubold, "The Homeric Text," *Ramus* 44 (2015): 5–28.

33. Albert Lord, *The Singer of Tales* (Cambridge, MA: Harvard University Press, 1960).

on the recurrence of elements at the level of language, theme, and story pattern in a fluid context of change.[34] Because they evolved from composition in performance, the Homeric poems, while drawing on an oral-formulaic past, were always being made anew in historically situated moments and through an extended diachronic process in which each performance yielded a different poem. The key artistic tool of the singer was the multiform, a compositional element that had an accumulated and deeply resonant meaning. It could take the shape of a repeated phrase (traditionally in English, "the wine dark sea," "οἶνοψ πόντος"), a type scene (rituals of hospitality), or even a narrative (the return tale). Improvisational flexibility over time and through the hands of various makers is its hallmark.

Even if scholars disagree about the extent of multiformity in the Homeric poems, the consensus is that there was no *Ur*-text from which derivations stem, and this renders problematic the notion that the poem is an *Ur*-text itself. As a composition in performance, the *Odyssey*, for example, not only moved in a crowded sea of oral tales, but it marginalized alternative odysseys, leaving signs of other tellings, mutable links with dissenting songs, and zones of opacity within complex systems of exchange. Even though its increasingly Panhellenic character allowed it to rise above local conditions of performance, as did the introduction of writing into the process of transmission, it never bore during the long centuries of its oral formation the title or the shape we now possess. There were other Penelopes, other Odysseuses, and even other epic traditions that had different ways of narrating the story of a cunning hero who got lost on his way home after a long war. This multiplicity was largely the result of epichoric story lines, often attached to hero cults, which developed over centuries. Such a plurality of tellings destabilizes the idea of Homer as an originary site.[35] Considerable cultural traffic surrounded the poem during the long period of its oral composition, and this means that it was already historically sedimented when a notional Homer came on the scene in the early archaic age. Indeed, research has turned up evidence that the *Odyssey* embraces elements from such disparate traditions as the Near Eastern epic

---

34. See John Foley and Justin Arft, "The Epic Cycle and Oral Tradition," in *The Greek Epic Cycle and Its Ancient Reception: A Companion*," ed. Marco Fantuzzi and Christos Tsagalis (New York: Cambridge University Press, 2015), 78–95.

35. See Jonathan Burgess, *The Tradition of the Trojan War in Homer and the Epic Cycle* (Baltimore: Johns Hopkins University Press, 2004); and Gregory Nagy, "Homeric Poetry and the Problems of Multiformity: The 'Panathenaic Bottleneck,'" *Classical Philology* 96.2 (2001): 109–19; and "Signs of Hero Cult in Homeric Poetry," in *Homeric Contexts*, ed. Montanari et al, 27–72.

of *Gilgamesh,* including the first-person narration of travel in foreign lands;[36] from such faraway places as the Pontic region, most notably the tale of the returning husband and the one-eyed ogre;[37] and from beyond the Pontic in the ancient lore of Scandinavia, which preserves memories of a Hyperborean culture.[38] Homer did not invent these characters and plot elements. They came to him in widely disseminated ways across centuries of cultural exchange, and he—or the collective associated with him—improvised upon them. The *Odyssey* is highly aware that "It's always the latest song, the one that echoes last / in the listeners' ears, that people love most" (1.404–5; "τὴν γὰρ ἀοιδὴν μᾶλλον ἐπικλείουσ' ἄνθρωποι, / ἥ τις ἀκουόντεσσι νεωτάτη ἀμφιπέλεται," 1.351–52), and it constantly historicizes its own narrative.

The Homeric Question thus endures, although in a more complex and fascinating form. One of the most productive strains of research along these lines has been an expanding body of scholarship on the epic cycle, poems in dactylic hexameter about the events leading up to and issuing from the Trojan War as Homer tells it, which have survived in only fragmentary and summary form, notably, in a digest known as the *Chrestomathy* by a certain Proclus whose identity is uncertain. While the dating of these works is still contested, many scholars agree that the stories they tell are pre-Homeric and thus that Homer had contact with some if not many of them.[39] The *Telegony,* for example, one of the poems in the epic cycle, tells of what happens to Odysseus, Penelope, and Telemachus after the end of the *Odyssey.* In this story, attributed to Eugammon of Cyrene (fl. 568 BCE), but probably part of an oral history that extended farther back than that date implies,[40] Odysseus travels to Thesprotia on the northern Greek mainland, marries the Thesprotian queen Callidice, who bears him a son Polypoetes, and travels back to Ithaca after the

---

36. On Homer and the East, see Walter Burkert, *The Orientalizing Revolution: Near Eastern Influence on Greek Culture in the Early Archaic Age,* trans. Margaret Pinder (Cambridge, MA: Harvard University Press, 1992); Martin West, *The East Face of Helicon: West Asiatic Elements in Greek Poetry and Myth* (Oxford: Clarendon, 1999); Bruce Louden, *Homer's Odyssey and the Near East* (New York: Cambridge University Press, 2011); and Johannes Haubold, *Greece and Mesopotamia: Dialogues in Literature* (New York: Cambridge University Press, 2013). See Damrosch, *What Is World Literature?,* 39–77, for an account of the conditions in which the cuneiform tablets of *Gilgamesh* were discovered.

37. West, *Making of the* Odyssey, 17–21 and 92–142.

38. Felice Vinci, "The Nordic Origins of the *Iliad* and the *Odyssey:* An Up-to-Date Survey of the Theory," *Athens Journal of Mediterranean Studies* 3.2 (2017): 163–86.

39. On the epic cycle, see Burgess, *Tradition of the Trojan War;* Martin West, *The Epic Cycle: A Commentary on the Lost Troy Epics* (New York: Oxford University Press, 2013); and Marco Fantuzzi and Christos Tsagalis, eds., *The Greek Epic Cycle and Its Ancient Reception: A Companion"* (New York: Cambridge University Press, 2015).

40. Burgess, *Tradition of the Trojan War,* 7–46.

queen dies in battle, with Polypoetes assuming the throne. On Ithaca once again, Odysseus engages in battle with an unknown intruder on his island, who turns out to be his son Telegonus from a union with Circe, and at Telegonus's unwitting hand he dies. Upon recognizing what he has done, Telegonus returns to Aeaea, where Odysseus is buried. There he marries Penelope, and Telemachus marries Circe.

This tale recounts a thick web of intrigue, mistaken identity, and incest that displaces the characters and values in the Homeric *Odyssey,* if we take them to be centered on a return tale that reestablishes bonds of kingship and family. The persevering Penelope ends up marrying her stepson and cohabiting with one of her husband's divine lovers. In a later work, the second-century traveler and geographer Pausanias speaks of another oral tradition with a promiscuous Penelope who bedded all the suitors and gave birth to the god Pan.[41] Contemporary reworkings of the Penelope and Circe figures in popular fiction have brought alive the vibrancy of the epic cycle and tales that diverge from the Homeric account.[42] We will return to the *Telegony* in later parts of this book.

Alternative and submerged odysseys are detectable not only through oblique references in the epic, but in the notorious lying tales within the *Odyssey.* There are four key ones that Odysseus tells when he returns to Ithaca in the guise of a beggar whose alleged home is Crete and who has suffered many of the same defeats the Ithacan Odysseus has: hardship in the Trojan War, treachery at home, shipwreck by sea, loss of a fortune. They reinforce the image of a hero who works by stealth and subterfuge rather than in the open air to achieve his ends.[43] It now seems that these tales are "lying" perhaps only from a Homeric point of view because they compete with his own story.[44] Rather than simply leaving them out of his tale, the poet maneuvers around them, creating tenuous links with other narratives of return, while simultaneously asserting the authority of his own performance.

---

41. Pausanias, *Description of Greece,* vol. 3., trans. W. H. S. Jones (Cambridge, MA: Harvard University Press, 1990), 8.12.5. The lustful Penelope is discussed by Barbara Dell Abate-Çelebi, *Penelope's Daughters* (Berkeley: University of California Press, 2010), 17–20.

42. See, for example, Margaret Atwood, *The Penelopiad* (Edinburgh: Canongate, 2005); and Madeline Miller, *Circe* (New York: Little, Brown and Company, 2018).

43. Casey Dué and Mary Ebbott, *Iliad 10 and the Poetics of Ambush, A Multitext Edition with Essays and Commentary,* Hellenic Studies Series 39 (Washington, DC Center for Hellenic Studies, 2010), part 1, accessed 8 September 2019, http://nrs.harvard.edu/urn-:hul.ebook:CHS_Due_Ebbott.Iliad_10_and_the_Poetics_of_Ambush.2010.

44. Gregory Nagy, "A Cretan Odyssey, Part 1," *Classical Inquiries,* 2015, accessed 8 September 2019, https://classical-inquiries.chs.harvard.edu/a-cretan-odyssey-part-1/; and "A Cretan Odyssey, Part 2," *Classical Inquiries,* 2015, accessed 8 September 2019, https://classical-inquiries. chs.harvard.edu/a-cretan-odyssey-part-2/.

FOUR (O)DYSSEAN TROPES

We are therefore better off talking about composition in performance in terms of "the paths of oral song" (οἶμαι, 8.479–81), a phrase drawn from the *Odyssey* itself, or "voices from the past."[45] Storytelling in such a vast and malleable context eludes the idea of textuality, which is enmeshed in notions of authorship and title. This is not to say that the Homeric poems were never canonized in antiquity, but the conditions of oral performance and their effect on the written text, which only stabilized over deep time, point to the problematic character of some fundamental ideas in reception studies. We cannot, for example, assume that in ancient art the depiction of figures and scenes associated with Odysseus and the Trojan War were drawn from Homeric epic rather than from material in the epic cycle. Where there was no text, there was no intertextuality, at least as we understand it in the era of artifactual objects within a tradition of reading and writing. Rather, there were nodes of narrative meaning in a dense network that could be activated from different directions and that were themselves neither fixed nor final but always shifting with the performance of living song.

In bringing Cavafy, Woolf, and Césaire together for the first time, *Modern Odysseys* makes use of these ideas in searching for alternatives to author- and text-based notions of influence, reception, and adaptation. It studies how these twentieth-century artists tap into, not the *Odyssey*, but a looser set of odyssean tropes that enable them to develop stories and create lyric sensibilities that drift in Homeric waters without coming into his wake. The metaphorical image is of a heavily tracked modern sea dotted by sporadic islands and loosely connected with the continents of canonical texts; here the most maneuverable crafts travel lightly, their form suited to chance encounters, accidental mishaps, and sometimes isolation in unknown harbors. Four tropes from this circulatory sea inform this study: diffusion and mixture; islands and isolation; passage and detour; and return and split endings. As used here, trope refers to nodules of meaning that are pliant enough to be "turned"—the basic meaning of *tropos*—in a process of poetic production. I distinguish tropes from multiforms because they are not constructs borrowed from Homeric oral theory, although they sometimes overlap with them. Taken together, they are meant to convey the sense of a journey marked by

1. a plethora of human experience that challenges normative categories by exerting a centrifugal force (diffusion and mixture);

---

45. Foley and Arft, "The Epic Cycle," in *The Greek Epic Cycle*, ed. Fantuzzi and Tsagalis, 83.

2. a withdrawal of exertion on the part of an agent as a consequence of trauma or loss (islands and isolation);
3. a need to reengage that brings with it the challenges of liminality (passage and detour);
4. and a movement toward recuperation that cannot be satisfied because the end is unavoidably vexed (return and split endings).

It is through these tropes that I trace a poetics of indirection. Because Cavafy does not typically write in narrative form, these tropes will be approached across a number of his poems, which taken together compose a picture of an odyssean-inflected imagination at work.

Diffusion is typically the product of travel away from home or of inter-rupted movement toward it, but it also brings the wandering subject into an awareness of the strangeness that constitutes identity. In the *Odyssey,* for example, diffusion is not only a consequence of getting lost after a war. It takes shape around scenes of hospitality, or *xenia,* that bring cultural differ-ence and psychic diffusion into view, that is, the fragmentation of the char-acter through disguise, withholding, or dissimulation. Key to this circulatory network is what Homer calls *kleos.* While that word is most commonly used for the medium of epic poetry, it can also refer to reports that circulate by word of mouth, functioning as a social glue but also leaving in its wake some-times contradictory stories. A good example may be found in the reports about Odysseus's whereabouts and safety: is he alive or dead, close to Ithaca or far removed from it, headed toward home or other seas? Circuitous and ever changing, *kleos* is another manifestation of diffusion in the *Odyssey.* In the poetry of Cavafy, a similar diffusion informs homoerotic explorations that combine sexuality and disparate Mediterranean ethnicities; in Césaire, it shapes a racially informed return tale that seeks to bridge, albeit tenuously, the Caribbean diaspora with Africa; and in Woolf, it motivates a transsexual adventure in the orient that critiques nationalism and empire as well as the construction of gender on which they depend.

Because wandering and exile are forms of separation and distance, they typically are interwoven with isolation, whether physical, psychic, or both. Geographical insularity in the form of island space is one manifestation of isolation, but an urban metropolis can also become metaphorically insular. In the *Odyssey,* the Calypso narrative, focused as it is on the desolation of the protagonist on Ogygia, the so-called "navel of the sea" (Robert Fagles has "at the center of the seas," 1.60; "ὀμφαλός ἐστι θαλάσσης," 1.50), plays a key role in developing Odysseus's isolation, even as it functions as a space of emer-gence from physical and psychic collapse. In Cavafy, Alexandria, the broken-down city states that surround it, and the provincial towns that imbue his poetic world with such color are often places of estrangement where loneliness and a sense of abandonment take shape around intoxicating but ephemeral homoerotic encounters. Woolf's geography of isolation in *Orlando* is more domestic, located as it often is in a gigantic mansion of a house that harbors a world. But it, too, is a place where ghosts wander corridors, ancestors stare out of painted portraits, and the family cemetery functions as the haunted foundation on which emotional breakdowns unfold. In Césaire's *Cahier*, the landscape itself is a prison, and isolation is as characteristic of the fragile Antilles as it is of the soul of a still colonialized people who inhabit a zombie land.

The experience of isolation and insular space is typically bound up with passage out of or into differentiated spaces, especially in cases where liminality is at issue. Narrative itself, a product of poetic composition, plays a key role in odyssean forms of passage because it relies on memory, the organizational work that goes on in it, and the uses of storytelling or lyrical remembering that attempt to recuperate what is lost. Odysseus's autobiography of the wanderings is a famous example of this mnemonic work, and so are his several Cretan tales. But Cavafy's closely honed recollections of the past also weave a way for his fictional personas to shape subjectivities in which bereavement and defeat can be partially overcome through an aesthetic rendering of loss. Writing becomes a form of passage in his work as it does in Woolf's *Orlando*, which features a second-rate author infatuated with the literary imagination. Much of the parody in the fictional biography emerges from the seriocomic ways the narrative uses writing as a passage into and out of psychic breakdown. In Césaire, the reader encounters serial enactments of passage, performed via shifting masks that are themselves a manifestation of a traumatized psyche working through the horror of the Middle Passage.

Passage, in turn, implicates home, a notion with both centripetal and centrifugal force in the works we will be examining. *Nostos*, Homer's word for homecoming, is a key dimension of the *Odyssey*, and yet the narrative treats it in a refracted manner, juxtaposing competing ways in which return may be understood and suspending the sense of a resolved ending. Césaire's *Cahier* introduces similar refractions, beginning with the title itself, which attenuates the notion of *retour au pays natal* by keeping a distance from Homer. Return, as he handles it, is essayistic and unclosed. A similar set of strategies is at work in *Orlando* where every return brings a new alienation. Woolf works creatively with the concept of the "phantasmagoria of the mind" in negotiating what homecoming might mean given the multiple subjectivities that circulate within her protagonist. While Cavafy is less focused on vagaries of consciousness, he writes poems of return that engage more loosely with itinerancy, shifting identities, and the displacements implicated in anomalous sexuality. These associations are provocatively worked out in poems that link eros, diaspora, and home.

It is through the four tropes of diffusion and mixture, islands and isolation, passage and detour, and return and split endings that this book formulates what I hope is a cogent approach to a poetics of indirection in Cavafy's lyrical homoeroticism, Woolf's novelistic explorations of transsexuality and gender relations, and Césaire's epic descent into the cauldron of racial consciousness and colonialism. These tropes open the way to backdoor strategies, invention by circumlocution, masquerades, devious forms of linguistic play, tricks with publishing, and sometimes outright coding to avoid the censor. Taking a long historical perspective on three writers who invite us to think about indirection as a manner of living, a form of thought, and a set of artistic strategies, this book seeks to generate new understandings of how modernists living at various sexual, ethnic, and racial margins shaped emergent subjectivities that have circulated more widely in late twentieth- and early twenty-first-century literature. In the process, it also aims to reorient our appreciation of the Homeric epic.

ORGANIZATION OF THE BOOK

Modern Odysseys is organized around four chapters that correspond to the four central tropes discussed above. Each contains discussions of the authors that inform this study, arranged around subheadings that indicate the main thrust of the argument. I open with readings that aim to develop fresh ways of engaging with the *Odyssey* and move on to discussions of Cavafy, Woolf, and Césaire, who rotate fluidly in the construction of each chapter. In order to make it easier for those who wish to read selectively on a particular author, I have included names in the subtitles of the table of contents. In this way, someone who is interested, say, in Woolf can locate relevant sections in the table of contents under the tropes, which tag her by name. One of the virtues of the groupings is that the chapters enable thematic clusters to emerge: homoeroticism, Greek orientalism, and the Mediterranean in Cavafy; transsexuality, gender, and British orientalism in Woolf; and racial consciousness and Antillean anticolonialism in Césaire.

While politics and imperial history are topics of recurring interest, the book does not aim to articulate an overarching account of either but rather draws on elements of both, chiefly through an examination of paratexts. Among the most common are epigraphs, diaries, letters, notebooks, and interviews. Details about the lives of Cavafy, Woolf, and Césaire that bear on the works studied will emerge in the four parts of the book. But it will help to have biographical sketches of the authors before embarking on a more intensive exploration.

MINI BIOS

Constantine Petrou Photiades Cavafy (1863–1933)—the literary name he chose was the anglicized Greek C. P. Cavafy—was born in Alexandria, Egypt, and grew up in a successful and wealthy merchant family.[46] He spent much of his childhood in Liverpool, Manchester, and London (it is said that he spoke Greek with a British accent), moved to Paris for a short while, and lived part of his young life in Constantinople, the capital of the Ottoman empire. His family tree included Phanariots, who were members of prominent Greek families in Phanar, which is the Greek section of Constantinople, and who held posts in the bureaucracy of the Ottomans. Through his well-to-do London relatives, he came into contact while still a youth with the British aesthetic movement and was exposed to the Pre-Raphaelites.[47] The Cavafy and Ionides families in London were business partners, but they also intermarried and assumed baptismal bonds together. The cousins Maria Zambaco and Aglaia Coronio, born Ionides, along with Marie Spartali, were known in Pre-Raphaelite circles as the Three Graces, and they sat as models or became painters themselves. When the Cavafy family lost its fortune, they moved back to Alexandria, but political unrest drove them away once again. Their home was destroyed in the British bombardment of the city in 1882, launched to quell an Arab nationalist uprising against the Anglophile Tewfik Pasha. When they returned in 1885, Cavafy took up residence there once more, this time for the rest of his life and in more modest economic circumstances.

He had a passion for history, which features prominently in his work, and he was fond of writing on obscure figures from late antiquity and the Byzantine period. He thought of himself as a poet-historian.[48] In 1915, he met

46. For a biography in English, see Robert Liddell, *Cavafy: A Biography* (London: Duckworth, 1974). For briefer synopses, see Manuel Savidis, "Biographical Note," accessed 5 May 2019, http://www.cavafy.com/companion/bio.asp; and Cavafy, *Complete Poems*, trans. Daniel Mendelsohn (New York: Knopf, 2012), xx–xxiv.

47. See Peter Jeffreys, *Reframing Decadence: C. P. Cavafy's Imaginary Portraits* (Ithaca, NY: Cornell University Press), 1–25.

48. Liddell, *Cavafy*, 123. On Cavafy as historian, see Vassilis Lambropoulos, "The Greeks of Art and the Greeks of History," *Modern Greek Studies, Australia and New Zealand* 11 (2003): 66–74; and Bruce Frier, "Making History Personal: Constantine Cavafy and the Rise of Rome,"

E. M. Forster, who served in the Red Cross during the First World War and was assigned to Alexandria. It was Forster who introduced his work to T. S. Eliot, D. H. Lawrence, and the Woolfs. In 1951, Hogarth Press published the first translation into English of *The Complete Poems of C. P. Cavafy*. Six years earlier, Leonard Woolf had written to Forster saying, "I have just had one of the great triumphs of my life. I have received from Singopoulo [*sic*; the heir to the Cavafy estate] a signed agreement giving me the right to publish Cavafy in Mavro's [John Mavrogordato's] translation. I shall do it complete. The triumph would be complete if you would write an introduction to it."[49] For most of his life, Cavafy earned a living from the salary he received in a government job at the Third Circle of Irrigation, and he also gambled. This money, along with the profits he earned from investments in the Alexandria Stock Exchange, enabled him to live comfortably, though not in the high style his family enjoyed while he was growing up. While he never discussed his homosexuality openly, he remarked on it indirectly in his "Notes on Poetics and Ethics," and it became an integral, if half-hidden, part of his poetry.[50] He also kept "self-commentaries" (*autoscholia*) on his poems and "confessional notes" of a sexual nature, sometimes referred to as "the masturbation diaries," which have yet to be published and which may turn out to be a fiction of overly exercised scholarly imaginations.[51] He only visited Greece four times in his life, the final sojourn motivated by a medical problem that was diagnosed as cancer of the larynx. After an unsuccessful round of treatment, he returned to Alexandria where he passed away in 1932. He is said to have remarked, "Where could I live better? Under me is a house of ill repute, which caters to the needs of the flesh. Over there is the church, where sins are forgiven. And beyond is the hospital, where we die."[52]

It was in 1886, within a couple years of the British bombardment of Alexandria, that Virginia Woolf was born in South Kensington, London, into a

---

Cavafy Forum (2010), accessed 5 May 2017. https://lsa.umich.edu/content/dam/modgreek-assets/modgreek-docs/CPC_Frier_Makinghistorypersonal.pdf.

49. Cavafy, *The Forster-Cavafy Letters: Friends at a Slight Angle*, ed. Peter Jeffreys (Cairo: The American University in Cairo Press, 2009), 115.

50. For an English translation, see Cavafy, "Notes on Poetics and Ethics," trans. Martin McKinsey, *Ploughshares* 11.4 (1985): 20–26. The work also appears in Cavafy, *Selected Prose Works*, ed. and trans. Peter Jeffreys (Ann Arbor: University of Michigan Press, 2010), 129–39. For the Greek text, see Cavafy, *Μικρά Καβαφικά Β*, ed. George Savidis (Athens: Hermes, 1987).

51. The *autoscholia* are currently being edited and translated into English by Diana Haas. On the "confessional notes," see Cavafy, *Clearing the Ground: Poetry and Prose: 1902–1911*, ed. and trans. Martin McKinsey (Chapel Hill, NC: Laertes, 2015), 135–44; and Dimitris Papanikolaou, "Days of Those Made Like Me: Retrospective Pleasure, Sexual Knowledge, and C. P. Cavafy's Homobiographics," *Byzantine and Modern Greek Studies* 37.2 (2013): 261–77.

52. Savidis, "Cavafy: Biographical Note."

well-off family of letters.[53] Her father, Leslie Stephen, was the first editor of the *Dictionary of National Biography*[54] and a friend of the novelist William Thackeray. Her mother, Julia Jackson, was known in Pre-Raphaelite circles, whose members, Holman Hunt and Thomas Woolner, had wooed her.[55] One of the most achieved portraitists in the history of photography, Julia Margaret Cameron (1815–79), was Julia Jackson's aunt, Virginia's great-aunt, and she had close connections with the Pre-Raphaelites.[56] This is one of the accidental links that connects the youthful Cavafy with Woolf. In her teens, Virginia was a student in the Ladies' Department at King's College, London, where she studied Greek, Latin, and German. She continued in Greek with a classical tutor, Janet Case, later coming under the spell of Jane Ellen Harrison (1850–1928), who was not only one of the first female professors of classics to teach at Cambridge in Newnham College but also one of the first to apply archaeological discoveries to the study of Greek religion.[57] She traveled to Greece in 1906 and wrote about it in a story called "A Dialogue on Mount Pentelicus," in which the British interlocutors express colonialist puzzlement about the modern Greeks, a "dusky, garrulous race," that does not comport well with their romanticized views of ancient Greek glory.[58] In addition, she kept a notebook that records her travel in Greece, Turkey, and Italy in 1906–9[59] and a Greek notebook, which contains notes on her reading from the works of Homer,

---

53. For biographies, see Quentin Bell, *Virginia Woolf: A Biography* (New York: Harcourt Brace Jovanovich, 1972); and Hermione Lee, *Virginia Woolf* (New York: Vintage, 1996).

54. Lee, *Virginia Woolf*, 50–78.

55. Lee, *Virginia Woolf*, 79–94.

56. Marion Dell, *Virginia Woolf's Influential Forebears: Julia Margaret Cameron, Anny Thackeray Ritchie, Julia Prinsep Stephen* (London: Palgrave Macmillan, 2016), 72–104; and Woolf's own essay, "Julia Margaret Cameron," in *The Essays of Virginia Woolf, 1925–1928*, ed. Andrew McNellie. Vol. 4 (London: Hogarth, 1994), 375–86.

57. For a recent study, see Jane Mills, *Virginia Woolf, Jane Ellen Harrison, and the Spirit of Modernist Classicism* (Columbus: The Ohio State University Press, 2014). On Woolf's Greek, see also Theodore Koulouris, *Hellenism and Loss in the Work of Virginia Woolf* (Farnham: Ashgate, 2011); Emily Dalgarno, *Virginia Woolf and the Migrations of Language* (New York: Cambridge University Press, 2011), 1–17; and Yopie Prins, *Ladies' Greek: Victorian Translations of Tragedy* (Princeton: Princeton University Press, 2017), 1–55.

58. For the story, see Woolf, "A Dialogue on Mount Pentelicus," in *The Complete Shorter Fiction of Virginia Woolf*, ed. Susan Dick (San Diego: Harcourt Brace Jovanovich, 1989), 63–68. For a treatment of the story within the context of Cavafy's poetry, see Martin McKinsey, "Where Are the Greeks: Revisiting Cavafy's 'Philhellene,'" *Cavafy Forum* (2010), accessed 5 May 2019, https://lsa.umich.edu/content/dam/modgreek-assets/modgreek-docs/CPC_Mckinsey_Philhellene_wherearethegreeks.pdf.

59. Woolf, *Virginia Woolf: Travel and Literary Notebook, 1906–1909*, held by the British Library, accessed 5 May 2019, https://www.bl.uk/collection-items/virginia-woolfs-travel-and-literary-notebook-1906-9.

Plato, Sophocles, Euripides, and others in the original.[60] A free thinker in a family with strong artistic and intellectual leanings, she married Leonard Woolf in 1912, a journalist, political writer, and sometime civil servant in Ceylon (now Sri Lanka). The two of them founded the Hogarth Press in 1917, distinguished among other things for its publication of the Standard Edition in English of the complete works of Freud.

They were central figures in Bloomsbury, a group of politically liberal artists and thinkers, many from Cambridge, who were joined by a spirit of rebellion against social convention, anti-imperialist views, deep interests in Hellenism, and complicated, polyamorous relationships with one another, often in ways that overlapped with their creative and scholarly work.[61] Vanessa Bell, Virginia's sister, was a painter at whose home in Gordon Square the so-called "Thursday evenings" started with a circle that included her husband Clive Bell, Lytton Strachey, Desmond MacCarthy, Maynard Keynes, Roger Fry, Duncan Grant, and, of course, the Woolfs. While Virginia's friend and lover Vita Sackville-West, a British aristocratic poet and novelist who inspired *Orlando*, was at the margins of Bloomsbury, both she and her husband, Harold Nicolson, an ambassador to Tehran and Constantinople among other places, had an open marriage and lived polyamorous lives like others in that group. Woolf suffered a number of mental breakdowns in her life, four between the ages of thirteen and thirty-three, and she was institutionalized as a consequence of some of them.[62] In her diaries, letters, and memoir, *A Sketch of the Past,* she writes of the episodes in some detail. While her bouts of mental illness were precipitated by numerous factors, she was severely depressed by World War II and the bombing of her London house in the Blitz. In 1941, she drowned herself in the River Ouse behind Monk's House, where she and Leonard Woolf lived.

Born in 1913 in Basse Pointe, Martinique, a village on the northeastern coast of the island exposed to the Atlantic, Aimé Césaire grew up in a plantation economy, about sixty-five years after the abolition of slavery in 1848.[63]

---

60. Woolf's Greek notebook is held at The Keep in East Sussex. See Theodore Koulouris, "Virginia Woolf's Greek Notebook (VS Greek and Latin Studies): An Annotated Transcription," *Woolf Studies Annual* 25 (2019): 1–197.

61. Christine Froula, *Virginia Woolf and the Bloomsbury Avant-Garde: War, Civilization, and Modernity* (New York: Columbia University Press, 2007); and Madelyn Detloff and Brenda Helt, eds., *Queer Bloomsbury* (Edinburgh: Edinburgh University Press, 2016).

62. Lee, *Virginia Woolf,* 170–96; Bell, *Virginia Woolf,* 35–36, 43–47.

63. For a full biography in French, see Romuald Fonkoua, *Aimé Césaire* (Paris: Perrin, 2010). There is a brief biography in English in Césaire, *Journal of a Homecoming: Bilingual Edition,* trans. N. Gregson Davis with commentary by Abiola Irele (Durham, NC: Duke University Press, 2017), 3–40; and a chronology in Césaire, *The Complete Poetry of Aimé Césaire: Bilin-*

Cavafy had already embarked upon what he considered the mature phase of his poetry, having completed his most famous poem, "Ithaca," in 1911, and Woolf had begun work on her first published novel, *The Voyage Out,* which was coincidentally set in a quasi-mythical Caribbean on a ship headed for South America. These details also suggest the weak links that connect them, islands and the sea being common elements. Having performed exceptionally well at the lycée in Fort-de-France, he went on to study in Paris at the École Normale Supérieure where he met Senghor, who introduced him to Africa, as Césaire would later say. It was a friendship that lasted all their lives. With Senghor and Damas, he created the student journal, *L'étudiant noir,* in which he published an early piece on racial consciousness and revolution. He participated in the cosmopolitan Parisian world of the Martiniquan Nardal sisters, Jane and Paulette, which included Suzanne Roussi, who would become his wife. Fed by the classics-heavy curriculum of the university, Césaire began writing *Cahier* while abroad. Like other black intellectuals in Paris at the time, he was attracted to Marxism and the promise it offered for an anti-imperial and anticolonial politics. He returned to his island in 1939 with his wife, Suzanne Roussi, and together with René Ménil, they founded the journal *Tropiques* whose purpose was to affirm Antillean culture and its partially lost African heritage. Suzanne, in particular, took an interest in German ethnographic theories and wrote about them in the journal. During the period of the Vichy regime when many French artists were in exile, André Breton visited Martinique where he discovered *Tropiques,* which he elevated into an icon of surrealist aesthetics. He hailed Césaire's *Cahier* as "nothing less than the greatest lyrical monument of the times."[64]

In 1945, Césaire began a long political career as mayor of Fort-de-France and was elected deputy to the French National Assembly, on a Communist ticket, cosponsoring the law in 1946 that made France's West Indian colonies into *départements d'outre mer.* He resigned from the Communist party in 1956, having reedited the year before his blistering essay, *Discours sur le colonialisme (Discourse on Colonialism),* which was published by Présence Africaine to wider audiences.[65] He was intensely active as a poet, dramatist, and essayist his whole life, and he collaborated with Breton, Picasso, and Wifredo

gual Edition, trans. James Arnold and Clayton Eshleman (Middleton, CT: Wesleyan University Press, 2017), xiii–xxvi.

64. See André Breton, preface of *Cahier d'un retour au pays natal / Return to my Native Land: Bilingual Edition* (New York: Brentano, 1947).

65. Césaire, *Discours sur le colonialisme* (Paris: Éditions Reclame, 1950; Paris: Présence Africaine, 1955); *Discourse on Colonialism,* trans. Joan Pinkham (New York: Monthly Review Press, 1972).

Lam, among others. He was among the first playwrights to adapt Shakespeare's *The Tempest* to a postcolonial Caribbean setting.[66] Having had six children with Suzanne Roussi, they were divorced after twenty-five years of marriage in 1963. She remains something of a mystery, having published nothing after 1945 and having died early at the age of fifty.[67] When her husband passed away at the age of 94, he had become *"père Césaire"* to the Martiniquans, one of the fathers who had taught at the lycée in Fort-de-France where Franz Fanon and Édouard Glissant were students.

Only recently has it become possible to think of three such different writers together—and in the company of Homer. So various are their backgrounds, languages, and cultural milieux that without the intense work being done in translation, global modernisms, black internationalism, and classical reception, this study would have been literally unthinkable, at least to this writer, even ten years ago, when it was so much sea foam. Whatever the limits of our new English lingua franca, and they are significant, it has enabled readers, writers, and critics to join in dialogues across previously closed or minimally porous boundaries. The challenges of keeping poetic language alive remain considerable, but this book has been written, in part, to contribute to the efforts.

---

66. Césaire, *Une tempête* (Paris: Seuil, 1969).

67. See Kara Rabbitt, "In Search of the Missing Mother: Suzanne Césaire, *Martiniquaise*," *Research in African Literatures* 44.1 (2013): 36–54.

~

Diffusion and Mixture

We are entirely made up of bits and pieces, interwoven so
diversely and in a form so changeable that each element at every
moment acts out its own role. And there is as much difference
between us and ourselves as between us and other people.

*Nous sommes tous faits de pieces et de morceaux, d'un arrangement
si varié et de forme si changeante, que chaque élément, à
chaque instant, joue son rôle. Et il y a autant de différence
entre nous et nous-mêmes qu' entre nous et un autre.*

—MONTAIGNE, "ON THE INCONSTANCY OF OUR
ACTIONS" (*"SUR L'INCONSTANCE DE NOS ACTIONS"*)

ONE OF THE CHIEF characteristics of odysseys is that they deal
in multiples often in combination with geographical expanses
that embrace a range of cultural differences. The Homeric prefix
"*poly*" is key in understanding this, particularly because the prefix is coupled
in the *Odyssey* with the notion of cunning intelligence (*metis*), as we see in
the epithets *polymetis* (crafty), *polytropos* (many-skilled), and *polymechanos*
(resourceful). The construction of fictional worlds as manifolds can look in
several directions: toward articulating plural selves; toward developing the
consequences of migration and colonization for a collective sense of identity;
or toward addressing divisions within a community that may be productive
or dysfunctional. Often such constructions are accompanied by a cartographic
sensibility that has both synchronic and diachronic dimensions. Places not
only change over time, but they have histories that shape the conditions in
which life on the margins is lived. Maps and visual geographies lend a certain
concreteness to this marginality. They pack layers of meaning, both personal
and communal, and foster the sense of a world that is, for better or worse,
far flung, tenuously connected, and constantly shifting under the pressures of
change. It is through diffusion and mixture, in other words, that sexuality, gender, and race may be troped and made available for imaginative exploration.

Chapter 1 traces this play, with special attention to Homer's Crete, Cavafy's Magna Graecia, Césaire's Antilles, and Woolf's country estate as microcosm.[1]

HOMER: THE *ODYSSEY* IN A SEA OF DIFFERENCE

Picture an ancient rugged palace with a hearth in a great hall made to offer warmth, welcome to strangers, and a sanctuary for domestic worship. It was filled with a rough lot of uninvited men helping themselves to the provisions of the house during the day, a behavior that has become a practice. But it's evening now, the intruders have scattered, and a fire burns, casting shadows in the dark. Before it, a man and a woman sit, exchanging stories of their past, she the queen, beautiful but troubled, he a vagrant who has suffered loss and draws her sympathy. They have known each other's presence in the palace before this encounter, but they have only just met, and the half-light expresses the curiosity and edginess they feel.

The intruders in the house are suitors of the queen, acting with impunity in the absence of a master. Having waited for a husband who has not returned after a twenty-year absence, the queen tells the vagrant that she has heard many tales about the man for whom she waits, all of which she regards with skepticism. A trick she has devised to defer a decision about remarrying has not worked: weaving by day and unweaving by night to fend off suitors she has promised to satisfy once the cloth has been finished, she has been found out. Her ruse discovered, she must now remarry. The vagrant admires her resourcefulness and fidelity and tells her they have won her acclaim abroad. But he is reluctant to reciprocate with his own narrative. When he does respond, he describes himself by opening with an account of where he comes from and a genealogy:

---

1. For the Greek *Odyssey*, I use Helmut van Thiel's edition (Hildesheim: Georg Olms, 1991), and for the English, the translation by Robert Fagles (New York: Penguin, 1996). In parenthetical citations, the book and line numbers cited first refer to the Fagles translation; the ones that appear second refer to the line numbers in the Greek text. For Cavafy, unless specified otherwise, I use *Collected Poems: Bilingual Edition*, ed. George Savidis; rev trans. Edmund Keeley and Philip Sherrard (Princeton: Princeton University Press, 2009). Reprinted by permission of Princeton University Press. For Woolf, I use *Orlando: A Biography*, annotated by Maria DiBattista (New York: Harcourt, Inc., 2006). For Césaire, quotations are from the bilingual edition *Journal of a Homecoming*, trans. by N. Gregson Davis with commentary by Abiola Irele (Durham, NC: Duke University Press, 2017), except where indicated; the text is based on the 1956 edition published by Présence Africaine, and stanza numbers are indicated in parenthesis.

There is a land called Crete . . .
ringed by the wine-dark sea with rolling whitecaps—
handsome country, fertile, thronged with people
well past counting—boasting ninety cities,
language mixing with language side-by-side.
First come the Achaeans, then the native Cretans,
Hardy, gallant in action, then Cydonian clansmen,
Dorians living in three tribes, and proud Pelasgians last.
Central to all their cities is magnificent Cnossos,
the site where Minos ruled and each ninth year
conferred with almighty Zeus himself. Minos,
father of my father, Deucalion, that bold heart.
Besides myself Deucalion sired Prince Idomeneus,
who set sail for Troy in his beaked ships of war,
escorting Atreus' sons. My own name is Aethon . . .

Κρήτη τις γαῖ’ ἔστι, μέσῳ ἐνὶ οἴνοπι πόντῳ,
καλὴ καὶ πίειρα, περίρρυτος· ἐν δ’ ἄνθρωποι
πολλοί, ἀπειρέσιοι, καὶ ἐννήκοντα πόληες·
ἄλλη δ’ ἄλλων γλῶσσα μεμιγμένη· ἐν μὲν Ἀχαιοί,
ἐν δ’ Ἐτεόκρητες μεγαλήτορες, ἐν δὲ Κύδωνες,
Δωριέες τε τριχάικες δῖοί τε Πελασγοί·
τῇσι δ’ ἐνὶ Κνωσός, μεγάλη πόλις, ἔνθα τε Μίνως
ἐννέωρος βασίλευε Διὸς μεγάλου ὀαριστής,
πατρὸς ἐμοῖο πατήρ, μεγαθύμου Δευκαλίωνος.
Δευκαλίων δ’ ἐμὲ τίκτε καὶ Ἰδομενῆα ἄνακτα·
ἀλλ’ ὃν μὲν ἐν νήεσσι κορωνίσιν Ἴλιον εἴσω
ᾤχεθ’ ἅμ’ Ἀτρείδῃσιν, ἐμοὶ δ’ ὄνομα κλυτὸν Αἴθων . . .

This scene occurs in Book 19 of the *Odyssey* (194–208; 172–83), and almost nothing is as it seems to be. Odysseus speaks through the persona of a broken-down Cretan, "telling lies that resemble the truth" ("ψεύδεα πολλὰ λέγων ἐτύμοισιν ὁμοῖα," 19.235; 19.203) to the wife whom he knows to be faithful and deserves his trust. Penelope sizes up the vagrant with her usual circumspection—she is attentive and cautious ("περίφρων")—but she does not acknowledge that he is her long-lost husband. Despite all signs pointing in that direction, there is no recognition scene. Instead, the intimate meeting on Ithaca opens up a completely different narrative about a bustling island in the south Aegean that the disguised Odysseus, who names himself Aethon, identifies as his own. There, he tells Penelope, is the land of his ancestors: they include Minos, the Cretan king Thucydides would later identify as the ruler who first created a great navy; a man the stranger claims as his grandfather, Deucalion, who survived the catastrophic flood that wiped out humankind; and Idomeneus who led a large contingent to Troy. At a late moment in the epic when the audience expects an intensification of the homing instinct, the conjugal pair move in separate directions, apart, not together. Not only does Odysseus's life story wander along other routes at this moment when he draws close to his wife. Penelope's own thoughts recede into an opacity that has long provoked audiences of the epic. Surely, she recognizes the man facing her. Eurycleia, the old maid who has raised Odysseus, is about to do just that when she bends to wash the beggar's feet and sees his scar.

What's happening here? I suggest the scene enacts one of the epic's chief dynamics: movement toward the center (home) is being interrupted by the contravening force of an alternative story that disrupts it (the foreign). The *Odyssey*, a return tale, is interfering with its own end, at both the fictional level of homecoming and the level of poetic composition, or narrative closure. In this passage, the story not only displaces the identity of Odysseus by giving him a different genealogy located on an island brimming with ethnicities, but it also estranges the couple in a scene of intimacy at the hearth, partly by inserting a lying tale. Diffusion on the large-scale geographical level of bustling Crete is being registered on the small-scale domestic level of an estranged married couple. The suitors, in other words, are not the only ones who stand in the way of a conjugal reunion. Framing the local situation are the conditions of life in a highly circulatory sea, and these conditions are linked by divergent tales. Much of the epic is bound up in this dynamic of alienation within the home and competing narratives. Penelope's web—the doing and undoing of it, the indeterminate character of its woven subject matter—is one of its key emblems. If the *Odyssey* is a foundation tale, diffusion and mixture are its "base." They loosely connect the lands that become Hellas, and they would eventually lead into a history of divisive quarrels between city states.

Let us take a closer look. The Crete that appears in *Odyssey* 19 is a teeming island surrounded by a wine-dark sea and "thronged with people / well past counting" (196–97; "πολλοί ἀπειρέσιοι," 174) who live in ninety cities and speak multiple languages, "language mixing with language side-by-side" (198; "ἄλλη δ' ἄλλων γλῶσσα μεμιγμένη," 175).[2] Crete's insularity does not isolate it,

        2. For discussions of Crete and the Cretan tales in the *Odyssey*, see Gregory Nagy, "Diachronic Homer and a Cretan Odyssey," *Oral Tradition* 31.1 (2017): 3–50; Olga Levaniouk, *Eve of the Festival: Mythmaking in* Odyssey 19 (Washington DC: Center for Hellenic Studies, 2011); Richard Martin, "Cretan Homers: Tradition, Politics, Fieldwork," *Classics@ 3, The Homerizon: Conceptual Interrogations in Homeric Studies* (2005), accessed 5 May 2019, https://chs.harvard.

but rather emphasizes its location in a network of sea crossings where strangers meet to conduct commerce and trade. In this picture, diffusion is productive, generative, and, by implication, enabled by *xenia,* the law of hospitality. Here we see the early Mediterranean as a place where interactive cultures come together in a colorful maritime marketplace of goods and ideas, a kind of peak period in which humans mingle peacefully in a sea of difference.

But this Crete does not occupy a place in the fictional time present of the epic; it is the Minoan island we see here before the rise of Mycenae to a position of Aegean hegemony. Although the proem in Book 1 of the *Odyssey* describes an Odysseus who saw "many cities of men . . . and learned their minds" (1.4; "πολλῶν δ᾽ ἀνθρώπων ἴδεν ἄστεα καὶ νόον ἔγνω," 1.3), the world of the wanderings offers no such thing.[3] That is a place of monsters, witches, and ogres. It is only in the Cretan tales, and this one told to Penelope, in particular, that we get an image of a cosmopolitan world of robust cities where people jostle and do business in multiple tongues. In other words, Homer's proem, which describes an odyssey that sounds like an adventure tale of extensive contact with foreign lands, does not precisely describe *this* odyssey, which tells a story of forced exile and suffering. From the outset, the narrative into which we are inducted intimates other tellings, toward which Odysseus's Cretan lie obliquely gestures.

The variety that characterizes the island of Crete gathers ethnographic depth from the peoples listed by name in the passage quoted above.[4] "Achaeans" is the word used most often in Homeric epic to describe the Greeks who collectively formed the expedition to Troy, that is, the Mycenaeans. Before them, there were the "native" or "true Cretans," who were the indigenous people, presumably the Minoans, after the name of their most famous king; and next, there were the Cydonians, who were inhabitants of the northwestern part of the island and, if not indigenous, then perhaps a mix of Minoan and Mycenaean. The Pelasgians, as the ancient Greeks themselves thought, were the prehistoric inhabitants of the land before the Greeks arrived, that is,

edu/CHS/article/display/1827; Steve Reece, "The Cretan Odyssey: A Lie Truer Than Truth," *American Journal of Philology* 115.2 (1994): 157–73; and Chris Emlyn-Jones, "True and Lying Tales in the *Odyssey*," *Greece and Rome* 33.1 (1986): 1–10. On alternative odysseys, see J. Marks, "Alternative Odysseys: The Case of Thoas and Odysseus," *Transactions of the American Philological Association* 133 (2003): 209–26.

3. On the proem of the *Odyssey,* see Irene de Jong, *A Narratological Commentary on the* Odyssey (New York: Cambridge University Press, 2001), 3–8; Jenny Strauss Clay, *The Wrath of Athena: Gods and Men in the* Odyssey (Princeton: Princeton University Press, 1983), 3–53; and Pietro Pucci, "The Proem of the *Odyssey,*" *Arethusa* 15.1–2 (1982): 39–62.

4. The ethnographic divisions listed in this passage are a topic of considerable scholarly dispute. For a fuller discussion with bibliography, see James Clackson, *Language and Society in the Greek and Roman Worlds* (New York: Cambridge University Press, 2015), 1–8.

non-Greeks. And the Dorians were a Greek-speaking people who arrived last in the land that would become Hellas. Within a few lines, the *Odyssey* calls up rolling pasts, now archaeologically identified as the Minoan-Mycenaean bronze ages, roughly the second millennium BCE, in which ancient peoples were already reflecting upon their own antiquity. The hallmarks of this memory are diverse ethnicities and multiple spoken languages, in functional relation to each other though suggestive of the friction that would lead to the eventual historical displacement of the Minoan empire by the Mycenaean.[5] That friction inheres as a trace element in the moment at which Odysseus remembers, a belated time marked by a fall from prosperity. This is the present time in the *Odyssey*, which is removed by multiple generations from the prosperity of bronze-age Crete.

The vibrant diversity of this large Aegean island may be described in terms of a particular kind of mixture, namely, syncretism. It is an island where scattered peoples—indigenous Cretans, Achaeans, Cydonians, Pelasgians, and Dorians—coexist and come together in encounters where difference is asserted but tolerance is also exercised.[6] That is one of the reasons why the list of names is important; these are not an assimilated people, and Crete is not a melting pot. Indeed, the island is referred to in the passage with a plural pronoun: "In them [Cretes], there is a large city, Cnossus" is a literal translation of line 178: "τῇσι δ᾽ ἐνὶ Κνωσός, μεγάλη πόλις." While this has been explained as "an elliptical plural" meaning "Crete and everything that belongs to it," the pluralizing illustrates a general tendency toward splitting and multiplication.[7] There are indeed several Cretes in the *Odyssey*.

In the *Iliad*, genealogy functions as a signifier of a unique patriarchal identity. But in *Odyssey* 19, it appears fungible. The authority it has outside the tale is displaced by the tale, which takes it over and uses it circumstantially to create an illusion of identity. In the process, the poem attenuates familial ties, transforming them from strong into weak or provisional bonds. Rather than exercising a natural power that derives from biological kinship, genealogy is subject to the superior force of Odysseus's storytelling art. Minos and Deucalion are divinely connected heroes who enjoy the privilege of Zeus. Yet it is a lying Odysseus, harassed by divine wrath, famous for his dubious morality, and brought low after fighting in the Trojan War, who says so. The family heritage he relates to Penelope is not only someone else's, but it goes against

---

5. See Nagy, "Diachronic Homer and a Cretan Odyssey."

6. On syncretism as both a lived experience and hermeneutic term, see Vassilis Lambropoulos, "Syncretism as Mixture and Method," *Journal of Modern Greek Studies* 19.2 (2001): 221–35.

7. See Nagy, "A Cretan Odyssey, Part 2."

the grain of the story that the *Odyssey* tells of its hero. Rather than focusing on the intrinsic veracity of the tale, the poet demonstrates Odysseus's ability to manipulate it as a fictional device.

When genealogy migrates from being a singular signifier of a patriarchal line to a convertible element in storytelling, it takes on other forms of diffusion, substituting alternative identities for biologically connected ones. In short, it becomes the product of narrative craft. The *Odyssey* foregrounds this dynamic of epichoric variations on the return tale, dramatizing the conditional circumstances in which collective narratives emerge. It provides a glimpse of how the Greeks saw themselves as a people in the course of their early settlements in southern Italy, the Aegean coast of Asia Minor, and the Black Sea, or what would later become Magna Graecia.[8] In so doing, it also illuminates the strains placed upon family bonds, which become attenuated through lateral movement, and upon the individuals who survive to tell their tales.

This point takes on greater depth if we consider the name Odysseus gives himself in the faux genealogy. He calls himself Aethon, a disputed word probably connected to a Greek term that means "fire" (αἶθος) or "burnt" (αἰθός). It may signify something like "the one who burns," but also "the one who is fiery by necessity."[9] Other connotations, however, are possible. Aethon—in Greek, Aithon—is linked with the word "*Aithiops*," or "Ethiopian," and the Ethiopians, or "burnished ones," in Homer are a people among whom Poseidon, Odysseus's nemesis, often sojourns.[10] In the first lines of the *Odyssey*, for example, while Zeus and Athena deliberate about how to handle the exile of Odysseus, Poseidon is said to be absent from Olympus, visiting "the Ethiopians worlds away, / Ethiopians off at the farthest limits of mankind, / a people split in two, one part where the Sungod sets / and part where the Sungod rises. There Poseidon went / to receive an offering, bulls and rams by the hundred" (1.25–29; "Αἰθίοπας, τοὶ διχθὰ δεδαίαται, ἔσχατοι ἀνδρῶν, / οἳ μὲν δυσομένου Ὑπερίονος, οἱ δ᾽ ἀνιόντος, / ἀντιόων ταύρων τε καὶ ἀρνειῶν ἑκατόμβης," 1.22–25). What is most important here is that the Ethiopians are those who live "at the farthest limits of mankind," some in the east, some in the west. In Homer, this extremity is connected, not with barbarism, but with their moral piety and extraordinary prosperity as mortals who are always feasting. This

---

8. See Irad Malkin, *The Returns of Odysseus: Colonization and Ethnicity* (Berkeley: University of California Press, 1998), 1–32; and Carol Dougherty, *The Raft of Odysseus: The Ethnographic Imagination of Homer's* Odyssey (New York: Oxford University Press, 2001), 3–18.

9. On the name, see Olga Levaniouk, "*Aithôn, Aithon*, and Odysseus," *Harvard Studies in Classical Philology* 100 (2000): 25–51.

10. See Alfred Heubeck, et al, eds., *Commentary on Homer's* Odyssey. 3 Vols. (Oxford: Clarendon, 1988), 1:74–76; and James Romm, *The Edges of the Earth in Ancient Thought: Geography, Exploration, and Fiction* (Princeton: Princeton University Press, 1992), 45–60.

explains the epithet that characterizes them: "*amumon*," or "blameless." When
Poseidon is among them, he moves not only into a land of plenty with pious
inhabitants but also behind an "opaque screen" where no one can see him and
where his own vision is limited.[11]

Interestingly, the extremity of the Homeric Ethiopians will later make
them the subject of an ambivalent ethnocentrism in Greek geography: the
center may be regarded as a position of superiority (foreigners are perceived
as less evolved and barbaric) or inferiority (foreigners are idealized, the farther away they are, the more so). In Homer, the Ethiopians are elevated, but
ironically, if we consider Odysseus's contrived name. He is driven by a scarcity
of food that is the inverse of Ethiopian abundance. What may be more significant, however, is that Aithon activates a weak, and oblique, link with visibility
and nonvisibility. For Penelope to be with a man who is a kind of Aithiops
is to be unable to see him, as he cannot clearly see her. The name assumes a
place within a broader diffusion associated with migration, wandering, and
the earth's edges.

From this perspective, Odysseus's bluffing is worth examining more
closely. While cunning and deceit are heroic aspects of his character that
enable survival in an unpredictable and hostile world, they also suggest a
pathology, a form of maladaptive behavior that intrudes into social interactions by arousing heightened defenses that block the very thing sought. His
dissembling, in other words, appears symptomatic at times, a consequence of
internal processes that are not discursively formulated in Homer's text, but
that appear immanent.[12] The *metis* in Odysseus's storytelling, which arguably
gives him room to maneuver in the risky environment of home, may also be
seen as a misplaced use of lying—the weaving of a tale before a woman known
for her own extraordinary weaving.[13] It is along these lines that the *Odyssey*
has been approached as a paradigmatic text for understanding war and war
veterans who are sometimes unable to reenter the social order after trauma
and engage in forms of malingering, avoidance, and mendacity that are self-

---

11. See Romm, *Edges of the Earth*, 46–47.

12. For a fuller treatment of "the symptom" in Homeric epic and the *sōma / psychē* distinction, see Brooke Holmes, *The Symptom and the Subject: The Emergence of the Physical Body in
Ancient Greece* (Princeton: Princeton University Press, 2014), 1–82. On the Homeric mind or
soul, see Joseph Russo, "Re-Thinking Homeric Psychology: Snell, Dodds, and Their Critics,"
Quaderni Urbinati di Cultura Classical 101.2 (2012): 11–28. The term "immanent Homer" is that
of Egbert Bakker, "Rhapsodes, Bards, and Bricoleurs: Homerizing Literary Theory," *Classics @:
Issue 3*, accessed 5 May 2019, http://www.chs.harvard.edu/publications.sec/classics.ssp.

13. On the associations between weaving, *metis*, and *nostos*, see Bergren, *Weaving Truth*,
especially chapters 1 and 4.

defeating.[14] In this context, the epic emerges as a poem whose scope embraces not only efficacious cleverness but also the detrimental consequences of prolonged violence upon the one who suffers it. The damaged wanderer cannot reenter the old order, which in any case is never the same. Every story is both a return and a deferral of return.

If geography, genealogy, character, and birth name are marked by forms of diffusion and mixture in *Odyssey* 19, so is *nostos* itself, which is usually translated into English as "homecoming." The word has been connected to the Indo-European root "*nes-*," which means "save oneself," and interpreted to signify in its earliest sense "a return from death and darkness to light and life."[15] In Homer it refers not only to the journey but also to the story one tells about it. Narrative is integral to the concept.[16] It often takes on a directional sense through such expressions as "*oikade,*" meaning "toward home," and in the *Odyssey,* especially, "toward home from the Trojan War." But the verb to which it is related, *neomai,* has both centrifugal and centripetal force. It can mean "come" or "go," and in the play of Homeric poetry, it gathers an energy that is based upon shifting perspectives. Coming may also be going and returning home may also be arriving alive in a place only to encounter further danger.

Kleos is intertwined with this itinerancy and diffusion, and in the *Odyssey,* it enables a view of island dynamics, especially as they involve Ithaca, which is topographically marginal to the Aegean. In the most basic sense, *kleos* refers to reports that circulate by word of mouth.[17] Beginning with local talk, it is typically spread by travelers, and ultimately it can lead to fame in oral

---

14. The most far-reaching study in this vein is Shay, *Odysseus in America.* Other studies elaborate upon Shay's ideas, for example, the essays in Meineck and Konstan, *Combat Trauma and the Ancient Greeks.* In the latter, see especially Kurt Raaflaub, "War and the City: The Brutality of War and Its Impact on the Community," 15–46, and Corinne Pache, "Women after War: Weaving *Nostos* in Homeric Epic and in the Twenty-First Century," 67–86. See also Dany Nobus, "*Polymetis* Freud: Some Reflections on the Psychoanalytic Significance of Homer's *Odyssey,*" *Comparative Literature Studies* 43.3 (2006): 252–68; Joel Friedman and Sylia Gassel, "Odysseus: The Return of the Primal Father," *Psychoanalytic Quarterly* 21 (1952): 215–23; and Arthur Wormhoudt, *The Muse at Length: A Psychoanalytic Study of the* Odyssey (Boston: Christopher, 1953).

15. See Donald Frame, *The Myth of Return in Early Greek Epic* (New Haven: Yale University Press, 1978), 28.

16. See Bakker, *Meaning of Meat,* 13–35; and Anna Bonifazi, "Inquiring into *Nostos* and Its Cognates," *American Journal of Philology* 130.4 (2009): 481–510.

17. For *kleos* in the *Odyssey* and its ambiguities, see Andrew Ford, *Homer and the Poetry of the Past* (Ithaca, NY: Cornell University Press, 1992), 57–67; Charles Segal, *Singers, Heroes, and Gods in the* Odyssey (Ithaca, NY: Cornell University Press, 1994), 85–109; and Douglas Olson, *Blood and Iron: Stories and Storytelling in Homer's* Odyssey (Leiden: Brill, 1995), 1–17 and 43–47.

song.[18] If Odysseus has already won *kleos* in the *Iliad*, it is in need of updating in the *Odyssey*. In the newer epic, his excellence, or *arete*, is dependent not upon performance in battle, but upon an ability to survive in a world that requires *metis*—practical intelligence, the adoption of different personas, and cunning perseverance. In the absence of her husband, Penelope has won *kleos* by weaving wiles that help her maintain her fidelity under duress.[19] Helen's own weaving is often connected, not only with her role in initiating the Trojan War but also with scenes of that war, which she crafts in her handiwork at the loom. When she offers Telemachus a robe as a guest-gift during his visit to the court of Menelaus in *Odyssey* 3, she puts it into circulation in the world beyond Sparta where it will augment her own *kleos*. As *kleos* ramifies, it may be absorbed into the most distinguished oral form of performance, epic song. The latter lays down heavier tracks, but in general, report in the *Odyssey* is poetically cultivated in ways that suggest tenuity and currency—a world bound by weak rather than strong links.

To sum up, by the time of Homer, Crete had already become associated with diffusion and mixture, which may have been elements in the formulation of the proverb that all Cretans are liars.[20] As for Odysseus, he had already become associated with alternative tales, a living embodiment of the epithets by which he is best known: *polytropos, polymetis,* and *polymechanos.*[21] The bard acknowledges such tales obliquely by alluding to them in the act of marginalizing them. As lies that resemble the truth, the Cretan tales may have a psychic dimension, pointing to *nostos* as a journey of the soul in which lying emerges as a symptom that defers the ostensible object of desire, a point to which we will return in chapter 3. If obliquity characterizes Odysseus, it extends to Penelope. Husband and wife maneuver around each other as spouses who are ironically joined by bonds of *xenia,* the guest-host relations that enable strangers to come together. These interwoven layers invite interpretations that respect the indirection with which the major characters in the *Odyssey* approach each other. They also invite the audience to appreciate the

---

18. See Michelle Zerba, *Doubt and Skepticism in Antiquity and the Renaissance* (New York: Cambridge University Press, 2012), 85–110.

19. See Melissa Mueller, "Helen's Hands: Weaving for *Kleos* in the *Odyssey,*" *Helios* 37.1 (2010): 1–21; and Marilyn Katz, *Penelope's Renown: Meaning and Indeterminacy in the* Odyssey (Princeton: Princeton University Press, 1991), 20–29, 192–95.

20. For a discussion, see Richard Thomas, "Cretan Homers: Tradition, Politics, Fieldwork," *Classics @3,* Colloquium at Center for Hellenic Studies, accessed 5 May 2019, https://www.chs.harvard.edu/CHS/article/display/1307.

21. For two influential formulations of Odysseus's *polytropos,* see John Peradotto, *Man in the Middle: Name and Narration in the* Odyssey (Princeton: Princeton University Press, 1990); and Pietro Pucci, *Odysseus Polytropos* (Ithaca, NY: Cornell University Press, 1987).

indirection of the epic itself and its ways of crafting stories that reflect the contested character of interwoven narratives. A similar dynamic is at work in the poems of Cavafy.

CAVAFY: DIASPORA, OBLIQUE ENCOUNTERS, AND HOMOEROTIC DESIRE

If the *nostoi* of the *Odyssey* are connected with the early ways the ancient Greeks envisioned their settlements abroad, they also illuminate how human relationships at home are strained to the tipping point by war and its aftermath. Of course, the pursuit of wealth, historically speaking, was a major factor driving some of the early *apoikiai*, literally, "homes away from home," and this determined their location on the littorals of the Mediterranean, especially in Sicily and Italy. Mercantile profit lay behind what could turn an *apoikia* into an *emporion,* a word that refers to a place where a typically transient population of traders became settled over time, often growing into a major center of affluence that spawned secondary foundations.[22] In some cases, wealth became associated with hedonistic practices, and the combination of the two lies behind some well-known poems of Cavafy. This dimension of his work takes on particular significance in light of his own family's wealth, which came from trade in the Mediterranean and England (London, Manchester, Liverpool), two regions he often intertwined in his poetry. It is ironic, in light of the itinerancy of his own family, that he chose to settle in Alexandria and to do very little traveling after he established himself there. Like Woolf, and to a lesser extent Césaire, the odyssean tonalities of his work were shaped by early journeys and by a life of intense reading, both of which had a lasting impact on his creative work.

He also lived in a cosmopolitan Alexandrian neighborhood of homes and shops owned by Greeks, Austrians, Italians, French, and British, and he cultivated, through afternoon conversations in his apartment with friends and visitors, a wide variety of individuals and families with whom he spoke Greek, French, and English. He knew only rudimentary Arabic, however, and he may never have visited the home of an Egyptian family, though the city was

---

22. For a wide-ranging treatment of the Mediterranean on which this discussion draws, see Peregrine Horden and Nicholas Purcell, *The Corrupting Sea: A Study of Mediterranean History* (Oxford: Wiley-Blackwell, 2000), 9–50. On *apoikia* and *emporion,* see Robert Garland, *Wandering Greeks: The Ancient Greek Diaspora from the Age of Homer to the Death of Alexander the Great* (Princeton: Princeton University Press, 2014), 34–38.

predominantly Muslim.[23] It was the Egypt of antiquity to which he was connected in his poetry, and he was, of course, geographically close to Crete.[24] Scenes drawn from remote corners of the past are ubiquitous in Cavafy's work. They mark the fact that he was not a poet of autochthony. In fact, he visited Greece only four times in his life, and rather than describing himself as a "Hellene" (Έλλην) or a "Hellenist" (ἑλληνίζων), he called himself "Hellenic" (ἑλληνικός)—a Greek by sensibility and culture rather than by blood or geographical location.[25] His Hellenism diverged from the European Enlightenment's view of Greek culture, which emphasized the achievements of the classical age in democracy, architecture, poetry, and ethical philosophy, and demoted Byzantium. Cavafy, on the other hand, embraced Byzantine culture, including the cult of the saints, which was marginalized in most Western views of Greece.[26] Living as he did on the rim of north Africa, facing the Mediterranean, he inhabited a site of mixture that extended back millennia, and his poetry is rich with the cultural heterogeneity of the region.

Archaeology was one of the lenses through which he saw some of this past. He argued for the return of the Elgin marbles, and he did so by calling out the disdainful opinion toward modern Greeks expressed in a British monthly review on the controversy as "the mixed little population which now lives upon the ruins of ancient Greece."[27] We get a less defensive point of view in a newspaper article Cavafy wrote in 1892 to mark the opening of the Museum of Alexandria. He recommends that excavations in the city continue, since "the ground on which we live undoubtedly hides many artifacts and many relics of ancient Alexandria."[28] What interests him, in particular,

---

23. For these details of Cavafy's Alexandrian life, I am indebted to Gregory Jusdanis, who is coauthoring with Peter Jeffreys a biography of Cavafy in English.

24. See Bettina Bader, "Egypt and the Mediterranean in the Bronze Age: The Archaeological Evidence," in *Oxford Handbooks Online* (2015), accessed 5 May 2019, doi: 10.1093/oxfordhb/9780199935413.013.35.

25. Recorded by Timos Malanos in *Περί Καβάφη* (Alexandria, 1935), 6.

26. See Martin McKinsey, *Hellenism and the Postcolonial Imagination: Yeats, Cavafy, Walcott* (Madison, NJ: Fairleigh Dickinson University Press, 2010), 21–35; Eleni Kefala, "Hybrid Modernisms in Greece and Argentina: The Case of Cavafy, Borges, Kalokyris, and Kyriakides," *Comparative Literature* 58.2 (2006): 113–27; Peter Jeffreys, "Cavafy, Forster, and the Eastern Question," *Journal of Modern Greek Studies* 19.1 (2001): 61–87; Sarah Ekdawi, "Cavafy's Byzantium," *Byzantine and Modern Greek Studies* 20 (1996): 17–34; Artemis Leontis, *Topographies of Hellenism: Mapping the Homeland* (Ithaca, NY: Cornell University Press, 1995), 1–39; Gregory Jusdanis, *Belated Modernity and Aesthetic Culture: Inventing National Literature* (Minneapolis: University of Minnesota Press, 1991), 1–12; and Diana Haas, *Le problème religieux dans l'oeuvre de Cavafy: Les années de formation, 1882–1905* (Paris: Université de Lille III, 1987).

27. James Knowles, "The Joke about the Elgin Marbles," *Nineteenth Century*, 29 (1891): 495–506.

28. Cavafy, "Our Museum," in *Selected Prose Works*, ed. and trans. Jeffreys, 41–42.

is the way the museum "speaks to the imagination [*phantasia*]" of Greeks about "the glorious Hellenism of Alexandria." Its collection "presents to us an image of that noble civilization that developed so robustly in Egypt, as in another Greece, injecting into the east [*Anatolia*] the Greek spirit and adorning eastern [*Anatolian*] ideas with the Greek refinement and grace with which it came into contact."[29] If these comments emphasize the vitality of Hellenism in Alexandria, many of his historical poems give expression to the vitality of Byzantium in relation to the Latin Middle Ages. Cutting a wide swath, Cavafy's poetic corpus navigates an array of Eastern and Western cultural contacts in a dialectic of exchange that recalls the brimming Crete of *Odyssey* 19. His poetic personas sometimes face the east from the angle of a superior western Greece and exoticize it. But they can also speak from the vantage of a hyphenated Greece-Egypt, which renders Hellas rather than the east distant and sometimes foreign.[30]

As these remarks suggest, at a time when nineteenth-century Greeks were engaged with the irredentist nationalism of the *Megale Idea,* or the "Great Idea," which sought to restore Magna Graecia, Cavafy followed different paths. Rather than embracing the emerging concept of a Greek nation, he was attuned to processes of cultural translation, and his poems reflect a range of attitudes related to authenticity, geographical boundaries, and inherited cultures. Significantly, his sense of what it means to be Greek is almost always inflected with the local, and he is fond of bringing an awareness of historical sedimentation into his works. Against this backdrop, a set of poetic strategies emerges. For Cavafy, diaspora becomes an imaginative medium for exploring the links that join a scattered people over space and time. Hellenism, in the process, becomes visible as a constructed site. Its competing voices give rise to multiply conceived collective identities that never resolve into a coherent synthesis, but instead remain suspended as possibilities within a larger exploratory framework of art.

From this perspective, Cavafy's creative work appears to enact a modern version of Homer's *Odyssey,* an epic that travels the byways and finds complex meaning in alluding to alternative versions. Greece in the nineteenth century, as it sought to shake off the five-hundred-year yoke of Ottoman rule, had to

---

29. Cavafy, "Our Museum," in *Selected Prose Works,* ed. and trans. Jeffreys, 42. For the Greek, see http://www.kavafis.gr/prose/content.asp?id=317&cat=6, accessed 5 May 2019.

30. For a fuller discussion, see Jeffreys, *Eastern Questions: Hellenism & Orientalism in the Writings of E. M. Forster & C. P. Cavafy* (Greensboro, NC: ELT Press, 2005), 88–114; Hala Halim, *Alexandrian Cosmopolitanism: An Archive* (New York: Fordham University Press, 2013), 56–119; and Dimitris Tziovas, "Beyond the Acropolis: Rethinking Neohellenism," *Journal of Modern Greek Studies* 19 (2001): 189–220.

reinvent itself in a world of evolved nations and crumbling empires where it had grown estranged from its own classical past.[31] This is how Cavafy's poetry takes on odyssean tonalities, testing narrative options and improvising identities. In his nuanced historical vision, homoerotic encounters take on some of the characteristics of contingency that he reads across the annals of Mediterranean time. They often arise from accidental crossings and oblique encounters in locales that are themselves at the edges of political power. Their deviancy is enhanced by a marginal geography that is not fantastical like the world of the wanderings in the *Odyssey*, but that is marked by itinerancy and risk, conceived in a unique register.

Cavafy's poetry certainly does not constitute anything like a founding tale, but it does approach the nineteenth-century challenges of imagining what Hellenism may be through a complex interweaving of hypothetical possibilities. These are worked out in the often gritty but sometimes aesthetically refined spaces where individuals of taste and erotic sensibility touch. Here, the glance, the sound beyond walls, the stir of an evanescent male form, convey an awareness of the strange within the familiar, of a fuller story only partly told, of cultural traces whose power lies in being suggestive rather than understood. Here, Cavafy's sense of a fragmentary history meets up with hidden sexual desire. Both may be positioned alongside the scene of the man and woman at the hearth in *Odyssey* 19, speaking in proximity but across distances in a language of indirection.

His compositional method, in significant ways, cultivates a poetics of weak links and oblique encounters. Cavafy was a chronic reviser, a fact George Seferis observes when he calls the writer's pieces "works in progress."[32] While there are 154 poems in the canon of "acknowledged" or "published" works ("ἀναγνωρισμένα"), we have an additional 27 published between 1886 and 1898 that were "repudiated" ("ἀποκηρυγμένα"), but that Cavafy never threw away; another 77 works that Cavafy completed but did not approve for publication and that are sometimes referred to as "hidden" ("κρυμμένα"); and yet another 25 poems known as "incomplete" ("ἀτελή") pieces that he was revising before he died. He also penned numerous prose writings and kept various notebooks on his work and private life.[33] None of the poems, even

---

31. See Jusdanis, *Belated Modernity,* 49–87.

32. George Seferis, *On the Greek Style: Selected Essays in Poetry and Hellenism,* trans. Th. D. Frangopoulos (Athens: Denise Harvey, 1992), 125.

33. Cavafy's methods of writing were intricate, and the experts do not always agree on the text. The authoritative source is George Savidis, *Οι Καβαφικές Ἐκδόσεις, 1891–1932: Περιγράφη και Σχόλιο* [The Cavafian Publications] (Athens: Tachydromou, 1966). Savidis's first edition of Cavafy, used in Keeley and Sherrard's bilingual edition, was later revised, and he substituted a monotonic for Cavafy's polytonic system of diacritical marks. On the need to reedit the Savidis

the "acknowledged" ones, were ever gathered in a collected edition that saw commercial distribution during his life, although in his last years, three privately printed collections circulated: *Poems (1905–1915)*, *Poems (1916–1918)*, and *Poems (1919–1930)* (or *–1931* or *–1932*).³⁴ The first two were thematically arranged into groups—the philosophical, the historical, and the hedonic. The third was chronologically arranged and never bound. Before his poems made their way into collections, Cavafy kept them in folders, with the pages held together by a brass pin in the upper left corner. The content of these folders was always changing, as poems were added, removed, and revised over time.³⁵ Cavafy's texts were not fixed, but open ended. As in the case of the *Odyssey*, but on a different scale, the trope of diffusion characterizes the process of artistic production itself.

It is possible to get a broader sense of how such tropes circulate in his poetry by examining a poem entitled "Poseidonians" ("Ποσειδωνιάται," 1906). This is a "hidden" piece, in which the speaker reflects upon what happens when migration from the native land entails settlement in proximity to other civilizations, which exert a transformative effect on the transplanted people. The work gives us a provocative view of the consequences of early colonial activity in the Greek world, and it does so by making us think about how Hellenism and barbarism might be conceived in a diasporic Mediterranean. In its use of an ancient epigraph by Athenaeus, a Greek rhetorician and grammarian of the third century CE, it also enables an examination of paratexts that obliquely import homosexual content. Such strategies are common in Cavafy's poetics of indirection.

The people of the poem's title were a colony established by the Greeks in the seventh century BCE in the southwestern Italian peninsula. This positions

---

text, see Cavafy, *The Collected Poems*, ed. Anthony Hirst and trans. Evangelos Sachperoglou (New York: Oxford University Press, 2007), xxxiv–xxxvi. Mendelsohn provides an overview of Cavafy's publishing in Cavafy, *Complete Poems*, trans. Mendelsohn (New York: Knopf, 2012), lviii–lxi.

34. For the Greek editions, see Cavafy, *Τα Ποιήματα Α (1897–1918)*, ed. George Savidis (Athens: Ikaros, 1991); *Τα Ποιήματα Β (1919–1933)*, ed. George Savidis (Athens: Ikaros, 1991); *Κρυμμένα ποιήματα (1877; –1923)*, ed. George Savidis (Athens: Ikaros, 1993); *Ατελή ποιήματα (1918–1932)*, ed. Renata Lavagnini (Athens: Ikaros, 1994); *Αποκηρυγμένα: Ποιήματα και μεταφράσεις (1886–1898)*, ed. George Savidis, 2nd ed. (Athens: Ikaros, 2013); *Τα Πεζά (1882; –1931)*, ed. Michael Pieris (Athens: Ikaros, 2003). Also see Sarah Ekdawi and Anthony Hirst, "Hidden Things: Cavafy's Thematic Catalogues," *Modern Greek Studies, Australia and New Zealand* 4 (1996): 1–34.

35. Aleko Senghopoulo inherited the poet's manuscripts, publications, and other documents. In 1963, he assigned the study and publication of these materials to George Savidis, who sold the archive in 1969. Ownership passed to his son Manuel Savidis in 1995, and in 2012 to the Onassis Foundation.

them in the wave of migration during the archaic age in which the Homeric epics were composed. Poseidonia was a colony twice removed since its founders were themselves Greek colonists of the town of Sybaris further south in Italy.[36] Sybaris was established about a century earlier than Poseidonia by the Achaeans and had become extremely wealthy by virtue of its location as a port city.[37] While it does not appear in the poem by name, it hovers at the margins as a twilight presence. A couple of final details: Poseidonia was taken over by the Romans in 273 BCE, and its name was Latinized to Paestum. The city went through numerous changes with the influx of Italic peoples and Oscan, a sister language to Latin. By the time of the geographer Strabo in the first century CE, it was in decline, and in later centuries, it was entirely abandoned.[38]

"Poseidonians"

> ... like the Poseidonians in the
> Tyrrhenian Gulf who, though of Greek origin,
> were completely barbarized, having become
> Tyrrhenians and Romans and having changed
> their language and many of their customs. But
> one of the Greek festivals they conduct even to
> this day, in which they come together and recall
> ancient names and customs, and after wailing
> loudly and weeping to each other, they go their
> ways. —Athenaeus

Their Greek tongue the Poseidonians
lost through centuries of intermixing
with Tyrrhenians and with Latins and other foreigners.
The only remnant that remained
was a Greek festival with beautiful rites,
with lyres and pipes, with contests and crowns.
They had a practice at the end of the festival
of enacting ancient customs and repeating Greek names,
which only a few still remembered.

---

36. On Poseidonia and Sybaris, see Strabo, *Geography*, trans. Horace Jones (Cambridge, MA: Harvard University Press, 1923), 5.4 and 6.1.

37. On the luxurious life of the inhabitants of Sybaris, see Athenaeus, *The Deipnosophists*, trans. Charles Gulick, vol. 3 (Cambridge, MA: Harvard University Press, 1929), 12.14–23.

38. Translation of the poem is by the author; for the Greek, see Cavafy, Ποιήματα, A, 145. For readings of the poem, see Gregory Jusdanis, *The Necessary Nation* (Princeton: Princeton University Press, 2001), 174–75; and Halim, *Alexandrian Cosmopolitanism*, 64–66.

And their festival always ended in a melancholy way.
For they remembered that they too were Greek,
They too were Italiotes once.
And now how far had they fallen, what had they become,
that they lived and spoke barbarously,
fallen—disastrously!—from Hellenism.

"Ποσειδωνιᾶται"

. . . Ποσειδωνιάταις τοῖς ἐν τῷ Τυρρηνικῷ
κόλπῳ τὸ μὲν ἐξ ἀρχῆς Ἕλλησιν οὖσιν ἐκβαρβαρῶσθαι
Τυρρηνοῖς ἢ Ῥωμαίοις γεγονόσι καὶ τὴν τε φωνὴν
μεταβεβληκέναι, τά τε πολλὰ τῶν ἐπιτηδευμάτων, ἄγειν
δὲ μιάν τινα αὐτοὺς τῶν ἑορτῶν τῶν Ἑλλήνων ἔτι καὶ
νῦν, ἐν ᾗ συνιόντες ἀναμιμνήσκονται τῶν ἀρχαίων ὀνομάτων τε
καὶ νομίμων ἀπολοφυράμενοι πρὸς ἀλλήλους καὶ δακρύσαντες
ἀπέρχονται. —Ἀθήναιος

Τὴν γλῶσσα τὴν ἑλληνικὴ οἱ Ποσειδωνιᾶται
ἐξέχασαν τόσους αἰῶνας ἀνακατευμένοι
μὲ Τυρρηνούς, καὶ μὲ Λατίνους, κι᾿ ἄλλους ξένους.
Τὸ μόνο ποὺ τοὺς ἔμενε προγονικὸ
ἦταν μιὰ ἑλληνικὴ γιορτή, μὲ τελετὲς ὡραῖες,
μὲ λύρες καὶ μὲ αὐλούς, μὲ ἀγῶνας καὶ στεφάνους.
Κ᾿ εἶχαν συνήθειο πρὸς τὸ τέλος τῆς γιορτῆς
τὰ παλαιά τους ἔθιμα νὰ διηγοῦνται,
καὶ τὰ ἑλληνικὰ ὀνόματα νὰ ξαναλένε,
ποὺ μόλις πιὰ τὰ καταλάμβαναν ὀλίγοι.
Καὶ πάντα μελαγχολικὰ τελείων᾿ ἡ γιορτὴ τους.
Γιατὶ θυμοῦνταν ποὺ κι᾿ αὐτοὶ ἦσαν Ἕλληνες—
Ἰταλιῶται ἕναν καιρὸ κι᾿ αὐτοί·
Καὶ τώρα πῶς ἐξέπεσαν, πῶς ἔγιναν,
νὰ ζοῦν καὶ νὰ ὁμιλοῦν βαρβαρικὰ
βγαλμένοι—ὢ συμφορά!—ἀπ᾿ τὸν ἑλληνισμό.

Athenaeus represents the Poseidonians as Greeks of Magna Graecia who went through multiple name changes. All are associated with a peninsula that the Greeks themselves colonized and that later powers in the region controlled. The renaming of the Poseidonians reflects a "complete barbarization" ("ἐκβαρβαρῶσθαι"), according to Athenaeus, as measured by two standards: language and custom. Change is conceived as a devolution from Hellenism:

the Greek colonists become Italiotes (Greek-speaking inhabitants of the Italian peninsula between Naples and Sicily); Tyrrhenians (Etruscans); and Latins (early inhabitants of the region around Rome). There are seven variations on the root *hellen-* in the short poem, and they affirm the value of a culture that the poem itself is recreating in vague outline. Like the passage in *Odyssey* 19 about Crete, Cavafy's poem presents us with layered histories—an ancient people reflecting upon its own antiquity. As in the *Odyssey*, too, the earlier society is presented as more vibrant and dynamic than the later. Moreover, Cavafy's text, like Odysseus's tale to Penelope, involves a bit of *metis*.

What do we know about the epigraph? Athenaeus of Naucratis (modern Egypt) wrote a work entitled the *Deipnosophists*, or *Dinner Table Philosophers*, in which he discusses at length the often sensually indulgent customs of the ancient Greeks at their legendary symposia.[39] Interestingly, while he tells us little about the Poseidonians, he speaks in some detail of the luxury of the Sybarites, connecting them with the Etruscans who were similarly given to sumptuous living and who, in addition to enjoying women erotically, were particularly keen on sex with boys and adolescents. Since the Poseidonians lived between the Etruscans and the Sybarites, we have here a weak link with homoerotic resonance.

This resonance carries over to the passage quoted in the epigraph where the Poseidonians are described as people who lost their Hellenism as they became Italianized, Etruscanized, and Latinized.[40] Significantly, the only trace of antiquity the latter-day Poseidonians retain is contained in a ritual of remembrance, which consists of repeating archaic words the people do not understand and describing customs they no longer comprehend—what these words and customs are, we do not know. The vagueness is already in the text of Athenaeus, and it reappears in the body of the poem. The exquisite Sybarites hover at the edges, accessible through lateral reading and weak links that obscure erotic content.

There are other points of interest. The passage from Athenaeus is itself a quotation from a work by Aristoxenus, a Peripatetic philosopher whose chief

---

39. See note 36. On Athenaeus and the Second Sophistic, see James Porter, "Ideals and Ruins: Pausanias, Longinus, and the Second Sophistic," in *Pausanias: Travel and Memory in Roman Greece*, ed. Susan Alcock et al (New York: Oxford University Press, 2003), 63–92; and David Braund and John Wilkins, eds., *Athenaeus and His World: Reading Greek Culture in the Roman Empire* (Exeter: University of Exeter, 2000).

40. On cultural mixing among the Poseidonians, see Maurizio Gualtieri, "Greeks, Lucanians, and Romans at Poseidonia/Paestum (South Italy)," in *A Companion to the Archaeology of the Roman Republic*, ed. Jane Evans (New York: Wiley-Blackwell, 2013), 369–86; and Michael Crawford, "From Poseidonia to Paestum via the Lucanians," in *Greek and Roman Colonization: Origins, Ideologies, and Interactions*, ed. Guy Bradley et al (Cardiff: Classical Press of Wales, 2006), 59–72.

interest was in music and who grieves over its decline during a period of recolonization of Greeks by Italic peoples.[41] None of his work remains except in fragmentary form, as is the case with the passage at hand. The epigraph, then, is doubly removed (it is a quotation of a quotation) rather in the same way that Poseidonia itself is doubly removed (it is a colony of a colony). More-over, Cavafy's quotation itself might very well have come from the English of John Addington Symonds, a British poet and cultural historian whose major work, a seven-volume set titled *Renaissance in Italy* (1875–86), was followed by the more personal *Sketches and Studies in Italy and Greece* (1879). In the latter, he describes a visit to Paestum in which he cites the passage from Athenaeus that we find in "Poseidonians."[42] This would make Cavafy's epigraph doubly removed: a borrowing from Athenaeus via Symonds. Interestingly, Symonds does more than simply cite the ancient writer. He comments on Athenaeus's quotation of Aristoxenus, pointing to the "strange pathos" of this fragment "tossed by the dark indifferent stream of time":

> The study of music was [Aristoxenus'] chief preoccupation; and he used this episode in the agony of an enslaved Greek city, to point at his own conser-vative disgust for innovations in an art of which we have no knowledge left. The works of Aristoxenus have perished, and the fragment I have quoted is embedded in the gossip of Egyptian Athenaeus. In this careless fashion has been opened for us, as it were, a little window on a grief now buried in the oblivion of a hundred generations.[43]

"The oblivion of a hundred generations": weak links and oblique relations, indeed. They reveal how diaspora and homoeroticism are linked in the poetry of Cavafy.

It is possible that the elegaic tone of the passage from Symonds condi-tioned Cavafy's own tone in "Poseidonians."[44] Because Symonds was homo-sexual—this might have motivated Cavafy's use of him as an intermediate source—the empathy he registers for the Poseidonians may have been sparked by the broader Sybaritic context of the passage, before "barbarization" set in. In this case, homosexuality, too, would be doubly removed in the poem

---

41. Aristoxenus, *Aristoxenus: Elementa Rhythmica: The Fragment of Book II and the Addi-tional Evidence for Aristoxenean Rhythmic Theory*, ed. Lionel Pearson (New York: Oxford, 1990).

42. See Cavafy, *Complete Poems*, trans. Mendelsohn, 564–66. For the passage quoted, see John Addington Symonds, *Sketches and Studies in Italy and Greece*. Third Series (London: Smith, Elder, and Company, 1879), 261–64.

43. Symonds, *Sketches*, 263.

44. Cavafy, *Complete Poems*, trans. Mendelsohn, 565–66.

through a displacement from Sybaris to Poseidonia and from Poseidonia to Symonds—or so it appears when following the paratexts. If Symonds enters the poem obliquely, we may reference even more obliquely his daughter, Margaret "Madge" Symonds Vaughan, who (importantly in this study) was a close friend Virginia Woolf particularly fancied when she was still a Stephen and studying Greek with Janet Case.[45] Cavafy would like this kind of happenstance.

What should we make of the poem's numerous displacements? One answer comes from the structure of the poem itself. The epigraph is substantially repeated in what follows, with important differences. Composed largely in demotic, the body of the piece plays with the ethnicity it describes by inviting the reader to reflect on how a move from the "high" dialect of ancient Greek (in the epigraph) to a "lower" linguistic register (in the body) reflects upon the speaker's views of barbarism. Cavafy's persona does not seem aware of his own fallenness, as it were, and the poem unfolds at his expense. The hyperbolic "disastrously!" ("ὦ συμφορά!") in the final line bears out the suspicion that he is a naïve narrator who thinks like a purist but speaks like a bastard. He misses how our access to culture derives from more or less proximate relations to a deep antiquity, which is only available in fleeting glimpses. From this perspective, the entirety of "Poseidonians" becomes a complex meditation on the vagaries of *kleos*—the talk that circulates in a city, that gets passed down but also lost in translation, and that speaks through the cracks about origins, loss, and sybaritic desire.

Cavafy's Hellenism grows up around these tenuous connections. It cultivates philhellenic sentiments, while also ironizing them around "the dark indifferent stream of time," to use Symonds's words. These silences have another dimension. In 1906 when Cavafy composed "Poseidonians," it would have been risky to write publicly about same-sex relations in a society that criminalized them. Thus "Poseidonians" enables reflection upon how oblique reading meets up with social restraints upon "the love that dare not speak its name."[46] This may overstate the censorship of the times, since Cavafy's own homosexuality was known in Alexandrian circles.[47] But such hidden knowledge of a public secret is its own kind of curse, and readers encounter this secrecy regularly in his poems.

"Poseidonians" surreptitiously links the lapse from Hellenism with a loss of erotic culture. Another poem, "The Glory of the Ptolemies" ("Η Δόξα τῶν Πτωλεμαίων") moves in an inverted way: it presents a claim to Hellenism

---

45. Lee, *Virginia Woolf*, 158–59.

46. The phrase is that of Lord Alfred Douglas, a lover of Oscar Wilde, in his poem, "Two Loves," and it was repeated in Wilde's trial on charges of sodomy.

47. Gregory Jusdanis has provided this information.

through direct participation in the hedonic life, which the poem puts into question. The name in the title—the Ptolemies—refers to the royal family that ruled Egypt in the Hellenistic period after the death of Alexander the Great. But the monarchs of the line were Macedonian Greeks, and they were the last dynasty of ancient Egypt. They were thus Greek-Egyptians whose ethnicity was complicated by their rivalry with the Seleucids, who were Macedonians, too, but from a line that governed the area of Anatolia, Persia, the Levant, and Mesopotamia. Both regions were intensely Hellenized in the third and second centuries BCE. But Seleucia and Egypt were Hellenized in different ways, and the conflict between them is a recurrent subject in Cavafy's poems. In the translation that follows,[48] Keeley and Sherrard use an orthographic rendering of "Seleucus" that reflects a demotic Greek pronunciation—"Selefkos"—which is inconsistent with the haughty tone and claim to origins that the poem seeks to convey. I keep the orthography with the caveat that it is an element of translation and not of Cavafy's Greek.

"The Glory of the Ptolemies"
I'm Lagides, king, absolute master
(through my power and wealth) of sensual pleasure.
There's no Macedonian, no barbarian equal to me
or even approaching me. The son of Selefkos [Seleucus]
is really a joke with his cheap lechery.
But if you're looking for other things, note this too:
my city's the greatest preceptor, queen of the Greek world,
genius of all knowledge, of every art.

" Ἡ Δόξα τῶν Πτολεμαίων"
Εἶμ' ὁ Λαγίδης, βασιλεύς. Ὁ κάτοχος τελείως
(μὲ τὴν ἰσχύ μου καὶ τὸν πλοῦτο μου) τῆς ἡδονῆς.
Ἡ Μακέδων, ἢ βάρβαρος δὲν βρίσκεται κανεὶς
ἴσος μου, ἢ νὰ μὲ πλησιάζει κάν. Εἶναι γελοῖος
ὁ Σελευκίδης μὲ τὴν ἀγοραία του τρυφή.
Ἄν ὅμως σεῖς ἄλλα ζητεῖτε, ἰδοὺ κι αὐτὰ σαφή.
Ἡ πόλις ἡ διδάσκαλος, ἡ πανελλήνια κορυφή,
εἰς κάθε λόγο, εἰς κάθε τέχνη ἡ πιὸ σοφή.

Rather than featuring a belated, melancholic speaker who looks back in time at a Greek past that was once splendid and voluptuous, this poem presents

---

48. Cavafy, *Collected Poems*, trans. Keeley and Sherrard, 64–65.

a ruler in his prime—a Ptolemy—who speaks in the present tense, boldly declaring himself an "absolute master" of physical pleasure and thus of Hellenism. His use of the term "Lagid" to identify himself is an indicator: the name is taken from the father of Ptolemy I, Lagus, the first, the source, the begetter of the line. The self-important ruler measures his superior hedonism against a rival Seleucid of the same ancestry (Macedonian) whose "cheap lechery" marks an excess, or a deficiency, depending on the perspective. In any case, the Seleucid is a baser creature. Nothing, however, is so visible as the hyperbole of the poem's speaker who regards Hellenism as a possession won in a zero-sum competition. The slur he directs at a competing dynasty rebounds upon him. Between this poem and "Poseidonians," Cavafy enables us to construct the Greek-barbarian split from opposite ends of a spectrum: a Hellenism diluted by colonization and a Hellenism imperialized in an attitude of proprietary ownership. Both are the subject of critique in his poetry.

"In a Town of Osroini" ("Ἐν Πόλει τῆς Ὀσροηνῆς") features a location that was originally part of the Seleucid dynasty, but here a different dynamic is at work.[49] This dynasty, too, was formed after the death of Alexander the Great and later came under the control of the Syriac empire, the Parthians, and the Romans. Osroini, which lies within it, was just the kind of place Cavafy preferred: syncretic, a bit rundown, a little decadent. Here the transliteration of the place name into demotic ("Osroini") is more in keeping with the tone. Unlike Poseidonia, which was a port town, and Alexandria, which dominated the Mediterranean for centuries, Osroini was landlocked. But the city controlled the east-west passage from Anatolia to Mesopotamia known as the Persian Royal Road, and thus it resonates with the commerce and multiple dialects that we find in Homer's description of Crete.

"In a Town of Osroini"
Yesterday, around midnight, they brought us our friend Remon,
who'd been wounded in a taverna fight.
Through the windows we left wide open,
the moon cast light over his beautiful body as he lay on the bed.
We're a mixture here: Syrians, migrated Greeks, Armenians, Medes.
Remon too is one of this kind. But last night,
when the moon shone on his sensual face,
our thoughts went back to Plato's Charmides.

---

49. Cavafy, *Collected Poems*, trans. Keeley and Sherrard, 128–29.

"Ἐν Πόλει τῆς Ὀσροηνῆς"
Ἀπ᾽ τῆς ταβέρνας τὸν καυγᾶ μᾶς φέραν πληγωμένο
τὸν φίλον Ρέμωνα χθὲς περὶ τὰ μεσάνυχτα.
Ἀπ᾽ τὰ παράθυρα ποὺ ἀφίσαμεν ὁλάνοιχτα,
τ᾽ ὡραῖο του σῶμα στὸ κρεββάτι φώτιζε ἡ σελήνη.
Εἴμεθα ἔνα κρᾶμα ἐδῶ· Σύροι, Γραικοί, Ἀρμένιοι, Μῆδοι.
Τέτοιος κι ὁ Ρέμον εἶναι. Ὅμως χθὲς σὰν φώτιζε
τὸ ἐρωτικό του πρόσωπο ἡ σελήνη,
ὁ νοῦς μας πῆγε στὸν πλατωνικὸ Χαρμίδη.

Recalling in the past tense a midnight hour of sexual wandering and drunken fun, the poem focuses on a singular figure the speaker saw one day earlier: a beautiful young man who was wounded in a tavern brawl. Memory has transformed experience in this brief lyric, both concretizing the moment and broadening it through lateral connections based on ethnicity and historical references that link it with a more remote antiquity. There is an Iliadic tone to this combination of beauty and a wound, which Cavafy plays upon in one of his early Homeric poems, "The Funeral of Sarpedon." Sarpedon was the imposing Trojan warrior and son of Zeus whose life could not be spared on the battlefield, not even by his father, since it was necessitated by fate. Like Sarpedon, Remon is named, but the difference, of course, lies between heroes and town rowdies.

Cavafy is moving against the bias of an epic fabric by presenting us with a singularity that is nonheroic and by connecting his subject, not with a patriarchal lineage, but rather with a multiplicity of ethnic identities whose "mixture" ("κρᾶμα") the poem invites us to admire. It may be an overreach for Keeley and Sherrard to give us "migrated Greeks" in line 5 instead of simply "Greeks," but they choose the phrase because Cavafy does not use the regular term "Hellenes" here, preferring instead the more diasporic sounding "Graikoi." If "Poseidonians" ends by pointing to the necessary and productive impurities of ethnic intermingling, "In a Town of Osroini" connects such mixtures with the transgressive allure of same-sex desire. We are miles away from a Lagid king in an opulent but static Alexandria.

The homoerotic suggestion, apparent in the moonlight that appears to privilege Remon, is intensified by the mention in the final line of Plato's Charmides, an aristocratic youth from Athens known for his exceptional beauty who appears in a dialogue of that name.[50] The aristocratic side of Charmides

---

50. See Panagiotis Roilos, *C. P. Cavafy: The Economics of Metonymy* (Urbana: University of Illinois Press, 2009), 78.

is partially undone in Cavafy's poem through a rewriting of it. Mixture is here elevated to an aristocracy of the flesh, or rather the wounded flesh. Remon undergoes two transformations: first, a rite of passage in which the wound symbolically signifies entry or initiation into a privileged group, the "we" ("μᾶς") of a fraternal band; and second, an injury that poetry heals through its aesthetic care of the body. Once again, the text is tricky in its oblique inclusion of homoerotic themes. It is oblique in another way as well because it takes the central argument in Plato's dialogue, which is about temperance, or *sophrosyne,* and lays it onto the poem itself. What counts as temperance in the text of "In a Town of Osroini" is not the conduct of Remon, but the subtle modulations that the poet works on his own artistic temperance. It is his poetic craft that takes "the body" ("τὸ σῶμα") and "the face" ("τὸ πρόσωπο") of the young man and brings them under the feminizing illumination of the moon, thereby making both "beautiful" ("ὡραῖο") and "sensuous" ("ἐρωτικό"). That this process also inverts Platonic love is very much to the point. If Plato privileges the upward ascent, Cavafy brings what is up down to the particular level of a person, place, and time, which take priority. Significantly, Oscar Wilde wrote a poem in 1881 entitled "Charmides," in which the motif of a young wounded male, lovingly cared for, figures prominently, a poem Cavafy was likely to have known, and if not, then one that surfaces in the play of accidental encounters we are tracing.[51] Wilde, then, like Symonds, shares an erotic attraction that may bear obliquely on the poem to which it is connected.

To summarize, the odyssean qualities of "In a Town of Osroini" include its conjuring up of a marginal Mediterranean that is culturally diffuse, transected by well-traveled trade routes, and possessed of a diachronic richness that connects east and west. Like "Poseidonians," it exhibits sensibilities toward a Hellenism that is always in formation, even if the movement is perceived as a devolving one, a culture with porous boundaries shaped by the turbulence of history and the connectivity of a dynamic sea. Both pieces invite slant ways of reading via paratexts, such as the epigraph or work cited, which take the reader on suggestive detours. The monological Lagid is a satirized voice that diverts diasporic currents by construing Alexandrian supremacy as a fixed achievement. In all three poems, the reader encounters intertexual references cleverly woven to shape a mixture of voices that comments indirectly on the speakers, turning them, at least in the case of "Poseidonians" and "The Glory of the Ptolemies," into examples of what they grieve or deplore. The technique of calling up multiple pasts that reflect ironically upon one another recalls the

---

51. See Cavafy, *Complete Poems,* trans. Mendelsohn, 451.

scene in *Odyssey* 19, as does Cavafy's tendency to distribute identities across geographical boundaries that call attention to shifting margins of power.

CÉSAIRE: THE COLONIAL ANTILLES AND A MAP OF ONE'S OWN SPILLED BLOOD

The odyssean tonalities of Cavafy may not be overtly archipelagic. He does not evoke a strong visual sense, for example, of such island configurations as the Cyclades, which present us with a visual model of cultural links in which separation is as important as connectedness. But the figures, towns, and customs we encounter in his work assume a land-dotted Mediterranean Sea with maritime routes that span three continents across deep time and through cataclysmic events: territorial wars, the overthrow of empires, religious crusades, and the massive displacement of peoples. This would have been a history in which Césaire was steeped at the École Normale Supérieure since it emerged from a region that Europe identified as the cradle of its own civilization. It was an autobiographical moment, however, that inaugurated his writing of *Cahier d'un retour au pays natal*.[52] Césaire claims to have found his native land in a foreign landscape off the Dalmatian coast as a consequence of the hospitality of a fellow student, Petar Guberina. After passing the rigorous entrance exams for the École Normale in 1935, he took up an offer from his friend to visit the Adriatic coast over summer break. Looking out to sea from a third-story apartment window, he was struck by a resemblance between the Croatian Martinska and the Antillean Martinique. Inspired, he commenced writing what would become a long poem—a lyrically intense tale of personal wandering and the wandering of a dispossessed people.

It is hard to say whether this beginning was bound up with the realization that the Mediterranean, too, is an abyssal sea at whose bottom lie the vestiges of those who inhabited its littorals. Césaire gives evidence of this history in his poem *"Depuis Akkad depuis Elam depuis Sumer."*[53] There he speaks of the "master of the three paths," inverting the slave figure into a position of paradoxical superiority by virtue of the ancient civilizations that were built upon the labors of his back. The phrase also looks to the tripartite Caribbean soul—part African, part European, part Carib—that he explores across the body of his work. In any event, *Cahier* was the first work of racial consciousness to bring alive the haunted depths of the Black Atlantic. It inspired

52. See Fonkoua, *Aimé Césaire*, 57–58.
53. Césaire, *Complete Poetry of Aimé Césaire: Bilingual Edition*, trans. A. James Arnold and Clayton Eshleman (Middletown, CT: Wesleyan University Press, 2017), 399.

what Edward Kamau Brathwaite would later call the "submarine unity" of the Middle Passage and what Édouard Glissant would theorize as "transversality," a way of thinking that resists universalist transcendence and cultural synthesis by remaining receptive to the resonant obscurities of the trans-oceanic route.[54]

The iconic image of such an orientation is "the open boat"—"*la barque ouverte*"—a repurposing of Odysseus's raft and the sail whose stitch work is a reminder of Penelope's weaving.[55] Glissant's image is itself inspired by Césaire's "proud pirogue" ("*fière pirogue*"), which figures prominently at the end of *Cahier,* a topic to which we will return in chapter 4. These images embody the diffusion and mixture that created the Caribbean. Without citing the *Odyssey,* the poem sets out on its own voyage of discovery and traces a way that is distinctly Antillean. It is the revolutionary aspiration of the poem that makes readings based on reception and influence tendentious. Césaire's poem practices a poetics of weak links and oblique relations, which distances source texts connected with Europe or an ancestral continent.

It is nonetheless understandable why some Antillean writers have been attracted to the idea of "the New World Mediterranean."[56] This is a topic that has drawn increasing attention since Derek Walcott's *Omeros* and his receipt of the Nobel Prize for Literature in 1992. In writing an epic linked with his birthplace, Walcott had to confront the contradictions of such an endeavor. In the Caribbean, he observes, "servitude to the muse of history has produced a literature of recrimination and despair" that has found it difficult to rise above the primordial cry and the bitterness of grievous wrongs. Moreover, the tropical archipelago lacks what epic requires—"the visible presence of ruins, wind-bitten or sea-bitten," offering instead only "midden fragments, artifacts, and the unfinished phrases of a dead speech."[57] Yet the Caribbean is in need of foundation tales precisely because it has been deprived of them, something that Césaire recognizes and that Glissant foregrounds in his own theorizing.[58] Both understand the risks of proximity to Europe in carrying through such a project, but Césaire more acutely. He not only studied classical languages and

---

54. Edward Kamau Brathwaite, "Caribbean Man in Space and Time," *Savacou,* Pamphlet 2 (1974): 1; and Glissant, *Le Discours Antillais,* 330.

55. On "the open boat," see Glissant, *Poetics of Relation,* 5–9; in French, 17–21. On the connections between the sea, travel, stories, and weaving in the ancient Greek Mediterranean, see Dougherty, *Raft of Odysseus,* 1–37.

56. See Benítez-Rojo, *Repeating Island,* 4; and J. Michael Dash, *The Other America: Caribbean Literature in a New World Context* (Charlottesville: University of Virginia Press, 1998), 11 and 82–106.

57. For this sequence of quotations, see Derek Walcott, "The Muse of History," in *What the Twilight Says: Essays* (New York: Farrar, Strauss, and Giroux, 1999), 44–46.

58. See Glissant, *Le discours antillais,* 326–47.

literatures while at the École Normale but he also taught the subjects once he returned to Martinique and became a teacher at the Lyçée Schoelcher in Fort-de-France. The intellectual labor of studying this monumental history in combination with his new thinking on Africa in the company of Léopold Senghor and Léon Damas, both of whom helped forge the concept of *négritude*, spurred Césaire's own early reflections in *Cahier*. The title accommodates the improvisational character of the composition: the poem is a "notebook," loosely linked in its parts, not a big book with a heroic tale to tell. It takes advantage of the modesty of the medium and allows the writer to find poetry by turning his back on it.[59] Césaire, then, invites a different way of thinking about Antillean foundation tales than does Walcott when he speaks of "poets of the New Aegean,"[60] although both have initiated a project of reading reciprocally between the two seas.[61]

From the opening stanzas of *Cahier*, it is clear that Césaire is waging an assault on the inherited language in forming an Antillean French that expresses a human catastrophe.[62] This is, at least in part, what makes the work difficult. Many editions include commentaries that are triple the length of the poem, and the work of editing *Cahier* has itself become a contentious space in which scholars debate the nature of the changes that the poem went through over the course of two decades.[63] The backbone of the first publication in 1939, which appeared in the French magazine *Volontés*, remains strong in all subsequent editions. It was the version translated into Spanish in 1943 by Lydia Cabrera—the first ever translation of *Cahier*—and it included illustrations by the Cuban painter Wifredo Lam. In the hiatus between the 1939 edition published in French and the 1947 bilingual French-English edition published in New York under the promotion of André Breton, numerous revisions made their way into the text. This was the period during World War II and its aftermath when Breton and other European intellectuals moved to New York, turning it into a hotbed of surrealism. There, Breton met Césaire in 1940, and

59. See Georges Ngal, *Aimé Césaire: Un Homme à la recherche d'une patrie*, 2nd rev. ed. (Paris: Présence Africaine, 2000), 471; discussed by Natalie Melas, "Poetry's Circumstance and Racial Time: Aimé Césaire, 1935–1945," *South Atlantic Quarterly* 115.3 (2016): 469–71.

60. Walcott, "The Muse of History," in *What the Twilight Says*, 42.

61. Greenwood, *Afro-Greeks*, 20–68.

62. See Césaire's interview with René Depestre at the Cultural Congress of Havana in 1967, which is included in *Discourse on Colonialism*, 83–84.

63. See A. James Arnold, "Beyond Postcolonial Césaire: Reading *Cahier d'un retour au pays natal* Historically," *Forum for Modern Language Studies* 44.3 (2008): 258–75; Christopher Miller, "Editing and Editorializing: The New Genetic *Cahier* of Aimé Césaire," *South Atlantic Quarterly* 115.3 (2016): 441–55; and Carrie Noland, "Translating Césaire," *Modernism/Modernity*, 26.2 (2019): 419–25.

later visited him in Martinique. Césaire would say in subsequent interviews that his poetry "did not emerge from Breton's *Manifestos of Surrealism*," but that the encounter with Breton was "a confirmation of the truth that [he] had found through [his] own reflections."[64] Again, the notion of a European source is considered, only to be qualified.

For his part, Breton was taken by the power of Césaire's poetry and wrote an introduction to the 1947 edition of *Cahier* entitled "A Great Black Poet" (*"Un grand poète noir"*). There he admires Césaire for "the gift of song, the capacity for refusal, the power of extraordinary transmutation."[65] Critics have remarked that the 1956 edition published by Présence Africaine, with an introduction by Petar Guberina, was shaped by Césaire's engagements with the French Communist Party and with the debate about whether surrealism could function as a revolutionary force.[66] Césaire attributed his resignation from the party to the fact that it was dogmatic and insufficiently tuned to "the Negro question."[67] This was not the last edition of the work. Présence Africaine published two later versions, one in 1968, which was a bilingual French-English text, and another in 1983, which included, among other things, revised stanza divisions.[68]

As this summary suggests, *Cahier* was for decades a work under construction. Although Césaire practiced a different kind of revision than did Cavafy, both adopted a provisional approach to composition and regarded their creative activity as work in progress. The complexity of the poem's publication

---

64. See, for example, *"Entretien avec Aimé Césaire par Jacqueline Leiner,"* in the collected edition of René Ménil and Suzanne Césaire, eds., *Tropiques: Revue Culturelle, 1941–1945* (Paris: Jean-Michel Place, 1978), vi. For a wide-ranging collection of texts on surrealism in Caribbean literature, including essays by Aimé Césaire and Suzanne Roussi Césaire, see Michael Richardson, ed., *Refusal of the Shadow: Surrealism and the Caribbean,* trans. Krzysztof Fijałkowski and Michael Richardson (New York: Verso Books, 1996). On broader connections between surrealism and politics, see Kelley, "Poetics of Anticolonialism"; Brent Hayes Edwards, "The Ethnics of Surrealism," *Transition* (1999): 132–34; A. James Arnold, *Modernism and Négritude: The Poetry and Poetics of Aimé Césaire* (Cambridge, MA: Harvard University Press, 1981), 124–54; and N. Gregson Davis, *Aimé Césaire* (New York: Cambridge University Press, 1997), 14–22.

65. See the preface to *Cahier d'un retour au pays natal* (Paris: Bordas, 1947), included in Césaire, *Notebook of a Return to the Native Land,* trans. Clayton Eshleman and Annette Smith (Middleton, CT: Wesleyan University Press, 2001), xv.

66. For the connection between Marxism and surrealism in Césaire's thought, see Depestre's interview with Césaire at the Cultural Congress of Havana in 1967, which is included in *Discourse on Colonialism.* Césaire resigned from the Communist Party in a public letter written to Maurice Thorez and translated into English by Chike Jeffers in *Social Text* 28.2 (2010): 145–52. For the French, see *"Lettre au Maurice Thorez du 24 Octobre 1956,"* accessed 5 May 2019, http://lmsi.net/Lettre-a-Maurice-Thorez.

67. See Césaire's interview with Depestre.

68. See the introduction by Irele in Césaire, *Journal of a Homecoming,* 41–42.

history challenges not only the idea of a definitive text but also the stability of the much-debated concept of *négritude*. Césaire appears to have first used the term in print in a student review entitled *L'étudiant noir* (1935), which he edited while in Paris with Senghor and Damas.[69] Thus *Cahier*, the most famous platform for the idea, metaphorically performs the return upon which it also reflects. As with Homer and Cavafy, in their different ways, Césaire incorporated the activity of journey and detour into his habits as a writer. Unlike Cavafy, however, Césaire crafted a poem that traveled quite remarkably in the world from the time it was first published.

Despite the political radicalism that shaped it, *Cahier* poses problems if it is treated as a manifesto. For one thing, the work is notoriously difficult. Part of the challenge arises from a predilection to name things concretely. This naming ranges from exact terms for flora and fauna on the island (*calabase, sapodilla, jubejube, cecropie*) to the instruments with which slaves were tortured (*carcan, brodequin, cep, chevalet*). Césaire said he used language in this way so that the people of the island could acquire "a sense of Martiniquan reality."[70] He also thought it restored what he called the "force value," or "*valeur-force*," to things, an energy in which he could himself participate as a poet.[71] The search for *le mot juste* was enabled by his long hours in the library of the École Normale on Rue d'Ulm where he studied dictionaries, encyclopedias, natural histories, and treatises on anthropology whose contents made their way into the extravagant vocabulary for which *Cahier* is famous.[72]

On almost every page, we find creolisms, snatches of song, technical terms, neologisms, and primordial cries that mingle and explode. Passages of searing power evoke a Martinique eviscerated by the brutalities of slavery and colonialism. They erupt into monologues and incantatory catalogues that are convulsive like the geology of the island itself whose volcano, Mont Pelée, erupted disastrously in 1902. Much of the poem is lost if the imagina-

---

69. Scholars have now revised the date on which the term *négritude* was first used in print. See Christopher Miller, "The Revised Birth of Negritude: Communist Revolution and the 'Immanent Negro,'" *PMLA* 125.3 (2010): 743–49; and Raisa Rexer, "Black and White and Re(a)d All Over: *L'étudiant noir*, Communism, and the Birth of *Négritude*," *Research in African Literatures* 44.4 (2013): 1–14.

70. See Césaire's interview with Leiner, *Tropiques*, 1941–45, eds., Ménil and S. Césaire, ix.

71. On "*valeur-force*," see Thomas Hale, *Les Écrits d'Aimée Cesaire, Bibliographie commentée* (Montreal: Les Presses de l'Universite de Montreal, 1978), 406; Davis, *Aimé Césaire*, 36; and Benítez-Rojo, *Repeating Island*, 4.

72. René Hénane, *Glossaire des termes rares dans l'oeuvre d'Aimé Césaire* (Paris: Jean-Michel Place, 2004), which attests to the recondite quality of the poet's language and an interest in taxonomic systems. For a broader treatment of Césaire's literary style, see N. Gregson Davis, "Forging a Caribbean Literary Style: 'Vulgar Eloquence' and the Language of Césaire's *Cahier d'un retour au pays natal*," *South Atlantic Quarterly* 115.3 (2016): 457–67.

tive dimension of its politics is traded off for slogans and positions. While the political experiment in *négritude* may have passed, Césaire's poem of *négritude* continues to stimulate debate because of its more complex treatment of the coined term.[73] As in the case of Cavafy's explorations of Hellenism and diaspora, *négritude* is a mobile concept that shifts depending upon the perspective from which it is treated.

The odyssean trope of diffusion and mixture that we have been exploring takes on two distinct aspects in *Cahier*. In the first case, we are dealing with a diffusion that is conceived in terms of the pathology of a dominated people without the will to live or to mingle in meaningful expressions of community. Here, diffusion is synonymous with collapse, desolation, and the mystified colonial mind. In the second case, we are talking about diffusion as an effect of mapping Martinique and the Antilles on a world grid where its fragility is visible, but its key position in the circulatory waters of an ocean is also strikingly apparent. It is the attempt to negotiate between these two kinds of diffusion that makes *Cahier* "an odyssey of a jolt into consciousness" ("*une odyssée d'une prise de conscience*"). This is a phrase Césaire uses in passing to describe his poem, and it should not be turned into a subtitle.[74] Suzanne Roussi Césaire illuminates this jolt when she speaks in her essay "*Le grand camouflage*" of how the "unbearable beauty" of the Antillean islands masks torment, abjection, and fears of being surpassed by the rest of world.[75] The Caribbean person, unable to accept his "*négritude*" and unable "to whiten himself" ("*se blanchir*"), resorts to "habits of trickery" ("*mesquineries*") in order to survive—"the great game of hide and seek" ("*le grand jeu de cache-cache*"). A vivid manifestation of this morbid psychic state is the poetry of "*doudouisme*," which submits Caribbean beauty to the myth of exoticism—exuberant greenery, quaint cottages, and locals with big white grins on their dark faces. The delusion circulates as a social poison, contaminating the very real ecological splendor of the Antilles.[76]

It is this lush but sickened world to which we are introduced in the opening of *Cahier*. The journey begins as a walk through hell, a *katabasis*, plung-

---

73. Natalie Melas, "Untimeliness, or *Négritude* and the Poetics of Contramodernity," *South Atlantic Quarterly* 108.3 (2009): 566.

74. The phrase occurs in Euzhan Palcy and Annick Thébia-Melsan, *Aimé Césaire: Une voix pour l'histoire*, Film (London: Saligna and So On, 1994).

75. Suzanne Césaire, "Le grand camouflage," *Tropiques* 13–14 (1945): 267–73. For an English translation, see Suzanne Césaire, *The Great Camouflage: Writings of Dissent, 1941–1945*, ed. Daniel Maximin and trans. Keith Walker (Middleton, CT: Wesleyan University Press, 2012), 39–48.

76. See Anny Dominique Curtius, "Cannibalizing *Doudouisme*, Conceptualizing the Morne: Suzanne Césaire's Caribbean Ecopoetics," *South Atlantic Quarterly* 115.3 (2016): 513–34.

ing us into a horrific landscape of decay and disease that resonates with a long line of katabatic descents without forging strong bonds with any. One is Rimbaud's *Une Saison en Enfer,* which begins by tearing out for Satan "a few ghastly pages from the notebook [*carnet*] of the damned."[77] As in Dante's *Inferno,* we find ourselves wandering with a guide in a liminal zone between darkness and morning, a place of half-dreams and nightmarish visions whose drag is felt through the repetition of a phrase that becomes the poem's refrain: "at the end of daybreak" ("*au bout du petit matin*").[78] Unlike Dante's Virgil, however, Césaire's guide is himself lost, and he stalls repeatedly on the poem's refrain. Instead of the exotic beauty evoked by touristic images, the reader is confronted with

> the starving Antilles, the Antilles pockmarked with smallpox, the Antilles dynamited with alcohol, run aground in the mud of this bay, in the dust of this town ominously grounded. (2)[79]

> *les Antilles qui ont faim, les Antilles grêlées de petite vérole, les Antilles dyna-mitées d'alcool, échouées dans la boue de cette baie, dans la poussière de cette ville sinistrement échouées.*

Welcome to paradise, an "outlandish, masking scar [*eschare*]" on "the wound [*blessure*] of the waters" (3); a "most fragile layer of earth [*plus fragile épaisseur de terre*]" (4); a town "flat—spread out: slipped, fallen from its common sense, inert [*plate—étalée, trébuchée de son bon sense, inerte*]" (5). Amid sprawling adjectival qualifiers, we hear again and again the scornful deictic pronoun "this," in the feminine form ("*cette*"): "this town" ("*cette ville*") and "this crowd" ("*cette foule*"), bound together, yet divergent.[80] The land is not soil, and those living on it are the mortally wounded; they will later be called, literally, "*mortiférés*" (42). In this place of abjection, even "the flowers of blood" ("*les*

77. Arthur Rimbaud, *A Season in Hell / Une Saison en Enfer: Bilingual Edition,* trans. Louise Varèse (New York: New Directions, 2011), 4–5.

78. This is the translation of Clayton Eshleman and Annette Smith, *Notebook of a Return,* 1 and *passim.*

79. On *katabasis* in the poem, see Davis, "'Homecomings without Home': Representations of (Post) Colonial *Nostos* (Homecoming) in the Lyric of Aimé Césaire and Derek Walcott," in *Homer in the Twentieth Century: Between World Literature and the Western Canon,* ed. Barbara Graziosi and Emily Greenwood (New York: Oxford University Press, 2007), 191–209.

80. On the use of deictics and demonstratives in the poem, see Césaire, *Cahier d'un retour au pays natal,* ed. Dominique Combe (Paris: Presses Universitaires de France, 1993), 47–64; and Emily Greenwood, "Dislocating Black Classicism: Classics and the Black Diaspora in the Poetry of Aimé Césaire and Kamau Brathwaite," in *African Athena: New Agendas,* ed. Daniel Orrells (New York: Oxford University Press, 2011), 362–72.

fleurs du sang") are said to "shrivel and scatter" (*"se fanent et s'éparpillent,"* 3).
Here in the opening stanzas of the poem, the same-sex gendering of two key
nouns suggests a broader problem: "this town" and "this crowd," both of them
feminine nouns, are, together, sterile. Sexual imagery is prominent, but it is
linked with barrenness, not community.

Striking images in stanza 8 underscore the point. This crowd that does not
know how to behave like a crowd is said to be

> like a woman you would have thought to be wholly in tune with her lyric
> cadence, who brusquely calls out to a hypothetical rain and commands it
> not to fall; or like one who makes a rapid sign of the cross without apparent
> motive; or like the unexpectedly stark animality of a peasant woman, urinat-
> ing upright, legs far apart and stiff.

> *à la façon dont une femme, toute on eût cru à sa cadence lyrique, interpelle*
> *brusquement une pluie hypothéthique et lui intime l'ordre de ne pas tomber;*
> *ou à un signe rapide de croix sans mobile visible; ou à l'animalité subitement*
> *grave d'une paysanne, urinant debout, les jambes écartées, roides.*

In a blighted landscape, we encounter an unlikely metaphorical female in the
act of sexual intercourse, absorbed in an elemental rhythm of the body seeking gratification. It bears repeating: who is the analogue of this female "in her
lyric cadence"? The crowd that does not know how to behave like a crowd, the
crowd that cannot mingle, the crowd that is alienated from its own possible
pleasure. The simile moves from lyricism at the moment of sexual consum-
mation to the alienation conveyed abruptly in "a hypothetical rain": the semen
cannot explode, or is forbidden to, by a woman who deceives. Having interrupted orgasm, she is pictured again, almost immediately, in another simile of
the crowd as "a peasant, urinating upright," her rain having stolen the rain of
the one she has tricked, his inseminating fluid rendered "hypothetical" by her
excretory audacity. What joins these two women is the woman in the middle
of the chain of similes, the woman who performs the sign of the cross in an
empty moment of distraction. Her gesture is an expression, not of faith, but of
meaningless religious practice, another kind of faking.

As others have remarked, female deception is prominent in the poem's
opening stanzas,[81] and this recalls the Homeric Penelope who is famous for

---

81. See Hedy Kalikoff, "Gender, Genre, and Geography in Aimé Césaire's *Cahier d'un
retour au pays natal," Callaloo* 18.2 (1995), 492–505; and Melas, *All the Difference in the World,*
192–94.

her trickery, especially with the suitors who have invaded her house. But the male speaker who uses this gendered imagery turns it back on himself from the beginning of the poem. One of the first gestures of *Cahier* is to dismiss figures of colonial authority in a masculine tone of contempt ("Buzz off I told the man, pig-snout, honkie-snout, buzz off," 1; "*Va-t-en, lui disais-je, gueule de flic, gueule de vache, va-t-en*"). Immediately after this banishment, the rough slang shifts into a more meditative tone:

> Then, more composed than the face of a woman telling a lie, I turned toward paradises lost to him and his kin, and there, lulled by the ebb and flow of a tireless thought, I nurtured the wind, I unloosed the monsters . . . (1)

> *Puis je me tournais vers les paradis pour lui et les siens perdus, plus calme que la face d'une femme qui ment, et là, bercé par les effluves d'une pensée jamais lasse je nourissais le vent, je délaçais les monstres . . .*

These lines may be loosely read as a substitute for the classical invocation to the Muse, and they mingle with the Christian undertones of Milton's *Paradise Lost* to produce a somber reference to the inadequacy of the classical tradition for the task ahead. But the self-declared mendacity of the speaker's composure is the most important element of the poem's self-initiation. *Cahier* seeks to demystify the lies of its speaker and the people he addresses as a form of false consciousness. It goes about this by undoing the binary of female deceit and male candor. If the crowd is adept at finding "the moment of disengagement, of escape, of evasion" ("*le point de désencastration, de fuite, d'esquive*," 8), so is our leader in the hellscape of the damned. He is, among other things, attempting to cut his own path without following the lead of Western precedent, and he is doing so by performing a complex act of engaging with reception while resisting it.

It is not surprising then as the poem pushes ahead that the female continues to mutate even as the speaker continues to respond to her signifying power. She becomes, among other things, a nondeceptive erotic figure of the earth, described as a "great vulva raised to the sun" ("*terre grand sexe levé vers le soleil*," 36); a generative site of "the vitelline membrane" ("*la membrane vitelline*") that must be breached if there is to be rebirth (76–77); and a symbol of "the femininity of the moon" ("*la féminité de la lune*"), her menstrual blood part of a wider natural order of life and death (118). As these metamorphic images multiply, so does the speaker whose consciousness is being enlarged through a studied contact with his self-delusions.

If the first form of diffusion in the poem is a pathology specific to the colonial situation, the second arises from a projection of the colonized mind into a global setting. This brings us to a famous passage on the geography of the Antilles. Here the reader is given a bird's eye view of the sea that links an external map of the slave trade with an internal map of the enslaved psyche, a personally constructed sense of longitude and latitude (42). Later in the poem, the speaker will refer back to this passage, describing it as "my original geography" ("*mon original géographie*")—"the world map made according to my own use, not tinted with the arbitrary colors of scholars, but with the geometry of my spilt blood" ("*la carte du monde faite à mon usage, non pas teinte aux arbitraries couleurs des savants, mais à la géometrie de mon sang répandu,*" 146). Significantly, it is in stanza 42, the mapping scene, that we first encounter the term *négritude* in the poem.[82]

What I call my own: these few thousand mortally wounded who go round and round in the calabash of an island and what is mine also this archipelago bowed as though in strenuous desire for self-denial, a maternal anxiety, you might say, to protect the exceedingly delicate, slender thread that separates one America from the other; and its flanks exuding for Europe the fine liqueur of a Gulf Stream, and one of the two incandescent zones between which the Equator walks on a tightrope toward Africa. And my island not confined, its open brashness upright at the rear of this polynesia; in front: Guadeloupe severed into the two halves at the dorsal bone and no less wretched than ourselves, Haiti where for the first time negritude stood up tall and straight and declared that it believed in its humanity, and the ludicrous little tail of Florida where the strangulation of a lynched nigger is being consummated, and Africa, gigantic caterpillar sliding up to the Hispanic foot of Europe, naked and exposed to death's sickle with its enormous swaths. (42)

---

82. The critical literature on negritude is vast. Works that have informed the present study include Maryse Condé, "*Négritude césairienne, négritude senghorienne,*" *Revue de Littérature Comparée* 3–4 (1974): 409–19; Tracy Denean Sharpely-Whiting, *Negritude Women* (Minneapolis: University of Minnesota Press, 2002); Abiola Irele, "The Poetic Legacy of Aimé Césaire," *French Politics, Culture & Society* 27.3 (2009): 81–97; N. Gregson Davis, "Negritude as Performance: The Interplay of Efficacious and Inefficacious Speech Acts in *Cahier d'un retour au pays natal,*" *Research in African Literatures* 41.1 (2010): 142–54; Ronnie Scharfman, "Aimé Césaire: Poetry Is/and Knowledge," *Research in African Literatures* 41.1 (2010): 109–20; Reiland Rabaka, *The Negritude Movement: W. E. B. Du Bois, Léon Damas, Aimé Césaire, Léopold Senghor, Frantz Fanon, and the Evolution of an Insurgent Idea* (Lanham, MD: Lexington, 2015); and Melas, "Untimeliness," 567–70.

Ce qui est à moi, ces quelques milliers de mortiférés qui tournent en rond dans la calebasse d'une île et ce qui est à moi aussi, l'archipel arqué comme le désir inquiet de se nier, on dirait une anxiété maternelle pour protéger la ténuité plus délicate qui sépare l'une de l'autre Amérique; et ses flancs qui sécrètent pour l'Europe la bonne liqueur d'un Gulf Stream, et l'un des deux versants d'incandescence entre quoi l'Equateur funambule vers l'Afrique. Et mon île non clôture, sa claire audace debout à l'arrière de cette polynésie, devant elle, la Guadaloupe fendue en deux de sa raie dorsale et de même misère que nous, Haïti où la négritude se mit debout pour la première fois et dit qu'elle croyait à son humanité et la comique petite queue de la Floride où d'un nègre s'achève la strangulation, et l'Afrique gigantesquement chenillant jusqu'au pied hispanique de l'Europe, sa nudité où la Mort fauche à larges andains.

The reader is given a striking visualization—a kind of camera scan—of the colonial Antilles, scattered like specks of dust across a massive expanse of water, almost invisible from on high.[83] But in reaching this point in the poem, the scale has also been widening laterally, and now a new dimension opens. Height is added to breadth, and the vertical intersects the horizontal. Continents and landmasses come into view: the Americas, Europe, Africa, all connected via the Gulf Stream exuded by the Antilles. While phallic imagery precedes the heady ascent—the speaker feels "male thirst and obstinate desire"—it is ironized, as usual in Césaire, by a diminution of the "I" in the act of self-assertion. Masculine vigor flickers as it meets "this modest nothing" of an island that cowers defensively to the crack of its "jailer," the colonizer (41). This moment, despite the view from above, is not about transcendence. It is about using the map in a way that personalizes its impersonality. Repeatedly connecting his archipelago to a worldwide network of exchange, built upon slave labor, the speaker effectively gives birth to the Antilles on a global stage. It is a deeply ambiguous act.

The vocabulary illuminates this. Not coincidentally, Césaire calls attention to language in this cartographic moment. The artful construction of words is integral to the artful imagining of the map. As others have observed, stanza 42 includes two neologisms—*mortiférés* and *négritude*.[84] *Mortiférés* means literally "death-bearing" or "lethal." *Négritude* is an abstraction formed from the

---

83. On "cartographic belittling," see Melas, *All the Difference in the World,* 170–73.

84. See Davis, *Journal of a Homecoming,* xi–xviii, who glosses the terms. He links *mortiféré* with a passage in Book 6 of the *Aeneid,* which tells of Aeneas's encounter with the figure of *mortifer Bellum* in his descent to the underworld.

suffix *-tudo* in conjunction with *nègre,* meaning "dark," thus bearing the sense of "the experience or condition of being dark or black." Both are constructed from Latin roots, informing a passage that resonates with a new consciousness of Africa. It is important to acknowledge that *négritude* is a diffuse signifier in this critical passage. In its first appearance in the poem, the word looks in different directions: toward a proud uprising in Haiti, toward "a lynched nigger" in Florida, and toward an Africa that "caterpillars" its way north toward the murderous sickle of Europe. In connecting the Antilles with the ancient mother country—two "zones of incandescence"—the umbilical tightrope stretches precariously over a yawning deep.

Nègre carries the weight of a long history. It is only recoverable through its traces on the Black Atlantic and on the islands of the Antilles, whose history has to be constructed from vast stretches of silence. The suggestions of the word are apparent in lines from Césaire's poem "Word" (*"Mot"*), which bring it alive:

> the word nigger
> all filthy with parasites
> the word nigger with roaming bandits
> with screaming mothers
> with crying children
> the word nigger
> a sizzling of flesh and horny matter
> acrid
> burning [85]

> *le mot nègre*
> *tout pouacre de parasites*
> *le mot nègre*
> *tout plein de brigands qui rôdent*
> *de mères qui crient*
> *d'enfants qui pleurent*
> *le mot nègre*
> *un grésillement de chairs qui brûlent*
> *âcre*
> *et de corne*

---

85. Césaire, *Complete Poetry of Aimé Césaire,* trans. Arnold and Eshleman, 480–83.

In these lines, we are given what a lynching smells like, what the cries of a continent sound like, what the view of an escape looks like—all fed through a Latin word, *niger,* that has become polluted by hate speech. While *négritude* can convey racial pride, it also packs the ugly punch of racism—a complexity built into the imaginative use of the map.

Let us stick to vocabulary a moment longer. The word for island, *île,* is used twice in the passage. Also derived from the Latin, *insula* means a place set apart, by itself. In both instances, the singular is connected with a word for a group of islands: "*île*" and "*archipel,*" in the first half of the passage, are counterbalanced by "*île*" and "*polynésie,*" in the second.[86] Archi- (*archē*), "chief, foremost, first," joined with *pelagos,* "high sea, open sea," means: "the chief, the most important sea." But the ancient Greeks did not use that word. First attested in Italian, it began circulating in that language around 1500 to refer to the Aegean, or what the Romans called *mare nostrum,* "our sea." Thereafter it came to be used of any sea with many islands, the prominent sense being that of a discrete body of water (*pelagos*) containing a plurality (*poly-*). "*Poly-,*" joined with "*-nésie,*" from *nēsos,* the Greek word for "island," was first used by Charles de Brosses in 1756 of all the Pacific islands, the emphasis here being upon multiplicity in an unbounded expanse of water, a connotation roughly the opposite of *archipel.*

The one and the many are at play in the diffusion and mixture of stanza 42. This is apparent not only in the charting of the Antilles, the external map, but in the speaker's own charting of the phenomenology of *Antillanité,* of being Antillean. Center and periphery shift, creating a pulsating effect of foreground and background, amplitude and concentration. Because images alternate, the rhythms of the stanza almost breathe. The speaker takes in air as he declares, "what is my own," tightens up with the arched archipelago in the grip of maternal anxiety, then exhales; he breathes in again with "the fine liqueur of the Gulf Stream," clenches on "the tightrope toward Africa," then exhales; breathes in once more as his island rears up in the "open brashness" of "non-closure," grimaces with the wretchedness of Guadaloupe, then exhales. At this point, the word *négritude* appears in the text, at a moment of deep inhalation that invests the coined abstraction with the physical breath of the body. Then, on the exhalation, lynching. The rhythm of ascent and descent is characteristic of the poem, which builds itself up to knock itself down, with renewed vigor and insight each time. This is the form that the decolonization of the soul—

---

86. For "archipelago," see the *Oxford English Dictionary* (2018), accessed 5 May 2019, http://www.oed.com.libezp.lib.lsu.edu/view/Entry/10387?redirectedFrom=archipelago#eid. For "polynesia," see the *Oxford English Dictionary* (2018), accessed 5 May 2019, http://www.oed.com.libezp.lib.lsu.edu/view/Entry/147256?redirectedFrom=polynesia#eid.

what Césaire calls the tripartite Caribbean soul, part African, part European, part Carib (39)—takes in the poem. It must travel out into the world that has wounded it in order to find healing.

In arguing for a poetics of weak links and oblique relations, this section has attempted to demonstrate how Césaire's poem distances itself from the long colonial arm of the Western canon. It is not that classical allusions are nonexistent in *Cahier,* but rather that they are mobilized within broader strategies of breaking the chains of reception. This in itself is an epic labor that the poem considers vital in the struggle for renewal. It is caught up with efforts to displace the concept of source, which in the Antillean context is deadening, at least at this early stage of self-declared revolution, which entails a profound demystification of a poet and of a people.

WOOLF: TILTING AT PAGANS' HEADS
IN A HOUSE THAT IS A TOWN

If diffusion looks at least two ways—toward dysfunction and renewal—in Césaire's exploration of racial consciousness, it does so in an enactment of an unending dialectic that moves along both synchronic and diachronic axes. The personas in *Cahier* must be flung across the comatose geography of the present and made to plunge into the bloody earth or the submarine depths to activate the memory of things past. Diffusion and going deep are complementary and ongoing movements in *Cahier,* and they shape the colonial predicament. Woolf's *Orlando,* on the other hand, brings us from the beginning into a world, not of comatose bodies and death, but of comic fecundity in a domestic space so sprawling that it constitutes a teeming microcosm of its own.

Unlike *Cahier* where the search for a meaningful personal and collective history discloses a lack related to the traumatic displacement of a people, *Orlando* presents us with the surplus weight of a history rooted in an aristocratic family and a great country house, wealthy and deeply grounded in normative gender roles.[87] In short, before the travel away from home begins, the claims of property and patriarchy prevail. They are manifest in a diffusion within the home and a self that constantly tests the limits of what a house can hold before it bursts through the walls in search of foreign travel. Like the palace on Ithaca and Penelope who weaves her wiles in its chambers, Orlando navigates his way through domestic crises that reveal the ambiguities of his

---

87. Alison Booth, "The Lives of Houses: Woolf and Biography," in *A Companion to Virginia Woolf,* ed. Jessica Berman (London: John Wiley, 2016), 13–26.

own role playing and the wayward bent of his sexuality. Cavafy makes inventive use of historical depth in exploring a similar sexual waywardness, but his tones are cooler, less expansive, and more meditatively layered than Woolf's, and they steer clear of the explosive effects Césaire seeks in his odyssey of racial consciousness, tending instead—with important exceptions—toward languidness, attenuation, and melancholy.

Before engaging more closely with Woolf's text, it is worth comparing her writing practices to those of the other two writers we are exploring because they illuminate the trope of diffusion and mixture. If Cavafy's poetry was work in progress because of the peculiar system of publication he adopted and if Césaire's was always under revision because of its ingestion of evermore material, Woolf's leaves a similar impression, but by virtue of how much she wrote. She has left us about 4,000 letters, 30 volumes of diaries, 400 essays, and 10 or so novels, depending on how one counts such pieces as *A Room of One's Own* (1929) and *Three Guineas* (1938). The two latter pieces focus on women, education, and politics, exploring how social exclusion has prevented women from entering into the professions, and why the modern structure of education, along with the professions it has generated, have been conducive to Fascism and world war. Together, these texts constitute not only an imposing body of work by a woman who wrote almost every day of her life, but a set of literary experiments whose mixed forms make this kind of tallying a challenge. *Orlando* presents yet other complications that arise from its somewhat chaotic publication history.

Woolf's fictional biography was first published not in England, but in the United States.[88] On 2 October 1928, Crosby Gaige, a Broadway producer and occasional printer of fine books, printed a limited edition of 861 copies, all autographed. A few days later, on 11 October 1928, the day on which Woolf ends the fictional biography, the Hogarth Press printed another edition. From stereotype plates of the Gaige limited edition, Harcourt Brace published its own edition on 18 October 1928. There was an important difference, however, between the Gaige edition and those that followed. The Gaige contained title chapters: Chapter One: Childhood and Youth; Chapter Two: Manhood, Ambassador at Constantinople; Chapter Three: The Age of Transition; Chapter Four: London, Life, Wits and Law Suits; Chapter Five: Marriage and

---

88. For fuller discussions of the complex publication history of *Orlando*, see Madeline Moore, "*Orlando*: An Edition of the Manuscript," *Twentieth Century Literature* 25.3/4 (1979): 303–55; Alison Scott, "'Tantalising Fragments': The Proofs of Virginia Woolf's *Orlando*," *Papers of the Bibliographical Society of America* 88.3 (1994): 279–351; and Amy Elkins, "Old Pages and New Readings in Virginia Woolf's *Orlando*," *Tulsa Studies in Women's Literature* 29.1 (2010): 131–36.

Home Life; Chapter Six: Later Years, Conclusion. This organization aligns the text not only with a personal life history, but also with the *Bildungsroman,* a coming-of-age tale.

The manuscript that Woolf presented to Sackville-West upon publication, however, was yet differently organized. It had four, not six chapters, and they bore different titles from the Gaige edition: Chapter One: Elizabethan and Jacobean; Chapter Two: Carolinian; Chapter Three: Restoration and Augustan; Chapter Four: Victorian and Modern.[89] Rather than emphasizing a developmental tale, this version orients the reader to the text as a commentary on, and parody of, the history of British literature. While the Gaige text provided the stereotype plates for the Harcourt Brace publication, the latter did not contain chapter titles, but only chapter numbers.

This is not the end of it. Page proofs were involved.[90] Not only were there multiple sets as a result of the Gaige, Hogarth, and Harcourt Brace editions being prepared for press within the same short period of time, but the final products were different. The American and English publications are not the same texts. More remarkable, perhaps, is that the proofs Woolf sent to the American publisher contained corrections of about eighty typographical errors and over 600 substantive changes.[91] *Orlando* was rewritten at some length in the final stages. The entire process illuminates the difficulty of pointing to a definitive text.

Woolf's predilection toward revising is apparent at several levels. She is well known for the hybrid form of prose and poetry she writes. But her treatment of genre presents us with similar mixtures. Among them is biography, a term she includes in the subtitle of the work—*Orlando: A Biography.*[92] In a letter to Sackville-West, Woolf remarks that the idea she was conceiving at the time could "revolutionize biography in a night."[93] What this means becomes more apparent in "The New Biography" (1927), an essay she wrote while embarked on *Orlando*:

---

89. Elkins, "Old Pages," 133.

90. See Scott, "'Tantalising Fragments,'" 281–84.

91. See Scott, "'Tantalising Fragments,'" 283.

92. On Woolf's views of biography in relation to fiction, see Ray Monk, "This Fictitious Life: Virginia Woolf on Biography, Reality, and Character," *Philosophy and Literature* 31.1 (2007): 1–40; Elena Gualtieri, "The Impossible Art: Virginia Woolf on Modern Biography," *Cambridge Quarterly* 29 (2000): 349–61; and Julia Briggs, "Virginia Woolf and the 'Proper Writing of Lives,'" in *The Art of Literary Biography,* ed. John Batchelor (Oxford: Clarendon Press, 1995), 245–65.

93. Woolf, *The Letters of Virginia Woolf,* ed. Nigel Nicolson and Joann Trautmann, 6 vols. (New York: Harcourt Brace Jovanovich, 1975), (9 October 1927), 3:429; hereafter, *Letters.*

On the one hand there is truth; on the other, there is personality. And if we think of truth as something of granite-like solidity and of personality as something of rainbow-like intangibility and reflect that the aim of biography is to weld these two into one seamless whole, we shall admit that the problem is a stiff one.[94]

In another letter she wrote to Sackville-West in the same year, she notes that the project she is making up will satirize her own "lyric vein"—"Everything mocked. And it is to end with three dots . . . so."[95] For the daughter of a man who was the first editor of the *Dictionary of National Biography* (1885–1900), a work of Victorian sensibility centered on larger-than-life men, there is mischief here. Leslie Stephen conceived of biography as presenting "the greatest possible amount of information in a thoroughly business-like form," and he aligned it with what is "historical, not conversational or discursive."[96] Woolf's emphasis on "personality" opens the door to the biographer's imagination and leads to artfulness, which can rapidly pass into artifice and fantasy.

Fantasy is at the heart of *Orlando* whose basic story is that of a male born in the Elizabethan age who lives 350 years, aging only thirty-six years in the process. Along the way, he goes through a mysterious sex change into a woman while on a journey abroad in Constantinople. Woven throughout is a commentary on the literary history of Britain, told through the protagonist's personal contacts with its chief representatives, who range from Marlowe, Jonson, and Shakespeare to Tennyson, Browning, and Carlyle. The tenuousness of temporal and bodily boundaries so crucial to *Orlando* is intensified through a parody of the follies of periodization. Texts constantly spill over the temporal boundaries built around them, which makes literary generalizations, like categories of sex and gender, comically reductive.

---

94. See Woolf, "The New Biography," in *The Essays of Virginia Woolf,* ed. Andrew McNeillie. 4 Vols. (London: Hogarth; New York: Harcourt; San Diego: Houghton Mifflin Harcourt, 1986–2010), 4:473; and Woolf, *Granite and Rainbow: Essays* (New York: Houghton Mifflin, 1975). On the topic of biography in the Bloomsbury group with attention to Woolf, see Max Saunders, *Self Impression: Life-Writing, Autobiografiction, Literature, and the Forms of Modern Literature* (New York: Oxford University Press, 2013), 438–83. For a closer reading of *Orlando* as biography, see Julia Briggs, *Virginia Woolf: An Inner Life* (New York: Harcourt, 2005), 191–94; and Suzanne Raitt, *Vita and Virginia: The Work and Friendship of V. Sackville-West and Virginia Woolf* (Oxford: Clarendon, 1993).

95. *Letters,* (6 March 1927), 3:342.

96. Leslie Stephen, "A New 'Biographia Brittanica,'" *Athenaeum* 23 (1882): 85–52.

Feeding Woolf's instinct to unsettle was the new genre of the Freudian case study,[97] which influenced fellow Bloomsbury companion (and one-time suitor) Lytton Strachey, notably, his book *Eminent Victorians: Cardinal Manning, Florence Nightingale, Dr. Arnold, General Gordon* (1918). This work took aim at iconic nineteenth-century biographies of figures whose ambitions he regarded as the product of neurotic Victorian views of sex, religion, and meaningful work.[98] Another significant influence, however, was no other than Sackville-West's husband, Harold Nicolson, an ambassador, diplomat, and writer whose *Some People* (1927) presents us not only with "rather below life size" figures but also with "devices of fiction in dealing with real life," namely, his own.[99] Her essay "The New Biography" is in fact a review of this book. In constructing *Orlando* as a biography, then, Woolf is taking on a controversial human subject, Vita Sackville-West, using literary strategies that deliberately blur historical fact and that take the genre in a fantastical direction. It was a copy of the family history, *Knole and the Sackvilles,* authored by Vita and given as a gift, that had stimulated Woolf's imagination to begin with.[100] But she immediately took her friend's history in the direction of playfulness, conceiving of it as a "writer's holiday" from "the serious poetic experimental books whose form is always so closely considered."[101] The plot of the fictional biography may be summarized in this way:

- a period of growing up in England followed by a self-imposed exile in Constantinople provoked by sexual crises;
- a carnivalesque sojourn in that city, which includes the sex change;
- wanderings with the "gipsies" through Turkey and Greece;
- the penning of an autobiographical poem, "The Oak Tree";
- a return to the homeland and loss of property, contingent upon the sex change;
- and an ongoing life of cross-dressing and assumption of multiple identities.

---

97. On this subject, see Nicole Jouve, "Virginia Woolf and Psychoanalysis," in *The Cambridge Companion to Virginia Woolf,* ed. Susan Sellers and Sue Roe (New York: Cambridge University Press, 2000), 245–72.

98. For a biography of Strachey himself, with a detailed treatment of his sexual life, see Michael Holroyd, *Lytton Strachey: A Critical Biography* (New York: Norton, 1995).

99. "The New Biography," 477.

100. See Briggs, *Virginia Woolf,* 451n42.

101. Woolf, *The Diary of Virginia Woolf,* ed. Anne Oliver Bell and Quentin Bell. 5 Vols. (London: Hogarth, 1977–85), 3:131; hereafter, *Diary.*

Broadly, Woolf presents us with a tale of exile, homecoming, and mixed iden-tity that critics have not linked with the *Odyssey* for good reason. The struc-ture is sufficiently loose that it does not constitute an adaptation, but the tale does drift in odyssean waters, picking up on the picaresque qualities of the ancient return tale while distancing itself from the canon.

It is the house, however, and not the ship that is the most visible embodi-ment of diffusion in Woolf's fictional biography, at least initially. Thus when the young protagonist, in the first pages of *Orlando,* navigates a residence "so vast that there seemed trapped in it the wind itself, blowing this way, blowing that way, winter or summer" (12), a house that was a "vast congeries of rooms and staircases" (16) with a banqueting hall "five acres distant on the other side" (16), the reader enters a large-scale geography. When we are told that this house has been the residence of male ancestors who had cut "many heads of many colours off many shoulders of pagans" while riding "in the barbarian fields of Africa" (11), we may hear traces of the many cities of many men that Homer references in the prologue to the *Odyssey,* mediated through a rich tradition of travel literature. And when the narrative lingers upon Orlando's ancestors as the conquerors of "barbarian" Africans, whose shrunken heads blow in a windy attic, it is apparent that the protagonist participates in a rac-ism that flows through the family line.[102] It is this monumental history of imperial conquest that is gradually dismantled in Woolf's narrative. The sex change, which brings into focus the role of gender and sexuality in the con-struction of empire, is key to the process. So is the brilliantly imagined nar-rator of *Orlando* who acts as both the vehicle for conveying Victorian social norms and site of satire. It is worth looking at the house before moving to the narrator.

In addition to its fabled 365 bedrooms, Orlando's house is "a town ring-ing with men at work at their various crafts": horse keeping, beer brewing, furniture fashioning, and so forth (14). From a hill on his property, he can see other mansions that belong to his family, and beyond them lies the Eng-lish Channel, leading to an even wider geography of rivers with ships headed out to sea. Patriarchal though the system he inhabits clearly is, the narrative

---

102. For treatments of Woolf's orientalism, see Sarker, "Woolf and Theories of Postcolonial-ism"; Steven Putzel, "Virginia Woolf and British 'Orientalism,'" in *Virginia Woolf Out of Bounds,* ed. Jessica Berman and Jane Goldman (New York: Pace University, 2001), 105–12; Hovey, "'Kiss-ing a Negress in the Dark': Englishness as a Masquerade in Woolf's *Orlando,*" *Proceedings of the Modern Language Association* 112.3 (1997): 393–404; Karen Lawrence, "Orlando's Voyage Out," *Modern Fiction Studies* 38.1 (1992): 253–77; and Helen Carr, "Virginia Woolf, Empire, and Race," in *The Cambridge Companion to Virginia Woolf,* ed. Sellers and Roe, 197–213.

offers signs early on that Orlando is both part of it and detached from it.[103] For one thing, he is an odd assemblage: a youth with dreams of conquest who likes solitude, a nobleman who wishes he were born a writer, a valiant lover of traipsing around who is easily disturbed by sights. It doesn't take long to see that, like space and time in Woolf's book, Orlando's brain, too, is a "roomy one" (13). The high-pitched busyness around him can easily spark a "riot and confusion of the passions and emotions" (13). This "welter of opposites" (18)— the rainbow side of life—often baffles the narrator, who believes it is his duty to stick in workman-like fashion to the facts. Woolf, however, complicates the facts at every twist and turn, thereby turning her protagonist into a vaguely polytropic Odysseus. One way to conceive of this tumult is in terms of multiple internal identities that can be played out externally through the use of clothing, gesture, and manner. Instead of a diasporic consciousness at work, as with Cavafy's homoeroticism, or a consciousness attuned to fragmented selves, as with Césaire's treatment of the colonialized mind, Woolf presents us with an evolving gender consciousness, which enters increasingly into a realm of polymorphous sexuality.

As the narrator maneuvers a way between the material dimension of Orlando's life, which can be verified through records, documents, and archival sources, and his mental processes, an amusing phenomenology of experience begins to emerge. Searching for ways to narrate hidden subjectivities, the biographer turns to two forms of granite-like evidence: the young Orlando's prodigious literary output, which includes a trove of poetic manuscripts on classical subjects, and his "liking for low company," revealed through adventures in the neighborhood of Wapping Old Stairs, a section of London frequented by sailors and women with names like Sukey (22). His writing speaks to his tendency toward solitude, his meanderings to his love of mingling across social boundaries. Though his house is a town and his estate a place from which the world may be seen, neither contains him. He's errant.

The world of *Orlando* in the first chapter, then, is one in which the amplitude of the protagonist is emphasized. Diffusion characterizes Woolf's mixing of genres and her fictionalized subject who seeks to expand beyond the domestic and national boundaries of Englishness. Her biographer continuously struggles with tools of the trade in fashioning this quirky figure. So frequently, in fact, is this narrator given to outbursts that he—or she, we can't

---

103. For the house in *Orlando*, see Sarah Edwards, "'Permanent Preservation for the Benefit of the Nation': The Country House, Preservation, and Nostalgia in Vita Sackville-West's *The Edwardians* and Virginia Woolf's *Orlando*" in *Modernism and Nostalgia: Bodies, Locations, Aesthetics*, ed. Tammy Clewett (New York: Palgrave Macmillan, 2013), 93–110.

be sure—soon passes into being a subject too, one we are asked to read with attention to the skew.[104] This is a strategically important facet of Woolf's fictional construction. The straitlaced biographer allows her to get sensational material into the record about Orlando's shifting sexualities, caste transgressions, and ethnic mixing. Onto this narrator much of the book's orientalism is displaced.

Such narrative migrations as we find in the opening chapter of *Orlando* are a recurring feature of odyssean fictions. We have seen them at work in the puzzles posed by the Cretan tales, in the rolling pasts of Cavafy's poetry, and in the fluctuating perspectives of Césaire's personas. Woolf, however, also ensures that grounding devices check the centrifugal energy of her protagonist. Even as Orlando takes in the panorama of travel when he steps out of his windy attic, he does so at the base of an oak tree that allows him to "feel the earth's spine beneath him" (15).[105] While the "hard root" has erotic connotations, it is also a potent double signifier. Roots stabilize identity and harness what might otherwise be rampant. But they are also part of a living and ramifying system that supports limbs, which grow over time.[106] The doubleness is important in understanding the "The Oak Tree," an autobiographical poem that Orlando pens over centuries. A close parallel is drawn between the object in nature and the object in art, a crafted thing and the product of *poiesis*. It reminds us of Césaire's "original geography" and the map made in the image of his own blood. And it becomes a site of writing in which diverse ethnicities and sexualities mingle, as they do in Cavafy's "Poseidonians" and "In a Town in Osroini."

The expansiveness of *Orlando* in the first chapter of Woolf's book does not end with the house, or with the landscape visible from the oak tree, or with his cross-class meanderings. Promiscuous as the protagonist is—he dallies both with Queen Elizabeth and the blowsier Sukey of Wapping Old Stairs—his heart has not yet gone abroad. That is what happens in his love affair with the Russian princess Marousha Stanilovska Dagmar Natasha Iliana Romanovitch,

---

104. See Susan Dick, "Literary Realism in *Mrs. Dalloway, To the Lighthouse, Orlando* and *The Waves,*" in *Cambridge Companion to Virginia Woolf,* ed. Sellers and Roe, 62–67; and Kathryn Benzel, "Reading Readers in Virginia Woolf's *Orlando: A Biography,*" *Style* 28.2 (1994): 169–82.

105. On geographical expansiveness and the impulse toward rooting, see Froula, *Virginia Woolf and the Bloomsbury Avant Garde,* 180–89; Anne Ronchetti, *The Artist, Society, and Sexuality in Virginia Woolf's Novels* (London: Routledge, 2004), 81–90; and Elise Swinford, "Transforming Nature: *Orlando* as Elegy," in *Virginia Woolf and the Natural World,* ed. Kristin Czarnecki and Carrie Rohman (Liverpool: Liverpool University Press, 2011), 196–201.

106. Robert Kohn, "Erotic Daydreams in Virginia Woolf's *Orlando,*" *Explicator* 68.3 (2010): 185–88.

whom Orlando, remembering the name of a favorite pet fox, calls Sasha.[107] It all begins on the frozen Thames when Orlando is confronted with a figure on skates whose sexual ambiguity piques him. Significantly, the Russian tunic and trousers that the person wears serve "to disguise the sex" of the one wearing them (27–28). The quoted phrase echoes the opening sentence of the book where Orlando himself is described as a "he" whose sexual identity might be confused by virtue of "the fashion of the time," which "did something to disguise it" (11). Woolf constructs the encounter as a recognition scene—one in which the object mirrors the subject. It thereby anticipates the sex change.

Names in *Orlando* have been well tracked in the critical literature, but Sasha's offers a broader insight into the way language functions in representing the foreign. The princess bears an amusing combination of first names and family names, mostly Russian, but with traces of Scandinavian (Dagmar) and of Greek and Roman ancestry via Spain and Romania (Iliana, Romanovitch). Most of the spellings are variants (Marousha and Stanilovska). In short, the name itself is wayward, and it points to a more basic waywardness in the person who bears it. Who is she? The question reduces Orlando to a hair-pulling struggle with words. "Ransack the language" (35) as he does, he can't find words that might help him understand this creature who has so completely enchanted him and brought him to the brink of madness. Linguistic impoverishment, a more general theme of the book, figures prominently in this episode, and it is partially overcome through an analogy that connects polymorphous sexuality with racial miscegenation.

Orlando's insecurity and bewilderment are enacted through a performance he sees on the ice involving a black Moor "waving his arms and vociferating" over a fair-skinned woman "in white laid upon a bed" (42). Identifying with the Moorishness of the male, he vicariously participates in the murder he beholds, fantasizing about killing Sasha in a discharge of jealousy after he sees her in someone else's embrace. Although neither Shakespeare nor *Othello* is named, same-sex desire (Orlando's) is racialized; black skin becomes a metaphor for moral darkness, an association already prominent in the Renaissance imagination and here amplified in a fictional Elizabethan age.[108] This displace-

---

107. On the name, see Natalia Solovyova, "The National and 'the Other' as a Biography of the Creative Mind: *Orlando* by Virginia Woolf," in *Woolf Across Cultures*, ed. Natalya Reinhold (New York: Pace University Press, 2004), 215–25.

108. On the racialization of color in the Renaissance, see Karen Hall, *Things of Darkness: Economies of Race and Gender in Early Modern England* (Ithaca, NY: Cornell University Press, 1995), especially 1–24. For readings of *Othello* and race in *Orlando*, see Karen Kaivola, "Revisiting Woolf's Representations of Androgyny: Gender, Race, Sexuality, and Nation," *Tulsa Studies in Women's Literature* 18.2 (1999): 235–61; and Celia Daileader, "Othello's Sister: Racial

ment of errant sexuality onto a person of color is not unlike what happens when the speaker of *Cahier* identifies his mendacity with females, only to recognize that he lies in the act of excluding himself from complicity. The colonialized black male who scapegoats women in Césaire's text and the privileged white male who displaces sexual anxiety onto blacks in Woolf's text are struggling with forms of immanent consciousness that challenge representation.

Assuming an alternative identity through a narrative that mirrors one's own also recalls Odysseus's use of the Cretan tales to negotiate difficult barriers in his home. In both cases, the identification contributes to the proliferation rather than the streamlining of selves; Odysseus is not only a Cretan, but multiple Cretans, and Orlando is not only an Othello, but as we will see, multiple other ethnic and racial selves. This multiplicity may be enabling, but it can also devolve into psychic dysfunction or chaos. Cavafy's poems, by contrast, do not so much move into the experience of diaspora as come onto the poetic scene already diasporic and mixed. His tonalities are cooler than those of Césaire and Woolf, his narratives more attenuated, his lyrical impulse more understated and melancholic. But the worlds he creates—the Poseidonia of Magna Graecia, the Lagid dynasty in Egypt, the outliers in Osroini—share with these writers a diffusion related to geographical expansiveness and plural subjectivities that can be, by turns, enabling and destabilizing. This brings us to the trope of islands and isolation in chapter 2.

Hermaphroditism and Appropriation in Virginia Woolf's *Orlando*," *Studies in the Novel* 45.1 (2013): 56–79.

CHAPTER 2

Islands and Isolation

Exile is more than a geographical concept. You can be an
exile in your homeland, in your own house, in a room.

—Mahmoud Darwish, interview

Over time as most people fail the survivor's exacting test of
trustworthiness, she tends to withdraw from relationships. The
isolation of the survivor thus persists even after she is free.

—Judith Lewis Herman, *Trauma and Recovery*

Isolation may be variously imagined in literary odysseys, but certainly one of the common forms it assumes is the insularity of islands. The boundedness of stretches of land in large bodies of water is, to an extent, dependent on how much land there is and whether it occupies a sea or an ocean. Tightly configured archipelagoes whose islands are visible to one another contribute to a sense of interconnectedness for those who inhabit them. Bits and pieces of earth scattered over a fluid blue may become steppingstones that enable exchange or foster a sense of community. The Aegean with its roughly 7,000 islands and islets contains several of such groupings, among them the Cyclades, the Dodecanese, and the Sporades, and land is almost always in sight. Though archipelagoes are not a dominant image in Cavafy's poems, his cityscapes often infer or present visual images of an interactive sea that churns up towns and imperial centers. Césaire's Antilles, by contrast, are situated at the intersection of the Atlantic and the Caribbean, and they are more diffuse. While a cartographic view from on high enables an appreciation of their vital position in systems of economic and cultural exchange, they also appear fragile and tissue-like. From Basse Pointe on the northeastern coast of Martinique where Césaire was born, the Atlantic looms, wild and windy, but in Fort-de-France one can feel a more heavily laden place of suffering that bears witness to human traffic in conditions of violence over centuries—the earth that figures so prominently at the opening of *Cahier*.

Islands, as we have seen, are vital to the world of Homer's *Odyssey*. Here they become associated with a wide range of experience marked, on the one hand, by the bustling, syncretic economy of an old-world Crete and, on the other, by the grittiness of an Ithaca that Odysseus calls home, a place considerably less rich in resources and overrun by a bevy of thuggish aristocrats. Within this spectrum, Ogygia, the island inhabited by Calypso, is more fantastical and symbolically weighted. It is from Ogygia that Odysseus emerges from the wanderings in a drama of rebirth. Homer's story shares narrative elements with Césaire's since *Cahier* endeavors to give birth to an island people by bringing them across the boundaries that isolate them in their suffering.

In the *Odyssey* and *Cahier*, we are presented with literal islands, but Cavafy and Woolf take us into metaphorical spaces on land that are island-like in their insularity—sites of exile that embody the sentiment of the epigraph by Palestinian poet Mahmoud Darwish that stands at the opening of this chapter. With Cavafy, the sea is never far away, either a reminder of a freedom that his personas do not have or a channel of escape from the shame inflicted by their sexual deviance. The image of the city as an island is an ancient one, an exemplary case being Thucydides's Athens, its long walls and port the markers of a strategic insularity.[1] Cavafy presents us with a particularly vivid reimagining of the trope. The isolation in Woolf's *Orlando* is even more restricted for it takes the form of a physical interior in the most secluded of places, a subterranean family crypt. The island-like character of this underground geography is suggested by the protagonist's movement out of it and into a sea across which he exercises a freedom that would otherwise be impossible. Rather like the cave of Calypso, the tomb in *Orlando* is ambiguously imagined as a womb enabling rebirth.

HOMER: FROM CALYPSO TO THE
THERAPY OF THE WORD

One way of approaching these topics is from the perspective of the person left behind—the one who awaits the arrival of a valued other in a place that becomes prison-like.[2] Penelope is an evocative example. Her waiting isolates

---

1. See Christy Constantakopoulou, *The Dance of the Islands: Insularity, Networks, the Athenian Empire, and the Aegean World* (New York: Oxford University Press, 2007), 61–89.

2. On the structure of the return tale and those left behind, especially the female, see John Foley, *Homer's Traditional Art* (University Park: Pennsylvania State University Park, 1999), 115–19, 137–42. On this topic in modern literature, see Victoria Reuter, "A Penelopean Return: Desire, Recognition, and *Nostos* in the Poems of Yannis Ritsos and Gail Holst-Warhaft," in

her, and in her isolation, she becomes a character linked to her environment by tenuous bonds. While she is famous for her marital fidelity, her motives are in fact rendered ambiguously in the epic, in response to the flow of stories that pass through the Ithacan court. Although she awaits her husband's return, she relates in the scene at the hearth with the beggar a dream she's had about twenty pet geese who are killed by an eagle and whose loss she mourns (19.603–24; 19.535–53). The disguised beggar interprets it to mean that the geese are the suitors and her husband the eagle who will kill them. But he misses or ignores a diverting implication: Penelope grieves their loss, and this suggests a more complex relationship with the suitors. While the text is obscure about her fondness, the dream points in the direction of a romantic engagement with the men who have taken over her house.

The ambiguities that surround Penelope are exemplified in her weaving trick.[3] In keeping open her options in remarriage, she looks in two directions: toward the husband for whom she longs, but also toward her best choice among the suitors. In Book 18 (181–85; 158–63), she is overcome by the longing to show herself in her beauty to the suitors, an act prompted by Athena, but one that is compatible with other signs of encouragement to the intruders who woo her with gifts. The bard describes the weaving trick in a repeated phrase: she leads on her admirers, "but all the while with something else in mind" ("νόος δέ οἱ ἄλλα μενοινᾷ; 2.100; 2.92 and 18.319; 18.283).

The notion of "something else in mind" or "thinking otherwise" is emphasized from the beginning of the epic. When Penelope first descends the stairs from the women's quarters in Book 1, her face veiled, she does so because Phemius, the resident bard, has been singing of the *nostoi* before the suitors and, while they listen enchanted, the sound of his songs saddens her—her "most of all" (394; "μάλιστα," 342). The intensifier sets her apart, at the margins of what draws the males in the house. Weeping, she asks Phemius to cease because his tales remind her that her husband has not yet achieved his *nostos,* though his fame, his *kleos,* has spread throughout Greece. But the only Odysseus who has won *kleos* in the sense of epic song is the Iliadic one; the Odyssean character is merely the subject of *kleos* in the sense of rumor and report at this point. Penelope must situate herself at the intersection of epic song and ordinary talk

---

Odyssean Identities in Modern Cultures: The Journey Home, ed. Hunter Gardner and Sheila Murnaghan (Columbus: The Ohio State University Press, 2014), 89–111; and Sheila Murnaghan, "The Misadventure of Staying Home: Thwarted *Nostos* in De Chirico and Rebecca West," in *Odyssean Identities,* ed. Murnaghan and Gardner, 112–32.

3. The critical literature on Penelope's weaving is substantial. See Bergren, *Weaving Truth*; Barbara Clayton, *A Penelopean Poetics: Reweaving the Feminine in Homer's Odyssey* (Lanham, MD: Lexington, 2004); and Maria Pantelia, "Spinning and Weaving: Ideas of Domestic Order in Homer," *American Journal of Philology* 114.4 (1993): 493–501.

to remain alert about the possibilities for *nostos,* and yet in doing so, she also attracts the desire of the suitors who wish "to lie beside her, share her bed" (421; "παραὶ λεχέεσσι κλιθῆναι," 366). Alone in her suffering, her appearance is nonetheless enticing to the men who surround her, and she knows it. Her isolation is in tension with her currency.

There are, in fact, alternative stories about Penelope that probably circulated in Homer's time. In an extant fragment of the poet Pindar (early fifth century BCE), Penelope is the mother of the god Pan via the god Apollo.[4] In a much later attestation, the Greek traveler and geographer Pausanias (second century CE) refers to a tale in which Odysseus, upon his return, charges his wife with bringing paramours into the house. Being cast aside by him, she travels to Sparta and Mantinea in Arcadia, where she eventually dies.[5] In yet other accounts, Penelope beds all the suitors, and this is how Pan is conceived, the etymology of his name meaning "all."[6] These accounts bring into view the ambiguities surrounding Homer's Penelope, suggesting the circulation of epichoric tales about her that had local color and meaning. While Penelope's emotional isolation is key to her fidelity in the *Odyssey,* her story is also crossed by other vectors, lending added force to the phrase used of her trickery—that she weaves the shroud "with something else in mind."

When Odysseus first comes into view in the epic, it is in a more radical scene of isolation and tears (5.165–75; 5.151–58). Like his wife, he mourns, but unlike her, he is not situated in the circuitous routes of *kleos.* Rather, he has been completely separated from them for ten years. What he does best, which is speaking artfully, has become an impossibility. While his wife is making her speech to Phemius in Ithaca, he is stranded on the island of Calypso, deprived of company and grieving as he looks out upon a limitless sea. This grief connects husband and wife across a great geographical divide, but Ithaca and Ogygia could not be more different. The latter is surrounded by an abyss. When Zeus sends Hermes to free Odysseus from exile, the wing-sandaled god wonders, "Who would willingly roam across a salty waste so vast, / so endless?" (5.112–13; "τίς δ᾽ ἂν ἑκὼν τοσσόνδε διαδράμοι ἁλμυρὸν ὕδωρ / ἄσπετον," 5.100–101).

---

4. See Pindar, *The Odes of Pindar,* trans. C. M. Bowra (Oxford: Oxford University Press, 1935), Frag. 90.

5. See Pausanias, *Description of Greece,* 8.12.5–6.

6. On this lustful Penelope, see Abate-Çelebi, *Penelope's Daughters,* 17–20; and Marie-Madeleine Mactoux, *Pénélope: légende et mythe* (Paris: Les Belles Lettres, 1975), 99.

What is remarkable about Odysseus when we first come upon him is his anonymity.[7] The name of the goddess who detains him underscores this. Calypso means "the concealer" (literally, "I will conceal"), and she inhabits a place distant from Mount Olympus and far outside the social order upon which the fame of epic song depends. In this encounter, Homer gives poetic expression to a mythical death, experienced after war and prolonged violence, and before the therapy of the word has intervened in the form of storytelling.[8] Odysseus will come to tell his tale and thereby construct a path back into a world he has lost; he will thereby win *kleos* in a more glorified sense. But he must be reborn to do so. The cave of Calypso functions archetypally as tomb and womb, its extreme location a symbol of death and its vine-covered cave a symbol of birth.[9] It provides a point of orientation for understanding the primal sense of *nostos* as a psychic journey out of the dark and into the light.[10] And it anticipates patterns we will examine in Cavafy, Woolf, and Césaire.

In an evocative passage that presents us with Hermes's view of Ogygia as he approaches it in flight, the audience is given details about Calypso's dwelling: she is weaving inside her cave; he smells a fire burning with two kinds of wood; he sees the woodland around the opening, blooming with alder, poplar, and cypress; he can almost taste the cool water flowing from four springs.[11] If the cave is a womb, it is a fashioned one, a cultivated place in a strange landscape somewhere between the Olympian gods and mortals where suffering can be treated without intrusion or threat of continued injury. In its lushness, life for Odysseus has been reduced to the most basic biological level: sex. The island is akin to a "halfway house" that enables healing by reducing ambi-

---

7. On these aspects of the Calypso episode, see Thomas van Nortwick, *The Unknown Odysseus: Alternate Worlds in Homer's* Odyssey (Ann Arbor: University of Michigan, 2008), 12–23; and G. E. Dimock, *The Unity of the* Odyssey (Amherst: University of Massachusetts Press, 1989), 14–16.

8. On storytelling as a Homeric form of psychic therapy, see Christensen, "The Clinical *Odyssey*"; Race, "Phaeacian Therapy in Homer's *Odyssey*," 47–66; and Pedro Laín Entralgo, *The Therapy of the Word in Classical Antiquity*, trans. L. J. Rather and John Sharp (New Haven: Yale University Press, 1970), 29–31.

9. On the Calypso episode and its symbolic character as a psychological journey, see Bergren, *Weaving Truth*, chapter 3; Egbert Bakker, "The Greek *Gilgamesh* or the Immortality of Return," *Eranos: The Proceedings of the 9th International Symposium on the* Odyssey (2000): 331–52; Bruce Louden, *The Odyssey: Structure, Narration, and Meaning* (Baltimore: Johns Hopkins University Press, 1999), 104–29, and *Homer's* Odyssey *and the Near East*, 124–34; and Segal, *Singers, Heroes, and Gods*, 37–64, 82–83.

10. See Frame, *Myth of Return*, for this sense of *nostos*.

11. For analyses of the landscape of Ogygia, see Norman Austin, *Archery at the Dark of the Moon: Poetic Problems in Homer's* Odyssey (Berkeley: University of California Press, 1975), 149–52; and de Jong, *Narratological Commentary on the* Odyssey, 128–29.

ent noise, as it were.[12] But if the nymph once pleased, she does so no longer. Calypso has become a captor, and Odysseus rejects the immortality she offers.

A visible sign of the hero's rebirth is his engagement in building the boat he needs in order to leave. This activates a certain kind of memory, namely, know-how, or *techne*. What he constructs is not a boat of the sort that got him to Troy or into the world of the wanderings—a *neus*—but a *schedie*, a word etymologically related to the adverb *schedon* and signifying something close at hand, makeshift.[13] What Calypso provides, among other things, is cloth—for the sail, but also as clothing. These two woven products, having been introduced, are almost immediately at odds in the narrative. The sail helps get the open boat out to sea, and the clothing protects its navigator from the elements. But when Poseidon unlooses a storm that shatters the craft, Calypso's robes prove to be so heavy that they nearly drown Odysseus. He must shed the garments. With the help of a sea nymph, Leucothea, the White Goddess, who lends him a diaphanous veil that takes him ashore, he is saved (5.366–90; 5.333–53). But the tension that is bound up with Calypso the concealer continues long after Ogygia.

From this moment on, one might say, Odysseus carries Calypso in him. In other words, he is drawn to garments (or metonymic substitutes) that conceal. Under threat, he will go into hiding, and so what saves him also ensures that he remains estranged. Here the audience is confronting the shadowy side of a heroic ethos of survival—a scarred man who must fit the pieces back together, but who does so never having completely overcome the catastrophes that have befallen him. That is why the figure of Odysseus in Greek literature veers unstably between the noble and the ignoble, the just and the unjust.[14] He comes to Homer in this ambiguous form already, as we know from his trickery in the *Iliad*, especially during the night raid on the Trojan camp with Diomedes in Book 10 but also from the story of the Trojan horse, which is told in the epic cycle and by Demodocus in Book 8.[15] Homer, however, galvanizes the image in the *Odyssey*, drawing connections between injury, concealment, and a tendency to relapse under pressure into anonymity. If Odysseus leaves

---

12. See Race, "Phaeacian Therapy in Homer's *Odyssey*," 47, who also uses the metaphor of "a halfway house."

13. On Odysseus's raft, see Dougherty, *Raft of Odysseus*, 32–37; de Jong, *Narratological Commentary*, 137–38; and Heubeck et al, *Commentary on Homer's* Odyssey, 1:274–75.

14. For a study of the permutations of Odysseus in later art and literature, see Silvia Montiglio, *From Villain to Hero: Odysseus in Ancient Greece* (Ann Arbor: University of Michigan Press, 2011).

15. Dué and Ebbott, Iliad *10 and the Poetics of Ambush*, Part 1, Essays 1 and 2. The tale of the Trojan horse is also told in summary form in *Odyssey* 8 in the songs of Demodocus.

Calypso behind in one sense, the verb and the actions connected with her name continue to wind their way through the narrative.

This is apparent in a well-known simile that ends Book 5, after Odysseus has finally reached the terra firma of Phaeacia, having been at sea twenty-one days:

> As a man will bury his glowing brand in black ashes,
> off on a lonely farmstead, no neighbors near,
> to keep a spark alive—no need to kindle fire
> from somewhere else—so great Odysseus buried
> himself in leaves and Athena showered sleep
> upon his eyes . . . sleep in a swift wave
> delivering him from all his pains and labors [literally, "covering his eyes"]
> (5.540–67)

> ὡς δ᾽ ὅτε τις δαλὸν σποδιῇ ἐνέκρυψε μελαίνῃ
> ἀγροῦ ἐπ᾽ ἐσχατιῆς, ᾧ μὴ πάρα γείτονες ἄλλοι,
> σπέρμα πυρὸς σῴζων, ἵνα μή ποθεν ἄλλοθεν αὕοι,
> ὣς Ὀδυσεὺς φύλλοισι καλύψατο· τῷ δ᾽ ἄρ᾽ Ἀθήνη
> ὕπνον ἐπ᾽ ὄμμασι χεῦ᾽, ἵνα μιν παύσειε τάχιστα
> δυσπονέος καμάτοιο, φίλα βλέφαρ᾽ ἀμφικαλύψας.
> (5.488–93)

The repetition of words for hiding, burying, or covering, including those that pun on Calypso (*kalyps-*), is one of the most striking features of the passage. While Odysseus's capacity to deliberate is prominent in the narrative of the shipwreck—he has moments on the high sea in which he debates with his "heart," or *thumos,* about what to do—the wordplay prefigures the dialectic of concealing while revealing that is enacted across the epic.

To hide flaming embers in black ashes far away from neighbors so that one doesn't have to ask for help is cunningly anticipatory for a man shipwrecked on an unknown shore; Odysseus is "overjoyed" (5.538; "γήθησε," 5.486) to find shelter. But the self-sufficiency may also be read as insularity, not just as a feature of the landscape, but as a precarious state of the psyche, a kind of interior insularity whereby a "firebrand" (associated with war) is kept alive in disconnection from "neighbors" (in peace), thereby creating weak interpersonal bonds.[16] Physical and psychic injury, hiding, and relapses into obscurity

---

16. Bergren, *Weaving Truth,* chapter 3, has a powerful analysis of this simile and others in Book 5; the reading proposed here draws different conclusions.

are linked, and the regressive element in this scenario appears in the characterization of the hiding place in terms typically used of a wild boar's lair.[17]
Odysseus's reputation as a trickster figure, well known from folklore, can hide
the links between wounding and the compensatory strategies by which he
protects himself. These reaction formations will be explored in chapter 3, but
for now I take them to be bound up with the evolution of a folkloric character
type in the more complex world of epic where moral conflicts, problems of
responsibility, and questions about the return from violence press hard. With
this pressure, the human mechanisms by which choice and action take shape
grow more complex as well.

CAVAFY: COSMOPOLITAN ISOLATION
AND SEXUAL SHAMING

Cavafy's cities, while often historically situated in a specific time that carries
geographical bearings, are also powerfully imagined places, located at the
intersections of multiple cultures and described in a lexical code that carries
underlying meaning. When the inner life is extroverted in his verse, becoming part of a citified or cosmopolitan setting, the space becomes evocative of
psychic states, and a sense of entrapment predominates, heightened by the fact
that the land in Cavafy is never far from the sea, which emerges as a route not
taken. Exile can become a paradoxically self-imposed condition that points
to damaged agency—a wound linked with social shaming. To put it this way
brings us close to a fact about Cavafy's own life.

In one of his personal "Notes on Poetics and Ethics" written on 28 April
1907, he describes his feelings about the city he has made his home:[18]

> I've grown used to Alexandria by now, and probably even if I were rich I'd
> go on living here. But even so, how it oppresses me. What a hardship, what a
> burden a small city is. What a curb on one's freedom [τι ἔλλειψις ἐλευθερία].
>
> I'd go on living here (then again, I'm not altogether certain that I would)
> because it's like a homeland to me [σαν πατρίς], because it's all bound up
> with my life's memories [ἀναμνήσεις].
>
> But how much someone like me—different as I am [σαν κ'ἐμένα τόσο
> διαφορετικό]—needs a big city.

---

17. See de Jong, *Narratological Commentary*, 147.

18. See "Notes on Poetics and Ethics," trans. McKinsey, 23. For the Greek text, see *Μικρά
Καβαφικά Β*, 115.

London, for instance. Ever since . . . P. M. left, I haven't stopped thinking about it.[19]

As is typical of Cavafy, even in his self-commentaries, the passage is oblique
in its references. Although Alexandria is identified by name as "a small city"
that "oppresses" because of its "curb on one's freedom," what kind of freedom remains unclear. London would be preferable because it is larger, but
also because P. M. has decamped there, which is why it's alluring. We do not
know who P. M. is. The identity is hidden, or rather, half hidden. What com-
pels the writer to remain in the insular city that marginalizes him is that it is
"like a homeland" that has engendered the "memories of [his] life." Similarly,
the writer is not an "I," but rather a man "different as I am," literally, "like me,
so different," in an oblique sense. The writer is not self-same but removed
by degrees of resemblance from a homeland and from himself. P. M. moves
within this network, ungendered and half named. The constraints of finance
("even if I were rich") shape a more basic dialectic of living at the margins.
Migration is an option that might enable a move away from confinement, but
the writer has "grown accustomed" to malaise. In his wavering between this
and that, holding open possibility while living a reality that undermines it,
one hears a skepticism that suspends ultimate judgment. The indirection of a
life lived on the edges is isomorphically constructed in a style of indirection.

With these remarks in mind, we can turn to "The City" ("Η Πόλις"), a
poem Cavafy began in 1894 and revised over a period of fifteen years, before
publishing it in 1910.[20] Interestingly, he chose this as the opening piece in his
first self-published collection, *Poems, 1905–1915*, and so he thought of it as an
introduction of sorts to his work up to that date. It is laced with references to
sea routes, foreign shores, lost opportunities, and entrapment, rendered in a
decadent register. I have transliterated the Greek word at the end of each line
in the following poem in order to make a point about rhyme in the discussion that follows.

"The City"
1 You said: "I'll go to another country, go to another shore [*thalassa*], a
2 find another city better than this one [*aute*].　　　　　　　　　b
3 Whatever I try to do is fated to turn out wrong [*grafte*]　　　　b

---

19. On the central role of Alexandria in the thought and poetry of Cavafy, see Edmund
Keeley, *Cavafy's Alexandria: Study of a Myth in Progress* (Cambridge, MA: Harvard University
Press, 1976).

20. See the note of Mendelsohn in Cavafy, *Complete Poems*, trans. Mendelsohn, 413. For
the translation, see *Collected Poems*, trans. Keeley and Sherrard, 50.

4 and my heart lies buried as though it were something dead
   [*thamene*].   c
5 How long can I let my mind moulder in this place [*menei*]?   c
6 Wherever I turn, wherever I happen to look [*do*],   d
7 I see the black ruins of my life, here [*edo*],   d
8 where I've spent so many years, wasted them, destroyed them
   totally [*chalassa*]."   a

9 You won't find a new country, won't find another shore [*thalasses*]. a
10 This city will always pursue you. You will walk [*gyrnas*]   b
11 the same streets, grow old in the same neighborhoods [*gernas*],   b
12 will turn gray in these same houses [*asprizeis*].   c
13 You will always end up in this city. Don't hope for things
   elsewhere [*elpizeis*]:   c
14 there is no ship for you, there is no road [*hodo*].   d
15 As you've wasted your life here, in this small corner [*edo*],   d
16 you've destroyed it everywhere else in the world [*chalases*].   a

"Ἡ Πόλις"

1 Εἶπες· "θὰ πάγω σ᾽ ἄλλη γῆ, θὰ πάγω σ᾽ ἄλλη θάλασσα.
2 Μιὰ πόλις ἄλλη θὰ βρεθεῖ καλλίτερη ἀπὸ αὐτή.
3 Κάθε προσπάθεια μου μιὰ καταδίκη εἶναι γραφτή·
4 Κ᾽ εἶν᾽ ἡ καρδιά μου—σὰν νεκρὸς—θαμένη.
5 Ὁ νοῦς μου ὡς πότε μὲς στὸν μαρασμὸν αὐτὸν θὰ μένει.
6 Ὅπου τὸ μάτι μου γυρίσω, ὅπου κι ἂν δῶ
7 ἐρείπια μαῦρα τῆς ζωῆς μου βλέπω ἐδῶ,
8 ποὺ τόσα χρόνια πέρασα καὶ ρήμαζα καὶ χάλασα."

9 Καινούριους δὲν θὰ βρεῖς, δὲν θἄβρεις, ἄλλες θάλασσες.
10 Ἡ πόλις θὰ σὲ ἀκολουθεῖ. Στοὺς δρόμους θὰ γυρνᾶς
11 τοὺς ἴδιους. Καὶ στὲς γειτονιὲς τὲς ἴδιες θὰ γερνᾶς·
12 καὶ μὲς στὰ ἴδια σπίτια αὐτὰ θ᾽ ἀσπρίζεις.
13 Πάντα στὴν πόλι αὐτὴ θὰ φθάνεις. Γιὰ τὰ ἀλλοῦ—μὴ ἐλπίζεις—
14 δὲν ἔχει πλοῖο γιὰ σέ, δὲν ἔχει ὁδό.
15 Ἔτσι ποὺ τὴ ζωή σου ρήμαξες ἐδῶ
16 στὴν κώχη τούτη τὴν μικρή, σ᾽ ὅλην τὴν γῆ τὴν χάλασες.

The formal aspects of the poem are illuminating. This is a piece in two equal stanzas of eight lines for a total of sixteen lines, and they are arranged by the following rhyme pattern: <u>abbc cdda</u>, repeated twice in both stanzas. Though it is a critical element of the poem, the translators, Keeley and Sherrard, have not tried to render the rhyme in English.[21] The pattern loosely follows a quatrain structure that evokes the sonnet while working against its traditional variations. Similarly, rather than a dramatic monologue, the reader is introduced to a dramatic dialogue in two voices, the first contained in quotation marks and introduced by a verb of speaking, the second dropping both the quotation marks and the verb.

The initial action word of the poem is the familiar form of the second person singular, apparently directing itself to itself: the "You said" is speaking to the "I" or the oblique "me"—the same persona, divided into confrontational voices. In the turn from stanza 1 to stanza 2, this is confirmed. The tone of first-person desperation gives way to second-person judgment: "You said you will leave, but you will not do what you said—you have chosen to stay, and you will be ruined." It is this judgmental voice that has the last say and that stamps the first stanza with the sense of being a self-fulfilling prophecy. Key rhymes in the Greek underscore the fatalism, a few of which are noted here:

- the end rhymes of the first and last lines of both stanzas (1 and 8, 9 and 16) are identical; *thalassa* (shore / sea) echoes *chalasa* (destroyed), a possibility of change impeded;
- "another country" and "another shore / sea," which promise something better than "this" (Greek "*afte*"), are already "fated to be wrong," literally, they are "written already" (*grafte*) in line 3;
- this fatefulness (*grafte*) in line 3 is likened to a dead heart already "buried" (*thamene*) in line 4;
- the dead heart already "buried" (*thamene*) in line 4 joins the mind that "will moulder" (*tha menei*) in line 5;
- "wherever I happen to look" (*do*) in line 6 is directed at the rubble that is "here" (*edo*) in line 7; and so forth.

In its entirety, the poem enacts a ruination already in progress and far along: the heart, both the motor of life and the site of passion, is not just "dead" in the first stanza, but, more vividly, a "corpse" ("*nekros*"). The simple and repetitive diction, the parataxis, the tendency toward end-stopped lines, the imprisoning rhymes of "*thalassa*" ("sea") and "*chalasa*" ("wasted")—all gather force until the last two devastating enjambed lines: "As you've wasted your life here, in this small corner, / you've destroyed it everywhere else in the world."

---

21. For a translation that attempts to use rhyme, see Cavafy, *Complete Poems*, trans. Mendelsohn, 5.

Although the reader gets a rough sense of the voices speaking through the persona of the poem, the identity of the city is not specified and the actions that provoke the brutal self-dialogue remain obscure. From the start, the reader is enshrouded in a lyrically evoked gloom where death stares from every corner and terror lurks. The overpowering mood recalls the ambivalence felt for Alexandria in the personal note we have examined. But in the arc from self-interrogation in the autobiographical reflection to the completed poem, the aporia has moved into a morally charged self-condemnation. This is a poem that plays upon an ancient motif one may find, for example, in the reflections of Seneca, among others: travel to foreign places cannot make you well if the problem you are seeking to escape is yourself.[22] Montaigne waxes philosophical on the problem: "We take our fetters with us; our freedom is not total; we still turn our gaze towards the things we have left behind; our imagination is full of them."[23] We are our own blighted island—our own hell.

Cavafy himself provides a brief explanation for the poem in a letter he wrote to one of his friends: "There is a class of poems whose role is 'suggestif.' My poem ["The City"] comes under that head. To a sympathetic reader—sympathetic by culture—who will think over the poem for a minute or two, my lines, I am convinced, will suggest an image of the deep, endless 'désespérance' that they contain 'yet cannot all reveal.'"[24] "The City" has much in common with the decadent sensibilities in Baudelaire's *Les Fleurs du Mal*, Rimbaud's *Une Saison en Enfer*, and Wilde's *The Picture of Dorian Gray*, which merge the inner and the spiritual with the external and material in rendering degeneracy and dissolution.[25] The entangled condition of Cavafy's city-dweller—his deafness to possibilities outside the infernal dialogue in his head—is one of several highly achieved effects in the poem. The reader is dealing with a constructed horror that reinvents the trope of isolation as a *katabasis* into a self-made hellhole from which escape is impossible. A poetics of indirection is at work in the piece, and it shapes an intense affective state whose depths cannot be fully plumbed. Strikingly, some of the same elements we find in the

---

22. See Seneca, *Moral Letters to Lucilius* (New York: CreateSpace Independent Publishing, 2016), Letter 28.

23. Michel de Montaigne, "On Solitude," in *The Complete Essays*, trans. M. A. Screech (London: Penguin, 1987), 269.

24. Quoted in English in Gregory Jusdanis, *The Poetics of Cavafy: Textuality, Eroticism, History* (Princeton: Princeton University Press, 1987), 72; taken from Michael Perides, Ο βίος και το έργο του Κωνσταντίνου Καβάφη (Athens: Ikaros, 1948), 312.

25. See Haas, "Early Cavafy and the European 'Esoteric' Movement," *Journal of Modern Greek Studies* 2.2 (1984): 209–24; Kostas Boyiopoulos, "The Darkening of the Mirror: Cavafy's Variations on *The Picture of Dorian Gray*," *Journal of Modern Greek Studies* 30.1 (2012), 21–43; and Jeffreys, *Reframing Decadence*, especially ix–xix.

simile of *Odyssey* 5—the heart that lies buried within, the black ruins, the fear of a new country, the sense of devastation—may be found here. But Cavafy's poem is much more clearly burdened by a sense of lost opportunities and self-blame than Homer's simile of Odysseus suggests, and his metaphorically shipwrecked life is the consequence of a self-imposed exile.

While isolation in "The City" is drawn in apocalyptic tones, other poems present the compulsion to hide as the effect of unnamed "obstacles" that check both speech and action. These consign the poem's persona to silence in a world blinkered by convention and the narrowness of socially acceptable trajectories for a life story. While Cavafy rarely speaks of homoerotic desire directly, and never divulges names or practices, the works are notable for the ways in which, failing to come out of the closet, they nonetheless indicate it. Their provocation lies in rendering secrets suggestively enough to allow the imagination to work on their spare evocative power. A good example is the poem "Hidden Things" ("Κρυμμένα").[26]

> From all I did and all I said
> let no one try to find out who I was.
> An obstacle was there that changed the pattern
> of my actions and the manner of my life.
> An obstacle was often there
> to stop me when I'd begin to speak.
> From my most unnoticed actions,
> my most veiled writing—
> from these alone will I be understood.
> But maybe it isn't worth so much concern,
> so much effort to discover who I really am.
> Later, in a more perfect society,
> someone else made just like me
> is certain to appear and act freely.

> Ἀπ᾿ ὅσα ἔκαμα κι ἀπ᾿ ὅσα εἶπα
> νὰ μὴ ζητήσουνε νὰ βροῦν ποιὸς ἤμουν.
> Ἐμπόδιο στέκονταν καὶ μεταμόρφωνε
> Τὲς πράξεις καὶ τὸν τρόπο τῆς ζωῆς μου.
> Ἐμπόδιο στέκονταν καὶ σταματοῦσε με
> πολλὲς φορὲς ποὺ πήγαινα νὰ πῶ.
> Οἱ πιὸ ἀπαρατήρητές μου πράξεις

---

26. Cavafy, *Collected Poems*, trans. Keeley and Sherrard, 360–61.

καὶ τὰ γραψίματά μου τὰ πιὸ σκεπασμένα—
ἀπὸ ἐκεῖ μονάχα θὰ μὲ νοιώσουν.
Ἀλλὰ ἴσως δὲν ἀξίζει νὰ καταβληθεῖ
τόση φροντὶς καὶ τόσος κόπος νὰ μὲ μάθουν.
Κατόπι—στὴν τελειοτέρα κοινωνία—
κανένα ἄλλος καμωμένος σὰν ἐμένα
βέβαια θὰ φανεῖ κ' ἐλεύθερα θὰ κάμει.

It is a solitary voice that speaks in these lines from an isolated space of self-censorship and self-alienation, the cause of which are obstacles that stand in the way. The words "let no one try to find out who I was" are part admonition and part invitation. The speaker plays hide and seek in the text, remaining tantalizingly open while seeming to close the gap. As in other poems by Cavafy, the dynamic of concealing while revealing figures prominently. Moreover, through the reference in the final lines to a "more perfect society" in which the current "obstacles" will be removed, the poem performs an incipient founding act, in the lyric rather than epic mode, that may enable the emergence of new identities, which can only be vaguely adumbrated in time present. The play with multiple personas, the need to conceal, and the obstacles that prevent disclosure are all key Cavafian themes, but they take on added resonance when placed in an odyssean context because in some poems, like "Hidden Things," they become exemplary acts within island-like cities that alienate and suffocate.

Another poem, this one organized in a more obviously narrative fashion, approaches half-hidden things through an itinerary of social and moral decline, in which isolation and insularity figure prominently. "Days of 1896" ("Μέρες τοῦ 1896"), composed in 1925 and first published in 1927, is one of five similarly titled poems (for example, "Days of 1901") that evokes a sense of peak experience, the ephemerality of pleasure, and the imprisoning demands of society upon the homosexual.[27] In its form, the poem figures among a group that uses a divided line, which makes the image on the page appear to have a fault running through it. What makes it particularly important for this study is that it introduces a figure who does not fit the social script, who is driven into vagrancy as a consequence of being shamed.

27. This reading builds upon Dimitris Papanikolaou, "Days of Those Made Like Me"; Sarah Ekdawi, "'Missing Dates': The 'Μέρες' Poems of C. P. Cavafy," *Byzantine and Modern Greek Studies* 35.1 (2011): 73–75; Diana Haas, "Around the Revisions of Cavafy's 'Σ'ένα βιβλίο παληό--('In an Old Book—), 1922–1929," in *Imagination and Logos: Essays on C. P. Cavafy*, ed. Panagiotis Roilos (Cambridge, MA: Harvard University Press, 2010), 245–62; James Faubion, "Cavafy: Toward the Principles of a Transcultural Sociology of Minor Literature," *Modern Greek Studies, Australia and New Zealand* (2003): 19–39; and Jusdanis, *Poetics of Cavafy*, 64–80.

"Days of 1896" begins abruptly with a verb in the past tense that declares the ruin of an unnamed "he" in the face of a community that has treated him disdainfully. Yet the poem is organized around a *volta* that not only reframes the subject, but that is also reframed itself at a higher level. There everything, including the revisionary judgment, is projected along an historical axis of discursive practices.[28]

"Days of 1896"

1 He was completely debased.   An erotic propensity,
2 highly forbidden   and regarded with contempt
3 (natural nonetheless)   was the cause.
4 His society   was very prudish
5 He gradually lost   his meagre resources;
6 then his standing,   and his reputation.
7 He was approaching thirty   without ever holding down
8 a job for a year,   at least that anyone knew of.
9 Sometimes he earned   his living from
10 deals that   were shameful.
11 He degenerated into a character   who, if they saw you with him
12 often, you'd likely   be greatly compromised.

13 But that's not all of it.   That wouldn't be right.
14 The memory of his beauty   deserves much more.
15 There's another way of seeing   and, if imagined that way,
16 he appears attractive.   He appears simple and true
17 a child of eros   who above and beyond his honor,
18 and his reputation,   without question put
19 the pure pleasure   of his pure flesh.

20 Above his reputation?   But society was
21 so prudish   and made such foolish connections.

"Μέρες τοῦ 1896"

1 'Εξευτελίσθη πλήρως.   Μιὰ ἐρωτικὴ ροπή του
2 λίαν ἀπαγορευμένη   καὶ περιφρονημένη
3 (ἔμφυτη μολοντοῦτο)   ὑπῆρξεν ἡ αἰτία:
4 ἦταν ἡ κοινωνία   σεμνότυφη πολύ.

---

28. Translation is by the author. The Greek text is from Cavafy, *Collected Poems,* trans. Keeley and Sherrard, 278.

5 Ἔχασε βαθμηδὸν   τὸ λιγοστό του χρῆμα·
6 κατόπι τὴ σειρά,   καὶ τὴν ὑπόληψί του.
7 Πλησίαζε τὰ τριάντα   χωρὶς ποτὲ ἔναν χρόνο
8 νὰ βγάλει σὲ δουλειά,   τουλάχιστον γνωστή.
9 Ἐνίοτε τὰ ἔξοδά του   τὰ κέρδιζεν ἀπὸ
10 μεσολαβήσεις ποὺ   θεωροῦνται ντροπιασμένες.
11 Κατήντησ᾽ ἔνας τύπος   ποὺ ἂν σ᾽ ἔβλεπαν μαζύ του
12 συχνά, ἦταν πιθανὸν   μεγάλως νὰ ἐκτεθεῖς.

13 Ἀλλ᾽ ὄχι μόνον τοῦτα.   Δὲν θἄτανε σωστό.
14 Ἀξίζει παραπάνω   τῆς ἐμορφιᾶς του ἡ μνήμη.
15 Μιὰ ἄποψις ἄλλη ὑπάρχει   ποὺ ἂν ἰδωθεῖ ἀπὸ αὐτὴν
16 φαντάζει, συμπαθής·   φαντάζει, ἀπλὸ καὶ γνήσιο
17 τοῦ ἔρωτος παιδί,   ποὺ ἄνω ἀπ᾽ τὴν τιμή,
18 καὶ τὴν ὑπόληψί του   ἔθεσε ἀνεξετάστως
19 τῆς καθαρῆς σαρκός του   τὴν καθαρὴ ἡδονή.

20 Ἀπ᾽ τὴν ὑπόληψι του;   Μὰ ἡ κοινωνία ποὺ ἦταν
21 σεμνότυφη πολὺ   συσχέτιζε κουτά.

The initial words—"Ἐξευτελίσθη πλήρως" (1)—sound a death knell. Mendelsohn's translation reads, "He debased himself completely." Evangelos Sachperoglou prefers "He was disgraced completely,"[29] while Keeley and Sherrard give us "He became greatly degraded."[30] The variants suggest different levels of agency, all of them possible in light of the middle-passive inflection of the Greek verb. Did the man choose a disgrace he could have avoided? Was he the passive object of social condemnation? Or was it some combination of these that led to his demise? These questions help frame alternative ways of understanding the relationship between the marginalized homosexual and the marginalizing society.

The values of Cavafy's third-person speaker, it is quickly clear, are not those of the group: he regards the society that condemns as "prudish," or more literally, "puffed up with a holier-than-thou attitude" (4, 21). Other poems

---

29. Cavafy, *Collected Poems*, trans. Sachperoglou, 167.

30. On Cavafy's use of pejorative terms to describe homosexuality, see Margaret Alexiou, "C. P. Cavafy's 'Dangerous' Drugs: Poetry, Eros and the Dissemination of Images," in *The Text and Its Margins. Post-Structuralist Approaches to Twentieth-Century Greek Literature,* ed. Margaret Alexiou and Vassilis Lambropoulos (New York: Pella, 1985) 157–96; Haas, "Around the Revisions," and "Νόμος καὶ Ἔγκλημα στὴν ἐρωτικὴ ποίηση τοῦ Καβάφη," *Μόλυβδο—Κόνδυλο—Πελεκητής* 7 (2000): 146–56.

by Cavafy echo the speaker's derogatory view of norms as so much "chattering about morality" ("περὶ ἠθικῆς λαλοῦντες").[31] Two sets of values collide in "Days of 1896": the moral code of society, on the one hand, which pronounces judgment upon an "erotic propensity" that is "highly forbidden," and the natural order to which the speaker appeals, on the other, which understands this orientation as innate. Informed by this doubleness, the first stanza traces a kind of tragic fall, measured in incremental loss—of money, position, reputation—all leading to an alienation cast as a contagious shame. Unable to be anything other than what he is by nature, he is trapped in a double bind and ultimately exiled. With its focus on the sordid and the furtive, the poem brings us into Cavafy's sensual city, a version of fin de siècle Alexandria with its drifters, who move from one shabby location to another, not unlike those of Homer's Ithaca, though for different reasons, leaving behind stories.

The colliding values of the social group and the speaker are registered in the first stanza by stylistic features. A cascade of feminine adjectives dominates the first several lines. These adjectives modify feminine nouns, which describe a subject whose male identity is conveyed through a single masculine pronoun at the end of line one: "him" ("του"). Gender, including the gender of the speaker, is caught up in equivocations. The natural and the social jostle, each pushing the other across the split of the divided line and, through enjambment, beyond line-end. As is often the case in Cavafy's closets, the public condemnation is hypocritical; the group is complicit in the behavior it disparages. The details are telling: the man was nearing thirty, he had never worked over a year or had a legitimate job, and he played a go-between in shady deals. Where are the wife and children? This conjures the world of rumor, and rumor ends up speaking what it means to silence.[32] Rather than hidden things, the first stanza presents us with "half-hidden things"—"μισοκρυμένα," to use a word from another of Cavafy's poems.[33] These are things already mediated in competing ways (the social versus the natural) in the historically identified moment of "Days of 1896." What is distinctive in the poem is that the natural is aligned with nonnormative sexuality, which from 1880 to 1920 was becoming part of the new discourse of sexual pathology in European medical

---

31. See "Theater of Sidon (A. D. 400)," in *Collected Poems*, trans. Keeley and Sherrard, 238–39, line 6, for the phrase, which Haas discusses in "Around the Revisions."

32. Michel Foucault, *The History of Sexuality: An Introduction*, trans. Robert Hurley (New York: Pantheon, 1978), 1:27; and Didier Eribon, *Insult and the Making of the Gay Self*, trans. Michael Lucey (Durham, NC: Duke University Press, 2004), 15–17.

33. See Cavafy, "When They Come Alive" ("Ὅταν Διεγείρονται"), *Collected Poems*, trans. Keeley and Sherrard, 122–23.

circles.[34] As already seen, Cavafy was writing at some of the same intersections of literature and "invertism" as were Virginia Woolf and the Bloomsbury group, whose interests in psychoanalysis, homosexuality, and androgyny were partly spurred by the work of Havelock Ellis, Richard von Krafft-Ebbing, and Heinrich Kaan's *Psychopathia Sexualis*.[35]

From the tensions in the poem's first stanza, the second stanza draws new energy. Its interruptive force is sounded by a counter declaration in the opening half line: the words "But that's not all of it" (13) undo the finality of "he debased himself completely." The reader is projected into a realm of sensuous beauty, mediated by memory. The object of shame is purified through a personal recollection that makes possible a rewriting of the life story along aesthetic lines. As the poem moves out of the past and into a present tense that reconstitutes meaning, the outcast becomes attractive. This attractiveness shines in the simple light of his physical desire, which he offers without contrivance or intrigue. There is a genuine purity here, conveyed through the ritual language of *katharsis*, applied to sexual pleasure and the body ("the unsullied [καθαρῆς] pleasure / of his unsullied [καθαρή] body," 19). The syntax flows in a single smooth sentence that moves across the space of the divided line. Memory is transformed into a practice—a mnemonics—that enlists the aid of writing to call the record of the past into question. Gesturing toward an alternative tale, Cavafy's speaker abandons common gossip to shape a new account of homosexual biography, free from the stigmatizing force of traditional morality. But even this new narrative does not elude the poem's insistent historicizing.

One must look to a metapoetic level. Stanza 2 is no less involved in the play of appearances than stanza 1: the poem does not move from seeming to essence or from semblance to truth. Cavafy emphasizes this by identifying the alternative perspective as "another way of looking" (15). The poem as a whole then is composed of alternative standards of value and divergent tales, no one of which cancels out the other. All are situated in the days of 1896. This positioning enables something like a suspension of judgment—a historically informed conception of ethical and aesthetic possibilities that qualifies its own preferred way of seeing. The distancing strategies are typically Cavafian.

---

34. For a more extended treatment of "half-hidden things," see Dimitris Papanikolaou, "'Words That Tell and Hide': Revisiting C. P. Cavafy's Closets," *Journal of Modern Greek Studies* 23 (2005): 235–60. On the influence of late nineteenth- and early twentieth-century sexology on Cavafy, see Papanikolaou, "Days of Those Made Like Me."

35. See Heinrich Kaan, *Psychopathia Sexualis: A Classic in the History of Sexuality*, ed. Benjamin Kahan and trans. Melissa Haynes (1884; Ithaca, NY: Cornell University Press, 2017).

Three consequences of the relativizing emerge. First, the social community is redefined by the poem's projection of the homosexual closet into it. Through rumor, the homosexual is both revealed and concealed.[36] Second, the natural order, though offering a defense of homosexuality, takes on the character of a historically bound discourse—one of several ways of thinking and speaking about the body. Third, aesthetically oriented art assumes the freedom of reinventing the subject, but it, too, is cast as one of several ways of seeing. In the poetry of Cavafy, there is a liberation that comes from such weighing and counterweighing. Here, it is not connected with the character of the young man whose story is being told, nor even with the third-person narrator, but with the poet himself. It is he who shapes the narrative in order to salvage the wreck of a personal life by remembering it in a revisionary fashion.

Other critics have noted that the year 1896 referenced in the title of Cavafy's poem very nearly coincides with the year of the Oscar Wilde trials involving charges of sodomy, or "gross indecency"—1895.[37] It is unlikely that Cavafy did not follow the story. While in court, Wilde was asked to interpret the phrase, "the love that dare not speak its name," which was from a poem penned by Lord Alfred Douglas, one of Wilde's lovers.[38] Although he characterizes the love as having "nothing unnatural about it," just as Cavafy does in "Days of 1896," he is nonetheless direct in speaking of it as an affection of an older male toward a younger.[39] This openness proved scandalous, and it allowed the prosecution to connect Wilde with the young—and notorious—men in Taylor's circle, much to the detriment of his case.

This was the kind of attention Cavafy sought to avoid by cultivating a poetics of indirection. While his poems are not, like the Cretan tales, lies that resemble the truth, they mask sexual identity through cunning strategies of half-hidden things. The "Notes on Poetics and Ethics" are paratexts that provide evidence of the displacement, and they capture some of what is lost in the process of bringing same-sex desire from experience to imagination and from imagination to the page, a topic that will be explored in chapter 4. Tropes of isolation function as literary devices that give form to the indirection. In "The City," they are cast in the shape of a nightmarish world of nonreferen-

36. See Eve Sedgwick, *The Epistemology of the Closet* (Berkeley: University of California Press, 1990), 67–90.

37. See Sarah Ekdawi, "Days of 1895, '96, and '97: The Parallel Prisons of C. P. Cavafy and Oscar Wilde," *Modern Greek Studies Yearbook* 9 (1993): 297–305; and Jeffreys, *Reframing Decadence*," 16–17.

38. The phrase is from the poem "Two Loves" by Lord Alfred Douglas, which was published in 1894. Douglas had an affair with Wilde.

39. See the Criminal Trial Transcript, accessed 5 May 2019, http://law2.umkc.edu/faculty/projects/ftrials/wilde/Crimwilde.html.

tial expression that feeds on its own compulsory silence. In "Days of 1896,"
they create a space for the necessary transience of those who incur shame by
engaging in natural acts that are nonetheless heavily stigmatized.

It is shame, at least in part, that lies behind Cavafy's creation of a homoerotic aesthetic, which is given expression in "Hidden Things," and it is this
aesthetic that elevates what the social order condemns as depraved. In the
context of entrapment, exile, and vagabondage that this part of the book has
been tracing, his Mediterranean becomes a site of itinerant sexual identities,
lived across dangerous borders, in need of masking, and compelled to rely
upon veiled writing that partially hides what it also seeks to expose. Although
the poems examined here are not overtly Homeric, they enact a Calypso-like
dynamic in a self-protective mode, constructing homoerotic subjectivities in
the space between what can be seen and what lies beneath or behind. Isolation
is by turns the condition that must be escaped, a consequence imposed against
choice, and the insularity needed for survival.

WOOLF: DOMESTIC *KATABASIS* AND
MOMENTS OF BEING

In turning from Cavafy to Woolf, this study once again focuses on withdrawal
and alienation in the context of sexual anomaly. It also continues to examine
how isolation can give way to moments of insight that enable the formulation
of a poetics dependent upon the very forms of silence that an oppressive social
order imposes upon speech and action. Readers of Woolf, however, have a
great many more paratexts upon which to draw than do readers of Cavafy.
These paratexts enable an intimate encounter with the ways in which the early
diaries and letters she wrote about her own psychic breakdowns are transformed in her fictional works.[40] In *Orlando*, these experiences first appear in
the events that follow the affair with Sasha, the Russian princess who opens
the door to mysterious flights across seas that are deeply transformative.

Chapter 2 of the fictional biography commences with a male protagonist who has been jilted by a female, though an ambiguous one, on what is
presumably her journey back to Russia. But the *nostos* tale told here recedes
behind the greater enigma of who Sasha is, why she has come to England at
all, and with whom she has departed. Unlike Odysseus, Orlando's experience
of isolation begins with his being in Penelope's position, watching a Muscovite

---

40. On the connection between Woolf's "poetics of loss" and Hellenism, see Koulouris,
Hellenism and Loss.

ship disappear in the swirling waters of a melting landscape whose itinerary he cannot imagine. His illicit erotic encounter with a supposed Russian princess under the cloak of night and amid rampant gossip (he was contracted in marriage before the affair) delivers him into a nowhere land of shame that alienates him from everyone he knows. But rather than drifting by virtue of social ostracism into unknown geographies like some of Cavafy's itinerant lovers, Orlando takes up wandering in his own house. It is filled with the ghosts of his forbears and bygone visitors who got lost in meandering hallways and never found their way back to common rooms. The chapter includes a mythical sleep, a *katabasis,* and the near fatal "disease" of obsessive reading and writing, whose onset is treated with macabre humor and whose progress is traced to a pollen that has blown, suggestively, out of Greece and Italy (55). Gothic elements shape the satire, suggesting that the ghosts haunting the house mingle with the ghosts haunting the head.

To approach Woolf's treatment of isolation in her return tale—of islandlike areas in settled places like houses—it is helpful to turn first to the magical sleep into which Orlando falls upon losing Sasha. Like later ones, this sleep is linked with an extreme event, in which the goings-on in "the chambers of [the] brain" (50) remain largely inscrutable to the biographer who continually backs down from trying to explain them. It recalls Odysseus's sleep on a ship provided by the Phaeacians who have promised him safe passage home. Upon his departure, the audience hears that they laid out a blanket for him on the deck, and as the ship set sail, "an irresistible sleep fell deeply on his eyes, the sweetest, / soundest oblivion, still as the sleep of death itself" (13.91–92; "καὶ τῷ νήδυμος ὕπνος ἐπὶ βλεφάροισιν ἔπιπτε, / νήγρετος ἥδιστος, θανάτῳ ἄγχιστα ἐοικώς," 13.79–80). A few lines later, the ship is said to be speeding along "bearing a man endowed with the gods' own wisdom / one who had suffered twenty years of torment, sick at heart / . . . but now he slept in peace, the memory of his struggles / laid to rest" (13.101–2, 104; "ἄνδρα φέρουσα θεοῖς ἐναλίγκια μήδε᾽ ἔχοντα / ὃς πρὶν μὲν μάλα πολλὰ πάθ᾽ ἄλγεα ὃν κατὰ θυμόν, / . . . δὴ τότε γ᾽ ἀτρέμας εὗδε, λελασμένος ὅσσ᾽ ἐπεπόνθει," 13.89–90, 92).

In the *Odyssey* and *Orlando,* these mythical sleeps share common features.[41] They are of extraordinary length, they call attention to the enigmatic border crossings made in their duration, and they are followed by episodes of amnesia. Odysseus has no recollection of his journey, and he fails to recognize Ithaca upon arriving. Whatever the dividing line that cordons off the realm of the wanderings from the rest of post-Trojan War Greece, it resists consciousness and the strong pull of the epic toward narration. Similarly, whatever the

---

41. On sleep and thresholds in the *Odyssey,* see Segal, *Singers, Heroes, and Gods,* 79–84.

nature of the psychic blow that plunges Orlando into a weeklong oblivion after the loss of Sasha, the nature of its violence exceeds the descriptive capacity of the biographer and resists representation. The thickening of texture around Orlando's "trance" (50) is a consequence not only of its profundity, but its aftermath. For one thing, the subject of the comatose state has no recollection of it; he has "an imperfect recollection of his past life" in general (50). In fact, after Orlando wakes, forgetting appears to be so much more important than remembering that we are made to wonder whether death must be dealt in "small doses" in order to survive. Posing a series of questions without answer, the biographer ponders whether such trances function as "remedial measures" that save us from premature mortality. Did Orlando die and come back to life? (50) Once again, the obscurity of the subject is approached through narrative devices that conceal as they reveal.

In her memoir, *A Sketch of the Past* (1939–40), Woolf describes what she calls "moments of being," highly memorable pauses in the flow of time, sometimes luminous and elevating, but more often accompanied by a "hopeless sadness" or a "horror" during which she becomes "passive under some sledgehammer blow," which exposes her to "a whole avalanche of meaning," while she stands "unprotected, with nothing to ward it off."[42] This "shock-receiving capacity," Woolf writes, "is what makes [her] a writer" because it draws her into formulating an explanation:

> I feel that I have had a blow . . . and I make it real by putting it into words. It is only by putting it into words that I make it whole; this wholeness means that it has lost its power to hurt me; it gives me, perhaps because by doing so I take away the pain, a great delight to put the severed parts together. Perhaps this is the strongest pleasure known to me.[43]

Creativity is the combined act of being struck hard and meeting the strike by putting together the severed parts of a psyche overcome by a surplus of meaning. This process is ongoing, and tenuously so, in Woolf's own life. Without pointing to the *Odyssey,* the fictional biography casts light upon how moments of being emanate from island-like spaces where safe harbor appears as a temporary space of *nostos*—of safe arrival on the far side of madness.

If unconsciousness is a way of checking out of a world that has become impossible to bear, it can also constitute a death-like state that is prolonged

---

42. Virginia Woolf, *Moments of Being: A Collection of Autobiographical Writings,* ed. Jeanne Schulkind, 2nd ed. (New York: Harcourt, 1985), 78. Woolf speaks at some length about these experiences in her letters and diaries; see Lee, *Virginia Woolf,* 182–91.

43. Woolf, *Moments of Being,* 72.

upon awakening. Rather than breathing fresh air when he comes to, Orlando's preoccupation with "death and decay" (53) continues to isolate him, and he descends into the underground of his monumental manor whose ancestors have been buried in a crypt, a gothic house of horrors with bones littered here and there.[44] The deep isolation of sleep is followed by a secondary manifestation, which reveals that the psychic collapse has not yet been integrated. Woolf's domestic *katabasis* emphasizes this. Walking the gloomy corridors of his mansion, her protagonist looks at "picture after picture as if he sought the likeness of somebody whom he could not find" (53), and he finally stops when he comes upon a Dutch snow scene.

> Then it seemed to him that life was not worth living any more. Forgetting the bones of his ancestors and how life is founded on a grave, he stood there shaken with sobs, all for the desire of a woman in Russian trousers, with slanting eyes, a pouting mouth, and pearls about her neck. She had gone. She had left him. He was never to see her again. And so he sobbed. And so he found his way back to his own rooms. (54)

The accident of coming upon an image with snow in it—not even a portrait, but a generic landscape scene—activates tears in a process that is affectively cathartic. The image triggers a repressed memory, which can then be revisited and released. The dynamic is familiar. Woolf's narrative is dramatizing a version of Aristotelian catharsis, which suggests that the arousal of powerful emotion from watching a mimetic image can issue in a discharge of emotion that alleviates the disturbance. But in *Orlando,* it is not enough to fall unconscious and later cry purgative tears. Severe blows require more.

Before seeing exactly what more, it is worth lingering a moment longer on mimetic images. Orlando's search for a picture after the severe blow of Sasha recalls a need that Woolf herself describes in a letter of 1915 to Margaret Llewelyn Davies after one of her early collapses[45]: "I wanted to say that all through that terrible time I thought of you and wanted to look at a picture of you, but was afraid to ask."[46] For Woolf, photographs could provide evidence of relationships that seemed spectral after a psychic breakdown. On her journey back from extreme isolation, they could function as a prompt for

---

44. On the themes of *katabasis* in modern literature, see Michael Thurston, *The Underworld in Twentieth-Century Poetry: From Pound and Eliot to Heaney and Walcott* (New York: Palgrave Macmillan, 2010); and Rachel Falconer, *Hell in Contemporary Literature: Western Descent Narratives Since 1945* (Edinburgh: Edinburgh University Press, 2007), 42–62.

45. Davies was general secretary of the Cooperative Women's Guild from 1899 until 1921.

46. Woolf, *Letters,* 2:60.

reweaving a narrative torn under the strain of a breakdown. While Davies
had not precipitated a crisis, she was a weak link back to a precrisis world
that Virginia was attempting to reconstruct through mimetic images of the
people in her past.

From the outset of her project, Woolf planned on incorporating visual
images into the text of *Orlando,* showing her character at various stages in life,
through both painted portraits drawn from the collection at Knole, the Sack-
ville estate, and photographs of Vita herself that Virginia planned on taking.[47]
These images were not the consequence of an emotional crash in her relationship with Sackville-West from which she was seeking to extricate herself. But
they do call attention to Vita's fear that she might herself precipitate such a
collapse in her friend.[48] They also suggest that if photographs or paintings
could provide tenuous links back to sanity, they might also be a weak form of
combat against a potentially aggressive force.

Vita understood this. Having given Virginia access to the Knole collection (and much of her personal life), she says in a letter to her, "You see, any
vengeance that you ever want to take will lie ready to your hand."[49] In the
ensuing events, Vita indeed felt framed in multiple senses by Woolf's project, especially the photo shoots she was talked into.[50] Upon completing the
manuscript, Virginia wrote her to say, "Did you feel a sort of tug, as if your
neck was being broken on Saturday last at 5 minutes to one? That was when
he [Orlando] died—or rather stopped talking, with three little dots . . ."[51] After
reading the finished manuscript, Vita wrote Virginia to say she had fallen in
love with Orlando, while also feeling "like one of those wax figures in a shop
window, on which you have hung a robe stitched with jewels."[52] Virginia's pen
had bitten, and the bite appears to have been, at least in part, a form of self-

---

47. Woolf, *Letters,* 3:430. For discussions, see Elizabeth Hirsh, "Virginia Woolf and Portraiture," in *The Edinburgh Companion to Virginia Woolf,* 171–75; Colin Dickey, "Virginia Woolf
and Photography," in *Edinburgh Companion to Virginia Woolf and the Arts,* ed. Maggie Humm
(Edinburgh: Edinburgh University Press, 2010), 375–91; Erika Flesher, "Picturing the Truth in
Fiction: Re-visionary Biography and the Illustrative Portraits for *Orlando,*" in *Virginia Woolf
and the Arts,* ed. Diane Gillespie and Leslie Hankins (New York: Pace University, 1997), 39–47;
and Lee, *Virginia Woolf,* 505–7. Vanessa Bell had a major hand in taking the photographs for
Orlando.

48. See Nigel Nicolson, ed., *Vita and Harold: The Letters of Vita Sackville-West and Harold
Nicolson* (New York: Putnam, 1992), 158–59.

49. See Vita Sackville-West, *Letters of Vita Sackville-West to Virginia Woolf,* ed. Louise
DeSalvo and Mitchell Leaska (New York: William Morrow, 1985), 238.

50. See Nicolson, *Vita and Harold,* 185; Sackville-West, *Letters of Vita Sackville-West to
Virginia Woolf,* 237–38; and Lee, *Virginia Woolf,* 505–6.

51. See Woolf, *Letters,* 3:474.

52. Sackville-West, *Letters of Vita Sackville-West to Virginia Woolf,* 288.

inoculation for the author of *Orlando*—a way of using aggression in art to protect the self from being radically undermined by a potential threat.

The strange limbo of mimetic artifacts such as paintings and photographs in *Orlando*—the mix of fact and fiction, granite and rainbow—recall the similar strangeness of the Cretan tales in the *Odyssey*, which also have a prophylactic dimension. No sooner is Odysseus delivered by the Phaeacians on the shores of Ithaca than he begins to enter into a period of extended obscurity in his own home where he tells tales of other Odysseuses who crossed the seas, met with hardship and shipwreck, and made and lost fortunes. The vivid painterly style of these tales—their *enargeia*—as well as the traces in them of autobiographical elements that overlap with Odysseus's life, as we know it in the *Odyssey*, suggest that they occupy a vaguely defined area between the psychic annihilation endured in the wanderings and the return to Ithaca. These tales are in obvious ways very different from Woolf's use of images, but both point to mimetic links between recovery and trauma.

Woolf plays out these effects by developing Orlando's own writerly side. In ascending from the isolation of the crypt, the protagonist moves toward processing his experience by putting it into words. This is how we are introduced to "The Oak Tree," a work loosely modeled on Sackville-West's *The Land* (1926), a georgic praising the beauty of the Kent countryside, which won the author the Hawthornden Prize. The manuscript is an important part of the narrative of *Orlando*. Among the fifty or so works the protagonist has penned by the age of twenty-five, almost all of them bearing Greek titles, including "The Return of Odysseus"; this is the only one with a sturdy Anglo-Saxon name.[53] It is an intimate text in every way. Secretive and alluring, the reader is never given access to it. While we occasionally hear obliquely about what the "The Oak Tree" contains, the biographer steers clear of its contents, through a combination of ignorance and alarm, thus suggesting its connection with the rainbow rather the granite side of life. I will return in chapter 4 to this tree in relation to the famous olive in *Odyssey 23*, which grounds the marriage bed of Odysseus and Penelope. But its importance here anticipates what is to come. Whether Orlando's clandestine manuscript is a bridge into or out of madness is ambiguous because writing can stimulate deep anxieties even as it enables psychic channeling.

What the reader does know is that when the still fragile protagonist sets to writing in Chapter Two, the moment is marked by a significant narrative pause. With the rise of the pen, memory is activated, and memory "may agi-

---

53. For a discussion of these manuscripts, and especially "Xenophila," see Maria DiBattista, *Imagining Virginia Woolf: An Experiment in Critical Biography* (Princeton: Princeton University Press, 2009), 119–21.

tate a thousand odd, disconnected fragments, now bright, now dim, hanging and bobbing and dipping and flaunting, like the underlinen of a family of fourteen on a line in a gale of wind" (58). Metaphorically, this faculty is a "she," cast in Penelopean imagery as a "seamstress, and a capricious one at that . . . who runs her needle in and out, up and down, hither and thither" (58). The very motion of dipping the quill sets her going. And so when Orlando dips, it is Sasha who first materializes before him—"Where was she; and why had she left him?" (59). These questions so agitate him that he manages to "squirt" ink all over the table in his quasi-erotic distraction.

Woolf has improvised a Rorschach test. While the Russian princess appears momentarily in the filmy liquid, it is not her face that Orlando begins to fathom in the spill. It is rather the vague image of a man he once saw sitting at the servants' table of his own house with ink and paper, whose identity was then, and is still, unknown (17). Was he a poet? So begins the adventure with Mr. Nicholas Greene. He is a fictionalized famous writer who lives in the age of Marlowe, Jonson, and Shakespeare (sometimes he transitions into being a parody of Shakespeare), but who regards all Elizabethans as hacks, slavishly turning out work that brings in money, but not "Glawr" (66), an English strangulation of the French "*Gloire*" (Vita spoke fluent French). Greene is a rather paunchy man who wears a stained ruffle and slobbers when he talks. But he is of the "sacred" rather than the "noble race" (62), and Orlando is infatuated with him. He will live for the entire duration of the story and be instrumental in the publication of the protagonist's work in the twentieth century, but not before unleashing damage. As we will see, Orlando's antagonistic relationship with him is not unlike Odysseus's relationship with Demodocus, the singer in the Phaeacian court who tells an abbreviated tale of the Trojan horse, making a path for the still anonymous Odysseus to relate the story of the wanderings. The rapport between Odysseus and Demodocus is strong, but there is competition between them, which raises the question of who is responsible for life stories—an important consideration when the hero is still alive and can tell his own tale.

For both Odysseus and Orlando, fame through storytelling is at stake. Herein lies the disease of the ink and quill for Woolf: the quest for "Glawr." Once it opens the breach, into it leap "Ambition, the harridan, and Poetry, the witch, and desire of Fame, the Strumpet" (60). Literary fame, of course, is a modern way of referring to what Homer calls *kleos,* which, as already seen, runs the gamut from gossip and report to tales of the great deeds of men and Penelope's weaving for glory. Orlando, then, during the protracted isolation of the Sasha affair, moves from deep sleep to a descent into the underworld, to the partially purgative effects of mimetic visual art, and finally to a passion for writing that is not unlike the construction of a *nostos* tale one might recount after returning from the dead. When he shares with Nick Greene a classically inspired piece he has written entitled "The Death of Hercules," dreaming of "Glawr," it goes with his romantic soul attached. And when Greene delivers a scathing review of it in a journal—"he found it wordy and bombastic in the extreme" (70)—Orlando suffers another blunt-force blow, this one directed at his second most vulnerable spot: a love of writing. Instead of entering into another deep sleep, however, Orlando enters into "obscurity" once again, a state that "rids the mind of the irk of envy and spite" and "sets running in the veins the free waters of generosity and magnanimity" (76–77). The entire traumatic episode in Chapter Two of Woolf's fictive biography enacts death and rebirth through a drama of concealing while revealing. The biographer's view, shaped as it is by a poetics of indirection, takes the form of a kind of peep show that offers sporadic insight into a murky psychic world of anxiety and resistance to the toxic side of literary *kleos*. While the psychology of this inner drama is modern, it captures the urgency in odysseys of telling one's own tale—and the inadequacies of a third-person narrative approach to experience, which can be hijacked, as we know from Homer.

CÉSAIRE: PELÉAN ERUPTIONS AND PORTRAITS OF BLOOD

While the *Odyssey* shows the protagonist a way back from death by opening a door for storytelling via the Calypso episode, *Orlando* enables a mode of survival by creating a form of personal life writing enabled by a katabatic descent among the ancestors. *Cahier,* by contrast, poses the question of where an enslaved people can turn for its own reimagined representations of hell in a society that is highly racialized. What Césaire offers as a response is the result of a poetic process that he describes in a 1978 interview in terms of a "descent into oneself" ("*une descente en soi-même*"), which can trigger an outburst of the imagination in verbal form.[54] Elsewhere in the interview, he speaks of poetry as an activity that "ascends from the deep" ("*monte des profondeurs*").[55] It consists in the double movement of going down into an abyss followed by rising back up, a pattern repeatedly enacted in his poetry.[56]

---

54. See the interview with Jacqueline Leiner in the collected edition of *Tropiques,* xvii.

55. *Tropiques, 1941–1945,* xi: "*La vraie poésie monte des profondeurs,*" which Césaire modifies by saying, "*toute poésie.*"

56. See Alfred Alexandre, *Aimé Cesaire: la part intime* (Montreal: Memoire d'Encrier, 2014); and Mamadou Ba, "*S'orienter dans l'histoire: Césaire entre mémoire et promesse,*" in *Aimé Césaire: oeuvre et héritage: colloque du centenaire,* ed. Christian Lapoussinière (Paris: Jean-Michel Place, 2017), 188–95.

From such plunges and upsurges, Césaire gathers fragments that enable him to visualize death and rebirth—for an individual and for a people. Islands here are both literal and metaphorical, and passing through them enables a certain resourcefulness, exercised at the limits of consciousness.

Césaire sometimes personalizes his descent by speaking of it in native terms borrowed from the active volcano on Martinique, Mont Pelée, whose eruption in 1902 destroyed St. Pierre, the capital of the island at the time (it subsequently moved to Fort-de-France). Speaking of Basse Pointe, the village where he was born on the far north of the island, not far from St. Pierre, he says, "I always had the sense that we were born from the mountain, that we were born from the volcano [on est né du volcan] . . . I feel that my poetry is peléan [peléen] . . . it builds up for a long time [s'accumule pendant longtemps], it builds patiently, it makes its course [fait son cheminement], one might think it is extinct [éteinte], and then suddenly, the great eruption [la grande déchirure]."[57] Access to an infernal space through a mountain whose cleft still steamed was a potent stimulus for the experience of katabasis in Césaire's poetry.[58] From this trope, he would draw sacral associations.[59] Jean-Paul Sartre acknowledged this dimension of black poetry, without singling out Césaire, in his 1948 essay "Orphée noir" ("Black Orpheus"). The ancient Greek myth suggested itself "because this untiring descent of the negro into himself causes me to think of Orpheus going to reclaim Eurydice from Pluto."[60] Sartre did no favor to the writers of whom he wrote when he called négritude "anti-racist racism" ("racisme antiraciste"). But his view of this body of work as a salient example of "poésie engagée" and his description of it in existentialist terms as a reflection of "the being-in-the-world of the negro" ("l'être-dans-le-monde du Nègre") helped bring wider attention to a literary corpus that might have not otherwise have reached larger audiences at the time.[61]

---

57. See the interview with Daniel Maximin, "La poésie, parole essentielle," Présence Africaine, 126.2 (1983): 10 (author's translation).

58. See Davis, "'Homecomings without Home'"; Scharfman, "Aimé Césaire: Poetry Is / Knowledge"; and Fardin, "Volcan: épouvante ou espérance: mythe et réalité," 309–16.

59. On Mont Pelée and the theme of sacrificial violence, see Daniel Delas, "Césaire et le sacré: poésie et sacrifice," in L'écriture et le sacré: Senghor, Césaire, Glissant, Chamoiseau (Montpellier: Presses Universitaires de la Méditerannée, 2002): 141–52.

60. Jean-Paul Sartre, "Black Orpheus," trans. John MacCombie, Massachusetts Review 6.1 (1965): 22, 33, 36 for quotations; originally published in French, "Orphée Noir" in Léopold Senghor, ed., Anthologie de la nouvelle poésie nègre et malgache (Paris: Presses Universitaires de France, 1948).

61. For the quotations, see Sartre, "Black Orpheus," 18, 33, and 36. For a commentary on Sartre's essay, see Abiola Irele, "A Defence of Negritude: À Propos of 'Black Orpheus' by Jean-Paul Sartre," Transition 50 (1975/76): 39–41.

One way to approach the question of how *Cahier* handles the trope of isolation and insularity is by examining two well-known passages in the poem that invite pairing. One is a description of an historical figure, Toussaint Louverture (1742–1803), a former slave who lived in Saint Domingue and led a successful slave revolt between 1791 and 1804 against French colonial rule, which resulted in an independent state, now Haiti. The other is a description of a nameless character referred to as the "pongo," a word used of an ethnic group in the Congo, but also slang for a giant ape or gorilla.[62] If Toussaint Louverture stands on one end of a spectrum of racial reference in the poem as a liberator of a dispossessed people, the pongo stands on the opposite end as a figure of racial abjection. Both appear in conditions of extreme isolation, and both are created in ways that make their "weakness" in a historical setting into a "strength" in the poetic narrative. The passages constructed around these characters address two distinct needs in *Cahier's* journey of coming into consciousness.

First, for a deracinated people with no history of its own and no ancestral heroes, there is a need for exemplary figures who can function as rebels against atrocities.[63] This history must be composed from the weak links that survive in the memory of a displaced people, and they are in need of imaginative invention. It is one of Césaire's major contributions to the literature of decolonization that he found ways of immersing himself in the obscure collective consciousness of a lost people and forging such imaginative figures. In *"La poésie et la connaissance"* ("Poetry and Knowledge"),[64] he contrasts the faculty of judgment with the image saying, "it is by means of the image, the revolutionary image, the distant image, the image that overthrows all the laws of thought that mankind finally breaks down the barrier" of what is merely perceived (*"C'est par l'image, l'image révolutionnaire, l'image distante, l'image*

62. See Cavafy, *Journal of a Homecoming*, commentary by Irele, 237.

63. See Celeste-Marie Bernier, *Characters of Blood: Black Heroism in the Transatlantic Imagination* (Charlottesville: University of Virginia Press, 2012); Cora Kaplan, "Black Heroes/ White Writers: Toussaint L'Ouverture and the Literary Imagination," *History Workshop Journal* 46 (1998): 33–62; Clément Mbom, *"Toussaint Louverture, Martin Luther King Jr., Léopold Senghor, Nelson Mandela, et Aimé Césaire: cinq mondes, un même idéal,"* in *Aimé Césaire: oeuvre et héritage*, 50–61; and Kalikoff, "Gender, Genre, and Geography." From the perspective of classical reception, see Graziosi and Greenwood, eds., *Homer in the Twentieth Century*, 1–20; McConnell, *Black Odysseys*, 39–70; and the contributions in Emily Greenwood, "Re-Rooting the Classical Tradition: New Directions in Black Classicism," *Classical Receptions Journal* 1.1 (2009): 87–103.

64. For the English, see Césaire, "Poetry and Knowledge," in *Lyric and Dramatic Poetry, 1946–1982*, trans. Clayton Eshleman and Annette Smith (Charlottesville: University of Virginia Press, 1990), xlii–lvi. For the French, *"La poésie et la connaissance," Tropiques* 12 (1945): 157–70.

qui bouleverse toutes les lois de la pensée, que l'homme brise enfin la barrière."[65] Toussaint, who cast aside his surname Breda, the name of the plantation on which he worked for Louverture, could be mythologized in this way, in other words, through the image.[66] Later characterizations—Black Spartacus, Black Napoleon, *Le premier des noirs*—reveal the pull he exerted on the imagination. William Wordsworth was not the only poet who wrote a tribute to him.[67] Toussaint's self-invented moniker, which reflects something of his cunning, means "the opening" (*"l'ouverture"*). He put it to good use in his life and his life writing.[68]

A complex figure who assumed multiple identities in a turbulent period of Caribbean history and who began the process of myth-making that still surrounds him by writing a memoir, Louverture remains in many ways a protean figure.[69] Recent biographers have expressed very different opinions of his status as a revolutionary. Some uphold Trinidadan C. L. R. James's view of him as a "Black Jacobin,"[70] a supremely gifted man possessed of the intelligence, physical stamina, and political skill to rise as a leader at a turning point in history. Others regard him as a follower of the *ancien régime,* a social climber or "a white black" who adopted the economic perspective of his masters and a pragmatic politics.[71] For Césaire, he is a figure of the "heroic Antilles, the African Antilles"—a protagonist in the first black epic of the New World, writ-

---

65. Césaire, "Poetry and Knowledge," li–lii; for the French, 166.

66. Bernier, *Characters of Blood,* 30–32.

67. William Wordsworth, "To Toussaint L'Ouverture." See Bernier, *Characters of Blood,* 28. Other poems of tribute include those of John Greenleaf Whittier, "Toussaint l'Ouverture" and Henrietta Cordelia Ray, "Toussaint L'Ouverture." C. L. R. James composed a play on him, *Toussaint Louverture: The Story of the Only Successful Slave Revolt in History: A Play in Three Acts,* and Derek Walcott was inspired by him to write *The Haitian Trilogy: Henri Christophe, Drums and Colours, and the Haytian Earth.*

68. See Kaplan, "Black Heroes/White Writers," 33–62.

69. "The Memoir of Toussaint Louverture Written by Himself" was first published by M. Saint Rémy in *Mémoires de la vie de Toussaint Louverture;* first English trans. by J. R. Beard, *Toussaint L'Ouverture: A Biography and Autobiography* (1863), accessed 5 May 2019, https://www.marxists.org/reference/archive/toussaint-louverture/memoir/index.htm. For a critical analysis of this memoir, see Daniel Desormeaux, "The First of the (Black) Memorialists: Toussaint Louverture," trans. Deborah Jenson and Molly Krueger Enz, *Yale French Studies* 107 (2005): 131–45.

70. C. L. R. James, *The Black Jacobins: Toussaint Louverture and the San Domingo Revolution,* 2nd rev. ed. (New York: Vintage, 1989), 145–62. For a recent biography that takes James's point of view, see Charles Forsdick and Christian Høgsbjerg, *Toussaint Louverture: A Black Jacobin in an Age of Revolutions* (London: Pluto, 2017).

71. See, for example, Philippe Girard, *Toussaint Louverture: A Revolutionary Life* (New York: Basic Books, 2016). Desormeaux sees Louverture as inhabiting a middle ground between the politics of the *ancien régime* and anticolonial rebellion.

ten in the blood of Haitians.[72] Important, however, as his revolutionary spirit
was for the poet in shaping black dissent, the transformation of his death
into a sacrificial act also meant it could take on a commemorative function,
keeping open (*"ouvert"* > L̲ouverture) the possibilities of a more expansive
future. This monumentalizing of a black male genealogy in the Caribbean
has elicited a correction in recent studies of the women of negritude.[73] Only
recently have such revisionary treatments taken shape. The heroizing of figures like Louverture would break barriers of race, while leaving barriers of
gender largely untouched. Nonetheless, Césaire's poem performs some stunning acts of masculine self-critique.

This brings us to a second need in *Cahier*'s odyssey. If the artful creation
of heroes is one of the motivating forces in the poem, Césaire is aware that
the literary concept of the hero is itself problematic because it emerges from
a colonial context. He thus simultaneously advances and undermines heroic
figures through the personas he creates. In doing so, he both taps into epic
while resisting its pull. *Cahier* has no protagonist. It has voices engaged in a
continuous dialectic of consciousness. When a larger-than-life character takes
shape from one of the voices of the poem, another follows, qualifying and
diminishing its exemplary force. It is through such oblique approaches to the
colonial situation—such essayistic advances and retreats from the sides—that
the poem works its demystifications.

The passage on Louverture in stanzas 44 and 45 appears in close proximity
to the one on the geography of the Antilles in stanza 42, which was examined
in chapter 1. It is there that the reader is first given a glimpse of Antillean
revolt through the singling out of Haiti "where for the first time negritude
stood up tall and straight and declared that it believed in its humanity." Just as
that stanza begins with the phrase, "what I call my own" (*"ce qui est à moi"*),
so do the two stanzas on Louverture.[74] After a bird's-eye view of the archipelago that captures the circulatory flow of the West Indies in a world-wide
economy, the speaker turns to "a tiny prison cell in the Jura Mountains" of

---

72. See Césaire's interview with René Depestre in *Discourse on Colonialism*, 90; also the
comments of Cheikh M. S. Diop, "Labilité et résilence: contours des notions," in *Aimé Césaire:
oeuvre et héritage*, 37–49. Césaire later wrote a biography of him: *Toussaint Louverture: La
révolution française et le problème colonial* (Paris: Présence Africaine, 2000).

73. See Jennifer Ann Boittin, *Colonial Metropolis: The Urban Grounds of Anti-Imperialism
and Feminism in Interwar Paris* (Lincoln: University of Nebraska Press, 2015); Tracy Denean
Sharpely-Whiting, *Negritude Women* (Minneapolis: University of Minnesota Press, 2002) and
Franz Fanon: Conflicts and Feminisms (Lanham, MD: Rowman and Littlefield, 1997), esp. ch.
1; and Dawn Fulton, *Signs of Dissent: Maryse Condé and Postcolonial Criticism* (Charlottesville:
University of Virginia Press, 2008).

74. See Doris Garraway, "'What Is Mine': Césairean Negritude between the Particular and
the Universal," *Research in African Literatures* 41.1 (2010): 71–86.

France, the location of Fort de Joux (44). This is where Napoleon Bonaparte imprisoned Louverture in 1803 and where the rebel died from pneumonia and malnutrition. Here are the first lines in Davis's translation, which have been slightly revised to reveal rhyme and word patterns in French.

1 What I call my own

2 a man alone incarcerated in white [*blanc*]

3 a man alone who defies the white screams of a white death [*la mort blanche*]

4 (TOUSSAINT, TOUSSAINT LOUVERTURE)

5 a man alone who captivates the white hawk of a white death [*la mort blanche*]

6 a man alone in a barren sea of sand, white [*blanc*]

7 an old black man [*un moricaud vieux*] up against the waters of the sky-god

(44–45)

The words capture Louverture in a state of isolation, removed not only from tropical Saint Domingue with its revolutionary turmoil but far from human company and confined in a "tiny prison cell."

Key to these lines is anaphora, a dominant feature of Césaire's poetic style, which often evokes the orality of ritual incantation.[75] In the passage under consideration, this figure of speech, rooted in repetition, places us at the intersection of poetry and religion by calling attention to words as a sacred form of making meaning. Fundamental to the transformation of Louverture is the reversal of Western color symbolism that we see in the passage quoted above: white is turned into the color of death, and black is wrested from its association with evil. In the repetition of "a man alone" at the beginning of successive lines (2–3, 4–5), we are made to see the solitude of the person suffering. So, too, in the repetition of the words "white death" at the end of successive lines (3, 5), the reader is drawn into the sense of a human killer's whiteness that merges with the color of a killer-snow. "White" is repeated twice more at line ends (2, 6), creating an interwoven pattern of masculine and feminine gendered adjectives. Between these anaphoric lines we find the key line, "(TOUSSAINT, TOUSSAINT LOUVERTURE)." The capitalization reinforces the figure's heroism in the face of death; the parenthesis is a syntactical strat-

---

75. On Césaire's use of anaphora, see Brent Hayes Edwards, "Aimé Césaire and the Syntax of Influence," *Research in African Literatures* 36.2 (2005): 1–18; and Patrice Somé, "The Anatomy of a Cosmogony: Ritual and Anaphora in Aimé Césaire's *Cahier d'un retour au pays natal*," *Journal of Ritual Studies* 7.2 (1993): 33–52.

egy for embracing the prisoner and keeping him alive. At the nadir of the struggle in the first seven lines, Louverture appears as "an old black man," "*un moricaud vieux*": his island "sands" have been exchanged for a "barren sea" of sand-like snow in a world whose gods drop freezing rain.

So begins the ironic anaphora of "death" ("*la mort*"), the overcoming of which is the purpose of the entire passage.[76]

8 Death inscribes a bright halo above this man
9 death is a star emerging quietly above his head
10 death breathes furiously in the mature cane-field of his arms
11 death gallops in the jail like a white charger
12 death glows in the dark like the eyes of a cat
13 death hiccups like the surf under the Keys
14 death is a wounded bird
15 death wanes
16 death is a shadowy peccary
17 death expires in a white pool of silence

8 *La mort décrit un cercle brillant au-dessus de cet homme*
9 *la mort étoile doucement au-dessus de sa tête*
10 *la mort souffle, folle, dans la cannaie mûre de ses bras*
11 *la mort galope dans la prison comme un cheval blanc*
12 *la mort luit dans l'ombre comme des yeux de chat*
13 *la mort hoquette comme l'eau sous le Cayes*
14 *la mort est un oiseau blessé*
15 *la mort décroit*
16 *la mort vacille*
17 *la mort est un patyura ombrageux*
18 *la mort expire dans une blanche mare de silence.*

The audience is pulled into another anaphoric sequence in which death is linked with different verbs in each line. This is not a description of a past event. It is an enactment in the moment, mobilized through poetic language, which now takes on a more explicitly sacral function. Lines 8 and 9 combine Christian and classical images: death delineates a halo that rises above the dying man, even as it softly studs the sky above his head with a star. Suddenly, the color symbolism shifts, white becoming light, black the night sky: the debased "*moricaud*" rises up through a canonization that is simultane-

---

76. For a commentary, see Irele in Césaire, *Journal of a Homecoming*, 198–201.

ously a metamorphosis into a constellation. Death itself is transfigured: it "breathes furiously"; "gallops"; "glows"; "hiccups"; "wanes"; "wavers"; and finally, "expires." Transferred epithet is a dominant figure in this litany: death hiccups, death wanes, death expires. Death dies. Louverture does not. Contributing to the downward spiral of a personified *Mort* is the gradual decrease of intensity in the animals named, from horse, to cat, to wounded bird, to peccary or patyura, "a little animal, whose presence is said to presage death, hence the adjective *ombrageux* [shadowy]."[77]

Césaire's portrait of Louverture liberates him from the prison in which he is confined. It does so by making poetry a power capable of overcoming, at least in part, the racial and colonial brutality that landed him in the Jura Mountains to begin with. Here, in an early stage of evolution in modern Caribbean thought, Césaire performs an act of sacralization that is in tune with a perceived need to bring heroic figures into the yet unspoken histories of a maligned race. The integrity of this heroizing, however, does not stand uncontested in the poem. It is sharply undermined by the episode of the pongo, which has sometimes been likened to the Cyclops episode in the *Odyssey*.[78] In the stanzas leading into what is perhaps the most excruciating moment in the poem, the speaker is caught up in self-recriminations for mimicking the very perceptions of the white colonials that he has been dismantling. Addressing the reader, he makes a confession:

> You should know just how far I pushed my cowardice.
> One evening in a streetcar opposite me, a nigger.

> *Il faut savoir jusqu'où je poussai la lâcheté.*
> *Un soir dans un tramway en face de moi, un nègre.*"

In a mere two lines, key points emerge, fleshed out in the stanza that follows: "opposite me a nigger" emphasizes the confrontational character of the situation, but the phrase also calls attention to a form of mirroring in which the speaker sees himself in the degraded other.[79]

---

77. See Irele in Césaire, *Journal of a Homecoming*, 201.

78. For interpretations, see Davis, *Aimé Césaire*, 20–61; and Sylvia Wynter, "'A Different Kind of Creature': Caribbean Literature, the Cyclops Factor and the Second Poetics of the *Propter Nos*," in *Sisyphus and Eldorado: Magical and Other Realisms in Caribbean Literature*, ed. Timothy Reiss, 2nd ed. (Trenton, NJ: Africa World Press, 2002), 143–67.

79. This reading builds upon Franz Fanon, *Peau noire, masques blancs* (Paris: Seuil, 1952), trans. Charles Markmann, *Black Skin, White Masks* (London: Pluto, 1986), 40–62; Stuart Hall, "Negotiating Caribbean Identities," *New Left Review* 1.209 (1995): 3–14; and Nick Nesbitt, *Carib-*

This encounter is constructed as a remembered journey through public space on a moving vehicle. On the page, it appears in blocks of prose that emphasize its narrative dimension. It is composed in the past rather than the present tense, which suggests that the speaker has had time to reflect on it. And rather than a reversal of Western color symbolism, we find the contrary: an insistence upon the worst connotations of *"nègre,"* drawn out at considerable length. Like the portrait of Louverture, however, this one is a study in isolation. In both cases, but more so in the second portrait, the audience is made aware of the crafting and molding that construct the racial subject. The passage is long, but it is famous and worth quoting at length. The underlined words highlight a vocabulary of crafting and artfulness.

A black man as huge as a great ape was trying to make himself small on the bench of a tramcar. He was trying to shed, on this filthy tramcar bench, his gigantic legs and his shaking, starved boxer's hands. And every bodily part had deserted, was deserting him: his nose, which resembled a peninsula adrift, even his blackness, which was becoming discolored under the action of a tireless tawing. And the tawer was none other than Poverty— an enormous bat from hell whose claw marks on his face had scarred it with islets of scab. Or rather, Poverty was an untiring artisan working on some grotesque cartouche. One could clearly make out how a sedulous and malevolent thumb had molded his brow into a hump, pierced his nose with two parallel, discombobulating tunnels, prolonged the lower lip out of all measure and, by a masterstroke of caricature, planed, polished and varnished the most delicate and dainty little ear in the whole world (French: *création*).

He was an ungainly black man without measure or proportion.

A black whose eyes rolled in gory fatigue

An indecent black and his toes sniggered in a very foul manner at the bottom of the cracked housing of his shoes.

Poverty—it was unspeakable—had gone to perverse lengths to construct him.

It had dug out the eye socket, then rouged it with a makeover of dust and mucous.

It had stretched empty space between the solid hook of the jaw and the bones of an old sordid cheek.

On top it had planted the tiny gleaming stumps of a beard a few days old. It had driven his heart to distraction, arched his back.

bean Critique: Antillean Critical Theory from Toussaint to Glissant (Liverpool: Liverpool University Press, 2013), 271–87.

The net effect was the <u>perfect image</u> of a hideous black, a sullen black, a melancholy black, a collapsed black, his hands joined in prayer on a gnarled stick. (99)

C'était un nègre grand comme un pongo qui essayait de <u>se faire tout petit</u> sur un banc de tramway. Il essayait d'abandonner sur ce banc crasseux de tramway ses jambes gigantesques et ses mains tremblantes de boxeur affamé. Et tout l'avait laissé, le laissait. Son nez qui semblait une péninsule en dérade et sa négritude même qui se décolorait sous l'action d'une inlassable <u>mégie</u>. Et le <u>mégissier</u> était la Misère. Un gros oreillard subit dont les coups de griffes sur ce visage s'étaient cicatrisés en îlots scabieux. Ou plutôt, c'était <u>un ouvrier infatigable</u>, la Misère, travaillant à quelque <u>cartouche</u> hideux. On voyait très bien comment le pouce industrieux et malveillant avait <u>modelé</u> le front en bosse, percé le nez de deux tunnels parallèles et inquiétants, allongé la démesure de la lippe, et par un chef-d'oeuvre <u>caricatural, raboté, poli, verni</u> la plus minuscule mignonne petite oreille de la <u>création</u>.

C'était un nègre dégingandé sans <u>rythme</u> ni <u>mesure</u>.

Un nègre dont les yeux roulaient une lassitude sanguinolente.

Un nègre sans pudeur et ses orteils ricanaient de façon assez puante au fond de la <u>tanière entrebâillée</u> de ses souliers.

La misère, on ne pouvait pas dire, s'était donné un mal fou pour <u>l'achever</u>.

Elle avait <u>creusé</u> l'orbite, l'avait <u>fardée d'un fard</u> de poussière et de chassie mêlées.

Elle avait <u>tendu l'espace</u> vide entre l'accrochement solide des mâchoires et les pommettes d'une vieille joue décatie.

Elle avait <u>planté</u> dessus les petits pieux luisants d'une barbe de plusieurs jours. Elle avait affolé le coeur, voûté le dos.

Et l'ensemble <u>faisait parfaitement</u> un nègre hideux, un nègre grognon, un nègre mélancolique, un nègre affalé, ses mains réunies en prière sur un baton noueux.

The passage begins in the descriptive voice of an observer who speaks in full sentences with punctuation. But the verbs in French ("*essayait*," "*semblait*," "*décolorait*") are in the imperfect tense, which confers upon the scene the sense, not only of the past, but of an ongoing past action, uncomfortably protracted and in need of an accommodation that would end the struggle of the man with the bench. Sprawling and ungainly, he was trying to fit in. But an external force has been at work upon him, and he doesn't have control of his body.

Likened to a creature that has long functioned as a nasty stereotype of the black African—the ape, for which the ordinary French word would be "*singe*"—the "*pongo*" is multiply devalued and alienated. His "*négritude*" is described as "discolored" and worn away, not proud and elevated, as in stanza 43, where it is linked with the courage of revolutionary Haiti. Here Poverty (*Misère*) has "molded," "constructed," "pierced," "planed," "polished," "varnished," "dug out," and "rouged" a figure whose body parts are catalogued in a cruel blazon: legs, hands, nose, brow, nostrils, lip, ear, eyes, jaw, nose, back. The reader is made to stare at a freak, an assemblage of loose and strange parts. The emphasis, however, is not on the phenomenology of the pongo. He is being deliberately objectivized through a process Césaire describes in *Discours sur le colonialisme* as "thingification"—"*chosification*"—and the forces operating upon him are being abstracted into an impersonal socioeconomic process with a capitalized name: Poverty, *Misère*.[80] The word that captures his affective state is "melancholy": he was "*un nègre mélancolique.*" Punning on the Greek word for black, "*melas,*" Césaire introduces "<u>mela</u>ncholy" as the black man's disease. A similar verbal effect related to color occurs in the image of "tawing" ("*mégie*"), the process of transforming the skin of an animal into white leather through the application of chemicals. The word is suggestive of a black pigment that has endured the corrosive effects of colonialism. But it may also evoke what Fanon would later call a "lactification wish," a desire to whiten the skin—a pathology, as we have seen, discussed by Suzanne Césaire in "*Le grand camouflage.*"[81]

The passage is fraught with tension. If Poverty is an artisan working on a "*cartouche,*" then the reader is invited to see in its craft not only inscriptions in flesh and blood but also associations with the oval-shaped artifacts of stone in ancient Egypt, which were used to inscribe a royal name. The word *cartouche* is derived from the ancient Greek *chartes*, meaning a sheet of writing paper made from papyrus. Here we are cued to suggestions of lost nobility in a figure whose scars point to a proud ancient past that has been brutally degraded. Thus *mégie* and *cartouche*, both terms of artistry, have countervailing force. Multiple sides of the "pigmentation crisis" are being played out.

There is a reason why the passage does not focalize the experience of the pongo. The scene is being set up for the speaker sitting "opposite," "*en face,*" and it is his psychology that comes into view in the second half of stanza 99. We pick up the passage quoted above with the lines that conclude Césaire's description of the black behemoth:

A black comical and ugly [he was], and some women seated behind me
snickered at the sight of him

---

80. Césaire, *Discourse on Colonialism*, 42.

81. Fanon, *Black Skin, White Masks*, 33, 83–84.

He was COMICAL AND UGLY
COMICAL AND UGLY that's for sure.
I spread a branching smile of complicity . . .
My cowardly self rediscovered!
I salute the three centuries that sustain my civil rights
and my devalued blood.
My heroism, what a farce!

Un nègre comique et laid et des femmes derrière moi ricanaient en le
*   regardant.*
*   Il était COMIQUE ET LAID,*
*   COMIQUE ET LAID pour sûr*
*   J'arborai un grand sourire complice . . .*
*   Ma lâcheté retrouvée!*
Je salue les trois siècles qui soutiennent mes droits
civique et mon sang minimisé.
Mon héroïsme, quelle farce!

The repetition of *nègre* and the phrase "COMICAL AND UGLY" are overt expressions of what the women's snickering signifies, channeled through the speaker's complicity with them. Echoing Baudelaire's use of the phrase in "The Albatross," the capitalized words "COMICAL AND UGLY" focus upon the winged beauty and grace of the bird in flight, which deflate into laughable clumsiness when sailors lay hold of the creature and mock its awkward movements, indifferent to its sky-borne majesty. Yet the whiteness of the bird in describing the abjection of the "nigger" points to the potential problems of allusion: black pigmentation is the problem that afflicts the pongo, and this fact is easily masked by the "accidental" whiteness of the analogical referent. In general, Césaire is highly alert to how poetic reception can import a whole load of such "accidents" and in the process weaken the force of critique by lowering the threshold of awareness.

This point is worth emphasizing because the pongo, with his dug-out eye socket and oversized body, has also been approached as a Cyclops-figure, but an inverted one who elicits sympathy rather than mockery.[82] If Césaire is here

---

82. Wynter develops what she calls a "Cyclopean poetics of reading" in "'A Different Kind of Creature.'" For a discussion of how the Cyclops has been reimagined over time, see Edith Hall, "Survival of Culture," in *Survival: The Survival of the Human Race*, ed. Emily Shuckburgh (New York: Cambridge University Press, 2008), 53–79. For a reading of the pongo as a Cyclops figure, see McConnell, *Black Odysseys*, 39–70; and of the Cyclops as a figure through whom black experience has been creatively constructed, Rankine, *Ulysses in Black*, 45–52, 128–48.

constructing an allusion, he is doing so in a more complicated way than such a reading suggests. The relationship between the pongo and the speaker is a mimetic one: that is, the persona whose point of view shapes the scene is beholding himself in the other, but he is doing so through the mediated form of the women who are onlookers. Significantly, we do not know their color. It is their gender that appears preeminent, and it has the effect of arousing sexual anxiety in the speaker who smiles collusively in public. When Fanon developed his views of the lactification wish, he identified it as a black woman's fear of "*la négraille*," or "niggerhood." Females, he thought, want to attach themselves to the lightest of males, and in doing so, they betray their own race. Against pathological female negrophobia, he posed a more normatively conceived black male self-alienation.[83] Césaire does not conceive of sex and gender in the way Fanon does. Through the triangulation of his poetic persona with "an ape man" and "women on the tram," he exposes male pathological phobia, and in doing so, he weakens the gender binary that Fanon upholds.

Narratively, the pongo is part of an alternative tale that seeks to undo the ideological violence of a colonial perspective. Césaire makes poetic use of Homeric elements to construct a different story. To a certain extent, the *Odyssey* itself contributes to such a reading by introducing sympathetic perspectives on the creature that it never fully renders in story form. Odysseus has himself violated the practices of hospitality by invading the cave of someone he does not know, thereby exposing himself to punishment. The Cyclops has a tender and nurturing relationship with his sheep, which contrasts with Odysseus's own instrumental treatment of his crew when he subordinates them to his desire for potential profit (guest-gifts) from a host he has not met and whose property he is transgressing. In depriving the Cyclops of his eye, he also takes away the only means by which the creature can sustain himself, a dimension of the episode that is emphasized in the brutality of the blinding, which approaches horror. Most significantly, his behavior occasions the curse of Poseidon, which stalks him forever. Since these details reach us via the narrative voice of Odysseus, who is speaking in the first person, it appears that he has himself come to understand, at least partially, his role in the offense.

In this chapter we have seen that Césaire taps into *katabasis* to create a drama of coming-into-consciousness with odyssean dimensions that do not rise to the level of being adaptations. He works in understated ways along a

83. See David Marriott, "*En moi:* Franz Fanon and René Maran," in *Franz Fanon's Black Skin, White Masks: New Interdisciplinary Essays,*" ed. Max Silverman (Manchester: Manchester University Press, 2005), 146–78; and Tracy Denean Sharpely-Whiting, "Anti-Black Femininity and Mixed-Race Identity: Engaging Fanon to Reread Capécia," in *Fanon: A Critical Reader,* ed. Lewis Gordon et al (Malden, MA: Wiley-Blackwell, 1996), 155–62.

network of weak links that avoid frontal engagement. These links enable the creation of portraits such as those of Louverture and the pongo that are vivid and shaped by diffusive effects. Both Woolf and Césaire present the audience with katabatic journeys involving damaged psyches that happen upon the healing potential of mimetic images—paintings, photographs, portraits "drawn in blood." Cavafy, by contrast, is not a poet of trauma. When he turns to the costs of anomalous erotic experience, it can be in the decadent and *suggéstif* mode of "The City" with its nightmarish images of entrapment. It may also be in the oblique mode of "Hidden Things" that thematizes concealing while revealing. Or it can be in the narrative mode of "Days of 1896," which elevates the outcast while not enshrining him in exile. Despite these differences, all three writers creatively use the trope of isolation in forging journeys of sexual and racial transformation that are marked by indirection and oblique forms of reference. Narrative is a key element in this drama and its stylistic resources capture the struggles of coming into language in resistance to psychic blockages, the near silence of an historical abyss, or forms of literary and cultural reception that sustain the very obstacles in need of change.

CHAPTER 3

Passage and Detour

The greater part of even the largest of dictionaries, with every page
in the most comprehensive of atlases, consists of relics and records
in the concisest [*sic*] of shorthands from bygone chapters in the tale
whereof we know neither the beginning nor the end—that of Man's
supreme venture into the world without, and into the world within.

—WALTER DE LA MARE, *DESERT ISLANDS*

W
HEN MONT PELÉE erupted on 8 May 1902, destroying the city of
St. Pierre and killing 29,000 people, among the dead were two
hundred residents of the Maison de Santé.[1] This was a sanato-
rium founded in 1838 as the first psychiatric establishment on Martinique, and
it sought to mandate government protocols for the commitment of patients
and to curb the practice of putting "the insane" ("*les aliénés*") into prison.[2]
By 1843, the facility had approximately eighty beds, and few slaves are likely
to have known about it, since in this period the expenses for their care were
borne by their masters. But after emancipation in 1848, the numbers at the
Maison de Santé swelled, with public funding covering the costs of treatment.
By 1902, the number had reached two hundred. When the volcano blew, many
of the residents of the institution were among the emancipated or their children, and they died down to the last person.

---

1. See Alwyn Scarth, *La Catastrophe: The Eruption of Mount Pelée: The Worst Volcanic
Disaster of the 20th Century* (New York: Oxford University Press, 2002) for a detailed description of the event and the corrupt politics that impeded efforts to evacuate.

2. For accounts, see Jules Vergeron, "*La Maison Coloniale de la Santé de Saint Pierre*,"
Revue Maritime et Coloniale, 4 (1844): 34–50; and Étienne Rufz de Lavison, *Mémoire sur la
Maison des Aliénés de Saint Pierre* (Paris: J.-B. Baillière, 1856). Most records were lost to the
lava and the fire.

The Maison de Santé prided itself on the modern therapeutic methods it used for the treatment of various conditions, including "*hydrothérapies,*" such as immersions and showers, and "*ergothérapies,*" such as education in reading, writing, and life skills, all of it, of course, under the direction of colonial rule. Chillingly, however, one of the only objects to have emerged from the site after the catastrophe was a twisted iron chair of the type used to treat the most violent of the patients who were strapped into one and placed in a subterranean cell in solitary confinement. Today, it is possible to visit the archaeologically excavated site. It is situated on the banks of the river Roxelane, surrounded by the lush greenery that feeds on volcanic soil. But the open terrace has views of the isolation cells, and in one of them sits "*la chaise de force,*" "the restraining chair," which survives as a grim reminder of a horrifying event. Its iron bars recall the Jura prison cell of Louverture, transported to the tropics. Césaire grew up in the shadow of a mountain whose violence he deeply personalized. His response, however, also reflected deeper racial ambiguities that surrounded the destruction. Because St. Pierre was both the political and social capitol of Martinique—it was known as "the Paris of the Antilles"—the shift of power to Fort-de-France after the eruption fostered a view in the black population that the natural disaster was also a kind of rebirth for people of color.[3]

If isolation, marked in an extreme way by the volcanic insularity of Martinique, is a recurring feature of the journeys under study in this book, so too is its apparent opposite: ceaseless wandering. In odysseys, passage often takes on the character of repeated or ongoing displacements. When compulsion takes on an inner dimension and appears driven by events from a personal past, it can emerge as compulsiveness. One of the claims of this part of the book is that the *Odyssey* connects external forms of agency from above—via divinities—with self-sabotaging behavior in the hero for which the narrative provides a background story. In the awareness it brings to the therapeutic power of the word, the epic also points to psychic disturbances that never quite heal, a central preoccupation of this chapter. To capture what is at stake, this part of the book moves briefly from the infernal insularity of the Maison de Santé in the colonial Antilles to the other side of the Atlantic and the colonizer's country for a different tale of travel madness.

Between the emancipation date of 1848 in Martinique and the catastrophe of Mont Pelée in 1902, there was an epidemic in continental France of a psychiatric disorder that came to be called "fugue state." Like hysteria, it was a

---

3. Lorelle Semley, "When Blacks Broke the Chains in 'The Little Paris of the Antilles,'" in *To Be Free and French: Citizenship in France's Atlantic Empire* (New York: Cambridge University Press, 2017), 115–59.

mental illness whose historical life was relatively short, with medical experts and sufferers coalescing to define a complex that was therapeutically treated, but only for a time, since its symptoms ceased being diagnosed.[4] In the fifth edition of the *Diagnostic and Statistical Manual of Mental Disorders* (DSM-5), fugue state appears in a revised form as a dissociative amnesia called dissociative fugue.[5] This epidemic, which peaked in the 1880s, overlapped with the period in which the Maison de Santé was developing, and it reflects the broader interest in France at that time in the neurology of mental illness. When it got its name, the definition of the condition varied, with professional disagreements about whether its aetiology was related to epilepsy, hysteria, or psychasthenia, and about how to treat it. But the symptoms most often observed were a compulsion to travel and amnesia, either total or partial, after the fugue episode, which might be overcome through talk therapy or hypnosis. The aim of rehabilitation was to attach the migrant to a proper place, to render him *habilis* in conditions he was attempting to escape, for reasons related to trauma or economic hardship. Typically, this was done through an intervention aimed at stimulating memory and shaping its bits and fragments into an integrated narrative.

If the Maison de Santé brings into view subjects who were multiply isolated during a catastrophe, mad traveler disease widens geographically to encompass distances unknown by the person who feels compelled to wander. These phenomena offer creative ways of thinking about how imprisonment and vagabondage may be related. Under what conditions is wandering an expression of the need for escape from debilitating life circumstances? What happens when it turns into involuntary exile? How can it become pathological? Under what circumstances is it a potential site for the constructive modeling of collective identities? If Homer's man of much suffering offers provocative ways of approaching these questions, so do Cavafy's explorations of hedonic passages, Woolf's creation of a travel narrative to Constantinople that includes sexual reembodiment, and Césaire's treatment of the enslaved consciousness in journeys connected with the Black Atlantic.

---

4. See Ian Hacking, *Mad Travelers: Reflections on the Reality of Transient Mental Illness* (Charlottesville: University of Virginia Press, 1998), 7–50.

5. See *Diagnostic and Statistical Manual of Mental Illness*, 5th ed., (Washington, DC: American Psychiatric Association, 2013), ch. 26. Hacking, *Mad Travelers*, offers an engaging account of the phenomenon. See also Jason Ramsay, "Mad Travelers: Book Review," *Journal of Mind and Behavior* 21.4 (2000): 261–65.

HOMER: ODYSSEUS'S WOUND AND
NARRATIVE DETOURS

On the face of it, Odysseus is more an unwilling exile than an adventurer, cursed by the Cyclops and hounded by the unrelenting anger of Poseidon. But there are other ways of thinking about his itinerancy, and they point to forms of self-interference that drift against rather than with the flow of *nostos*. While deferral and delay have long been recognized as integral to the *Odyssey*, discussions emphasizing their relation to the psychic dimension of homecoming have yet to play out extensively.[6] The mythic and folkloric dimensions of the epic provide a framework for understanding why Homer's *nostos* tale is also a tale about ends that cannot be reached because they are vexed from the beginning. In order to understand this, the present section does not look to the most obvious stretch of narrative dealing with passage in the epic: Odysseus's narration of the wanderings in Books 9 through 12, upon which a great deal has been written. The focus is rather on the chronologically earliest *nostos* of the protagonist while still a youth, which brings us into the realm of deeply compromised family bonds.

Homer's verbs for "wander" are *alaomai* and *planomai*, both in the middle voice. This means that the action to which they refer has special reference to the subject and points to reciprocal or self-reflexive relations as well as to bodily and mental engagement in the exertion. The middle voice conveys the sense that the subject is affected by an event or activity.[7] In the *Odyssey*, this is an important feature of the words for wandering: *alaomai* and *planomai* capture a sense of amorphous or multidirectional movement, which is imposed, but also suffered and incurred, and which has effects upon the subject.[8] Typically, the space most closely connected to wandering is the sea, the navel of which is associated with a liminal geography, as we have seen in the exploration of Calypso's cave. "*Pontos*," one of the frequent words for sea in Homer,

---

6. Treatments of postponement in the *Odyssey* have a long history, but two insightful early studies include S. Besslich, *Schweigen—Verschweigen—Übergehen: Die Darstellung des Unausgesprochenen in der* Odyssee (Heidelberg: C. Winter, 1966); and Bernard Fenik, *Studies in the* Odyssey: *Hermes Einzelschriften 30* (Weisbaden: Steiner, 1974). See also Sheila Murnaghan, *Disguise and Recognition in the* Odyssey, 2nd ed. (Lanham, MD: Lexington, 2011). On the psychic journey and detours, see Shay, *Odysseus in America*; also Christensen, "Clinical *Odyssey*"; and Race, "Phaeacian Therapy." For a more literary reading of these themes, see van Nortwick, *Unknown Odysseus*.

7. See Rutger Allan, *The Middle Voice in Ancient Greek: A Study in Polysemy* (Amsterdam: Brill, 2003), 248–50.

8. See Silvia Montiglio, *Wandering in Ancient Greek Culture* (Chicago: University of Chicago Press, 2005), 1–4.

is related to the Indo-European root *pent-*, which refers to a difficult passage from one point to another, with strong connotations of danger and suffering in the crossing.[9] So, too, *thalassa* and *pelagos*: both are used with adjectives that mean broad, vast, or unlimited.[10] Wandering at sea is more primordial than living life on land. As soon as the audience is introduced to the hero in a wild and deserted expanse of water, it is clear that he has regressed and must start over again if he is to win his own *kleos*.[11]

When Odysseus and his crew first set sail after the war, their initial encounter is with the Cicones in Ismarus, a port city of Thrace, which is close to Troy, and on the map (9.42–63; 9.40–61). Pillaging the town to collect booty, a motive familiar from the *Iliad,* they arouse the locals, who descend upon them with fatal consequences: six men from each of the twelve ships are killed. It is while they make their way south across the sea in retreat that Zeus stirs up a cloud-gathering north wind, and he follows it with a devastating storm (9.75–80; 9.67–69). As the fleet tries to round Cape Malea at the tip of the Peloponnesus between the mainland and the island of Cythera, a notoriously difficult place to navigate, they drop off the map.[12] The wanderings, then, are constructed as a large-scale detour from the path to homecoming. Provocatively, the verb Odysseus uses to describe the giant clouds that enshrouded them when they disappear is the aorist "*kalypse*" (9.76; 9.68). The verb, as discussed in chapter 2, is related to the name Calypso. In chronological time, the goddess has not yet appeared in the action, but in the narrative, at the point when Odysseus tells his story as a flashback, she is in time past. Thus Odysseus, post-Calypso, tells of his lapse into a strange, otherworldly place, pre-Calypso, using a verb that is highly activated in the story. The first encounter he has is with the Lotus Eaters, who spend their life eating from a plant that destroys memory. He has disappeared down the rabbit hole. Immediately, he is made to remember that he cannot forget or he will never make it out.

---

9. See Émile Benveniste, *Problèmes de linguistique générale 1* (Paris: Gallimard, 1966), 297; and Marie-Claire Beaulieu, *The Sea in the Greek Imagination* (Philadelphia: University of Pennsylvania Press, 2015), 25.

10. See Montiglio, *Wandering in Ancient Greek Culture,* 7–11; and Beaulieu, *Sea in the Greek Imagination,* 21–58.

11. See Gregory Nagy, *Ancient Greek Hero in 24 Hours* (Cambridge, MA: Belknap Press), 275–95; and Bakker, *Meaning of Meat,* 13–35. For a fuller discussion of the range of *kleos* in the *Odyssey* that bears on the discussion in this section, see Ford, *Homer and the Poetry of the Past,* 57–67; and Segal, *Singers, Heroes, and Gods,* 85–109.

12. See Montiglio, *Wandering in Ancient Greek Culture,* 9; and François Hartog, *Memories of Odysseus: Frontier Tales from Ancient Greece,* trans. Janet Lloyd (Chicago: University of Chicago Press), 2.

By presenting us with a detour into a more primitive state—with a fall off the edge—the poem also shifts generic registers. It takes us into tales about monsters, witches, and cannibals, which incorporate aspects of the fabulous not found elsewhere in the poem or in the Iliadic tradition. Importantly, the Olympians, although they have knowledge of this place, do not frequent it, and there are no heroes who circulate in its waters. It is a world whose strange creatures are connected by weak links that defy geographical plotting as does the hero's journey itself. One must get out of it in order to establish a *kleos* for having survived it. Within this alternative reality, the danger of forgetfulness posed by the Lotus Eaters will be repeated in the Circe episode on Aeaea. There Odysseus and his men remain for a year, feasting with a goddess whose harm lies in the bewitching call to pleasure. During his sojourn, the goddess warns him of the Sirens, whose beckoning song of ancient Iliadic glory could lure them back to a world from which they have already departed. What we call forms of altered consciousness are represented in the *Odyssey* in terms of a journey through a treacherous sphere of monsters and oddities that signify a dissociation from ordinary cognitive states.

The wanderings require a closer look at the genre of the folktale.[13] By contrast with oral epic, which is about heroes, folktales are about ordinary people, and they circulate by word of mouth rather than through bardic song. They typically take place in vaguely defined locales; feature characters, including animals, that do not have a name; and transpire in an unspecified past. Studies have shown that the basic story patterns in folktales may be found internationally across very different times and places.[14] In fact, the protagonist of Homer's poem is himself folklorish, borrowed, as we have already seen, from the popular tradition of the trickster or the wily lad. In the *Odyssey*, Odysseus must come into epic, that is, out of the anonymity of the folktale and into a more complex moral sensibility. This passage is never complete. The personas

---

13. See Denys Page, *Folktales in Homer's* Odyssey (Cambridge, MA: Harvard University Press, 1973). On the generic distinctions between myth, folklore, and epic, see William Hansen, "Homer and the Folktale," in *A New Companion to Homer,* ed. Ian Morris and Barry Powell (Leiden: Brill, 1996), 444–45; and Lowell Edmunds, "Epic and Myth," in *A Companion to Ancient Epic,* ed. John Foley (Hoboken, NJ: Wiley-Blackwell, 2005), 31–44.

14. See Vladimir Propp, *Morphology of the Folktale,* trans. Laurence Scott, 2nd ed. (Austin: University of Texas Press, 1968); Algirdas Greimas, "*La déscription de la signification et la mythologie comparée,*" *L'Homme* 3.3 (1963): 51–66; and Claude Lévi-Strauss, "The Structural Study of Myth," *Journal of American Folklore,* 68 (1955): 428–44.

of Homer's hero often fluctuate with his folkloric avatar, who lacks a strong connection with social order, but is efficacious in his crafty plots.[15]

To get a better sense of how folklore and epic interact in Odysseus's passage, it helps to turn to a *nostos* in the *Odyssey* that occurs in the hero's youth and that is told in Book 19 of the poem. The tale begins not with a return, but with a scene of naming. When a child was born to Laertes and Anticleia, Autolycus, father of Anticleia and the child's maternal grandfather, visited Ithaca. The third-person narrator tells us that he was one who "excelled / the world at thievery, that and subtle, shifty oaths" (9.438–39); the Greek is "ὃς ἀνθρώπους ἐκέκαστο / κλεπτοσύνῃ θ᾽ ὅρκῳ τε" (19. 395–96). In a scene that configures the genealogy of the child, theft and deceit have a major role. Autolycus, the trickster, whose name means something like "Lone Wolf," is in Odysseus's bloodline, and he exercises an ongoing undertow in the struggles of the protagonist. This becomes apparent in the scene of Odysseus's naming, for it is Autolycus who names his grandson, saying to Anticleia and Laertes,

> Just as I
> have come from afar, creating pain for many [*odyssamenos*]—
> men and women across the good green earth—
> so let his name be Odysseus . . .
> the Son of Pain, a name he'll earn in full.
> And when he has come of age and pays his visit
> to Parnassus—the great estate of his mother's line
> where all my treasures lie—I will give him enough
> to cheer his heart, then speed him home to you.
> (19.460–68)

> πολλοῖσιν γὰρ ἔγωγε ὀδυσσάμενος τόδ᾽ ἱκάνω,
> ἀνδράσιν ἠδὲ γυναιξὶν ἀνὰ χθόνα βωτιάνειραν·
> τῷ δ᾽ Ὀδυσεὺς ὄνομ᾽ ἔστω ἐπώνυμον. αὐτὰρ ἔγωγε,
> ὁππότ᾽ ἂν ἡβήσας μητρώιον ἐς μέγα δῶμα
> ἔλθῃ Παρνησόνδ᾽, ὅθι πού μοι κτήματ᾽ ἔασι,
> τῶν οἱ ἐγὼ δώσω καί μιν χαίροντ᾽ ἀποπέμψω.
> (19.406–12)

---

15. For a fuller treatment of folklore and epic in Homer's poem on which this discussion draws, see Clay, *Wrath of Athena*, 54–74.

These lines make an opening for a *nostos* tale: the child will visit his grandfather when he is older, and he will return home. But the entire prospect bristles with danger because Autolycus, far from being a supportive genealogical link in the chain of ancestors, insinuates deceit and trickery into the family setting, actively disrupting the trust on which filial relations depend.

In naming Odysseus, Autolycus explicitly transfers his own "odiousness" to his grandson.[16] While the root of the participial verb *odyssamenos*, which is in the middle voice, may mean anger or hatred, scholars have argued for each and for both together. To turn to alternative translations, Fitzgerald renders *odyssamenos* periphrastically and makes Autolycus say, "my hand / has been against the world of men and women; / odium and distrust I've won. Odysseus / should be his given name." Fagles has, "Just as I / have come from afar, creating pain for many— / men and women across the good green earth— / so let his name be Odysseus / the Son of Pain." Anger, hatred, and pain are clustered early in Book 1 of the epic when Athena, challenging Zeus to intervene in the lost hero's homecoming asks, "Why is [Odysseus] so *odious*, Zeus?" The verb *odusao* ("ὠδύσαο," 1.62) and the name of the hero are explicitly linked. It is not difficult to draw connections between the two emotions of anger and hatred, and critics have done so. The words cover a resonant semantic range.

If Autolycus effectively curses his grandson, he also later endangers the boy when he comes to receive the gifts he has been promised. During the visit, he launches a boar hunt, in which his grandson and his sons participate. While the activity of going into the wild to kill animals may suggest an ephebic rite of passage, it is also one that endangers the boy's life. When Odysseus rushes at the boar with his spear, he hits it, but the animal simultaneously charges him, "lunging in on the slant, a tusk thrusting up / over the boy's knee, gouging a deep strip of flesh / but it never hit the bone" (19.509–11; "ὃ δέ μιν φθάμενος ἔλασεν σῦς / γουνὸς ὕπερ, πολλὸν δὲ διήφυσε σαρκὸς ὀδόντι / λικριφὶς ἀίξας, οὐδ᾽ ὀστέον ἵκετο φωτός," 19.449–51). After these events, the wounded hunter travels back to his mother and father who rejoice in his "return," his *nostos* (19.524; νοστήσαντι, 19.463). There he tells them his story, "how the white tusk of a wild boar had gashed his leg / hunting on Parnassus with Autolycus and his sons" (19.527–28; "ὥς μιν θηρεύοντ᾽ ἔλασεν σῦς λευκῷ ὀδόντι, / Παρνησόνδ᾽ ἐλθόντα σὺν υἱάσιν Αὐτολύκοιο," 465–66). *Nostos*—the

---

16. For extended discussions of the name, see Erwin Cook, "Active and Passive Heroics in the *Odyssey*," *Classical World* 93.2 (1999): 149–67; Peradotto, *Man in the Middle*, 120–70; and Clay, *Wrath of Athena*, 58–68. The disagreement about the verb and the name related to it is exemplified in two important scholarly articles in the 1950s: W. B. Stanford, "The Homeric Etymology of the Name Odysseus," *Classical Philology* 47.4 (1952): 209–13; and G. E. Dimock, "The Name of Odysseus," *Hudson Review* 9.1 (1956): 52–70.

word is contained in the participle that means "returning"—combines physical travel and storytelling.

In the poem, this tale is a flashback, which Erich Auerbach has made famous in his discussion of "Homeric foregrounding" in *Mimesis*.[17] He reads the episode of Odysseus's scar in terms of the epic's orientation toward a fictional world of "clearly outlined, brightly and uniformly illuminated, men and things," and he considers the long inset narrative on the boar hunt an example of a style that "knows no background." In Homer, "a continuous rhythmic procession of phenomena passes by, and never is there a form left fragmentary or half-illuminated, never a lacuna, never a gap, never a glimpse of unplumbed depths." But the scene of Odysseus's scar, far from being an instance of foregrounding, is dense with background.[18] It is told in the third person, and it clarifies Eurycleia's recognition of her master: she is engaged in an act of *xeinia*, namely, ritual foot washing, when she sees the scar, and remembers how it was incurred. Eurycleia's recognition is withheld from Penelope, who does not see the scar, and it is a recognition Odysseus wants to avoid.

Postponed recognition in this context is not simply a matter of Odysseus eluding notice for strategic purposes of managing revenge. It is associated with a return tale in his youth, which is implicated in treacherous family bonds. When the moment of *anagnorisis* between master and nurse occurs, the bard tells us Odysseus "hid his scar beneath the beggar rags" (19.573; "οὐλὴν δὲ κατὰ ῥακέεσσι κάλυψε," 19.507). The verb is *kalypse*. Calypso surfaces once again, underscoring the dynamic of concealing while revealing, which winds its way through the Ithacan books. His identity unwittingly disclosed, Odysseus moves laterally rather than teleologically in the drama of homecoming, taking a detour from the end at which the return tale is aimed.

It is worth recalling that in Book 19 where this recognition scene between master and nurse occurs, Odysseus as beggar is speaking with Penelope for the first time and is engaged in one of his Cretan tales. The revelation about the source of the wound is embedded in a broader story that the bard calls a lie. This is more than accidental: the truth of the wound and the lie that defers *nostos* are closely intertwined. Odysseus is, effectively, delaying his own return while the bard is suggesting via a third person narrative why he has reason to

---

17. Erich Auerbach, *Mimesis: The Representation of Reality in Western Literature*, trans. Willard Trask (1946; Princeton: Princeton University, 2003), 3–23.

18. For other readings that take issue with Auerbach's critique of Homer, see James Porter, "Erich Auerbach and the Judaizing of Philology," *Critical Inquiry* 35.1 (2008): 115–47; and Johannes Haubold, "Beyond Auerbach: Homeric Narrative and the Epic of Gilgamesh," in *Defining Greek Narrative*, eds. Douglas Cairns and Ruth Scodel (Edinburgh: Edinburgh University Press, 2014), 13–28.

do so.[19] As for Penelope, Athena has "turned her attention" or "diverted her mind" (19.542; "νόον ἔτραπεν," 19.479) so that she does not "catch the glance" in Eurycleia's eyes (19.541; "νοῆσαι," 19.478) and see a mark that would identify her husband—so that she might not "come to." The word used here for the mental act of perception is *noeo*, and the noun related to it is *noos*, both used within two consecutive lines.[20] Significantly, *nostos* and *noeo* are formed from the same Indo-European root, *nes-*, which, as we have seen, has the basic meaning of a return from darkness to light—a return construed by some as a coming into consciousness.[21]

In this paradigmatic scene of postponed recognition, the audience cannot be certain whether Odysseus is cognizant of the link that the bard draws between Autolycus's curse, his name, and the wound. He is not said to have *noos*, or mindfulness, of his own first *nostos*; it is Eurycleia rather than her master who focalizes the third-person tale.[22] In fact, a meaningful gap opens between the event and the one who suffered the wound—a gap that reflects a memory that the bard has displaced onto an adjacent party. Odysseus's immediate instinct, under the eye of Eurycleia and Penelope, is to cover up rather than expose who he is, and this places the episode within the Calypso complex. He avoids home as he attempts to recover it. This is why his Cretan lie—the one in Book 19 and others—has been particularly troublesome to audiences of the poem, and why critics have gone out of the way to make cases for an early recognition between Odysseus and Penelope.[23]

The pattern of self-concealment in scenes of *xeinia* such as the one in *Odyssey* 19 is already familiar to the audience of the poem. In the Phaeacian episode, Odysseus defers disclosure of his identity to king Alcinous and queen Arete for three books, despite their promises to ensure his *nostos*.

19. For a more detailed discussion of the complex narrative perspectives in this scene, see Adolf Köhnken, "Odysseus' Scar: An Essay on Homeric Epic Narrative Technique," in *Homer's Odyssey: Oxford Readings in Classical Studies*, ed. Lillian Doherty (New York: Oxford University Press, 2009), 44–61.

20. See Nagy, *Ancient Greek Hero*, 296–313, following Frame, *Myth of Return*.

21. In addition to Nagy and Frame, see Egbert Bakker, *Pointing at the Past: From Formula to Performance in Homeric Poetics* (Cambridge, MA: Harvard University Press, 2006); L. H. Lesher, "Perceiving and Knowing in the *Odyssey*," *Phronesis* 26.1 (1981): 2–24; and Austin, *Archery at the Dark of the Moon*, 110–14. For a broader consideration of consciousness in Homer, see Richard Seaford, "The *Psuchē* from Homer to Plato: A Historical Sketch," in *Selfhood and the Soul: Essays on Ancient Thought and Literature in Honour of Christopher Gill*, ed. Seaford et al (New York: Oxford University Press, 2017), 11–32.

22. de Jong, *Narratological Commentary on the* Odyssey, 475–78.

23. For recent discussions of early recognition in Book 19, with citations of earlier scholarship, see the special edition of *College Literature* 38.2 (2011), especially Bruce Louden, "Is There Early Recognition Between Penelope and Odysseus? Book 19 in the Larger Context of the *Odyssey*," 76–100.

They, too, have a resident bard like Phemius—Demodocus—and during the communal feasting, he sings two lays in which Odysseus is featured. One is about a quarrel between Agamemnon and Odysseus before the start of the Trojan War, another about the Trojan horse at the end of the war—bookend tales. Odysseus covers up both times. In the first lay, it is said that he "drew [his cape] over his head / and buried his handsome face" (8.101–2; "κάλυψε δὲ κάλα πρόσωπα," 8.85), and within a few more lines, "he hid his face and wept" (8.109–10; "ἂψ Ὀδυσεὺς κατὰ κρᾶτα καλυψάμενος γοάσκεν," 8.92); in the second lay, the concealment is repeated and Odysseus's tears are said to have "gone unmarked" (8.598; "ἐλάνθανε," 8.532) of the Phaeacians. Only Alcinous—in Greek, "alki-<u>noos</u>," he of the sharp or perceptive mind—witnesses the weeping.

What is happening here? The minor *nostos* in Phaeacia anticipates the major *nostos* in Ithaca. It does so in part because around it circulate, on the one hand, such terms as *noos* and *noeo*, also in the *nes*-group, and on the other, forms of the verbs *kalypto*, *krypto*, and *lanthano*. In short, Odysseus never simply passes over a boundary from darkness to light in leaving Calypso, but instead enacts strategies of avoidance as he winds his way toward an end he never reaches.[24] Significantly, when he does finally introduce himself in the Phaeacian court, it is not through the epithet "much suffering," or *polytlas*, but through the phrase "known to the world / by every kind of craft" (9.21–22; "πᾶσι δόλοισιν / ἀνθρώποισι μέλω," 9.19–20). In other words, he identifies himself with his devious grandfather. A great deal of the tension between centrifugal and centripetal forces in the *Odyssey* is played out along these semiotic routes of approaching and avoiding home.

In Book 5, the trickster from folklore, who lacks essence, is being partially sublimated, his cunning turned in the direction of storytelling skill. Odysseus is entering the epic. He is doing so by taking hold of his name—a name accursed from his birth and multiply accursed after the Cyclops—and bringing his own *noos* to the act of narration. In rendering his experience in a story, he must discern and perceive who he is. What the audience is watching, then, is a scene that discloses the artfulness of the word as a therapeutic instrument. Under the guidance of the bard, Odysseus enters a medium that enables him to interweave his Iliadic and Odyssean identities. The king and queen, in the course of his performance, praise him for his story: "What grace you give your words, and what good sense within! / You have told your story with all a singer's skill" (11.416–17; "σοὶ δ᾽ ἔπι μὲν μορφὴ ἐπέων, ἔνι δὲ φρένες ἐσθλαί, / μῦθον δ᾽ ὡς ὅτ᾽ ἀοιδὸς ἐπισταμένως κατέλεξας," 11.367–68).

---

24. Contrast with Bergren, *Weaving Truth*, ch. 3.

Now one of the great conundrums of the *Odyssey* confronts us. The epic would have the audience take as true the story Odysseus tells strangers about a fabulous world of monsters and witches in which he wandered for ten years, a story dependent on folklore. It explicitly characterizes as false the quite credible Cretan stories he tells on Ithaca, which feature commercial travel, family infighting, shipwreck, loss of property, and a known geography. Why does the Homeric bard go out of his way to make Alcinous and Arete praise their guest's storytelling as orderly, well told, and trustworthy, while later characterizing his protagonist's more realistic tales as false and deceitful? If in Books 9 through 12 storytelling functions as a form of narrative therapy, what do the fragmentation of identity and the seemingly retrograde character of Odysseus's spun tales on Ithaca say about his return from darkness into light?

By protracting return, the Cretan tales take the audience through a rich exploration of the various roles Odysseus must fill if he is to reinstate himself on Ithaca. Moreover, as earlier discussions have shown, they reflect the generic tendency of the *Odyssey* as epic to ingest epichoric versions of its own return tale in a process that resembles what Césaire later terms literary cannibalism, a topic of the next section. Nonetheless, there remains something disjunctive about Odysseus's lies that resemble truth, especially in a story of homecoming, and they have puzzled audiences of the epic, leading many to conclude that he is precisely the liar and the cheat that Alcinous and Arete take the trouble to say he's not.

CÉSAIRE: LAGOONS OF BLOOD AND LITERARY CANNIBALISM

The wound and the word, passage and detour: in its sedimented layers, the *Odyssey* preserves a culture's response to the aftereffects, both physical and psychic, of a prolonged exposure to war and the hardships of coming back from it. While Odysseus's narrative of his wanderings has therapeutic value as a form of cognitive integration, the Cretan lies disrupt its integrity through alternative tales that reflect not only a more fractured set of collective narratives but also psychic detours in Odysseus's own troubled *nostos*. Passage and detour are no less a consideration in *Cahier,* but rather than presenting us with hidden wounds and dissimulating stories, the poem constructs its personas around successive immersions into an abyssal loss on the premise that reliving the scene of violence is vital to recovering from it. These descents turn out to have a demiurgic potency: the poet is graced by a heightened vision that enables him to see into a fragmentary past and into a future that holds the promise of a newly regenerated people. He has the ancient power of the seer-poet, the *vates*, but his movements aren't always progressive. Every ascendancy Césaire accords his personas is coupled with a return to the heart of the volcano.[25] Memory is errant and works in shadow spaces; hence the need for repetition, revision, and the renewal of what is remembered—a ritual act with sacred dimensions.

The most significant of the routes on which the poem sets its various personas is composed of a loop between Martinique and Europe, which then enables Africa to emerge as a vital detour. The structure of this passage is worth remarking because it calls attention to how the poem resists configuring Africa as the site of return. The Africa of *Cahier* is not the destination of the poem or the enshrined mother land. It is a mysterious, indirectly understood, and not yet visited continent that is always in active formation in the poem. As an element of the three-souled Antilles, it is brought into focus through multiple lenses that are tentative and essayistic—"notebookish"—rather than restorative and final. Africa thus continuously complicates the dialectic of colonizer and colonized, which it is the task of the poem to understand, and it thereby interrupts the *retour* of the poem's title by exposing its multiple possibilities and contradictions.

Europe must be dealt with first. Removal from the *pays natal*, after walking the inferno of its local terrain, is marked in the poem by the infinitive "To leave" ("*Partir*," 33), which functions as a verbal noun without person or number attached. The "I" is not directly engaged in an action but in the imagination of an action, and this is an important difference. The poem, in fact, never changes the geographical location of its persona. Rather, it traces hypothetical passages, moving laterally across space and bringing back material from its travels. The first of these passages is ambiguously conceived as a form of self-exile from a diseased Caribbean Sea. But the colonizer's continent that appears as the destination is ominously characterized as "this other break of dawn of Europe" ("*Cet autre petit matin d'Europe*," 32)—a repetition of the landscape of the damned.

> To leave:
> As there are hyena-men and panther-men, I would be a jew-man,
> A kaffir-man,
> A hindu-man-from-Calcutta,
> A Harlem-man-who-does-not-vote.
> (33)

---

25. This perspective builds upon and revises the views of Davis, "'Homecomings without Home'" and "Negritude as Performance"; and Greenwood, "Dislocating Black Classicism."

Partir.
Comme il y a des hommes-hyènes et des hommes-panthères, je serais
un homme-juif
un homme-cafre
un homme-hindou-de-Calcutta
un homme-de-Harlem-qui-ne-vote-pas

Identifying with populations outside the Antilles, the speaker approaches Europe by expressing a global solidarity in suffering that is seen through the totem. This is an image that links the holocaust of the Jews, the imperialist abuse of Kaffirs in South Africa, the abject poverty of Hindus in India, and the racial discrimination against blacks in the United States.

Europe, in other words, is mediated through identities seen in dialectical relationship with it. The totem imaginatively joins peoples who have been subjugated by the ironized superiority of this so-called cradle of civilization. The orthography and style of the lines are worth observing. Hyphens are used to create chains, chains become quasi-neologisms, and the quasi-neologisms slide into one another through rhetorical asyndeton: loose links, oblique relations, tentatively joined in an exercise of global interconnection. There is a double significance in the image. If departure enables such forged bonds, it also reveals that leaving the Antilles is a form of returning to, not escaping from, suffering and brutality. The Europe that comes into view is a continent of war atrocities.

Unlike Odysseus, however, Césaire's persona willingly immerses himself in the struggle of passage, and he does so in the posture of self-sacrifice. Compensating for his departure, he carries the burdens of his people with him as psychic material he must process before understanding its collective consequences. His chief strategy is to invent masks that empower him to identify not only with the oppressed, but with one of the most degrading forms of violence on the spectrum of abuse: the random murder of someone you can "lay hold of . . . pummel . . . with blows, kill . . . actually kill, without having to account to anyone, without having to make excuses to anyone" (*"le saisir le rouer de coups, le tuer—parfaitement le tuer—sans avoir de compte à rendre à personne,"* 34). Jews, Kaffirs, Hindis, and American blacks exist in the state of exception. The laws protecting constitutional rights have been denied them through acts of power imposed by a government that asserts its sovereignty to operate outside the law.

In this context, the speaker assumes the mask of a visionary who tries to access a world order through "the secret code of grand communications and of grand conflagrations" (*"le secret des grandes communications et des grandes combustions,"* 36). Here Césaire channels an ancient view of poetry, revitalized by surrealism, as vatic knowledge, inaccessible to science and technology. In *"La poèsie et la connaissance"*—"Poetry and Knowledge"—he speaks of "The unconscious that all true poetry calls upon" and characterizes it as "the receptacle of original relationships that bind us to nature" (*"le receptacle des parentés qui, originelles, nous unissent à la nature"*).[26] He quotes André Breton, who writes, "It is the poets over the centuries who have made it possible to receive, and who may have enabled us to expect, the impulses that may once again place humankind at the heart of the universe . . . reminding us of an indefinitely perfectible place of resolution and echo for every pain and joy."[27] Subsuming the social and the political, poetry functions as an initiatory rite into esoteric knowledge that may be conveyed to a people by an inspired leader who is the medium of a higher spiritual truth. Integral to this notion is the fantasy of a prehistoric time in which the roles of king, prophet, warrior, and priest were joined, with poetry providing the medium of expression. Césaire is conjuring elements that coalesce in the creation of foundation tales. He is doing so by bringing images from the African diaspora, such as the totem, into contact with Western traditions that have cultivated the figure of the poet-prophet-king.

It is worth taking a closer look. As the discussion in chapter 2 bears out, the power of poetic language for Césaire is closely related to the "force value" (*"valeur-force"*) that lies coiled in words. In an essay on Leo Frobenius in the journal *Tropiques*, Suzanne Césaire connects this notion with the spiritual core, the soul of a culture conceived as an organic entity that lives, breathes, and undergoes change through the life and creative work of a people, channeled through its land and history—its *paideuma*, Frobenius's term.[28] By raising a rallying cry, she challenges Antilleans "to dare" (*"oser"*) to know themselves, to avow who they are, to ask what they want to be. A response to this challenge is vividly sounded in a passage of *Cahier* where the speaker tries to arouse himself into action after the departure from the *pays natal*, testing the possibilities of mantic speech.

> I would say hurricane. I would say river, I would say tornado. I would
> say leaf. I would say tree. I would be soaked with all the rains,
> moistened with all the dews. I would circulate like frenetic blood on
> the slow current in the eye of storming words . . . And you, ancestral
> ghosts, rise alchemical blue . . .
> (36)

---

26. "Poetry and Knowledge," xlviii; in French, *"La poèsie et la connaissance,"* 162.

27. "Poetry and Knowledge," xlvii; in French, *"La poèsie et la connaissance,"* 161.

28. Suzanne Césaire, *"Léo Frobenius et le problème des civilisations,"* *Tropiques* 1 (1941): 27–36.

Je dirais orage. Je dirais fleuve. Je dirais tornade. Je dirais feuille. Je dirais arbre. Je serais mouillé de toutes les pluies, humecté de toutes les rosées. Je roulerais comme du sang frénétique sur le courant lent de l'oeil des mots . . . Et vous fantômes montez bleus de chimie . . .

The very act of speaking words for earth, air, fire, and water suddenly reanimates the life that lives in them. Speech becomes both incantatory and necromantic. It calls forth the ancient powers that inhabit the material world as well as ancestral phantoms that loom within them, in a process likened to alchemy. The spoken language is being invested not only with the capacity to conjure but also with an aggressive force that makes words into "miraculous weapons" ("*armes miraculeuses*") for fighting the enemy—the intimate enemy of French colonialism.[29]

Having crossed the oceanic divide, the speaker, in a sudden sweep of the sort that is not uncommon in *Cahier,* is galvanized into imagining a rebirth with "earth great vulva raised to the sun / earth great delirium of the divine phallus," giving life to "the earth where all is free and fraternal, my earth" ("*terre grand sexe levé vers le soleil / terre grand délire de la mentule de Dieu . . . la terre où tout est libre et fraternel, ma terre,*" 36). The pansexual images resonate with the tonalities of Africa that will be developed in passages yet to come, and the female is imagined as an erotically inflected *terre maternelle*—but not unequivocally so, as is soon clear. Significantly, it is at this point of the poem that the memory of slavery first surfaces, a product of vatic access to a violent past. This memory merges with references to Nazi horrors: "a basket of oysters of eyes" ("*un panier d'huîtres d'yeux*") and "the beautiful sisal of human skin" ("*le beau sisal d'une peau d'homme,*" 36). Ghosts of the dead rise in a haze of alchemical blue, the barbarism of slavery merging with that of the Second World War.

But the sequence of stanzas under discussion (36–38) is composed in the conditional mood. It is an imaginary passage, inflected by a still incipient Africa, and its altruistic mission is undercut in the very act of articulation. Having no sooner envisioned a return in which he would say, "I have wandered for a long time and I am coming home to the abandoned ghastliness of your <u>sores</u>" ("*J'ai longtemps erré et je reviens vers la hideur désertée de vos*

---

29. The phrase is derived from the title of one of Césaire's poetry collections, *Les armes miraculeuses* (Paris: Gallimard, 1946). On "intimate enemies," see Maryse Condé and Richard Philcox, "Intimate Enemies: Conversation Between an Author and Her Translator," in *Intimate Enemies: Translations in Francophone Contexts,* ed. Kathryn Batchelor and Claire Bisdorff (Liverpool: Liverpool University Press, 2013), 89–97.

plaies," 37), the speaker now identifies with the prodigal son. What Suzanne Césaire conceives as a *paideuma* in the Frobenius vein for the redemption of a people is enacted hypothetically in *Cahier* as an experiment. The voice that would be "the mouth of adversities that have no mouth" ("*la bouche des malheurs qui n'ont point de bouche,*" 38) weakens into contrition, and the sacrificial narrative is exposed as formulaic role-playing. The hollow theatricality of the production is acknowledged in some of the poem's most quoted lines:

> Beware of crossing your arms in the sterile pose of a spectator, for life
> is not a show on stage, for a sea of troubles is not a proscenium, for a
> screaming human being is not a dancing bear . . .
> (38)

> *gardez-vous de vous croiser les bras en l'attitude sterile du spectateur,*
> *car la vie n'est pas un spectacle, car une mer de douleurs n'est pas un*
> *proscenium, car un homme qui crie n'est pas un ours qui danse . . .*

The Caribbean may be the backdrop for a tragic drama that must be performed if it is to enter the world. But "life is not a show," and the speaker, in becoming an actor, has caught himself in the histrionic pose of *vates*. Interwoven as it is with biblical overtones, the self-unmasking deflates the masculine grandiosity of passage. Back in the *pays natal,* whose grim shades are even grimmer, it is the same "limping life" ("*vie clopinante*") that Césaire's persona sees before him.

It is now possible for us to revisit the *terre maternelle,* the hyphenated Antilles-Africa that the poem traces in fits and starts. One of the most prominent reflexive moves of *Cahier* is to degrade a figure that has been elevated and to do so in proximate stanzas. The exoticism expressed in the line "earth great vulva raised to the sun" sits close to another image linked with the colonial abuses the vatic poet would seek to reverse. And with this image, the audience is brought back to the figure of the hypocritical or deceptive female. In the struggle to overcome the oppressor,

> does one ever kill Chagrin, as fair as the startled face of an English
> lady who peers into her soup tureen to find a Hottentot skull?
> (35)

> *mais est-ce qu'on tue le Remords, beau comme la face du stupeur d'une dame*
> *anglaise qui trouverait dans sa soupière un crâne de Hottentot?*

Davis translates "*Remords*" as "Chagrin" because he wants to capture the trivializing attitude of the female-as-colonial who finds the skull annoying or embarrassing rather than morally reprehensible. *Hottentot* is a derisive Dutch term to describe the non-Bantu people of South Africa who are now called Khoikhoi. And the English woman staring into her soup tureen is yet another example of the female whose ostensible culture disguises a grotesque insensitivity to colonial violence. Once again, in a section of the poem where passage is explicitly enacted as a psychic journey, the ambivalence of gender—the toxicity and fertility of the female—is made to reflect a similar ambivalence about masculine potency.

The evocation of cannibalism in the scene with the Hottentot skull brings us to another Césairean reclamation. Like madness and irrationality, the term cannibalism has been used to denigrate the people of the Caribbean since Europeans first began to colonize the region. Picking up on this history, the speaker turns it against the colonial culture:

> Because we detest you, yes you and your reason, we repossess
> ourselves in the name of demential praecox of flamboyant madness of
> inveterate cannibalism.
> (48)

> *Parce que nous vous haïssons vous et votre raison, nous nous*
> *réclamons de la démence précoce de la folie flambante du*
> *cannibalisme tenace.*

The alleged "inveterate cannibalism" of those with African ancestry, underscored by the asyndeton of the lines, is taken hold of and transformed into literary cannibalism—the engorgement of the texts of colonial writers in an act that is simultaneously destructive and reconstitutive.[30] Shreds of past writing, like pieces of flesh, are consumed and digested in creating something that combines the eater and the eaten. As recent studies have emphasized, it was Suzanne Césaire who first gave the term cannibalism conceptual clout. In another essay she published in *Tropiques* titled "*Misère de la poésie: John Antoine Nau*," she develops the notion through an attack on the poetry of *doudouisme*, which sentimentalizes the charm of Creole life without recogniz-

---

30. See Valerie Loichot, *The Tropics Bite Back: Culinary Coups in Caribbean Literature* (Minneapolis: University of Minnesota Press, 2013), 141–42; Maryse Condé, *Histoire de la femme cannibale* (Paris: Mercure de France, 2005); trans. Richard Philcox, *The Cannibal Woman* (New York: Washington Square Press, 2007); and Marie-Agnès Sourieau, "Suzanne Césaire et Tropiques: *de la poésie cannibale à une poétique créole,*" *French Review* 68.1 (1994): 69–78.

ing its profound self-estrangement, a point already taken up in earlier sections of this book.[31] Such poetry assimilates itself (renders itself "like" or "*similis*") to the culture that has violated it, while she imagines a poetry engaged in an aggressive act of eating the violator. She ends the essay epigrammatically saying, "Martiniquan poetry will be cannibal or it will not be at all" ("*La poésie martiniquaise sera cannibale ou ne sera pas*").[32]

Literary cannibalism takes a cultural stereotype of the mixed-race Caribbean as less than human, and by killing and consuming the stereotype, it attenuates its power. In *Cahier*, particularly, cannibalism is itself an example of what it seeks to name: it enacts through ingestion the need "to bite back" ("*mordre en retour*"), in Maryse Condé's words.[33] By conjuring up savages digging their teeth into human meat, Césaire takes hold of a derisive lexeme and turns it back on those who use it. One way to understand the pongo discussed in chapter 2 is to see the creature as a Cyclops that the poet has cannibalized in an Antillean setting, thereby reclaiming and reinventing Homer's man-eating giant. The abjection of the Cyclops in the *Odyssey* becomes the flip side of an enabling act of literary consumption on the part of the modern, racially marginalized poet. The trickster turns out to live vibrantly through the creature tricked.

It is partly via cannibalism that the reader reaches one of the first extended stanzas on Africa in the poem. In leaving a Europe "all convulsed with cries" ("*toute révulsée de cris*," 81), Césaire's persona comes to see "[his] puerile fantasies of old" ("*mes anciennes imaginations puériles*"), particularly, the adolescent notion of the poet as prophet who returns to redeem. He therefore goes about reinventing them. One of the consequences of this self-correction is apparent in a stanza that features, by contrast with the prophetic voice, a more historical and ethnographic mode of passage to Africa and its great ancient kingdoms. Here the tone of negation mimics the excision of these cultural centers from Western history books in the paradoxical act of overcoming it.

No, we have never been Amazon squadrons of the king of Dahomey,
nor princes of Ghana with eight hundred camels, nor scholars of
Timbuktu under the reign of Askia the Great, nor architects of Djenné,
nor Madhis, nor famed warriors. We do not feel under the armpit the
itch of those who bore the lance in former times.
(93)

---

31. See Suzanne Césaire, "*Misère de la poésie: John Antoine Nau*," *Tropiques* 4 (1942): 48–50. For a discussion, see Curtius, "Cannibalizing *Doudouisme*."
32. See especially Loichot, *Tropics Bite Back*, 141–76.
33. Quoted in Loichot, *Tropic Bites Back*, 188n12.

*Non, nous n'avons pas jamais été amazones du roi du Dahomey, ni
princes de Ghana avec huit cents chameaux, ni docteurs à Tombouctou
Askia le Grand étant roi, ni architectes de Djenné, ni Madhis, ni
guerriers. Nous ne nous sentons pas sous l'aisselle la démangeaison
de ceux qui tinrent jadis la lance.*

In a vivid instance of antiphrasis, what is historically true is affirmed through
rhetorical denial, an ironic form of parroting European racism. There were
indeed such kings, princes, scholars, architects, and warriors as those referenced.[34] The Dahomey kingdom, which was located in what is now southern
Benin, endured from about 1600 to 1900 CE, and it included all-female military regiments. The Ghana Empire flourished as a center of trade much earlier
between the ninth and eleventh centuries CE and was located in an area that is
now southeastern Mauritania and western Mali on land rich in gold. During
the Latin Middle Ages, Timbuktu, also in Mali, was a center of learning and
a flourishing manuscript culture whose scholars produced work on a wide
spectrum of subjects from mathematics and astronomy to law and geography. Jenne, the modern Djenné, was one of the oldest cities of sub-Saharan
Africa, especially well known for its Islamic mud architecture and linked with
Timbuktu as a prosperous center of learning and trade. Mahdis were and are
religious figures in Islam, regarded as eschatological leaders with the power to
rid the world of evil.

Stanza 93 renders explicit what Western history has suppressed, and in the
process, it conveys knowledge that has been obliterated in the consciousness
of colonialized Antilleans. Africa once again functions as a vital detour to a
continent that lies outside the passage that loops the Antilles and Europe. It
triangulates a binary relationship by deepening the terms in which it may be
understood and extending the purview of history. In so doing, it offers a new,
lateral perspective upon a passage already discussed—the aerial view of the
geographical Antilles, which is similarly triangulated (42). It also recasts the
negatively charged reference in stanza 39 to the three-souled Caribbean whose
"impure" blood is a curse.

Shortly after this, the slave ship, *le négrier,* comes into view, and it will
dominate the last sections of the poem. Through another strategy of provocative self-debasing, this ship is imagined as the vessel of the "vomit"
("*vomissure*") it contains, namely, the slaves who begin to be heard from the
monstrous hold.

---

34. See entries in Henry Louis Gates and Kwame Anthony Appiah, *Africana: The Encyclopedia of the African and African-American Experience,* 5 vols., 2nd ed. (New York: Oxford
University Press, 2005).

I hear rising from the hold the curses in chains, the hiccuping [*sic*] of the
dying, the sound of a slave being thrown overboard . . . the baying of a
woman in labor . . . the scrapings of fingernails groping for throats . . .
the tauntings of the whip . . . the rummaging of vermin amid the spells
of exhaustion.
(96)

J'entends de la cale monter les malédictions enchaînées, les
hoquettements des mourants, le bruit d'un qu'on jette à la mer . . . les
abois d'une femme en gésine . . . des raclements d'ongles cherchant
des gorges . . . des ricanements de fouet . . . des farfouillis de vermine
parmi des lassitudes.

The "vomit-that-is-slaves" slowly metamorphoses into "the slaves who vomit."
A deobjectifying—a reverse "thingification"—is being dramatized. The use
of hyphens intensifies the effect, and ellipsis suggests something inchoate yet
portentous in the offing, the stirrings that will soon issue in the poem's enactment of mutiny. It is at this point, when denigration of the race is strongest
and signs of a rumble begin to be heard, that Césaire interjects the scene of
the pongo. The creature comes out of the depths of Africa, not a continent of
savagery, but a proud and vibrant panorama of cultures.

It is now possible to make better sense of the undertones of nobility in the
portrait of the "ape-man" and add them as a supplement to the discussion in
chapter 2. Controversial as Césaire's strategies of self-abasement have been for
critics of *Cahier*—Condé, for example, sees them as a form of masochism[35]—
they are the means by which the poet enacts a coming-into-consciousness.
While self-abasement and revolt are also closely linked in Odysseus's passage
through the ironized home of Ithaca, his famous cunning, which sometimes
slides into self-obstruction, is not so clearly exposed. *Metis* can be morally
ambivalent, riddled (as in the Cyclops episode) with self-defeat, and even contrary to the notion of *nostos* as a teleological trajectory to a point of safety.
Césaire, by contrast, unmasks a set of attitudes and practices whose cunning
side often veers into pathological delusion, and in doing so, he confounds in
a different way the notion of a *pays natal*. In the ancient text, physical detour
brings in tow an originary scenario that illuminates psychic detour; in the
Caribbean text, psychic detour must go in search of a geography.

---

35. See Condé, "*Négritude césarienne, négritude senghorienne.*"

WOOLF: CONSTANTINOPLE AND EXILE AS CARNIVAL

Coming into consciousness is not a bad way to understand the tropes of passage and detour in *Orlando,* especially since the book loosely incorporates the structure of a bildungsroman, as does *Cahier,* though less obviously so. But Woolf deliberately eschews the interior stream of consciousness style of *Mrs. Dalloway* and *To the Lighthouse,* finding in what she calls the "externality" of her fictional biography a method by which to bring psychological processes into a visible space where a reader can see how they are experienced and performed in social contexts.[36] In other words, she crafts a narrator who steers well clear of "that riot and confusion of the passions and emotions which every good biographer detests" (13) and aims instead to record feats and noble deeds. Masculine-gendered as this traditional orientation toward biography is—Leslie Stephen is never far from Woolf's satire—it becomes increasingly difficult to sustain during and after the sex change when movements across sex, gender, and sexuality are complicated by movements across language, class, and nationality.

This is how the phantasmagoria of the mind emerges as a site of narrative production in *Orlando.* Through it, the story engages in a dynamic of concealing and revealing that is typical, as we have seen, of odyssean tales. An orientalized east plays a prominent role in this process. It opens an imaginary space in which what is forbidden at home can be performed abroad. In other words, the narrative links the "trans" in transsexual with the "trans" in transnational, showing how sex, gender, and sexuality are integral to nationalist ideas about normative womanhood.[37] Trans movements characterize not only the sex change, but many other crossed borders in Chapter Three of Woolf's satirical biography, suggesting how enmeshed the metamorphosis of Orlando's body is in social, political, and psychological change.

These issues, and the journeys they entail through Turkey and Greece, are the chief interest of this section of the book. Once more, cunning is integral to the narrative at several levels. Woolf's rendering the narrative voice in *Orlando* naïve is itself crafty, a strategy designed to protect the subject—a nontraditional, sexually ambiguous male—at the same time that it partially discloses what it seeks to hide. This is roughly the obverse of the *Odyssey* where "the newest song" is the best (1.371). In the epic, narrative techniques, rather than rendering the third-person bard naïve, call attention to the novel ways he complicates the traditional meaning of *nostos. Cahier's* odyssey is

---

36. On the "externality" of *Orlando,* see *Diary,* 3.164.
37. See Berman, "Is the Trans in Transnational the Trans in Transgender?"

more overtly confessional and self-disclosing than Woolf's, but both writers attempt to access marginalized forms of experience through daring ventures in literary form.

If the wound and the word figure prominently in the dramatization of the trope of passage in the *Odyssey* and *Cahier,* Woolf's *Orlando* features a physical mutation without surgical intervention and introduces texts such as letters, legal records, and private papers to explore the puzzles of Orlando's metamorphosis. Ultimately, the experience of sexual transformation leads back around to autobiographical writing as a form of psychic healing. One of the distinguishing features of such therapy in Woolf's work is that it produces a text, "The Oak Tree," whose content is hidden from the reader. Whatever it is that the straitlaced fictional biographer cannot or does not say takes the form of a remainder stored in a secret object, which draws the reader into a prurient relationship with the text within the text. On the basis of hints and clues, we are expected to draw our own conclusions. What is Orlando writing in this manuscript that grows longer as the story advances? How closely does it resemble the more traditional poetic works he crafts—the adolescent tragedies and epic tales that Nick Greene torches? As an object she later carries in her bosom, it takes on the qualities of a talisman and becomes increasingly prominent after the sex change as a substitute object. It thus resembles the totem, which Césaire uses to signify a magical unity-within-difference of Jews, Kaffirs, Hindis, and American Blacks. Like the totem of *Cahier,* too, it is connected with trauma.

The orient of Woolf's fictional biography is a fabrication based on several sources. She traveled to Turkey herself when she was twenty-four and kept a diary in which she recorded her impressions.[38] With the contacts she had through Leonard Woolf's civil service position and his editorial work for *The Nation* and *The Political Quarterly,* she was closely attuned to the military activities of the British Empire in the late stages of the Ottoman collapse. But perhaps more important were the details she derived from the letters and memoirs of Sackville-West, based upon her sojourns in Constantinople and Tehran while Harold Nicolson was an ambassador there.[39] In 1926, Vita took a circuitous route via Egypt and India before sailing across the Persian Gulf

38. See the online text, *Virginia Woolf's Travel and Literary Notebook, 1906–1909,* accessed 5 May 2019, https://www.bl.uk/collection-items/virginia-woolfs-travel-and-literary-notebook-1906-9.

39. On Britain's covert imperialist operations in the East and their impact on nineteenth- and early twentieth-century views of such regions as Turkey, see Pryia Satia, *Spies in Arabia: The Great War and the Cultural Foundations of Britain's Covert Empire in the Middle East* (New York: Oxford University Press, 2009), 3–22. For a view of orientalism and empire pertinent in understanding Woolf's orientalism, see Lisa Lowe, *Critical Terrains: French and British Orientalisms* (Ithaca, NY: Cornell University Press, 1992), especially 1–29.

to Tehran. Her voyage home was through communist Russia and Poland during a period of revolution. Hogarth published a travelogue of the journey under the title *Passenger to Teheran*.[40] Thus what emerges in Chapter Three of *Orlando* is an encounter that both exploits and creatively undermines stereotypes about the people, customs, and beliefs of an area that figured prominently in Britain's own imperial conquests. If questions of race and ethnicity help connect Woolf's work with Césaire, orientalism helps associate it with Cavafy's provocative realignments of Hellenism along eastern vistas, which will be the topic of the next part of this chapter.

The displacement of sexual nonconformity onto an exotic other, as in Orlando's encounter with the Russian princess, is repeated when a second attack of erotic desire strikes in the form of the Archduchess Harriet Griselda of Finster-Aarhorn and Scand-op-Boom. Her outlandish name reminds the reader of the no less concocted Princess Marousha Stanilovska Dagmar Natasha Iliana Romanovitch. The archduchess threatens to open the wound that has still not healed from the loss of the princess. But unlike Césaire's damaged wanderer whose departure takes him into the heart of colonial power in Europe, Woolf's wounded protagonist flees directly into the metropolitan center of the East and loses himself there—literally—in a sex change. The biography therefore unfolds contrasting orientalisms, one that looks to immersion in a foreign culture via the protagonist, the other to suspicion of strangeness via the narrator.[41] Orlando mingles in Constantinople, while the biographer, who emerges as a British colonialist at heart, and increasingly more male than female in his attitudes, often regards his subject's proclivities with scandalized incomprehension. The difference is, in part, a narrative strategy, which allows Woolf to get material into the story that might otherwise have come under the axe of the censor.

Perhaps the most economical way of delving into the material is to begin discussion with a particularly disruptive mode of the comic on which Woolf draws, namely, the carnivalesque, which is used to construct Constantinople as a site of inversion at multiple levels.[42] Suggestively positioned at the inter-

---

40. See Vita Sackville-West, *Passenger to Teheran* (1926; London: Taurus Parke, 2007).

41. On orientalism, homoeroticism, and the libidinous East in *Orlando,* see Julia Briggs, *Reading Virginia Woolf* (Edinburgh: Edinburgh University Press, 2006), 152–61; Kaivola, "Revisiting Woolf's Representations of Androgyny"; Karen Lawrence, *Penelope Voyages: Women and Travel in the British Literary Tradition* (Ithaca, NY: Cornell University Press, 1994), 179–206; and David Roessel, "The Significance of Constantinople in *Orlando,*" *Papers on Language & Literature* 28.4 (1992): 398–416.

42. On the carnivalesque in *Orlando,* see Hediye Ozkan, "The Spirit of Carnival: Virginia Woolf's *Orlando* and Constantinople," *Interactions* (2017), *HighBeam Research,* 30 September 2018, accessed 5 May 2019, https://www.highbeam.com.

section of Europe and Asia, the action that unfolds there cannot be wholly retrieved, the biographer tells us, since only "tantalising fragments" (93) of evidence remain after the revolution against the Sultan and the fire in the ambassadorial chambers that breaks out during Orlando's sojourn. The whole episode is framed by a major political upheaval that reflects and amplifies the sex change. The action of Chapter Three may be outlined this way, with key terms in bold calling attention to the carnivalesque dimension of the narrative.

Rank—Diplomacy—Hierarchy

The first section presents the reader with the activities of Orlando in his ceremonial public role after he has asked King Charles to send him as "Ambassador Extraordinary to Constantinople" (87). So effectively does he conduct affairs of state that he is inducted into the Order of the Bath and granted a Dukedom, public honors the biographer can narrate without anxiety.

Mingling—Sexual Border Crossing—Inversion of Hierarchy

There ensues a grand celebration of these honors, which combines the British, the Turks, and visiting dignitaries—"people of all nationalities" (93)—gathered to do homage to Orlando. A violent disturbance breaks out at the party—who is involved and why are unclear, there are only charred shreds of evidence—but it is quelled, and Orlando withdraws into his private quarters. There, a deed of marriage is later found, witnessing his union with a certain Rosina Pepita who never materializes in the story. Sometime that night, Orlando falls into a deep sleep and undergoes a change of sex, how we are not sure.

Mingling—Class Related Border Crossing—Inversion of Hierarchy

After sleeping for at least a week, during which time there is a Turkish rebellion, Orlando awakes, finds he has changed into a woman, and without the knowledge of anyone—they think he is dead—descends from his room to meet up with an old gypsy. "Attended by a lean dog, riding a donkey, in company of a gipsy, the Ambassador of Great Britain at the Court of the Sultan [leaves] Constantinople" (104).

Low Rank—Liminal Space—Nomadic Life

There follows an indeterminate period of time in which Orlando, now a she, wanders with the "gipsies" as one of their own, travels through Broussa near the Black Sea, and from there into Greece. The psychic aftermath of the sex change is handled in terms of literal and metaphorical wandering. Eventually, the good will of her newly acquired nomadic family turns against

her—they begin to feel she isn't one of them—and she makes her exit on a
merchant ship back to England.

The carnivalesque character of the sequence should be apparent in the inversion of the high, which is associated with diplomacy and matters of state, and
the low, which is associated with a superior nomadism of gender and class.

In the first glimpse we have of Orlando as ambassador, he is standing on
a parapet in "a long Turkish cloak" with a "cheroot" in his hand, looking out
on Constantinople from on high. Within his purview are the domes of Santa
Sofia, the Galata Bridge, and Pera on the opposite shore, with the teeming
masses of "green turbanned pilgrims," "shawled women," and "men on horses"
(89). Significantly, the district called Pera is taken from the Greek word that
means "on the other side," and it is a locative shifter, pointing to Europe, not
Asia, as the "other" upon which Orlando is gazing. In other words, he has
already undergone a kind of migration that renders the continent and country
from which he has departed into foreign land. Moreover, Santa Sofia, an epit-
ome of Byzantine architecture, is a symbol of religious and cultural intermingling. Built by the Emperor Justinian in 537 CE, it was for centuries a Greek
Orthodox cathedral before being converted in 1453 to a mosque.

The noble spectator on his balcony whom the biographer describes as
"English root and fibre" is in the habit of passing out of the gates of his pre-
cinct at night so that he can "mingle with the crowd on the Galata Bridge, or
stroll through the bazaars, or throw aside his shoes and join the worshippers
in the Mosques" (91). Fancying "darkness in his complexion," Orlando imagines he has an ancestry linked with the people who form this "wild panorama"
(89). The facility he exhibits in changing his appearance and passing as one
of the locals, along with his fluency in the Turkish language (96)—a glance
at Vita Sackville-West's fluency in languages—suggest that Woolf has shaped
the protagonist as a trickster figure. Like Homer's Odysseus and the maker of
masks in *Cahier,* he can experiment across boundaries and assume multiple
identities. Ethnicity and class are the registers in which his first border crossings are recorded.

As Orlando circulates, so does the rumor around him, much of it ambiguously gendered: "He became adored of many women and some men" (92), the
biographer tells us, though his "romantic power" combined with "a nature of
extreme reserve" (92). Despite his ambassadorial tasks, he tends to be reclu-
sive, and though he roams freely in the city, he makes no friends. If Woolf
creates a biographer who exoticizes Orlando, thus enabling an audience with
conservative moral sympathies to participate in the book's escapades from
afar, she also makes him into the unwitting voice of a satire through which the

British colonial perspective itself is taken down. For example, when the naval commander John Fenner Brigge, in a heavily verticalized scene, is driven up a Judas tree in order to watch the new duke's coronation, admiring as he climbs "our countrymen and women, dressed in the highest elegance and distinction," he gets distracted and falls off the branch (93–94).[43] Soon after that, a whole squad of British bluejackets is deployed during the ceremonies to quell an indoor disturbance, turning the palatial chambers into a field of battle protected by comically depicted military personnel (97). It is not only the action of Chapter Three that is carnivalesque, but the narration too, which is punctuated with ellipses that require an audience to fill in the blanks of letters and records that have holes big enough "to put your finger through" (88). Unlike Césaire's *Cahier* whose historical lacunae are tragically cast, *Orlando* describes a topsy-turvy world whose many inversions of hierarchy leave no wounds. Both works, however, engage in different ways with an odyssean practice of concealing while revealing.

These effects are extended in the report of Orlando's marriage to Rosina Pepita. The audience is told later in the narrative that they have three sons, but we never see the children or their mother. Introducing marriage into a scene involving a sex change may have provided Woolf another way to escape the censor by masking lesbianism with a normative social institution that at least partially hides it. But the doubling also reflects, to a certain extent, the life of Sackville-West, whose affairs with other women may have strained, but never ended, her marriage to Harold Nicolson. As for the elusive Rosina Pepita, we learn from the biographer that she is "a dancer, father unknown, but reputed a gipsy, mother also unknown but reputed a seller of old iron in the marketplace over against the Galata Bridge" (98).

Between the lines, we are invited to imagine a marriage of the high and the low, a Duke and a peasant woman, an English noble man and a gypsy from parts unknown, with a biological lineage composed of weak links. These movements up and down the social scale are literalized, not only with Pepita's ascent but also with Orlando's descent. After he awakens from a trance, she "[descends] the shattered and bloodstained staircase, now strewn with the litter of waste paper baskets, treaties, dispatches, seals, sealing wax, etc.," and takes flight (104). She does so after handily sticking two pistols in her belt.

Spectral lineages, weak links. These are, of course, the ways in which Woolf would have us see biography—as a form of giving life to ghostly remnants through narrative. It turns out that Rosina Pepita is not only a historical

---

43. On the parody of British colonialism in the Constantinople episode, see Jean Kennard, "Power and Sexual Ambiguity: The 'Dreadnought' Hoax, *The Voyage Out, Mrs. Dalloway*, and *Orlando*," *Journal of Modern Literature* 20.2 (1996): 149–64.

personage but also the actual grandmother of Vita, whose grandfather, "Old" Lord Lionel Sackville-West, took up with the dancer of Spanish heritage and begot several children with her.[44] One of them was Victoria Josefs Dolores Catalina, who assumed her father's surname and married the "Young" Lord Lionel Sackville-West, her cousin. She was the mother of Vita. It was Vita who researched and wrote a biography of her grandmother, a highly engaging dancer with a reputation as a charmer, although she never married a duke as Victoria and Vita would have wanted to claim (Rosita's husband was a barber of Malaga). We are in the land of granite and rainbow.

The deep sleep into which Orlando falls in Chapter 3 is not altogether like that of Chapter Two. Importantly, however, the sex change is neither trauma-inducing like the disappearance of Sasha nor the product of a tortured sense of being born into the wrong body.[45] It involves no surgery or other form of medical intervention. Nor, when Orlando awakens and looks into a mirror, does he show signs of "discomposure" (102). Though a woman, _he_ remains precisely as _he_ was. And so when _her_ memory goes back through the events of _his_ past life, it does so without encountering any obstacle: "The change of sex, though it altered _their_ future, did nothing whatever to alter _their_ identity" (102). _He_ is at home in _her_ body, and as time goes on, the reader sees that both undergo psychic shifts that belie the apparent stability of morphological binaries. Still, the genitals remain the site, if not of a wound, then of a transformative change.

Since Orlando shows no surprise at the change—s/he does not undergo "recognition" or an "identity crisis" upon awakening from a long sleep—the grammatical jostling registers the shock at a systems-level, namely, language as it intersects with traditional constructions of sex and gender. These systems cannot adequately express the change. Indeed, because Woolf's narrator never exposes Orlando's physical attributes to the audience—we are not told what he, upon awakening as a she, sees in the mirror—the body never becomes the site of unambiguous sexual dimorphism. The transsexual change is constructed as an interrupted mirror scene that excludes the audience from spectatorship and renders prurient its desire to see. "Obscurity" and "opacity"

---

44. See Nigel Nicolson, _Portrait of a Marriage_ (New York: Atheneum), 47–58.

45. For recent treatments of transgender and embodiment, see Susan Stryker, Paisley Currah, and Lisa Jean Moore, "Introduction: Trans-, Trans, or Trangender?," in _Women's Studies Quarterly_ 36.3/4 (2008): 11–22; Ryan Anderson, _When Harry Became Sally: Responding to the Transgender Moment_ (New York: Encounter Books, 2018); and Jack Halberstam, _Trans*: A Quick and Quirky Account of Gender Variability_ (Berkeley: University of California Press, 2018). On _Orlando_, in particular, see Pamela Caughie, "The Temporality of Modernist Life Writing in the Era of Transsexualism: Virginia Woolf's _Orlando_ and Einar Wegener's _Man into Woman_," _Modern Fiction Studies_ 59.3 (2013): 501–25.

(99)—the biographer's words—characterize the entire scene, and they extend to Orlando's unconsciousness. Significantly, Woolf does not avail the biographer of the concept of androgyny. Since that term appears as a category in *A Room of One's Own*, which she was writing almost concurrently with *Orlando*, the withholding of it is purposeful, and the reader should not override it.[46] "Let other pens treat of sex and sexuality; we quit such odious subjects as soon as we can" (103), says the narrator. And the author agrees, though for different reasons.

Woolf's are not related to shame, as are those of her fictional biographer. While they have partly to do with the censor, they have perhaps more to do with the conviction that poetic language has a force that nomenclature lacks when it comes to sex, gender, and sexuality. In this context, verbal invention shapes what it brings into view, without assuming there is an existing state that ontologically subtends the experience rendered. In the process of crafting a language of sexuality in *Orlando*, Woolf is also crafting sexuality, attuning us to how the biographer's obtuseness gestures toward possibilities that lie beyond it. *Androgyny* is not her chosen term. The reader must activate the imagination to construct what the narrative keeps hidden.

Not surprisingly, in the aftermath of the metamorphosis in Constantinople, the question of what "nature" is becomes central in the narrative, and it is worked out through Orlando's eastern wanderings with the gypsies, which are configured as a detour. In other words, the sex change calls into question the biologically given difference of male and female, and this opens the way to a wider set of questions about what is by nature and what is by culture. Importantly, language, which has already been foregrounded as a limited medium for conveying the sexual change, continues to present challenges, now in the sphere of ethnicity. This serves to highlight the multiply marginal status of Orlando who takes up with a group that is displaced in several senses. Their migratory ways are not teleologically structured in terms of a journey that ends once an end is attained, and thus they invite a consideration of what home means for those who are perpetually on the move, as a mode of life. Moreover, they enable an audience to see that such movement is not compelled by external forces. The gypsies are not in exile, nor are they wanderers.

---

46. Lisa Rado, *The Modern Androgyne Imagination: A Failed Sublime* (Charlottesville: University of Virginia Press, 2000), adopts the term in her discussion of *Orlando*, 138–78. Kaivola, "Revisiting Woolf's Representations of Androgyny," opts for the concept of "hybridity" over "androgyny" as the more radical "third term" for characterizing nonbinary sex and gender mixtures. Berman, "Is the Trans in Transnational the Trans in Transgender," argues for the fluidity of the sex, gender, and sexuality in *Orlando*, and extends the concept to transnationalism.

They displace themselves, perhaps, or better, they do not regard space (its extension) in terms of place (a settled location).

By introducing another orientalized ethnic group into Orlando's eastern journey, Woolf again opens a distance between Orlando's mingling with a people who happily welcome her into their company and the narrator's more prejudicial views (gypsies are vagabonds, they are inclined toward theft, they dislike bathing, and so forth). Yet the symbiosis of the protagonist with this newly acquired tribe is short lived. Alienation sets in as the gypsies become suspicious of the ways in which she relates to the mountains, rivers, and trees through which they pass in their nomadic existence. This nature, which is the nature they inhabit in the absence of houses, is an unpredictable and danger-ous deity that unleashes violence upon those who make their life in it. While they can weave baskets, produce cheese, and snare birds, their crafts reflect a pragmatic relation to a realm that Orlando poeticizes by turning it into a divinely infused green world whose hidden truths may be rendered in meta-phor. Transported by what the narrator calls "the English disease,"

> she likened the hills to ramparts, and the plains to the flanks of kine. She compared the flowers to enamel and the turf to Turkey rugs worn thin. Trees were withered hags, and sheep were grey boulder. Everything, in fact, was something else. (106)

What feels to Orlando like a process of creating meaning through an expres-sion of mystical oneness with the elements and a common humanity is felt by the gypsies to be a way of conjuring ghostly presences that peek from behind the thing itself. Western metaphysics is reduced to a shadow show. And so in concocting ink from berries and in scratching expressive lines at the margins of "The Oak Tree," she falls more and more under the suspicion that when she milks goats, gathers firewood, and herds animals, she does so not for the sake of doing, but for some other reason. Suddenly, the gypsies feel as if they inhabit a haunted world stirred up by mischievous ways of seeing.

Revealing contempt for the gigantic house that Orlando describes to them and her illustrious genealogy, they make her wonder how her 365 bedrooms could ever amount to much, when they have the whole earth to call their own. What are a few hundred years of ancestry when their own people go back thousands? The tension reaches a peak one day when Orlando strains for a word to describe as "beautiful" a scene that opens before her: mountains, and in the distance, the Acropolis and the Parthenon. She comes up empty and must resort to the closest expression the gypsies have for the idea of "beauti-ful": "How good to eat!" (106) How good to eat the Parthenon is. This is not an instance of literary cannibalism. It is an appreciation so foreign to the gypsies that the idea of consumption renders it comically unimaginable. Confronted with hostile stares upon uttering the sentence, Orlando is thrust into profound doubt about whether "Nature" was "beautiful or cruel; and then she asked herself what this beauty was; whether it was in things themselves, or only in herself" (107). In this intense encounter between East and West, orientalism and occidentalism collide in a moment of nontranslatability that bristles with hostility. Who is the "barbarian" in the scenario? Significantly, the word migrates in Chapter Three.

The dynamic is played out in a moving scene at the end of the chapter that anticipates return. On the bone-dry peninsula of Mount Athos in northern Greece and in the heat of a summer day, Orlando sees a shadow on the slope, but nothing there to cast it. The fears her metaphysical musings have introduced into the gypsy camp seem to have migrated uncannily into her. The shadow deepens into a scene of England, first in the green summer with grassy lawns and oaks, then in the snowy winter, the landscape "marked with violet shades instead of yellow sunlight" and the icy roads crossed by lorries carrying firewood. The vision expands into a veritable snow globe until suddenly it is swallowed up, and the sight becomes a "blazing hill-side" once more (111). Home appears within the foreign as a longing for return, and yet the color tones—yellow and violet—already feel bruised, just as the enchanting vision of home will turn out to be an illusion. This moment in *Orlando* recalls Césaire's experience on the Croatian coast, imagining Martinique in Martinska, and returning to a *pays natal* that is a nightmare, not a home.

Just as *Cahier* raises questions about passage through such strategies as the conditional mood and the use of shifting personas in composing the three-souled inhabitant of the Caribbean, so too *Orlando* explores cross-dressing in order to understand better the relationship between clothing and identity. A famous passage in the book sets out three responses to its protagonist's erratic play with garments that are never resolved and remain suspended as possibilities (138–39). The narrator first observes that there is much to support the view that "it is clothes that wear us and not we them." Gender shapes the physical body, according to this way of thinking, "mould[ing] our hearts, our brains, our tongues to their liking." This is the performative thesis: gender is shaped through forms of dramatic enactment. It turns out to be the view of "some philosophers and wise ones," not the biographer, who rather inclines to think that clothes are "a symbol of something hid deep beneath." This is the essentialist thesis: it is nature that shapes the outward style in accordance with an inner being. Both perspectives lead to a third that combines them: "Different as the sexes are, they intermix. In every human being a vacillation from one sex to another takes place, and often it is only the clothes that keep the male or female likeness." Once again, such vacillations tend toward plural and ambiguous mixtures. There may be as many as "two thousand and fifty-two" people stirring in the phantasmagoria of the mind, that "meeting-place of dissemblables," which registers incessant change (130).

It is this experience of the difference between time on the clock and time in the mind that drives the narrative's central conceit: that of a character who ages only thirty-six years over a 350-year history. Biography may not be able to account for this seething multitude, but the image of a phantasmagoria goes some way in evoking a sense of trans-ing as a multidirectional process at work on several levels. If passage in *Orlando* turns out to shed light upon the diffuse character of sex and gender—its weak links with social law and custom—passage in *Cahier* rehearses multiple roles for its personas, thereby illuminating the diffuse meanings of negritude. Neither Woolf or Césaire upholds essentialist views about sex, gender, and race, instead using fictional devices associated with the trickster figure to mark layered border crossings.

CAVAFY: MEDITERRANEAN ROUTES AND
EPHEBIC VISIONS

It is one of the ironies of Cavafy's life that although his poems often deal with travel and faraway places, he himself lived a stationary life in Alexandria after the itinerancy of his youth. From his perch on the Rue Lepsius, he imagined other places he never visited and crafted a cosmopolitan body of work through his Anglo-European contacts and the deep reading he did, particularly on antiquity and the Byzantine period. During the itinerant phase of his life as he was growing up in London, Manchester, Liverpool, and Constantinople, he developed a British sensibility—and accent—that stayed with him his whole life. He also took pride in his patrician roots as a descendent of Phanariots, the wealthy Greek class of merchants of Byzantine descent who held positions of power in the Ottoman Empire. Throughout his life, he sought to maintain contacts with the elite Greeks of Alexandria that his family had formed when they enjoyed financial prosperity. But like other Greeks of the diaspora living in Egypt, he did not mingle with the Arab population. Rather than going out in the world, the world came to Cavafy, and his apartment became a meeting place for intellectuals, writers, and artists who spoke Greek, English, and French.

One of the biographical aspects of his life that enables us to approach the trope of passage in his work is to consider it from the perspective of these visitors to the Rue Lepsius. Typically, they were escorted from the chaotic din of the city along a dim, cramped, and book-lined hallway into a parlor lit by candles that the host used to create an evocative space described by one of his acolytes as "phantasmagorical."[47] The echo of Woolf is uncanny. Here, in an apartment that had no electricity and that was packed with dark and dingy furniture, the poet entertained his guests, holding forth on topics that enabled him to display his impressive historical knowledge. E. M. Forster describes his speech as cutting a passage of its own through an ever-shifting ambience of light and shadow: Cavafy would form "an immense complicated yet shapely sentence, full of parentheses that never get mixed and of reservations that really do reserve; a sentence that moves with logic to its unforeseen end, yet to an end that is always more vivid and thrilling than one foresaw."[48] This picture of a winding sentence forging a detoured path captures an important dimension of Cavafy's poetic style as a whole and of how he imagines the symbolically charged act of passage through, over, or beyond. Like Césaire and Woolf, his writing conceals as it reveals, often holding us either in a dream space or a vividly imagined moment of transitory experience, charged with erotic energy.

The friendship of Forster and Cavafy, which has long garnered attention, was itself complex, shaped by bonds that linked a European cosmopolitanism, a love of the Greek past, and a homosexual identity that required various forms of masquerade in its time.[49] But their versions of Hellenism were considerably different. Living as he did in the Greek diaspora in Alexandria, Cavafy's Hellenism was not only Asian inflected. It also embraced dimensions of Greek history that Forster, following such influential historians as Edward Gibbon in *The Rise and Fall of the Roman Empire* (1776–89), did not integrate into his Hellenism: the late antique and Byzantine eras and Christian Egypt.[50] Cavafy drew from these histories and had a deep interest in Orthodox hagiography. For him, a Hellenism that embraced only ancient Greece—the Greece of the European Enlightenment—was an orientalism that effectively colonized the postclassical by downgrading the Greece of Asia Minor, the Pontus, the Levant, and Egypt. His Hellenism embraces a diversity of elements, some grounded in the historical syncretism of Greece and the East, and some tending toward Hellenocentrism.[51]

---

47. These details have been supplied by Jusdanis in his biography in progress on Cavafy.

48. Forster, *Pharos and Pharillon*, 91–92.

49. Cavafy, *The Forster-Cavafy Letters: Friends at a Slight Angle*, edited by Peter Jeffreys (Cairo: University Press of Cairo, 2009).

50. See Diana Haas, "Cavafy's Reading Notes on Gibbon's *Decline and Fall*," *Folia Neohellenica* 4 (1982): 25–96; and Ekdawi, "Cavafy's Byzantium."

51. See Halim, *Alexandrian Cosmopolitanism*, 56–119; and Jeffreys, *Eastern Questions*.

Like Woolf, Cavafy finds in the East the kinds of settings that are conducive to writing on transgressive sexualities. Like her, too, he creates voices
that both reveal and conceal. Time warps and shifting temporalities figure
centrally in the writings of both. The immersive orientalism of *Orlando* draws
attention to the probable reason for Woolf's decision not to set the sex change
in Greece, though the protagonist travels through it. In her imagination,
Greece was more familiar than foreign, or, alternatively, the modern, colonialized Greece she encountered in her travels was not conducive to the kinds of
fantasy she wanted to concoct in *Orlando*. Cavafy's often historically engaged
expressions of homoeroticism contrast strongly with Woolf's more fanciful
imaginings of a sexual life lived on the edge. Her character's adventurousness,
which drives the plot of *Orlando*, could not be less like Cavafy's more cau-
tiously framed excursions into the nightlife of places located in Egypt, Syria,
and Cyprus. They involve imagination and memory, but not the marvelous.

One of Cavafy's unpublished poems, "Going Back Home from Greece"
("Επάνοδος από τὴν Ἑλλάδα," 1914), whose central trope is passage by sea,
explores these intersections. Homer is never referenced, but the work has an
odyssean sensibility and fleshes out the diasporic character of Cavafy's Mediterranean. Like "Poseidonians" and "A City in Osroini," which were discussed
in chapter 1, "Going Back Home from Greece" plays in between cultures and
ethnicities. And while its sexuality is muted into more broadly homosocial
tones, the erotic peeps out here and there, which is suitable for a poem in
which peeping turns out to be important activity.[52]

"Going Back Home from Greece"
1 Well, we're nearly there, Hermippos.
2 Day after tomorrow, it seems—that's what the captain said.
3 At least we're sailing our own seas:
4 the waters of Cyprus, Syria, and Egypt,
5 the beloved waters of our home countries.
6 Why so silent? Ask your heart:
7 didn't you too feel happier
8 the farther we got from Greece?
9 What's the point of fooling ourselves?
10 That would hardly be properly Greek.

11 It's time we admitted the truth:
12 we are Greeks also—what else are we?—

---

52. Cavafy, *Collected Poems*, trans. Keeley and Sherrard, 368–69.

13 but with Asiatic affections and feelings,
14 affections and feelings
15 sometimes alien to Hellenism.

16 It isn't right, Hermippos, for us philosophers
17 to be like some of our petty kings
18 (remember how we laughed at them
19 when they used to come to our lectures?)
20 who through their showy Hellenified exteriors
21 Macedonian exteriors (naturally),
22 let a bit of Arabia peep out now and then,
23 a bit of Media they can't keep back.
24 And to what laughable lengths the fools went
25 trying to cover it up!

26 No, that's not all right for us.
27 For Greeks like us that kind of pettiness won't do.
28 We must not be ashamed
29 of the Syrian and Egyptian blood in our veins;
30 we should really honor it, take pride in it.

"Ἐπάνοδος ἀπὸ τὴν Ἑλλάδα"
1 Ὥστε κοντεύουμε νὰ φθάσουμ᾽, Ἔρμιππε.
2 Μεθαύριο, θαρρῶ· ἔτσ᾽ εἶπε ὁ πλοίαρχος.
3 Τουλάχιστον στὴν θάλασσά μας πλέουμε·
4 νερὰ τῆς Κύπρου, τῆς Συρίας, καὶ τῆς Αἰγύπτου,
5 ἀγαπημένα τῶν πατρίδων μας νερά.
6 Γιατί ἔτσι σιωπηλός; Ρώτησε τὴν καρδιά σου,
7 ὅσο ποὺ ἀπ᾽ τὴν Ἑλλάδα μακρυνόμεθαν
8 δὲν χαίροσουν καὶ σύ; Ἀξίζει νὰ γελιούμαστε;—
9 αὐτὸ δὲν θά᾽ταν βέβαια ἑλληνοπρεπές.

10 Ἄς τὴν παραδεχθοῦμε τὴν ἀλήθεια πιά·
11 εἴμεθα Ἕλληνες κ᾽ ἐμεῖς—τί ἄλλο εἴμεθα;—
12 ἀλλὰ μὲ ἀγάπες καὶ μὲ συγκινήσεις τῆς Ἀσίας,
13 ἀλλὰ μὲ ἀγάπες καὶ μὲ συγκινήσεις
14 ποὺ κάποτε ξενίζουν τὸν ἑλληνισμό.

15 Δὲν μᾶς ταιριάζει, Ἔρμιππε, ἐμᾶς τοὺς φιλοσόφους
16 νὰ μοιάζουμε σὰν κάτι μικροβασιλεῖς μας

17 (θυμᾶσαι πῶς γελούσαμε μὲ δαύτους
18 σὰν ἐπισκέπτονταν τὰ σπουδαστήριά μας)
19 ποὺ κάτω ἀπ' τὸ ἐξωτερικό τους τὸ ἐπιδεικτικὰ
20 ἑλληνοποιημένο, καὶ (τί λόγος!) μακεδονικό,
21 καμιὰ Ἀραβία ξεμυτίζει κάθε τόσο
22 καμιὰ Μηδιὰ ποὺ δὲν περιμαζεύεται,
23 καὶ μὲ τί κωμικὰ τεχνάσματα οἱ καΰμένοι
24 πασχίζουν νὰ μὴ παρατηρηθεῖ.

25 Ἄ, ὄχι, δὲν ταιριάζουνε σ' ἐμᾶς αὐτά.
26 Σ' Ἕλληνες σὰν κ' ἐμᾶς δὲν κάνουν τέτοιες μικροπρέπειες.
27 Τὸ αἷμα τῆς Συρίας καὶ τῆς Αἰγύπτου
28 ποὺ ῥέει μὲς στὲς φλέβες μας νὰ μὴ ντραπούμε,
29 νὰ τὸ τιμήσουμε καὶ νὰ τὸ καυχηθοῦμε.

The poem is set sometime after Greece has fallen from political power, although its cultural dominance in the region remains strong. But dates are not provided, as they sometimes are in Cavafy. Reference to "our petty kings" suggests a Hellenistic or early Roman context in which Greek philosophers and wise men traveled extensively to do their teaching. In any case, the poem is attempting to navigate a discourse of Hellenism—a way of encoding the attitudes, values, and comportment of those who are or aspire to be Hellenic in the aftermath of its political ascendency. And it is using the trope of passage to do so.

Locating Greece at the intersection of colonizer and colonized, conqueror and vanquished, the poem gestures in the direction both of its fallen greatness and its continuing dominance as a purveyor of culture. The reader knows this because the poem takes the form of a dramatic monologue spoken by a Greek philosopher of some sort. Cavafy was much influenced by Robert Browning,[53] and he manipulates the irony associated with the literary form that Browning honed in order to capture tensions between multiple Hellenic identities. The root "_hellen-_" (ἑλλην-) is used six times in the poem, and together these instances explore the question of what is "befitting" or "becoming" for a Greek.[54]

---

53. See Evgenia Sifaki, "Self-Fashioning in C. P. Cavafy's "Going Back Home from Greece," *Synthesis* 5 (2013): 29–48; David Ricks, "How It Strikes a Contemporary: Cavafy as a Reviser of Browning," *Kambos: Cambridge Papers in Modern Greek* (2003): 131–52; and Maria Tombrou, "Καβήσης και Μπραουνινγκ," *Νέα Ἑστία* 153 (2003): 787–809.

54. For a discussion of ethnicity and race in the poem, see Halim, *Alexandrian Cosmopolitanism*, 66–69.

Tonally, the language is familiar, even breezy, with phrases that suggest a conversation between intimates picked up in mid-flow. The title refers not just to a "return," but to "a return home from." Cavafy uses the demotic *epanodos* instead of the ancient *nostos*. And because the speaker and his implied interlocutor are themselves Greeks of some sort, it is therefore paradoxical. How does a Greek return home from Greece? Because we are not informed of either the origin or the destination of the voyage, the geography is approximate rather than specific. The location is within "the waters of Cyprus, Syria, Egypt," (4–5)—plural "waters"—and the area encompasses not one but multiple "home countries" or "fatherlands" (5)—also plural. The ship is a key image, and it conveys circulatory movement rather than fixity.

The first stanza thus emerges from an action of passing through, of getting closer without arriving, as the first line indicates. Another way to put this is that the poem expresses geographical location in the form of relation: proximity and distance depend upon perspective. Relationally, the poem brings into view mainland Greece (but no city), the Greek diaspora (conceived in terms of the Levant and Egypt, but not clearly delimited), and the various realms of small kings who are regarded as pretenders masking as Greeks through "comical contrivances."[55] Geographically in between, the poem hinges on masquerades that disclose at least a bit of what they are trying to hide. *Orlando* is full of this kind of hide and seek, played out across the fluid boundaries of sex, gender, and sexuality. So are Odysseus's Cretan tales and the experiments with racial shape shifting in *Cahier*.

From the beginning, Cavafy's poem points to its own status as a dramatic dialogue: the speaker's companion, Hermippos, is silent, despite the speaker's efforts to elicit answers from him. This silence turns out to be strategic. "We are Greeks also," says the speaker returning home from Greece, "what else are we?" (11). In claiming Hellenic identity, he also puts it into doubt with the interrogative and the adversative "but": "but with Asiatic affections and feelings . . . affections and feelings / sometimes alien to Hellenism . . ." (13–14). Cavafy often engages in this kind of play with words on the pleasure scale. On the one hand, "affections and feelings"—or "loves and emotions"[56]—are aligned with oriental sensuousness and said to be "alien" ("ξενίζουν") to "Hellenism." On the other hand, they would have been accepted within the context of the Greek philosophical schools, which typically cultivated homosocial and homosexual bonds. One thing comes across loud and clear: Cavafy's speaker feels he is masquerading, and Greeks don't do that. His performance in the

---

55. For the latter phrase, see Cavafy, *Complete Poems,* trans. Mendelsohn, 323.
56. See Cavafy, *Complete Poems,* trans. Mendelsohn, 323.

poem is an extended attempt to "[admit] the truth" (11), to do what is becoming or befitting of a Greek, which means, above all, not pretending (9, 15, 25). But we are not sure what kind of Greek the speaker is. Has he migrated from the mainland to Asia, which is now his home, or does he take his Hellenic identity from a life in a Hellenized Asian city? The indeterminacy is calculated, and it informs the poem's drama.

At the heart of Cavafy's piece lies an anxiety about imitation and the real thing. This emerges even more strongly in stanza 3 where the speaker turns from himself to mock lesser Eastern kings who mimic a culture they have conquered but still emulate.[57] These kings are the ones who visit Greek academies not to acquire knowledge, but because knowledge, being both highly valued and Greek, elicits a concocted Hellenization performed through clothing and dress. In putting on Western ways, they cannot help it—"a bit of Arabia peep[s] out every now and then, / a bit of Media they can't keep back" (21–22). In fact, their extravagance lands them in a look that the speaker finds positively Macedonian, in other words, overwrought, outrageous. Eastern contrivances, poorly performed, break the credibility of the façade and become comic. These laughable kings, however, are also "ours" (16), and the "we" associated with them are the speaker and, presumably, Hermippos. But the Greek schools from which the interlocutors are returning are also "ours." The attempt to define that which is Greek founders on the pervious borders of west and east, Greek philosophers and lesser kings, the colonizer and the colonized, all of whom are bound in intricate networks of performing the other.[58]

Having mocked the east while expressing happiness in returning to it, the speaker in the final stanza issues an exhortation to Hermippos that the two of them should not be ashamed "of the Syrian and Egyptian blood / in our veins." Blood in the veins is new information: it suggests a Greek of Syrian-Egyptian extraction who protests too much and, in belittling "our petty kings," lets his own "Arabia" and "Media" peep out. But another way to read the ending is to say that Greeks who have "affections and feelings" sometimes foreign to Greek culture should not be ashamed of the "Arabia" and "Media" that flows in their bodies. The words are code for a valued sexuality that one should not have to express through an orientalist masquerade: "For Greeks like us that kind of pettiness won't do" (26). And yet what to do about it? The poem opens up multiple Hellenisms and links them loosely with alternative sexualities. Hermippos might have had something to say about this, but that is left up to the

---

57. Cavafy, *Complete Poems*, trans. Mendelsohn, 57.
58. Jeffreys, *Eastern Questions*, 89–91.

reader to ponder.[59] His silence is performative; it is part of the discursive range of the poem, which is constructed as a voyage in passage.

There is another form of passage one encounters in Cavafy's poetry, and it takes shape around the notion that the ancient Greek gods, though overthrown in history, nonetheless inhabit a landscape bristling with their elusive presence. "Ionic" ("Ἰωνικόν"), a lyrical piece that Cavafy revised in three different versions (1896, 1905, 1911), is constructed as an apostrophe to the "land of Ionia," a geographical area on the Aegean coast of Asia Minor from which Homer is reputed to have come. Its speaker may be a figure from the late classical or early Christian period who has witnessed the destruction of pagan antiquities.[60] But the voice is sufficiently general to allow a number of other speakers who could bear witness to the attempted razing of a culture that cannot be exterminated. For purposes of this study, the piece is important because it captures an exemplary Cavafian moment: the brief passage through space of an ephebe who embodies a rare sensuality.[61]

"Ionic"

1 That we've broken their statues,

2 that we've driven them out of their temples,

3 doesn't mean at all that the gods are dead.

4 O land of Ionia, they're still in love with you,

5 their souls still keep your memory.

6 When an August dawn wakes over you,

7 your atmosphere is potent with their life,

8 and sometimes a young ethereal figure,

9 indistinct, in rapid flight,

10 wings across your hills.

---

59. See Diskin Clay, "The Silence of Hermippos: Greece in the Poetry of Cavafy," *Greek, Roman, and Byzantine Studies* 3 (1977): 95–116.

60. Several critics see in the poem's reference to destruction the Christian demolishing of pagan temples in the fourth century CE. See Sarah Ekdawi, "Cavafy's Mythical Ephebes," in *Ancient Greek Myth in Modern Greek Poetry: Essays in Memory of C. A. Trypanis*, ed. Constantine Athanasius and Peter Mackridge (London: Frank Cass, 1996), 37. Mendelsohn refers us to the Roman emperor Attalus (d. after 416), while Jeffreys points to the invasions into Greece of the Goths in 396 CE. Jusdanis contextualizes the poem within the terms of the Asia Minor Disaster of 1922 and the expulsion from Turkey of the Greek population, which had inhabited Ionia since antiquity.

61. Cavafy, *Collected Poems*, trans. Keeley and Sherrard, 62–63.

" Ἰωνικόν"

1 Γιατί τὰ σπάσαμε τ᾽ ἀγάλματα των,
2 γιατὶ τοὺς διώξαμεν ἀπ᾽ τοὺς ναούς των,
3 διόλου δὲν πέθαναν γι᾽ αὐτὸ οἱ θεοί.
4 ᾿Ω γῆ τῆς Ἰωνίας, σένα ἀγαποῦν ἀκόμη,
5 σένα ἡ ψυχές των ἐνθουμοῦνται ἀκόμη.
6 Σὰν ξημερώνει ἐπάνω σου πρωῖ αὐγουστιάτικο
7 τὴν ἀτμοσφαίρα σου περνᾶ σφρῖγος ἀπ᾽ τὴν ζωή των·
8 καὶ κάποτ᾽ αἰθερία ἐφηβικὴ μορφή,
9 ἀόριστη, με διάβα γρήγορο,
10 ἐπάνω ἀπὸ τοὺς λόφους σου περνᾶ.

The poem is divided into two halves: the first five lines refer to the breaking of pagan monuments ("statues" and "temples") and the "driving out" of the gods thought to inhabit them; the second five lines reverse the action and redeem the loss through a claim that the gods still live. As is often the case in Cavafy, the divine life that endures is conceived in the idealized form of a youth, one who passes ethereally above a hill when the light is right, as on an August morning. The verb expressing the action of passing through is *"per-nao,"* and it signifies not only passage, but also detour—the gods' evasion of or escape from attempts to eradicate them. Others have noted that Cavafy's wording echoes the *Homeric Hymn to Hermes,* in which the god is at one point captured in his swift movement to "the bright crests of Mount Cyllene" ("καλὸν δὲ φόως κατέλαμπε Σελήνης") and in his entry "through a key-hole in a cave's door, like the autumn breeze, even as mist" ("δοχμωθεὶς μεγάροιο διὰ κλήιθρον ἔδυνεν / αὔρη ὀπωρινῇ ἐναλίγκιος, ἠΰτ᾽ ὀμίχλη," 140–50).[62]

The collective first-person voice of this poem—the "we"—splits over the course of ten lines.[63] While the speaker feels complicit in the destruction of ancient Ionia's architectural and sculptural treasures, he also celebrates the enduring vitality of its divinities. In the ambience of sun-struck hills at the height of summer, the Greek gods live, and occasionally one of them materializes, if only ethereally. Much of the power of this lyric arises from the simplicity of the evocation. Whoever he is, the speaker sees in a special way, and the present tense renders his perception timeless. The "we" who compose the audience are carried up in the "we" who have destroyed, and whatever doubts there might be about celestial beings, they are overcome. Because they are still

---

62. Cavafy, *Complete Poems,* trans. Mendelsohn, 439–40, citing Diana Haas.

63. For different readings of the irony in the poem, see Roderick Beaton, "C. P. Cavafy: Irony and Hellenism," *Slavonic and East European Review* 59.4 (1981): 516–28; and Edmund Keeley, "Cavafy's Voice and Context," *Grand Street* 2.3 (1983): 157–77.

"in love with" Ionia, the gods endure, and in an eternal present, "their souls still keep your memory." The poem situates the audience in the presence of a visionary acuteness that transcends historical catastrophe.

"Going Back Home from Greece" and "Ionic" lead us into the fuller exploration of passage, detour, and young male beauty that we find in "One of their Gods" ("Ένας Θεός τῶν," 1917). The ephebe is a distinctive figure in Cavafy's poetry, and before exploring how he is treated in this poem, he may be approached generically.[64] In antiquity, he was a male between the ages of about seventeen to twenty who underwent a military initiation rite into manhood. Cavafy's ephebe is young too, but he is also handsome, intoxicatingly fragrant, lithe, and boyish rather than muscled. His hair is typically black, his movement graceful and alluring, and he is Greek, or someone who has command of the Greek language, regardless of ethnicity. Not only is he aesthetically pleasing to look upon, but he is often an aesthete himself, given to a love of poetry, painting, sculpture, and the arts. This brings him close to the connoisseur. Though he may live at the margins of power, his social class does not define him; he typically exists in the past tense. But he may be reclaimed from anonymity through the poetry that memorializes his extraordinary qualities.

"One of Their Gods" features all these elements of the Cavafian ephebe. Its setting is Seleucia, which we have already encountered, the name of numerous cities under the rule of the Seleucid kings of Asia Minor who came to power after the death of Alexander. Its homoeroticism is more explicit than in "Ionic," and it makes use of coded words that Cavafy associates with decadence. It also features heightened vision.[65]

"One of Their Gods"

1 Whenever one of them moved through the marketplace of Selefkia
        [Seleucia]
2 just as it was getting dark—
3 moved like a young man, tall, extremely handsome,
4 with the joy of being immortal in his eyes,
5 with his black and perfumed hair—
6 the people going by would gaze at him
7 and one would ask the other if he knew him,
8 if he was a Greek from Syria, or a stranger.
9 But one who looked more carefully
10 would understand and step aside;

---

64. See Ekdawi, "Cavafy's Mythical Ephebes."
65. Cavafy, *Collected Poems*, trans. Keeley and Sherrard, 134–35.

11 and as he disappeared under the arcades,
12 among the shadows and the evening lights,
13 going toward the quarter that lives
14 only at night, with orgies and debauchery,
15 with every kind of intoxication and desire,
16 they would wonder which of Them it could be,
17 and for what suspicious pleasure
18 he had come down into the streets of Selefkia [Seleucia]
19 from the August Celestial Mansions.

" Ἕνας Θεός τῶν"
1 Ὅταν κανένας των περνοῦσεν ἀπ' τῆς Σελευκείας
2 τὴν ἀγορά, περὶ τὴν ὥρα ποὺ βραδυάζει
3 σὰν ὑψηλὸς καὶ τέλεια ὡραῖος ἔφηβος,
4 μὲ τὴν χαρὰ τῆς ἀφθαρσίας μὲς στὰ μάτια,
5 μὲ τ' ἀρωματισμένα μαῦρα του μαλλιά,
6 οἱ διαβάται τὸν ἐκύτταζαν
7 κι' ὁ ἕνας τὸν ἄλλονα ρωτοῦσεν ἂν τὸν γνώριζε,
8 κι ἂν ἦταν Ἕλλην τῆς Συρίας, ἢ ξένος. Ἀλλὰ μερικοί,
9 ποὺ μὲ περισσοτέρα προσοχὴ παρατηροῦσαν,
10 ἐκαταλάμβανον καὶ παραμέριζαν·
11 κ' ἐνῶ ἐχάνετο κάτω ἀπ' τὲς στοές,
12 μὲς στὲς σκιὲς καὶ μὲς στὰ φῶτα τῆς βραδυᾶς,
13 πιαίνοντας πρὸς τὴν συνοικία ποὺ τὴν νύχτα
14 μονάχα ζεῖ, μὲ ὄργια καὶ κραιπάλη,
15 καὶ κάθε εἴδους μέθη καὶ λαγνεία,
16 ἐρέμβαζαν ποιὸς τάχα ἦταν Αὐτῶν,
17 καὶ γιὰ ποιὰν ὕποπτην ἀπόλαυσί του
18 στῆς Σελευκείας τοὺς δρόμους ἐκατέβηκεν
19 ἀπ' τὰ Προσκυνητά, Πάνσεπτα Δώματα.

The poem is structured in three parts: 1) lines 1 through the near end of line 8 bring the male subject into view in a crowded Eastern agora across which he is passing while being watched by people who gaze at him (the verb related to "passage" is the same as the one in "Ionic," *pernao*); 2) lines 8 through 10 identify a small group of spectators with an alert sense of who he is and what he is doing; and 3) lines 11 through 19 describe the sector of the city into which he is descending and speculate about which of "Them" (16)—the ones who inhabit the "August Celestial Mansions"—the young male might be. Keely and Sherrard do not capitalize "Them" in line 16, but Cavafy does, just as he capital-izes the place of residence in line 19. These words single out the figure as one among a select few. While the verse is not rhymed, it makes use of a long line, multisyllabic words, and sound effects rooted in assonance and alliteration. The past tense suggests a memory aroused through reflection upon a subject who is distanced from the speaker, but not a phantom as in "Ionic."

In its illumination of an elevated ephebe, "One of Their Gods" recalls Homeric similes that feature a human being likened to a divinity. A good example appears in *Odyssey 6*, the Nausicaa episode, in which Odysseus reaches land after departing from the island of Calypso and having survived a storm sent by Poseidon. The bard describes his arrival as a *nostos* (5.347; 5.344), not a final, but an intermediate one, among people who come to per-ceive his distinction. Shipwrecked, Odysseus is shown hospitality by Nausi-caa, and after washing and clothing himself in the garments she lends him, he emerges from the brush transformed, his appearance described in a simile:

> . . . Zeus' daughter Athena made him taller to all eyes,
> his build more massive now, and down from his brow
> she ran his curls like thick hyacinth clusters
> full of blooms. As a master craftsman washes
> gold over beaten silver—a man the god of fire
> and Queen Athena trained in every fine technique—
> and finishes off his latest effort, handsome work,
> so she lavished splendor over his head and shoulders now.
> And down to the beach he walked and sat apart,
> Glistening in his glory, breathtaking, yes,
> and the princess gazed in wonder . . .
> (6.253–63)

> . . . τὸν μὲν Ἀθηναίη θῆκεν, Διὸς ἐκγεγαυῖα,
> μείζονά τ᾿ εἰσιδέειν καὶ πάσσονα, κὰδ δὲ κάρητος
> οὔλας ἧκε κόμας, ὑακινθίνῳ ἄνθει ὁμοίας.
> ὡς δ᾿ ὅτε τις χρυσὸν περιχεύεται ἀργύρῳ ἀνὴρ
> ἴδρις, ὃν Ἥφαιστος δέδαεν καὶ Παλλὰς Ἀθήνη
> τέχνην παντοίην, χαρίεντα δὲ ἔργα τελείει,
> ὡς ἄρα τῷ κατέχευε χάριν κεφαλῇ τε καὶ ὤμοις.
> ἕζετ᾿ ἔπειτ᾿ ἀπάνευθε κιὼν ἐπὶ θῖνα θαλάσσης,
> κάλλεϊ καὶ χάρισι στίλβων· θηεῖτο δὲ κούρη.
> (6.229–37)

In Homer's simile, Athena is compared to a craftsman of precious metals who has learned his skill (*techne*) from Athena (also Hephaestus). In other words, the simile is circular: Athena crafts like the craftsman who has learned from Athena. It captures Odysseus within a sphere of artistic form that divinizes him. The word "*charis*," from which we get charm and charisma, is repeated three times in four lines, emphatically raising the bar on standards of physical attractiveness. *Charis*, in turn, is linked with *techne*: things that bear this quality do so through artifice. Thanks to Athena, Odysseus appears taller and more muscled, with hair that falls like hyacinths. His beauty requires the complementary act of spectating, and Nausicaa finds him stunning.

"One of Their Gods" performs a number of feats, but among them is a strategic inversion of the Homeric simile. If Odysseus is a man made to look like a god, Cavafy's ephebe is a god made to look like a man: he comes from above, spatially—from "August Celestial Mansions," in which a select few reside. Rather than being characterized in terms of strength and bulk, his height is a signal quality. He stands "tall, perfectly handsome" (3). In both cases, the hair receives special mention: it tumbles like hyacinth flowers in the *Odyssey*, and it is fragrant (5) in "One of Their Gods," the latter a poetic line that caresses with its assonance of the *mu* sound. Because the word for "hair," which is "*mallia*" (5), rhymes with the word for "eyes," which is "*matia*" (4), the reader is invited to look more carefully at the phrase that Keeley and Sherrard translate as "with the joy of being immortal in his eyes"; Mendelsohn prefers "the joy of incorruptibility in his eyes" (4), and the line condenses the complex tonality of the whole poem.[66] The word "joy" translates "*chara*," a modern Greek variant of the Homeric *charis*, and the word "immortality" is a translation of "*aphtharsia*," which can also signify "incorruptibility." By saying that the ephebe has "the joy of *aphtharsia* in his eyes," Cavafy's speaker is playing on the idea that the sexually deviant is divine, pure, eternal. In doing so, he is taking hold of a passage conceived as a *katabasis*—a descent into another world—and using it to craft a realignment of values. It is the "night, with orgies and debauchery, / with every kind of intoxication and desire," that is godlike (14–15). This is the life one finds "under the arcades / among the shadows and the evening lights" (11–12). The dirty is the pure, the dark is the resplendent, down is up—oxymoronic combinations that resonate with "Days of 1896."

These realignments are a consequence of how the poem shapes the act of spectating. The speaker who sees the ephebe as a god is one of the initiated. It is from his perspective that the viewers in the poem divide into two groups:

---

66. Cavafy, *Complete Poems*, trans. Mendelsohn, 65.

those who see but cannot recognize the figure passing before them and the few, identified at the end of line 9, who know he is holy but wonder which of "Them" he is. In a line that pops with the *pi* sound, the latter are said not only to "look more carefully" ("περισσοτέρα προσοχὴ παρατηροῦσαν"); they also understand who he is and step aside to let him pass. They are the ones who sense they are beholding a divinity.

Passage in Cavafy—the literary use of it in metaphorically conceived journeys or crossings—can sometimes turn on the image of a wound; one thinks of Remon in "A Town in Osroini," although that is not really a poem about passage. One is much more likely to find this trope connected with explorations of diaspora, as in "Going Back Home From Greece," or with ephebic imagery, as in "Ionic" and "One of Their Gods," which makes sense since in the ancient world the ephebe is by definition in a liminal state between boyhood and manhood—in transit, as it were. Stirring behind the young male Cavafian body is the touch of divinity or the aura of an epiphanic moment whose allure lies partly in the impossibility of possession. Accidental though the connection is, the young Odysseus in the boar hunt is ephebic as well, but he is much more emphatically associated with a wound, as we have seen in the episode of Eurycleia's footwashing, which in turn suggests psychic blockages that divert rather than facilitate *nostos*. Rebirth in the epic—the passage from anonymity into another life—is in tension with a proclivity to withdraw, enacted in scenarios where Odysseus avoids self-disclosure.

Mutating identities emerge in *Cahier* as well, often in connection with the three-souled Antillean, part African, part European, part Carib; they are bound up in detours that are sometimes demystifying and sometimes psychically regressive. Césaire uses shifting personas to enact the decolonization of the mind from the forces that bury it in debilitating states of inferiority and submission. Here masks are a poetic composite of African and Western forms of expression that access identities in a cyclical process of ascent and descent. In *Orlando*, transsexuality and cross-dressing serve similar purposes, enabling mobility across the boundaries of sex, class, and ethnicity. Caught up in carnivalesque movements, they produce a spectrum of orientalisms that by turn affirm and undermine Western views of normative embodiment. Metaphorical *katabasis* is key for both Woolf and Césaire, just as it can be for Cavafy, who performs his own transvaluations of sexuality through descents that are also immersions in the sublime world of homoerotic pleasure.

CHAPTER 4

Return and Split Endings

Happy endings are best achieved by keeping the right doors locked.
—Margaret Atwood, *The Penelopiad*

Through the diasporic Mediterranean of Cavafy, the orientalized Constantinople of Woolf, and the triangulated soul of Césaire's
Caribbean, the trope of passage and detour winds its way, linking
the wound with the wandering word or inverting *katabasis* into a movement
of ascent. While the *Odyssey,* and notably the episode of Odysseus's scar, isn't
foregrounded in these lateral journeys across space and time, a poetics of indirection—of alternative tales, shifting masks, essayistic venturing, stories half
told—once again shapes much of the action. Telling it slant is not only characteristic of the personas and characters we encounter within the literary works
but of the poets who craft them.

It won't be surprising then that endings are enigmatic in the works we
have been examining, or in the case of Cavafy, since we are dealing with multiple poems, a sense of how journeys of pleasure and of personal trial sus-
pend teleology. Return is a conundrum for our writers, and by troping it as
such, they leave us contemplating enigmas. The *Odyssey* confronts the audience with a split ending so dramatic that it not only undermines the entire
notion of *nostos* as homecoming but raises questions, once again, about second odysseys. So do the poems by Cavafy that we will be examining in this
part, chiefly "Ithaca" and "Ships," which offer ways of articulating both the
hedonic voyage and the treacherous metaphorical journey of the imagination into print. Like Cavafy, Césaire, too, makes use of nautical imagery in

negotiating the open ending of *Cahier*, particularly in his image of the fierce pirogue on rough waters. He couples it with the incised tree of life, which lives on despite the lacerations it endures, its bark productive even as it continues to sustain injury. Provocatively, Woolf's *Orlando* presents us with its own boat and a tree, the former related to the maritime life of the man whom the protagonist marries, the latter associated with the oak tree—the organism in nature and its life in a book whose publication is deeply ambiguous. Both may be productively coupled with the famous tree linked with the marital bed in *Odyssey* 23.

HOMER: MURDER IN THE HOME AND SPLIT ENDINGS

Because ancient epic developed in a long oral history of transmission, the bard may be imagined as a storyteller with narrative latitude, working in an environment where he was aware of multiple ways of telling tales. He could shape these stories around the conditions of performance, thereby adapting to different platforms for acknowledging local interests in the stories he chose to tell.[1] As the various strains of epic song emerged in an early stage of diffusion, so did the Trojan *nostos* tales, Homer's among them, and ultimately the one that dominated the wider competition. The *Odyssey*, as we have seen, preserves evidence of a Cretan rather than an Ithacan Odysseus. In addition, Homer is likely to have known whole stories or elements of stories that took shape around works that compose the epic cycle.[2] This includes the *Telegony*, which tells of what happens to Odysseus and Penelope after the hero recovers his kingdom. While that epic has not survived, a summary of its plot has.[3] Provocatively reaching beyond its own borders, Homer's epic opens outward to touch alternative traditions even as it moves toward its own end. In doing so, it renews questions about the meaning of *nostos*, the broader question of

---

1. See Nagy, *Poetry as Performance: Homer and Beyond* (New York: Cambridge University Press, 1996); and *Homeric Questions* (Austin: University of Texas Press, 1996). Scholars building upon his work, especially with respect to the final two books of the *Odyssey*, include Burgess, *Tradition of the Trojan War*; and J. Marks, *Zeus in the* Odyssey (Washington, DC: Center for Hellenic Studies, 2008), ch. 3.

2. For a general treatment of the epic cycle, see Fantuzzi and Tsagalis, "Introduction," in *Greek Epic Cycle*, online without pagination; Gregory Nagy, "Oral Traditions, Written Texts, and Questions of Authorship," in *Greek Epic Cycle*, online without pagination; Burgess, *Tradition of the Trojan War*, 1–6; and Malcolm Davies, *The Greek Epic Cycle*, 2nd ed. (London: Bristol Press, 2001).

3. See Proclus, *Chrestomachy*, in *Hesiod, the Homeric Hymns, Epic Cycle, and Homerica*, trans. Hugh G. Evelyn-White, rev. ed. (Cambridge, MA: Harvard University, 1970).

the relationship between humans and gods, and the fundamental need for storytelling, both personal and collective.

In many ways, the *Odyssey* seems poised to present the audience with a satisfying conclusion to the wanderings of Odysseus. Having struggled ten years to get back home, the hero finally arrives on Ithaca. After a series of recognition scenes in which he tests the fidelity of his wife and loved ones, he takes his revenge upon the suitors and is reinstated as king, husband, and father. Reinforcing the sense of closure is the narrative use of ring composition: just as Book 1 of the epic begins with a council of the Olympian gods in which Zeus and Athena strategize on getting the hero off the island of Ogygia where Calypso is holding him captive, so, too, Book 24 ends with a divine council in which the two Olympians devise a way to ensure peace on Ithaca after the slaughter of the suitors. Yet the end of the epic is notoriously vexed, and the problems only begin with the judgment of two great ancient editors of Homer's poems, Aristophanes of Byzantium (ca. 257–185 BCE) and Aristarchus of Samothrace (ca. 220–143 BCE). In their view, Book 24 of the epic and the last seventy-six lines of Book 23 are later additions to the *Odyssey*. The judgment rests on the scholia, linguistic elements, and narrative structure.[4] According to this view, the Homeric epic ends immediately after the recognition scene of Odysseus and Penelope when the couple return "to their bed / and the old familiar place they loved so well" (23.337–38; "λέκτροιο παλαιοῦ θεσμὸν ἵκοντο," 23.296). The critical literature on this topic is substantial, and it cannot be summarized here. Instead the focus will be on the competing "romantic" and "apocalyptic" endings that the poem holds open, the first of which prominently features Penelope, the other Odysseus.

An overview of the final books of the epic will help flesh out the different ways in which the received text may be interpreted. In rough outline, these are the major episodes:

> Book 22: After winning the contest of the bow, Odysseus slaughters the suitors. The disloyal maids are then hung, and the evil herdsman Melanthius is mutilated and killed. At this point, Odysseus calls for "fire and brimstone" (22.521; "πῦρ καὶ θήιον," 22.493) to purify the great hall and sends Eurycleia to awaken Penelope and bring her downstairs.

---

4. We have the reports on Aristophanes's and Aristarchus's views from the scholia for the *Odyssey*. For discussions of where the *Odyssey* ends, see Heubeck, *Commentary on Homer's Odyssey*, 3:353–54; Richard Seaford, *Reciprocity and Ritual: Homer and Tragedy in the Developing City-State* (Oxford: Clarendon, 1992), 38–42, 72–73; Christos Tsagalis, "*Odyssey* 24.191–202: A Reconsideration," *Wiener Studien* 116 (2003): 43–56; and Marks, *Zeus in the Odyssey*, ch 3.

Book 23: In the megaron, while Odysseus is still covered in gore, the long recognition scene between husband and wife unfolds and concludes with his revelation that his journeys are not over. He must set out again. The two turn to love making, and here the shorter *Odyssey* ends. In the longer *Odyssey*, pillow talk ensues, and Odysseus relates the tale of his wanderings in summary form to a captivated wife, while she tells of events on Ithaca in his absence.

Book 24: A second *nekuia*, or book of the dead, follows (the first is Odysseus's visit to Hades in Book 11), in which the ghosts of the suitors meet up with the Greeks killed in the Trojan War. The recognition scene between Odysseus and Laertes follows, and the two of them, together with Telemachus, face a standoff with the surviving members of the suitors' families who want revenge. It takes the intervention of Zeus and Athena to resolve the dispute.

To sum up, the shortened form ends happily, if not ever after, at least with a restored household, a saved marriage, and prospects of future peace. Or so it seems. Penelope is given a privileged place as the character who culminates the theme of homecoming, and through her the epic fashions a notion of what marital fidelity under duress can deliver in the way of social redemption. In this case, the epic rests its eye on the rather narrow ground of domestic order where the like-mindedness of the spouses becomes subordinate to household management. Laertes is not part of this picture since his recognition scene is in Book 24.

Romance, though the term had not yet been invented, is a useful way of characterizing such a narrative ending, which softens blows, washes away blood, and brings harmony to the bittersweet labors of survival. Even so, the shorter text of the *Odyssey* makes one pause. It would bring the epic to an end just a few lines after Odysseus explains to his wife that he must leave again. Not only does this disrupt the sense of *nostos* as achieved homecoming, but it also makes the audience focus on Odysseus's impending departure just as he is about to slide into bed with his long-suffering wife. Intimacy is disrupted by a new alienation, all the more so since the journey it anticipates is described as a labor "boundless, laden with danger, great and long, / which [he] must brave out from start to finish" (23.283–85; "ἀμέτρητος πόνος ἔσται, / πολλὸς καὶ χαλεπός, τὸν ἐμὲ χρὴ πάντα τελέσσαι," 23.249–50). The estrangement is deepened by Odysseus's addition of an important detail to the prediction of the future journey that is not found in Teiresias's original words to him during the visit to the underworld (11.136–56; 11.118–37). There the prophet says that upon his return, after killing the suitors, he must set out again carrying an oar on his shoulder until he comes to people who know nothing of the sea. When he sees a traveler who mistakes his oar for a winnowing fan, he has to plant it in the earth and sacrifice to Poseidon. Upon his return to Ithaca, a peaceful death will come to him "from the sea" ("ἐξ ἁλός," 23.281). What he tells Penelope, by contrast, is that he will have to travel "through towns on towns of men" (23.305; "πολλὰ βροτῶν ἐπὶ ἄστεα," 23.267) before finding these people, and this suggests an extended journey by land that would rival the one on water he has survived.[5] The meaning of "from the sea," as scholars have shown, is ambiguous since it may signify death coming from out of the sea or death coming far away from the sea, in an inland location identified with the planted oar.

Just as Homer points in the direction of a Cretan odyssey earlier in the Ithacan books, he points in the direction of yet another odyssey here as Penelope, having pressed her question, replies rather distantly, "If the gods grant you a happy old age, / There is hope that someday a release from your troubles will come" (author's translation; "εἰ μὲν δὴ γῆράς γε θεοὶ τελέουσιν ἄρειον, / ἐλπωρή τοι ἔπειτα κακῶν ὑπάλυξιν ἔσεσθαι," 23.286–87). The conditional mood, the vague reference to time, and the rather cool tone bring into view an unclosed gap between husband and wife in the aftermath of a lengthy *anagnorisis*. Is the *Odyssey*, as it nears the moment when Penelope drops out of its narrative—she does not appear in Book 24—indicating that she has a life in another odyssey where her husband's struggles will not be hers, a narrative in which she enters new identities and narrative horizons? Some see in these lines an oblique reference to alternative tales that connect Odysseus with Thesprotia on the Greek mainland and that coalesce with the *Telegony*.[6] This is an epic that breaks loose from the values of marital fidelity, Ithacan patriarchy, and even the primacy of Odysseus. It follows, among other things, the fortunes of Penelope who marries Telegonus, Odysseus's son by Circe; Telemachus who marries Circe; and Odysseus who dies at the hands of his unwitting son Telegonus. The *Telegony* is an incest-cum-patricide tale that rivals the horrors of Greek tragedy. In this alternative odyssey, Penelope and Telemachus, in sharp contrast with Odysseus, are eventually granted immor-

---

5. For recent discussions of Odysseus's second journey, see Jonathan Burgess, "The Death of Odysseus in the *Odyssey* and the *Telegony*," *Antiqua* 7 (2014): 111–22; and Christos Tsagalis, *The Oral Palimpsest: Exploring Intertextuality in the Homeric Epics* (Washington, DC: Center for Hellenic Studies, 2008), ch. 4.

6. See Rebecca Rohdenberg and J. Marks, "Taphians and Thesprotians within and beyond the *Odyssey*," *Kyklos* 1 (2012), accessed 5 May 2019, https://chs.harvard.edu/CHS/article/display/5194; and Marks, *Zeus in the* Odyssey, ch. 4.

tality. If Homer's poem is looking beyond itself in the act of indicating its own limits, its insistence on an eventual happy end for its hero may be working against the undertow of a rival epic tradition that insists otherwise. That is, it is imagining an epic whose topography, values, and life experiences are sufficiently different from those of the *Odyssey* that they could not be told in the language of *this* epic.[7]

From such a perspective, Penelope's skeptical approach to Odysseus in the recognition scene of Book 23 looks two ways: towards a past in which belief in rumors could have, but did not, undermine the marital fidelity that the epic supports, and toward a future in another return tale once the *Odyssey* is finished. Significantly in Homer's epic, she is spared direct contact with the slaughter of the suitors. Athena has averted her mind, or *noos,* once again, this time not away from Odysseus's scar and the wound that produced it, but away from bloodshed in the great hall. In being removed from acts of violence connected with *nostos,* her own role in bringing it about is more fully defined by *metis* than is Odysseus's. She continues to use ruses; he resorts to killing. She has clean hands; he doesn't. Their *homophrosyne* is actually weakening as centrifugal forces continue to pull them apart.

The twists and turns of the recognition scene in Book 23 bear witness to how choppy the waters in fact are between the spouses. As Penelope is awakened and Eurycleia informs her that Odysseus has returned and killed the suitors, she both advances and withdraws from the act of meeting him.[8] She thinks that the gods have driven the nurse crazy. Giving momentary rein to her sense of joy as the nurse presses her, she asks how one man could kill so many others, to which Eurycleia replies, she is not sure, but when she returned to the great hall, "[she] found Odysseus in the thick of slaughtered corpses; / there he stood and all around him, over the beaten floor, the bodies sprawled in heaps, lying one on another . . ." (23.48–50; "εὗρον ἔπειτ' Ὀδυσῆα μετὰ κταμένοισι νέκυσσιν / ἑσταόθ'· οἱ δέ μιν ἀμφί, κραταίπεδον οὖδας ἔχοντες, / κείατ' ἐπ' ἀλλήλοισιν," 23.45–47). Not even the nurse's report that she has seen Odysseus's scar wins over her mistress. Consequently, it is hardly surprising that Penelope, rather than running to greet her husband, tentatively descends the stairs into the great hall. What follows is an extraordinary scene that is controlled, not by Odysseus, but by Penelope.

---

7. See Alex Purves, "Unmarked Space: Odysseus and the Inland Journey," *Arethusa* 39 (2006): 1–20.

8. For a fuller discussion of skepticism and deferral in this recognition scene, see Zerba, *Doubt and Skepticism,* 108–10.

As soon as she stepped across the stone threshold,
slipping in, she took a seat at the closest wall
and radiant in the firelight, faced Odysseus now.
There he sat, leaning against the great central column,
eyes fixed on the ground, waiting, poised for whatever words
his hardy wife might say when she caught sight of him . . .
One moment he seemed . . . Odysseus, to the life—
the next, no, he was not the man she knew,
a huddled mass of rags was all she saw.
(23.100–110)

ἣ δ᾽ ἐπεὶ εἰσῆλθεν καὶ ὑπέρβη λάινον οὐδόν,
ἕζετ᾽ ἔπειτ᾽ Ὀδυσῆος ἐναντίον, ἐν πυρὸς αὐγῇ,
τοίχου τοῦ ἑτέρου· ὃ δ᾽ ἄρα πρὸς κίονα μακρὴν
ἧστο κάτω ὁρόων, ποτιδέγμενος εἴ τί μιν εἴποι
ἰφθίμη παράκοιτις, ἐπεὶ ἴδεν ὀφθαλμοῖσιν.
ἣ δ᾽ ἄνεω δὴν ἧστο, τάφος δέ οἱ ἦτορ ἵκανεν·
ὄψει δ᾽ ἄλλοτε μέν μιν ἐνωπαδίως ἐσίδεσκεν,
ἄλλοτε δ᾽ ἀγνώσασκε κακὰ χροῒ εἵματ᾽ ἔχοντα.
(23.88–95)

This is literally a threshold moment. The entry of Penelope across physical space is conceived as liminal with respect to the great hall; the word for this boundary is "*oudos*," and it is repeated later in the scene, thus underscoring the divisions of the domestic interior. While Odysseus is not exactly hiding from her, he is hanging his head protectively in dirty rags that continue to disguise him, Calypso-style. The semantic field of the goddess is conveyed in the description of his clothings as "κακὰ εἵματα," words that recall the garments of the Concealer.

It is not so much the rags that put Penelope off as the fact that they are spattered, like the man before her, with blood and gore, signifying that he has not undergone ritual purification and therefore is, in a literal sense, untouchable. Visually mediating the moment of first contact between husband and wife are material signs of a mass killing—within the home. Where are all those bodies? The audience hears that they have been propped against each other "under the courtyard colonnade" (22.474; "κὰδ᾽ ἄρ᾽ ὑπ᾽ αἰθούσῃ τίθεσαν εὐερκέος αὐλῆς," 22.449) and later that they are "all stacked at the courtyard gates" (23.53; "οἳ μὲν δὴ πάντες ἐπ᾽ αὐλείῃσι θύρῃσιν / ἀθρόοι," 23.49). In the second *nekuia*, one of the ghosts, Amphimedon, says they are still unburied (24.206; 24.186–87), and near the end we finally hear that the families

have recovered the bodies for burial (24.461–64; 24.417–19). Homer emphasizes their spatial location between the worlds of the living and the dead, and
they haunt the scene between husband and wife. Penelope sees the man with
his head bowed low, but has trouble recognizing him. He remains effectively
undisclosed, obscure, as she tests him. He understands this because as he
waits to be acknowledged by his wife, he turns to Telemachus and observes,

> But you and I,
> put heads together. What's our best defense?
> When someone kills a lone man in the realm
> who leaves behind him no great band of avengers,
> still the killer flees, goodbye to kin and country.
> But we brought down the best of the island's princes,
> the pillars of Ithaca. Weigh it well, I urge you.
> (23.132–39)

> ἡμεῖς δὲ φραζώμεθ᾽, ὅπως ὄχ᾽ ἄριστα γένηται.
> καὶ γάρ τίς θ᾽ ἕνα φῶτα κατακτείνας ἐνὶ δήμῳ,
> ᾧ μὴ πολλοὶ ἔωσιν ἀοσσητῆρες ὀπίσσω,
> φεύγει πηούς τε προλιπὼν καὶ πατρίδα γαῖαν·
> ἡμεῖς δ᾽ ἔρμα πόληος ἀπέκταμεν, οἳ μέγ᾽ ἄριστοι
> κούρων εἰν᾽ Ἰθάκῃ· τὰ δέ σε φράζεσθαι ἄνωγα.
> (23.117–22)

Think about that indeed. Deliberately pointing to civic institutions—the
words *demos* and *polis* are used by Homer within a couple of lines of each
other—Odysseus acknowledges that he and his son should be exiled for the
slaughter. What kind of *nostos* is that? The audience is brought back to the
inland journey.

The oar in Teiresias's prophecy about a second odyssey is described in
Greek as a *sema*, a "sign," (23.310; "σῆμα," 23.273) of how Odysseus will know
where he must "plant [the] oar in the earth" (23.315; "καὶ τότε δὴ γαίῃ πήξαντ᾽
ἐκέλευσεν ἐρετμόν," 23. 276).[9] He will meet a traveler who thinks he is carrying a winnowing fan, and in that place, he must ground this object connected
to the fluid element. Because he will come across this traveler only after wandering to many cities, the *sema* as winnowing fan also becomes a mark of a
certain kind of society, one that lives not by water, but by the land it cultivates.
This land is so far away from water that boats are foreign to it. In this sense,

---

9. See Purves, "Unmarked Space," 11–8; and Burgess, "Death of Odysseus."

the prophecy, as Odysseus relates it to Penelope, echoes the first words of the epic, which introduce the hero as one who "[saw] many cities of men . . . and learned their minds" (1.4; "πολλῶν δ᾽ ἀνθρώπων ἴδεν ἄστεα καὶ νόον ἔγνω," 1.3). As already observed, these lines do not accurately represent *this* odyssey. The Odysseus who comes closest to matching the figure described in the proem is the worldly traveler who encounters cities with ways of life alien to a sea people—the Odysseus of the prophecy. If the epic points obliquely away from itself in Book 23 even as it moves toward wrapping up, it also begins that way by alluding to a hero from another epic tradition who has traveled the paths of song. That would embed the *Odyssey* within a wider range of non-Homeric *nostos* tales—tales that cross cultural and semantic boundaries, the planted oar being a symbol of this crossing.

In folkloric studies of the *Odyssey*, critics have shown that "the sailor and the oar" is a traditional tale in which a teller is likely to be evaluating the differences between two ways of life, the sea being associated with greater hardship and risk than the land.[10] The act of planting the oar evokes an existence marked by relative calm over time. From this perspective, as already seen, the prediction that Odysseus will experience a death "from the sea" is ambiguous since the phrase could mean either "coming out of the sea" or "existing apart from the sea." The cunning ambivalence, of course, is Odyssean. But in the case of the prophecy, it is arguably not Odysseus himself who is equivocating. It is the poem speaking through him about alternative tales, against which it asserts its own authority by marginalizing them. In the epic cycle, these cluster around the *Telegony* and the land of Thesprotia.

Now this semiotically rich oar in Book 23 that signifies another journey abroad appears in the text only fifty lines or so after another semiotically rich image connected to *nostos*, and that is the famous marital bed. Having built it himself around the large and sturdy trunk of an ancient olive tree, Odysseus has crafted an object that is "planted firm" or "immovable" (23.227; "ἔμπεδον," 23.203), in other words an object that symbolically represents conjugal fidelity. Like the oar, it, too, is described as a *sema*—a "*mega sema*" (23.212; "μέγα σῆμα," 23.188), that is, a particularly revealing and meaningful one.[11] Something else about it makes it special: no one knows about its history except Odysseus and Penelope. It is one of their "secrets," or "*krummena*," a word

10. See Tsigalis, *Oral Palimpsest*, ch. 4; and William Hansen, "Odysseus and the Oar: A Comparative Approach to a Greek Legend," in *Approaches to Greek Myth*, ed. Lowell Edmunds, 2nd ed. (Baltimore: Johns Hopkins University Press, 2014), 247–79.

11. See Froma Zeitlin, "Figuring Fidelity in Homer's *Odyssey*," in *The Distaff Side: Representing the Female in Homer's* Odyssey, ed. Beth Cohen (New York: Oxford University Press, 1995), 117–54.

related to that other provocative semiotic chain linked to Calypso / *kalypto* / *krypto*. Because only the two spouses (and one maid) have knowledge of it, the bed is central to the trick Penelope uses as a final test. She pretends it has been moved and thereby arouses the ire of Odysseus who launches into a speech about how he made it. This tale constitutes the proof Penelope needs to acknowledge him as her husband. At this point, one feels a mighty pull in the narrative toward closure. Even the retrograde movements of self-dissimulation, manifest chiefly in the Cretan tales, seem to have issued in a secret well kept and well understood. The man of much cunning can emerge from hiding; his wife can too.

And then comes the oar. Dramatically juxtaposed in the poem, the *semata* of bed and oar create new tension. Both are described in images of planting and grounding. But the stability of the first depends on an Odysseus whose travel supports the wealth of a primary home to which he remains bound. The oar, on the other hand, suggests more radical mobility. The voyage it portends may be a consequence of the murder of the suitors, which the epic takes seriously. It is possible other song traditions such as the *Telegony* associated Odysseus's ongoing wanderings with an act of bloodletting on Ithaca that required exile and purification. In such a case, the *Odyssey* itself would be pointing obliquely to different outcomes, which it sidelines. We will return to the semiotic systems of trees when we explore Césaire's image of the wounded tree of life and Woolf's elaborate play upon Orlando's oak tree, both the thing in nature and the book so closely bound up with it. Despite the differences between these organic objects, they are part of larger narrative drifts that work against a sense of closure.

If Penelope remains strongly aligned with *metis* in the final scenes of the epic, as evidenced in the ruse of the marriage bed, Odysseus turns to force—and force of Achillean proportions. Having stepped up to the threshold of the megaron after the contest of the bow in Book 22, he proceeds to shoot his first arrow directly into the neck of Antinous, the nastiest of the suitors, who literally doesn't see it coming. For the audience, not to mention the archer, there is satisfaction in this long-delayed act. But the picture grows murkier when Odysseus picks up a shield, dons a plumed helmet, and takes two bronze-tipped spears in his hands as he goes on a rampage that could come right out of Homer's war epic. Others have catalogued the Iliadic elements of the slaughter: the formulaic character of the arming scenes (22.116–33, 22.108–25); a challenge to a duel (22.64–71, 22.60–68); divine interventions (22.212–52, 22.205–40); pleas for pity (22.324–41, 22.310–29; 22.346–73, 22.330–60); and a mass of similes (22.311–24, 22.297–309; 22.408–14, 22.383–89; 22.426–30,

22.401–5; 22.494–99, 22.468–72).[12] The irony is thick: Odysseus comes closest
to assuming the role of Achilles at the moment he most dramatically moves to
reclaim his own home, the home from which he has been repeatedly detoured
and that he is now confronting as the space of the enemy, a battlefield. *Nostos*
in the epic could not be more at odds with itself.

On many levels, the slaughter is an act of transgressing in morally ambiguous ways.[13] Odysseus could have accepted compensation, or *time,* from the
suitors for their reckless and wanton acts (*atasthala*) rather than demanding *tisis* and slaughtering them.[14] After Antinous goes down, this is exactly
what the suitor Eurymachus proposes: that Odysseus spare his people and
accept restitution or pay back for his losses (22.57–63; 22.54–59). The response
Eurymachus gets couldn't be more Achillean: "No Eurymachus! Not if you
paid me all your father's wealth—/ no, not even then would I stay my hands
from slaughter / till all you suitors had paid for all your crimes!" (22.65–68;
"Εὐρύμαχ', οὐδ' εἴ μοι πατρώϊα πάντ' ἀποδοῖτε, / ὅσσα τε νῦν ὕμμ' ἐστὶ καὶ
εἴ ποθεν ἄλλ' ἐπιθεῖτε, / οὐδέ κεν ὣς ἔτι χεῖρας ἐμὰς λήξαιμι φόνοιο, / πρὶν
πᾶσαν μνηστῆρας ὑπερβασίην ἀποτῖσαι," 22.61–64). The audience is transported to the embassy scene in *Iliad* 9 when Achilles refuses Agamemnon's
offer of compensation, substantial though it is. While a social mechanism,
then, is available to stem the tide of violence in the *Odyssey, time* is not what
the hero wants. He wants vengeance, or *tisis.* Nowhere in the epic does he live
up so fully to his name—man of hatred and anger (active), but also man hated
and made the target of anger (passive)—as when he stands at the threshold of
the great hall intent upon killing.

Everything in the *Odyssey* seems to support his standing there. The suitors
have acted without fear of the gods or of *nemesis* from men (22.40–42; 22.39–
40). Athena has backed him in seeking revenge (*tisis*) (22.245–46; 22.234–35),
and Zeus himself has backed Athena (5.24–31; 5.23–24 and 24.527–30; 24.479–
80). But what is going to happen when the families of the suitors demand
their own revenge for another lost generation of men, one having already been
picked off in the Trojan War and the journey home, the other now slaughtered
by the returning king? While revenge may taste sweet, even in the blood that
so Homerically "smokes" ("θῦε," 22.309) from the ground, it is so only before

---

12. See de Jong, *Narratological Commentary on the* Odyssey, 524–25.

13. See Michael Nagler, "Odysseus: The Proem and the Problem," *Classical Antiquity* 9.2
(1990): 335–56.

14. On the *time/tisis* relationship in the *Odyssey,* see Alexander Loney, *The Ethics of
Revenge and the Meanings of the* Odyssey (New York: Oxford University Press, 2019), 13–76;
and Marks, *Zeus in the* Odyssey, ch. 3.

the fallout. And it is the fallout that divides the ending. If the *Odyssey* stops at 23.296 (in the Greek text), as Hellenistic editors and some later critics think it does, then the entire standoff dissipates into a cloud of bedroom romance. If the moral dilemma is allowed to take its course, then the audience is facing an apocalyptic end in which virtually everything connected with Ithaca goes to ruin. When the families of the suitors gather at Odysseus's palace to retrieve the bodies, the father of Antinous, Eupeithes, makes a speech on behalf of all of them in which he lays the problem out clearly, saying they will suffer "disgrace" ("λώβη") unless "[they] seek pay back" ("τισόμεθα") from the murders of their sons (24.478–80; 24.433–35).

The gods themselves have been complicit in bringing the crisis to this culmination. In the face of an ongoing blood feud they have fed, Athena intervenes with the backing of Zeus to bring an end to the hostilities—and a puzzling end it is. On the one hand, Zeus requires that the people swear "solemn oaths" (or "seal their pacts," 24.534; "ὅρκια πιστά," 24.483) to let Odysseus be king, and on the other, he will bring them "forgetfulness of the murder" ("a purging of memory," 24.535; "φόνοιο / ἔκλησις," 24.484). That, however, is a radical solution. It goes against the very grain of epic whose purpose lies in remembering. If it is the Ithacans who must be made to forget, then it is only Odysseus who can keep his own tale alive. But he will have to exit the Homeric sphere to do so.

WOOLF: TIME WARPS AND WILD GOOSE CHASES

As the epic nears its end, the plot of the *Odyssey* is increasingly driven by the necessity of revenge upon the suitors for their reckless violations of hospitality. While the necessity emanates from Odysseus's personal grievances, it reflects the crisis of a community, and it has the backing of the gods. Nonetheless, divine approval does nothing to minimize the contradictions posed by the returning king's near obliteration of the male line on Ithaca. Making the survivors forget the slaughter is a poetic device with narrative appeal, but the *Odyssey* covers its bases by engineering an inland journey after the violence that effectively puts Odysseus in exile. Already heavily strained by a twenty-year absence, the marriage of Odysseus and Penelope, which is at the heart of the *nostos* tale, must confront another obstacle that cannot help but crush it. A conjugal bond between partners who are rarely present to one another is a bond in appearance only. This makes the semiotically rich olive tree, which grounds the marriage bed, into a paradox that means other than what it apparently signifies.

The plot of *Orlando* is similarly driven by necessity as the narrative progresses. But here the imperative derives from marriage itself—the oppressive social institution of it, which functions as a mandate to partner for life, according to the prevailing morality. This is the key theme of the Victorian period in Chapter Five of Woolf's fictional biography, and it extends in Chapter Six into the twentieth century. Revenge enters the plot metaphorically through the devices the author introduces to disrupt "divine" laws governing heterosexual coupling, and they come into play via Orlando's continued wanderings after the return to England. As a man, the protagonist could set out for Constantinople and a life of action in the larger world. As a woman, she is more restricted, and the biographer, disturbed by having to deal with the phantasmagoria of the mind, must enter into the psyche of the subject with more depth and understanding.

Now the role of traveler splits, with Orlando exploring the psychic territory of sex, gender, and sexuality on British soil and her ultimately wedded husband, Marmaduke Bonthrop Shelmerdine, extending the geographical journey as a risk taker traveling at the edges of the world. A boyish figure reminiscent of the youthful protagonist, Shelmerdine is said to spend his life "in the most desperate and splendid of adventures—which is to say to voyage round the Cape of Horn in the teeth of a gale" (185). It is partly through him that Orlando comes to grasp the elementary delusions of her youth. His comic book simplicity is a foil to her growing complexity. As in the *Odyssey,* the physical separation of the spouses will keep them only nominally married. But nominally married is all Orlando and Shelmerdine want to be, and so the Cape of Horn rescues both from what might otherwise be a disastrous match.

This brings about a curious turn. While Homer's epic ideologically supports marriage, it continues through the end to estrange husband and wife, not least of all by necessitating other journeys. By contrast, while *Orlando* ideologically questions marriage, it finds paths for the characters to survive an unlikely union. It allows them to remain sexually indeterminate in ways that are agreeable to both, and it endows them with the gift of inventing a private language while enjoying the distance that keeps them apart. Like the *Odyssey,* however, *Orlando* has a split ending, just as almost everything leading up to it involves games of dissembling and indirection that recall the Cretan tales. Marriage, then, as a conventional literary form of the comic ending, is conspicuous for its ruse-like character in both works. This brings us around to another important tree—the oak, which in *Orlando* is both a living organism connected to home and an analogue of a living organism in the form of a manuscript that records wandering from home. If the olive tree is a semiotic

site for rootedness, though an ironized one, the oak tree is a semiotic site of
rootlessness for a subjectivity that in some sense looks for grounding.

This becomes clear upon Orlando's return to England. Because of the legal
suits brought against her, s/he returns to England "in a highly ambiguous
condition, uncertain whether she [is] alive or dead, man or woman, Duke
or nonentity" and lives "incognito or incognita as the case might turn out to
be" (125). Like Odysseus, Orlando's homecoming is not a return, although her
household attendants remain devoted to her, and she must adopt disguises
while precariously tipped at the threshold of the social order. Her estate cannot accommodate her, and she immediately goes in search of "life and a lover,"
continuing to wander after the wanderings. "When we are writing the life of
a woman," remarks the narrator, "we may, it is agreed, waive our demand for
action and substitute love instead" (198). Hemmed in directly upon her arrival
in the motherland, Orlando finds a new kind of vagabondage in Blackfriars
where her errant desires are given free rein. With its back alleys and vibrant
nightlife, this neighborhood is associated both with the Dominicans and the
seedier theater world of Shakespeare, and it provides the setting in which the
consequences of the Constantinople episode play out.

Woolf not only provides Orlando with a more sprawling urban setting for
experimentation, she expands time by placing her in the eighteenth century
when she arrives (in Constantinople she transitions from the sixteenth to the
seventeenth century), and she dramatizes the expansion through intervals of
temporal foreshortening in which "dissemblables" amass in a mental phantasmagoria. With these distensions and contractions—"an hour, once it lodges in
the queer element of the human spirit, may be stretched to fifty or a hundred
times its clock length; on the other hand, an hour may be accurately represented on the timepiece of the mind by one second" (223–24)—Woolf explores
a psychic field that resists the "housing" not only of temporal but of linguistic
categories as well.

While the wasting away of her estate in legal suits diminishes Orlando
economically, it also enables a continuing mobility over class lines that is revi-
talizing. Cross-dressing in her old black velvet suit trimmed with Venetian
lace, she descends in a sexually suggestive *katabasis* into the streets of London, searching out "the tribe which nightly burnishes their wares" (158). Not
only is her suit with its lace flourishes ambiguously gendered from the outset,
reminding us that the male protagonist was already girlish, her midnight wanderings typically end in the intimate company of other females—Nell, Prue,
and Kitty, women of the night—with her garments strewn on the floor. Sexuality in the form of erotic acts is indicated only obliquely. Emphasis falls on
the intimate intercourse that women in each other's presence can have with

one another when left alone. This is incomprehensible to socialized British males of the time who think they are catty and vindictive—an attitude Woolf mocks in *A Room of One's Own* by exploring the counternormative views embraced by the simple sentence "Chloe liked Olivia."[15] Not only do women like each other, they can explore intimate depths that a misogynist history misunderstands and misrepresents.

If one compares Orlando's nocturnal descents with that of the ephebe in Cavafy's poem, "One of Their Gods," it is clear that Woolf is not interested in either divinizing her character or exceptionalizing her. Ever open to the comically low, Orlando prefers to mingle, when she is not in deep hibernation after suffering a blow. She is a writer and an admirer of literature in general without being an aesthete, and she does not inhabit the esoteric worlds of Hellenic ephebes, even though her house is a town. Like Cavafy, however, Woolf uses the trope of erotic descent as a kind of detour through which she can disrupt heteronormative values, redefine gender roles by scrutinizing fashion, and bring a measure of personal freedom to a life bound by laws about what is sexually permissible.

In keeping with this broadening of narrative scale, Orlando's cross-dressing becomes ever more theatrical in the last two chapters. On any given day, she might wear a "China robe of ambiguous gender among her books"; knee breeches while clipping "the nut trees" when she takes to the garden; a "flowered taffeta" to a proposal of marriage "from some great nobleman" in Richmond; "a snuff-colored gown like a lawyer's" to visit the courts and get updates on her litigation; and when night comes, the velvet suit of a nobleman once more "in search of adventure" on the streets (161–62). These are socially crafted roles in which a literal closet becomes a metaphorical one where clothes assume the status of costumes (161). When Woolf has the biographer observe, "[Orlando's] sex changed far more frequently than those who have worn only one set of clothing can conceive" (161), she is reaching toward a phenomenology of polyamorous sexuality in search of a language. Constructed as they are around "dissemblables"—things disparate yet compounded and in a process of "incessant change" (130)—the body and desire can mutate dynamically in the course of a single day.

In her fluid treatment of sex, gender, and sexuality in *Orlando*, Woolf was going against the grain of the science of the time, which was engaged in extensive taxonomizing. This included the Freudian project of codifying sexual instincts in relation to fixed orientations. Despite the fact that Hogarth Press published the Standard Edition of Freud in English, Woolf expressed skepti-

---

15. Woolf, *A Room of One's Own* (New York: Harcourt Brace, 1929), 142–47.

cism of Freud's work and the push toward classification, which assumed that bodily identities were there to be discovered like the workings of the digestive tract and that nonnormative sexualities were pathologies.[16] She not only felt that fiction, or rather poetry, could more richly search out the questions that psychoanalysis was opening, she also regarded linguistic creativity as a more promising way to put words to what had not yet been named. Woolf's resistance to nomenclature was part of a wider resistance she displayed to nineteenth-century scientific excursions into the sexually anomalous.

As discussed in chapter 3, this resistance, in turn, was bound up with her critique of British imperialism and the standards of heterosexual womanhood it enforced in defining national identity. The antipathy may be contrasted with Césaire's embrace of taxonomical uses of language in *Cahier*. The difference is illuminating. He was working within colonial contexts whose alienating effects upon the people of the Caribbean were so deeply embedded that poetic language took on for him the demiurgic function of naming that the imperialist state had sought to monopolize in the centuries of slavery. This included the deliberate use of words for the flora and fauna of Martinique, which were particular to the island and bound up with Creole, and it extended to the cataloguing of instruments of torture that turned enslavement into a twisted kind of baroque art. Different aims guided Césaire and Woolf's choices about nomenclature.

In *Orlando,* and especially in Chapter Five, Woolf depicts a world driven not only by the heteronormative pressure to marry but by the hypermasculine environment of literary competitiveness, captured in the figures of Pope, Addison, and Swift. As caricatures of Restoration poets, these figures by turn shoot darts of "wit," let flow ripples of bland "urbanity," and unleash an "iron pelt of words" (154) that disabuse her, as Nick Greene once did, of her fanciful notion of what a writer is. Moreover, their misogyny illuminates for Orlando the "cannibal" instinct of their intellect—the ways it feeds upon the "Heart" and the gentler "Senses," which confer kindness and tolerance in a world that lacks both. This is not the literary cannibalism of Césaire whose revolutionary writer devours and digests an intimate enemy in order to create something bold, iconoclastic, and generative. It is the envious flesh eating of keen minds that lodge "in the most seedy of carcasses" (156). Having once participated in a masculine society of letters in the Elizabethan age and been devoured herself in a broadside by Nick Greene, Orlando is predisposed to favor the company

---

16. On Woolf and psychoanalysis, see Elizabeth Abel, *Virginia Woolf and the Fictions of Psychoanalysis* (Chicago: University of Chicago Press, 1989); and Sanja Bahun, "Woolf and Psychoanalytic Theory," in *Virginia Woolf in Context,* ed. Bryony Randall and Jane Goldman (New York: Cambridge University Press, 2012), 92–109.

of Nell, Prue, and Kitty, whose night time whisperings over a punch bowl offer solace from the vain egotism and rapacity of men who think women are mere "trifles" to "play with" (156).

If touches of nostalgia begin to enter the story after Orlando's wanderings abroad, it is because of the deep impressions made upon her mind and body in Constantinople. But it is also because the sixteenth and seventeenth centuries turn out in many ways to be freer than do later centuries. There is no principle of progress in Woolf's fictional biography. The eastern voyage is about breaking loose in an exoticized orient; Orlando's life in the three subsequent centuries is about forms of social oppression and literary censorship that threaten to kill her unconventional life at home. The narrative that takes shape around these constraints highlights the notion of "the spirit of the age" whose indomitability is such that it "batters down anyone who tries to make a stand against it far more effectually than those who bend its way" (178).

While Woolf makes use of this notion to mock the oversimplification of literary periodizing (another form of the overreaching impulse to classify), she also effectively engages with it in order to highlight aspects of Orlando's ongoing induction into the intricacies of gender.[17] This is especially apparent in the nineteenth century, which is said to be "antipathetic to [Orlando] in the extreme" (178). With its heavy crinolines, forced heterosexual coupling, and looming monuments of an ever-breeding Queen Victoria, it requires that she find a man she can "lean upon" (179). Faced with the imperative to conform, she strategizes ways "to resist and to yield; to yield and to resist" (115), cutting the corners of the law and using half-truths to forge alternative paths.

Odyssean and Penelopean cunning runs like a thread through these episodes in Chapter Five, the penultimate chapter of Woolf's book. It is a quality that enables Orlando to pick her way through the booby-traps of gender norms, which assume a highly visible national form in the figure of the reigning monarch. In the "dampness" of the Victorian age (a sense of stultifying seepage shapes the ambience of the time), she becomes mysteriously pregnant and sets about preparations for a birth with a bassinette and layers of crinoline to hide the bump, which embarrassingly announces the sexual intercourse that put it there (172). How Orlando comes to conceive a child remains obscure since the men in her life, so far as the reader knows, are restricted to the literary luminaries who both allure and repel her. This is one of her several clandestine lives, another being her marriage to Rosina Pepita, which also produces children. If pregnancy marks obedient acquiescence to the times,

---

17. On Woolf's treatment of periodization and the concept of the spirit of the age, see Jane de Gay, *Virginia Woolf's Novels and the Literary Past* (Edinburgh: Edinburgh University Press, 2007), 132–59.

an illegitimate child does not. After hormonal flashes, which are described in terms of "the spirit of the age blowing, now hot, now cold, upon her cheeks" (172), Orlando sits down to write one day, another equivocal act since women, especially pregnant ones, cannot be poets.

What begins, however, as an errant pen and an inkblot on the page turns into a full-blown adventure. The liquid first mutates by its own volition into monstrous curlicues and stanzas of insipid melancholy verse; migrates toward a spill of the entire inkpot on the page; and triggers a physical seizure of the body that settles on the quivering second finger of Orlando's left hand. Naked and bare as it is, she can only stop the paroxysms by placing a gold band upon it. As is often the case, sexual identities mingle, ink being a metaphorical medium for men to give birth, contractions being a female form of pushing out a baby. The inkblot both disrupts writing and is itself hijacked by a social dictate so invasive that it produces psychosomatic symptoms.

Warned but still husbandless, Orlando sets out wandering the streets of London once again, this time in search of a spouse. Overtly linking prostitution and marriage as street-walking acts, Woolf presents her protagonist's dilemma as a mock-tragic fall: while perambulating in a state of distraction, Orlando stumbles and breaks her ankle, sinks to the ground unable to walk, and, near death (she imagines), melodramatically decides to wed "the moor," that is, the earth on which she lies (182). At this moment, while she is in a swoon, Marmaduke Bonthrop Shelmerdine appears to her on a horse in a heroic style that conjures up a host of literary prototypes. Among them are Emily Brontë's Heathcliff and Shakespeare's Othello, the latter of whom figures, as already seen, in the early episode of Sasha and the great frost. Shelmerdine is a Moor of a different sort. While his sexual ambiguity is not immediately racialized, it will be, as Orlando's has already been.[18] The action is no longer unfolding in Constantinople, but the delirious swirl of events in London has an air of the carnivalesque about it.

Language, which by this point has become a character in the narrative, now moves in two directions that are crucial to how the book ends: first, toward the speech of the newly matched pair, and second, toward "The Oak Tree," Orlando's memoirish manuscript whose fate is decided in the final pages. Speech first. Once the inkblot has detoured writing, Woolf guides it in the direction of the conversational exchange between two nonheteronormative subjects who meet by accident, lack a common history, and yet immediately "recognize" each other. This recognition is linked, not with knowledge, as is the case, for example, with Eurycleia discovering Odysseus's scar, but

---

18. Daileader, "Othello's Sister."

with "understanding." That implies empathy, awareness of intended meanings, and levels of compatibility inaccessible to others (188–89). So well do Orlando and Shelmerdine move into this cognitive groove that when one blurts out the question, "Are you positive you aren't a man?," the other replies, "Can it be possible you're not a woman?" (189). In the language of rounding the Horn in the teeth of a gale, "they would go on talking or rather, understanding, which has become the main art of speech in an age when words are growing daily so scanty in comparison with ideas that 'the biscuits ran out' has to stand for kissing a negress in the dark when one has just read Bishop Berkeley's philosophy for the tenth time" (189).

Orlando "understands" that when Shelmerdine refers in his tales of the Cape to "running out of biscuits," he is implying a shortage of standard supplies, namely, white female heterosexuals. Reciprocally, when she speaks of "kissing a negress in the dark," he understands she is using the image of miscegenation for lesbian sex.[19] Both are code for a deviant sexuality understood in terms of socialized norms of skin color. They refer obliquely by displacing such aberrance onto racial stereotypes that function as distractions or scapegoats. The move resembles Césaire's use of the female as a site of displacement for racial delusion. In both cases, the extremity of the subject matter leads toward the instrumentalizing of alternative marginal groups.

Returning to the private language of the lovers, we can see that when Orlando, having donned a ring and conceived a child, acquiesces to marriage (in that order), speech in the text is effectively silenced for the reader. Paradoxically, however, it continues with great animation between the two encoders. Woolf sums up the cunning of their bond in the amusing cipher, "Rattigan Glumphoboo," which the reader is told conveys "a whole spiritual state of the utmost complexity," whose details are left, of course, to understanding—ours (208). These games of hide and seek perform what it means to resist while yielding, to conceal while revealing. Orlando's acquiescence to the spirit of the nineteenth century and its attendant social prejudices, which are sometimes taken as a sign of Woolf's assimilationist views in the last chapters of her fictional biography, should not be over emphasized. In Chapter Five, the British Empire, whose foundations rest upon the reproductive power of the woman who "married at nineteen and had fifteen or eighteen children by the time she was thirty" (168) is very much a target. Race enters the picture as part of a politics of the oppressed, although it is unevenly critiqued in the book and has laid Woolf open to charges of racism, even as she cuts wide swathes through the double standards that girdled nineteenth-century womanhood (168).

---

19. Hovey, "'Kissing Negresses in the Dark.'"

The conjugal bond between Orlando and Shelmerdine, based as it is on geographical distance, is purposefully weak. It has no association with erotic desire of the sort we find in the Sasha episode. The wedding ceremony itself obscures the vows, which take place amid "a clap of thunder" and the sound of a bird "dashed against the pane" (192–93). If the bird suggests a damaged capacity to fly, the thunder mutes the most important word in the wedding rite for a woman: "No one," the reader is told, "heard the word Obey spoken or saw, except as a golden flash, the ring pass from hand to hand" (193). The only people present on the occasion, in any case, are the loyal servants in the manor. There is no congregation that represents the social public toward which Orlando feels such ambivalence. What Woolf has contrived for Vita Sackville-West through her fictional protagonist is an arrangement whereby she can remain sexually deviant with impunity, bear a child without having to care for it, and win most of the suits in litigation because she is married (Sackville-West actually lost Knole in litigation over entailment).

The writing of "The Oak Tree" is interwoven throughout this excursion into speech and understanding. If Chapter Five begins with an explosion of ink and a blot that diverts the protagonist from unburdening herself via writing, Chapter Six begins with a hesitation that the pen might be up to "some of its involuntary pranks again" (195). As Orlando sits down at her inkpot, she expects interference from the spirit of the age, but that is not what happens. Marriage, masquerade though it is, turns out to be a highly convenient act of "obeisance" (196) to the times that considerably extends Orlando's range of movement. Having arranged things sufficiently well to pass the surveillance of the Victorian era, Orlando can continue to "travel" (write) carrying "contraband" (sexually deviant subject matter) without having "to pay the whole fine" (being prosecuted for obscenity, 196). With a fluent pen and in a ready state of mind, she finishes the manuscript she has been composing for centuries and announces its completion on a fine spring day with a resounding, "Done!" (200). Shortly thereafter, at the instigation of the manuscript itself, which beats about her breast with the imperative that "it be read," "The Oak Tree" is published through no less an intermediary than the three-hundred-year-old Sir Nicholas Greene. He is the Renaissance hack writer who turns out to have survived as long as Orlando and is now "the most influential critic of the Victorian age" (204).

Woolf has chosen to make the publication of *The Oak Tree* coincide with her own publication of *Orlando*. She has done so in a resounding reference to time in the text. With a striking of the bell at ten o'clock on the eleventh of October in 1928, Orlando finds herself violently cast into "the present moment" (219). Without the manuscript that has enabled her to trace with however fragile a thread the narrative of her days, she drifts in the blaring roar of the London streets, a pit of chaos. Nor does the apparent fame she wins through the publication of *The Oak Tree* assuage the near paralyzing dizziness she feels as she walks into that most modern of inventions, the multilevel department store with a lift. Dissociated from past and future, Orlando experiences the present as "an incessant shower of numerous atoms" (Woolf's phrase in "Modern Fiction"),[20] a torrent that threatens to swallow her whole. She walks it like a "narrow plank" (219) over the gaping maw of death.

Here at Messrs. Marshall & Snelgrove, where she shops for "boy's boots, bath salts, [and] sardines" (220)—it is the only other reference in the text to the son to whom she has given birth—her life passes before her. Scents that drift out of the elevator door as it opens at each landing remind her of the smells from the ships at Wapping Old Stairs. She is brought back to the sailor-girl Sukey with whom she used to lie in the hold of a ship among sacks of rubies. Then there are those royals who slept in the bed for which she is now buying silver sheets. And lo, if it is not a "fat, furred" Sasha she sees walking toward her—the horror of it makes her turn away for fear of recognition (222). Turkey, India, Persia, the voyage back to England—they all mingle in the small space and short time of a ride up the lift. This moment functions as a catalogue, a summing up of peak episodes, not unlike Odysseus's own summary of his voyage in a postcoital moment with Penelope.

But Woolf's angle is altogether different than Homer's. The voice of the Victorian biographer who guides the story in the first four chapters gives way to a modernist narrator who attempts to capture the phenomenology of moments of being. In previous eras Orlando has been drawn into a deep sleep at such points in time, and the biographer could beg off such an attempt. But she is here present to herself in her multiplicity. Impaired by the sudden flood of consciousness, she is coming undone in the twentieth century, and Woolf captures this in a symbolic return journey from the department store to her ancestral home: "the process of motoring fast out London so much resembles the chopping up small of body and mind, which precedes unconsciousness and perhaps death itself that it is an open question in what sense Orlando can be said to have existed at the present moment" (225). Something saves her from completely dissipating. She looks into her right rearview mirror and sees the shreds of herself peeling away like rapidly falling scraps of paper. The frame of the mirror enables a partial recovery, but to what? To the "seventy-six different times all ticking in the mind at once" and the "two thousand

---

20. See Woolf, "Modern Fiction," in *Essays*, 4:160. For a fuller treatment of time in Woolf's fiction, see Banfield, "Time Passes: Virginia Woolf, Post-Impressionism, and Cambridge Time," *Poetics Today* 24.3 (2003): 471–516.

and fifty-two" people that lodge there with them (225). Her condition is wild, precarious.

And Woolf protracts it. As Orlando approaches her estate, the multiples that proliferate arouse in her the sense that she, like the house into whose sepulcher she has descended, is haunted, inhabited by personas from different pasts that clamor to speak. Preserved in a 350-year memory, which inhabits a thirty-six-year-old body, they appear helter-skelter. It is at this moment that the famous wild goose appears for the first time, in flight and soaring away from her. Untamed and elusive, it has appeared to Orlando before in her foreign travels, though it is mentioned for the first time in the final chapter:

> I've seen it, here—there—there—England, Persia, Italy. Always it flies fast out to sea and always I fling after it words like nets (here she flung her hand out) which shrivel as I've seen nets shrivel drawn on deck with only seaweed in them. And sometimes there's an inch of silver—six words—in the bottom of the net. (229)

Flight and capture are here in tension, the sea a fluid signifier of an ever-flowing stream of consciousness from whose expanse and turbulence little can be caught or arrested. The bird itself transforms into fish as it wings away, suddenly slippery. Writing comes into view, this time in the form of "words like nets" that draw forth "only sea-weed." Appearing as it does while Orlando glides into the driveway of her estate, the wild goose visualizes what has just been described in the vertigo of multiple selves: the possibility that there is "the Captain self, the Key self," which "amalgamates and controls them all" (227), the self that may be taken hold of, if only for a moment, in the net of words.

This brings us back to *The Oak Tree*. As a manuscript, it has been an embodiment of a living, growing self, closely associated with an actual tree. During the wanderings, it becomes diary-like and takes on talismanic qualities that protect Orlando from harm. Upon the return to England, and after the sex change, she feels compelled by an increasing sense of modesty to hide it whenever she is interrupted in the act of writing. As a repository of experience across a radical reembodiment, it charts a growing awareness of what the gender expectations are for a British woman of the eighteenth and nineteenth centuries, and they do not include writing. A blood-stained patchwork of emotion, thought, and imagination, "The Oak Tree" remains alive until the moment it passes into the hands of Sir Nicholas Greene in his dapper gray suit who promptly sees it into press. It is then *The Oak Tree*. Publication, however, kills it, depriving it of its character as "a secret transaction, a voice answering a voice" (238). An attempted burial of the now dead object never comes off. To use a Césairean term, Orlando's life story has undergone "thingification" (*"chosification"*). When in 1928 she carries a signed first edition of her book to the tree she has not revisited since 1588, she can still ride the roots as if she were "riding the back of the world" (237). But these very roots forbid a commemorative interment by virtue of binding the earth and rendering it impervious. In the end, Orlando must let the book go, "unburied and dishevelled on the ground" (238). It has won her the "Glawr" she sought when she was a young man, but at the cost of losing its capacity to give expression to a life lived out over the deep mutabilities of time.

What makes *The Oak Tree* particularly important to this discussion is that, like the *Odyssey*, it plays with narrative frames: "The Oak Tree" as manuscript is embedded in *The Oak Tree* as published book. Both run parallel not only with Sackville-West's writing of her Hawthornden award-winning *The Land*, a long epic-like poem about the beauty of the Kentish countryside, but with Woolf's writing of *Orlando*. One might go so far as to say that Woolf is overwriting Sackville-West by making her fictional character's work a phantom text associated with a moribund English poetry of bucolic splendor, which her own more experimental biography submits to parody. Woolf's trenchant side is especially apparent at this point in *Orlando*, and it marks a competitive streak in her relationship with Sackville-West that has already been discussed in chapter 2.

Since Homer's literacy continues to be in question, it would be inaccurate to say that he overwrites Odysseus's tale, but he legitimizes it by incorporating it into the language of dactylic hexameter verse. While this is a kind of subordination, Homer frames it provocatively as an encounter between a late hero who got lost and an early bard, Demodocus (Homer's stand-in), who cannot sing of the *nostoi* because he has not yet come into contact with survivors of the Trojan War or singers beyond Scheria who sing of them. Here, too, the competitive edge between bard and storyteller is apparent, but "publication" in the Homeric text is less life killing than it is in *Orlando* since it ensures epic *kleos*—or does it? There is that enigmatic lightning bolt cast by Zeus at the end of *Odyssey* and a *deus ex machina* that ends retributive violence through the act of making people forget what the return of Odysseus means.

As Woolf's narrative winds its way to the finish, Orlando experiences something like a moment of being. She stands on a hill where the oak itself stands, and in the dark of night, she is absorbed into a vision that recalls the mystic appearance of an English snow scene on another hill, one she encountered with the gypsies in the withering heat of a Greek summer day long ago. Her life passes before her again, and suddenly—

everything was partly something else, and each gained an odd moving power
from this union of itself and something not itself so that with this mixture of
truth and falsehood her mind became like a forest in which things moved;
lights and shadows changed, and one thing became another. (239)

Moods and modes clash. Orlando, whose eyes have been brimming with tears
for most of Chapter Six, hears a plane in the sky and sees that it is Shelmerdine
who has returned by air and not by sea, her phosphorescent pearls his landing
lights. While the reader is told that it is a matured man who leaps from the
plane onto the earth, a cartoonish image of him persists. At the moment of
hitting the ground, a "single wild bird" (241) with an elongated neck comically
shoots up like a phallus over his head. But it quickly disappears into the horizon. The fictional biography appears to be moving toward a wild goose chase
of an end whose future is unpredictable. Whatever it may be, it will require,
like the second odyssey of Homer's epic, a new language and a visionary sense
of the possibilities for poetry in recreating sex, gender, and sexuality in the
aeronautic age.

CÉSAIRE: THE INCISED TREE, THE SLAVE SHIP,
AND THE PIROGUE

The love of nature that is perceived as "an English disease" in Orlando's wanderings and that becomes associated upon her return with the ambiguous
status of the oak tree may be productively compared with the diseased Martiniquan landscape in *Cahier*. When Césaire's speaker refers to "the red flesh of
[Antillean] soil" ("*la chair rouge du sol*") and "the dark accretions that weigh
down its righteous patience" ("*l'accablement opaque de sa droite patience*," 115),
he is pointing to the toxicity of the land, a reminder that African organicism
is being constructed from a site of displacement and a soil whose depths are
blood-steeped. This is why nature in *Cahier* is less an ecological site for charting environmentally sensitive relations with the vegetal world than a highly
charged symbolic landscape that is already humanized. The audience knows
this from the beginning when it is escorted onto an island whose topography registers the illness of those who inhabit it. The taxonomical richness of
Césaire's vocabulary for the flora and fauna of Martinique, which, as we have
seen, is connected with the "*valeur-force*" he finds in naming things local and
particular, is also an index he draws on in rendering a journey through hell.
    An understanding of Césaire's way of shaping the natural world may be
approached from yet another angle: the recurrent image of the tree, which

invites comparison with the *Odyssey* and *Orlando.* Among the numerous instances of trees in the poem, an iconic one appears in stanza 126, which marks a point where the speaker begins to turn, if not fully, then more optimistically, toward a process of liberation and healing. This means that the image is bound up with the final movements of an ostensible homecoming:

> And see this tree our hands have formed!
> it revolves, for all, the wounds incised
> in its trunk,
> the land labors for all
> and onrush of fragrant sap towards its branches!
> (126)

> *Et voyez l'arbre de nos mains!*
> *il tourne, pour tous, les blessures incises*
> *en son tronc*
> *pour tous le sol travaille*
> *et griserie vers les branches de précipitation parfumée!*

Two exclamatory sentences present us with a whole tree, generic, but among those that secrete liquid from the bark. Emphasis lies on the branches that reach up to the sky and the "incised" trunk whose "wounds" ("*blessures*") stimulate the rise of sap to the arboreal green, a visible sign of life and growth. The vigor and productivity of this organism are the paradoxical consequence of lacerations made to the body, which quicken rather than kill. Analogically, the wounds of slavery and colonization are imagined as the injuries inflicted on the Caribbean people, conceived now as an organically united collective with the capacity to self-heal. This "tree of our hands" ("*l'arbre de nos mains*")—in other words, made *by* "our hands" but also offered *from* "our hands"—is a kind of gift brought to the table of a meeting of world cultures in which the Antilles have a distinct role. It is in some such sense that the tree may be said to "revolve for all." The descent into the nightmarish world of the colonialized self—into the "cloistered intimacy" ("*intimité close,*" 125) of the deepest wounds—is here inverted, and the psychic divagations that have absorbed the poem are exposed to the open air where they take the form of growth. This marks the moment in the text when the "I" becomes "we," not in the conditional voice heard earlier as the speaker adopts masks, but in the present indicative, which carries through the poem's last lines.

Césaire, then, like Homer and Woolf, constructs a semiotically suggestive tree around tropes of return, but all three authors have their own emphases and purposes. The famous marriage bed in the *Odyssey* is not incised in the tree, but constructed around an augered and bored trunk, which functions as a sturdy bedpost. The audience is asked to imagine an already ancient olive that has endured, not whole, but as the product of *techne*. Césaire's and Homer's trees are simultaneously natural and crafted, though in different ways. The sap-fed branches of the former are the consequence of forced growth through an artful injury, with the dripping liquid of the trunk suggestive of blood and tears. The *Odyssey*'s tree, by contrast, has no branches or bark because they have been cropped to allow for a roof and walls, the enclosure emphasizing the intimacy of a personal bond. If Homer's tree is a domesticated stump, which points to a symbiotic union between nature and the social institution of marriage grafted onto it, Césaire's is made into an image of a personal ordeal, externalized into a collective enterprise, which it seeks to project onto a world stage. The *Odyssey* looks back in time, remembering events that through its own medium have become foundation tales. *Cahier* looks forward to a time when there will be a past that can be remembered because it has been lifted from the depths by a poetic soul that offers itself to an oppressed people. Although the sacrificial tonalities of the poem are ironized, they persist in the theater of masks that is the poem as a whole.

Woolf's oak tree is neither incised nor augered, but it is associated with Orlando's inscribed manuscript, which is organically connected to her deepest thoughts and emotions. It also has the kind of longevity associated with Homer's olive tree. But unlike the conjugal tree of the *Odyssey*, distinguished by its sturdy trunk, and the collective tree of *Cahier*, whose scored bark feeds the green crown, the most distinctive characteristic of Woolf's tree is its root structure. Orlando rides the knotty hardness of it in an erotically charged act of self-grounding. By keeping the poem associated with the oak a secret, however, Woolf moves in different ways than does *Cahier*, which dredges the depths in order to bring the sludge into the oxygen of poetry. While Césaire struggles to break the French language in order to forge a new Antillean dialect, Woolf ransacks the English language to craft new forms of life writing. Race, as already seen, can function as a site of displacement for the surveilled territory of white respectable English womanhood, and in Woolf's *Orlando* such displacements call attention to the strategies by which backdoor sexual relationships can be represented without threat of legal intervention.

It is significant that on the front end of stanza 126, which presents us with the wound-incised tree, Césaire frames the speaker in an act of prayer. On the back end of it, he delivers us to the marine element once again, through two images of sailing vessels. The prayer itself is worth remarking, before we return to the sea, since it asks a higher power to bring moderation where there may be hostility and an impulse toward revenge:[21]

> . . . heart of mine, preserve me from all hate
> do not make of me that man of hate for whom
> I have only hate
> for though I am quartered in this unique race
> you know nonetheless my domineering love
> you know that it is not from hatred of other races
> that I make myself the husbandman of this unique race . . .
> (125)

> . . . *mon coeur, préservez-moi de toute haine*
> *ne faites point de moi cet homme de haine pour qui*
> *je n'ai que haine*
> *car pour me cantonner en cette unique race*
> *vous savez pourtant mon amour tyrannique*
> *vous savez que ce n'est point par haine des autres races*
> *que je m'exige bêcheur de cette unique race . . .*

These often-quoted lines lead to the vision of the wound-incised tree, which picks up on the notion of a "husbandman" ("*bêcheur*") of a race. After the blistering journey of decolonializing that the poem has enacted, it is extraordinary to hear such devout words. On the one hand, the speaker calls his prayer "*virile*"—"robust" and "possessed of manly vigor" (122). The characterization is borne out by images that the one praying does so with a "fist at the end of an outstretched arm" ("*le poing à l'allongée du bras*," 123) and a "prow's head" ("*une tête de proue*," 122) that will fearlessly meet forces of resistance. On the other hand, these very images are contained in a supplication that acknowledges impotence and a need for help.

As is usual with Césaire, an affectively shaded idea—deliverance from enmity as a condition of healing—is personalized and deepened through cross-gendered connotations. The plea for a cessation of hostility coexists with the agonistic spirit required to fight the good fight. Biblical tones are overt, and they echo both the exhortation in the Old Testament's Book of Job "to gird one's loins" (38.3) for the struggle and the injunction of the New Testa-

---

21. For a fuller contextualizing of the prayer, see Keith Walker, "The Transformational and Enduring Vision of Aimé Césaire," *PMLA* 125.3 (2010): 756–63.

ment to refrain from returning hate for hate. Because the prayer is embedded
in a context that brims with images of a fertile and organically conceived
Africa, it aims to bridge religious and cultural traditions. It is at this moment,
as the speaker collects himself in an invocation to the divine, that the poem
declares one of its highest aspirations:

> . . . what I most desire is to
> to meet the universal hunger
> the universal thirst . . .
> (125)

> . . . *ce que je veux*
> *c'est pour la faim universelle*
> *pour la soif universelle* . . .

Evocative rather than declarative, these lines suggest a generalized need for
a people to be recognized and respected on the world stage as the possessors
of a distinct culture with a rich past. The Antilles have been deprived of what
Césaire calls "the historical initiative" for addressing such a need.[22]

It is fitting that the lines quoted above were used in a poster designed in
1956 by the Pan-African literary and artistic quarterly, *Présence Africaine*, for
the First Congress of Black Writers in Paris. The poster featured an image of
Picasso's well-known illustration, *Tête d'un Nègre*.[23] Césaire's words were chosen as an expression of a desire on the part of those who gathered to unite
around the themes of slavery, colonialism, and negritude at the same time that
they implied the importance of reaching across the divides of nationality and
race. In a speech delivered at the event titled "The Spirit of Civilisation, or the
Laws of African Negro Culture," Senghor echoed Césaire, saying that it was
not just Africans, but Afro-Asiatic peoples who were

> strengthen[ing] their personality by asserting it, so that they should not
> come empty-handed to "meetings of give and take." For world civilization,
> and, in the first instance, Peace, will either be the work of all, or it will not
> come about at all. . . . Experience has proved it: cultural liberation is an
> essential condition of political liberation.[24]

---

22. Césaire, "Culture and Civilisation," *First International Conference of Negro Writers and
Artists* (Paris, Sorbonne, 19–22 September 1956), *Présence Africaine*, 8–10 (1956): 203–5.

23. See *The First International Conference of Negro Writers and Artists*.

24. Léopold Senghor, "The Spirit of Civilisation or the Laws of African Negro Culture,"
First International Conference of Negro Writers and Artists, 8–10.

As a work that seeks such liberation through a politically inflected poetics, *Cahier* crafts the wound-incised tree as an Antillean version of the tree of life around which a larger mission unfolds. The *"amour tyrannique"* associated with it has militant connotations that mingle with the humility of prayer.

This humility is accompanied in a subsequent stanza (133) by a declaration of acceptance as a precondition to a declaration of independence for "this singular race" (*"cette unique race,"* 125). Once again, an agonizingly drawn out expression of more than thirty lines brings to life the most violent practices that were inflicted upon the slaves of the Antilles. And like all such catalogues in *Cahier,* this one cuts more than one way. In the act of accepting this violence—*"j'accepte"* is anaphorically repeated—the speaker also points the fist in the face of the perpetrators, evoking details of torture and punishment under the infamous Code Noir issued in 1685. Acceptance is premised upon rendering grievances in words. In this way, the apparent masochism of reliving the past is transformed into an experience of dialogue within a public space where it becomes possible to conceive the universal within the particular.[25]

I accept . . . I accept . . . entirely, without reserve . . .
. . . the flogged nigger who pleads: "Beg pardon massa"
and the twenty-nine legal lashes of the whip
and the four-foot high dungeon
and the iron collar with spokes
and the severed hamstring for daring to run-away
and the fleur-de-lys leaching into my shoulder fat from the red-hot brand-
   ing iron
(133)

j'accepte . . . j'accepte . . . entièrement, sans reserve . . .
. . . le nègre fustigé qui dit: "Pardon mon maître"
et les vingt-neuf coups de fouet légal
et le cachot de quatre pieds de haut
et le carcan à branches
et le jarret coupé à mon audace marronne
et la fleur de lys qui flue du fer rouge sur le gras de mon épaule

Césaire's *"j'accepte"* is a powerful and multidirectional signifier. The repetition of the word ironically recalls the title of an open letter Émile Zola wrote in 1898, *"J'accuse,"* which targeted the anti-Semitism of the French government

---

25. Mamadou Ba, *"S'orienter dans l'histoire"*; and Garraway, "'What Is Mine.'"

in its treatment of the Alfred Dreyfus case. It also reminds us of the *"homme-juif"* of stanza 34. Césaire is exhuming history from the depths of forgetfulness through the taxonomic specificity of words (*"mots"*) applied to objects that were invented to inflict harm (*"maux"*). The French rhyme of the homonyms *mots / maux,* played out in a number of poems that echo the themes of *Cahier,* suggests the particularly vivid way Césaire gives materiality to wounds by imagining them in such a metaphor as "the red flesh of [Antillean] soil."[26] Once again, in the absence of a recorded past that remembers and commemorates, the poet gives form to an inchoate mass of fragments and dismembered pieces.[27] As he descends into blood, he also ascends through the wound-incised tree. "The weakness of many men," Césaire says in the poem, "Preliminary Question," which is part of *Solar Throat Slashed* (*Soleil cou coupé*), "is that they do not know how to become either a rock or a tree" (*"La faiblesse de beaucoup d'hommes est qu'ils ne savent devenir ni une pierre ni un arbre"*).[28]

In a typically Césairean way, the injuries sustained by the individual and the collective are closely intertwined, and the process of understanding takes place through writing and rewriting, as *Cahier* was written and rewritten over many years. One of the most vivid formulations of the necessity of "living with" the ordeal may be found in a piece entitled "lagunal calendar" (*"calendrier lagunaire"*), which forms part of the poem sequence *moi, laminaire*[29] (in English, *i laminaria*). *Laminaire* is a kind of algae that takes the form of long ribbons, enabling a steady flow of water through its layers and thereby decreasing resistance:

> i inhabit a sacred wound
> i inhabit imaginary ancestors
> i inhabit an obscure will
> i inhabit a long silence
> i inhabit an irremediable thirst
> i inhabit a thousand-year voyage

> *j'habite une blessure sacrée*
> *j'habite des ancêtres imaginaires*
> *j'habite un vouloir obscur*
> *j'habite un long silence*

---

26. See *"calendrier lagunaire"* discussed below and *"Mot"* in *Lost Body* (*Corps perdu*), in *Complete Poetry of Aimé Césaire,* trans. Arnold and Eshleman, 480–83.

27. See Diop, *"Labilité et résilience."*

28. *Complete Poetry of Aimé Césaire,* trans. Arnold and Eshleman, 430–31.

29. *Complete Poetry of Aimé Césaire,* trans. Arnold and Eshleman, 652–53.

j'habite une soif irremediable
j'habite un voyage de mille ans

The "*moi laminaire*" of the poem sequence is the oblique form of the pronoun, indicating a subject that is both acted upon or affected and also charged with agency, and Césaire deliberately choses the lower case of his title. If this were in Greek, the verbal complexity would be marked by the middle voice. Here, the algae functions as a fluid medium that is simultaneously passive (water moves through it) and active (it transforms turbulence into a poetry that finds "*mots*" for "*maux*"). Only after prolonged and intimate immersion—among the ancestors, over the course of a long silence, in a voyage of a thousand years—does the "i" come to know its hidden history. It must "inhabit the wound," reverentially, if it is to elicit a collective meaning from it. As Césaire says in his interview with Daniel Maximin:

> I believe that the sacred exists in us, but it is a sacred that has been profaned [*profané*], that has been clichéd [*galvaudé*]. . . . One must find it again by the paths of art [*voies de l'art*], one must find it by the paths of language, by the paths of poetry. . . . To find the sacred again means to restore its energy; in other words, to restore to the sacred its revolutionary dimension, in the strict sense of the word.[30]

In the constantly mutating images of *Cahier* as it moves to its end, the universal hunger and thirst expressed in the figure of the incised tree shifts to the more concrete, local, and quotidian activity of Antillean fishermen who hazard the sea as a livelihood. It is "the proud canoe and its seagoing strength" ("*la fière pirogue / et sa vigueur marine*") that emerges as a complement to the sacrificial tree, first as it ventures out upon "a diverse ocean" and then, in the poem's vivid present tense, "rising and falling on the / pulverized wave . . . dancing the sacred dance before the flat gray backdrop of the village" ("*La voici avancer par escalades et retombées sur le flot pulvérisé / la voici danser la danse sacrée devant la grisaille du bourg*," 128). This, too, is a kind of return, performed daily and at risk. But now the tripartite Caribbean soul of stanza 39, a Carib-African-European agglomeration of parts that do not fit, converge in a triangulation bound up with larger impulses toward social and cultural healing.

As the proud canoe suggests, *Cahier* remains invested in an ethics of labor and merit—the extended journey—and it does so, in part, to moderate the

---

30. See the interview with Maximin, 21.

idealism of universals by reclaiming them in terms of a local culture with practices specific to it. The capacity for perseverance in conditions of instability, emblematized in Odysseus's raft, resonates in these sections of *Cahier*. So does the vital role of *polymechania*, of resourcefulness and cunning, in finding ways to survive. But the visual description of the *pirogue* rising and falling also suggests the life-preserving activity of yielding while resisting that is central to Orlando's return. In all three texts—the *Odyssey, Orlando,* and *Cahier*—retour demands resilience, openness to renewal in the aftermath of injury, and an understanding that homecoming is a vexed process whose protraction ironically generates the vitality of the ongoing journey.

If the wound-incised tree provides a sense of how the sacred is constructed in *Cahier* and if the proud *pirogue* bears testimony to the endurance of a debased but resilient people, the slave ship that dominates the last stanzas brings both together. The ocean-going vessel is not merely a literary image of a historical journey. It is a powerfully cathectic object that provides a site for the convergence of multiple movements in the poem. Stirrings from its bowels may be heard in the stanzas leading into the passage on the pongo. But from stanza 151 to the end, an explosive revolt breaks out. The ship careens as "the horizon falls apart, shrinks and expands," sundered by "the portent of a lightning flash as it tears asunder the clouds" ("*l'horizon se défait, recule et s'élargit / et voici parmi des déchirements de nuages la fulgurance d'un signe,*" 162). The audience is taken into a mutiny on the high seas of the Middle Passage, intensified by the eruption of natural forces. "The nigger scum," or "*la négraille,*" the most demeaning of French terms for the Africans transported across the Atlantic and repeatedly used at the end of the poem, is made the subject of another repeated phrase: "the old negritude is gradually becoming a cadaver" (156; "*La vieille négritude progressivement cadaverise,*" 162). Bloody revolt, which issues in the death of the slavers, is also the death of the perverse form of life into which the enslaved have been forced. Here negritude is a condition of abjectness overcome. As in the oxymoronic case of Toussaint Louverture in a cell of the Jura Mountains, "death dies" on the *négrier* for those who have stood up to protest the violence of transport.

The wound-incised tree, the fierce pirogue, and the slave ship enable us to reflect upon the uses of ritual in the final stanzas of *Cahier,* two of which are particularly important: trial by ordeal and lustration. Anthropologically, the ordeal is a judicial practice of traditional societies. The application of pain is thought to prove the guilt or innocence of the accused, survival being a sign of innocence. The sacred is an important aspect of trial by ordeal for it is thought to offer proof of a divine will at work and thus to validate both the infliction of pain as well as the cohesion of the group through the testing of one of its members. In stanza 154 of *Cahier*, it is used with reference to the speaker's recognition that his own suffering and the suffering of his people are an *"ordalie"* ("ordeal"). He interjects an example from Bambara ritual to illuminate the sense in which he so conceives it.

> I grasp now the meaning of my ordeal: my country is the "night lance" of my Bambara ancestors. It shrinks and its tip recoils desperately toward the hilt if it is moistened with chicken blood, and it declares that its temperament calls for human blood, human fat, and liver, and heart, not chicken blood.

> *Je tiens maintenant le sens de l'ordalie: mon pays est la "lance de nuit" de mes ancêtres Bambaras. Elle se ratatine et sa pointe fuit désespérément vers le manche si c'est de sang de poulet qu'on l'arrose et elle dit que c'est du sang d'homme qu'il faut à son tempérament, de la graisse, du foie, du coeur d'homme, non du sang de poulet.*

Chicken blood: the expression conveys cowardice and a failure of nerve. The "night lance" of the Bambara, an ethnic group living in what is now the Republic of Mali, is central to a ritual in which the weapon of war is said to recoil at the touch of anything but human blood. In the poem's time present, as the slave ship cracks and its masters are overthrown, the reference has several functions. What marks the violence of revolt as political is that it contests the power of a sovereign; what marks it as moral and judicial is that the supposed conquerors go down in the ordeal; and what marks it as sacred is that the aggressors become surrogates for those who bought and sold slaves. In this scene of revolt on the Atlantic, Césaire invests violence with a foundational purpose, making the *négrier* ("the slave ship") a metonym for *"mon pays"* ("my country").

Because the idea of a bloody revolt is key to the concluding stanzas of *Cahier*, it is perhaps not surprising that the complementary idea of lustration is closely connected with it. In stanza 167, after the "nigger cargo" (*"la négraille,"* once again) is depicted as standing upright (*"debout"*) "in the hold . . . / in the cabins . . . / on the bridge . . . / in the sun . . . in the blood" (166), it is not the slave ship that advances but "the lustral vessel" (*"le navire lustral,"* 167). Lustration is a term for purification by ritual sacrifice.[31] Its range

31. Robert Parker, *Miasma: Pollution and Purification in Early Greek Religion* (Oxford: Clarendon, 1996), 18–31, 257–80.

of application is wide, and it may embrace experiences ranging from birth to death. What is most important in the context at hand is that it pertains to a revolutionary act in which the blood of the agents of an older order is being purged from the hands of those who shed it—a righteous purgation because the violence has been part of a trial by ordeal. Lustration has numerous functions, all of which are pertinent in the final stanzas of *Cahier*. It separates the "good" from the "bad," and thus has the effect of marking a new community united around a common ethos, but not an exclusive or univocal one.

The uses of ritual at the end of *Cahier* point to fundamental differences with the *Odyssey*, which is similarly preoccupied with trial by ordeal, lustration, and foundational violence. At a time when the ancient Greek polis and its institutional structures were undergoing expansion, the epic was pushing up against the limits of archaic cathartic rituals, anticipating the gradual centralization of retributive violence within a judicial system in the sixth century BCE. This is a process dramatically rendered in Aeschylus's *Oresteia*. By contrast, *Cahier* has recourse to ritual at a time when the emancipatory promise of the Declaration of the Rights of Man and the various abolition decrees in the French West Indies were unfolding in the grim aftermath of the Second World War. Césaire's turn to ritual is part of the attack on "a collective hypocrisy that cleverly misrepresents problems, the better to legitimize the hateful solutions provided for them."[32]

Perhaps the greatest jolt for a reader of Homer and Césaire, however, comes with the recognition that what the *Odyssey* seeks at the end is that most un-epic of things: forgetting. The paradox of an Ithaca that will not remember an ancestral horror is unsettling. How can one explain the survival of the *Odyssey* in light of the *deus ex machina*? Is it Odysseus himself who disseminates it in a second odyssey? Césaire's *Cahier* poses the opposite problem. If the history of a 300-year catastrophe has been largely lost to the submarine depths, how can one remember it? To what can memory attach itself? In the near absence of records, it is a broken history of oral poetry that helps bridge the great divide between Africa and the Caribbean. If the *Odyssey* is a poem that becomes more definitively set in writing with the waning of orality, *Cahier* is a poem that turns from writing, which is associated with European magisterial history, to orality for recuperating a lost past. As for *Orlando*, orality disappears into written records of which only tantalizing fragments remain. In evading the censor, the text also plays out a prurience that it pushes to an extreme by inventing an opaque system of encoded speech for its polyam-

---

32. Césaire, *Discourse on Colonialism*, 32.

orous couple. Under conditions of this sort, the very idea of history is mocked because it emerges from the eclipse of an unspeakable past event and the hiddenness of a personal discourse that is never made public.

CAVAFY: HEDONIC SHIPS ON POLICED WATERS

Whether it appears as a body of water or as a region, Cavafy's Mediterranean offers complementary but sharply contrasting views of the marine voyages of the *Odyssey, Orlando,* and *Cahier.* In the poems explored in this final section, the ancient trope of *nostos* intersects with the hedonic, shaping new homoerotic subjectivities that are linked once again with the Hellenic diaspora. If desire seeks satisfaction, it also aims at its own prolongation. For Cavafy this means the eternally renewed journey whose initiating force is either loss or unfulfilled yearning. Memory plays a vital role in this poetic process of renewal. It is developed most fully in "Ithaca," an overt adaptation, but also in a more elusive piece, "Ships" ("Πλοῖα"), which is among the unpublished works. The latter meditates upon the craft of poetry in metaphorical terms of commercial travel on a policed sea. Because these two poems exemplify the difference between acts of literary appropriation and a poetics of indirection and weak links, they also enable a retrospective view of the ground that has been covered in this book.

Following a period of experimentation with Homeric subject matter drawn mostly from the *Iliad,* "Ithaca" goes considerably beyond Cavafy's efforts in an early piece called "Second Odyssey" (1894).[33] That is an unsuccessful poem, self-consciously cast as a response to Dante's and Tennyson's Ulysses, featuring a figure who represents odyssey not as return, but as the beckoning to travel beyond Ithaca and even outside the Mediterranean. This reflects Cavafy's intertexual thinking in an essay he wrote the same year titled "The End of Odysseus" ("Τὸ Τέλος τοῦ Ὀδυσσέως"), expressing caution about the rewriting of Homer: "Furthering the sentence from the place where Homer decided to end it by placing a period is a difficult and risky thing for another poet to undertake" ("Ἐκεῖ ὅπου ὁ Ὅμερος ἀπεφάσισε νὰ σταματήση καὶ ἔθεσε τελεῖαν, εἶναι δύσκολον καὶ ἐπικίνδυνον πρᾶγμα νὰ θελήση ἄλλος

---

33. Cavafy, *Complete Poems,* trans. Mendelsohn, 275. Also see Michael Paschalis, "Cavafy's 'Iliadic' Poems," in *Imagination and Logos: Essays on C. P. Cavafy,* ed. Panagiotis Roilos (Cambridge, MA: Harvard University Press, 2010), 153–72.

νὰ ἐξακολουθήσῃ τὴν φράσιν").[34] In that essay he probes the journey as an experience of adventure and a quest for new lands, not as a tale of exile and suffering. Dante's Odysseus, in the company of a small group of surviving crew members, sails westward toward the pillars of Hercules, desiring new knowledge, and dies in a whirlwind. Tennyson's Odysseus grows bored with the petty life on Ithaca and dreams of arriving at the Elysian fields and meeting Achilles. In both cases, Cavafy thinks the poets understand the "psychology" of the Homeric Odysseus in a way that questions the suitability of the ending in the ancient epic. But he also knows the story of the *Telegony* in the epic cycle, which takes Odysseus on a second voyage after arriving in Ithaca, and it is this alternative odyssey that most interests him. Going beyond the "period" of Homer's *nostos* tale, however, is a risky endeavor, as the quoted lines indicate, and yet that is exactly what Cavafy does, to great effect, in "Ithaca," which appeared in 1911, seventeen years after "Second Odyssey" and "The End of Odysseus."

"Ithaca" is not a dramatic monologue, nor is it written in the third person. Instead, it adopts the quasi-didactic mode of the informal second-person singular. The speaker is a worldly, lifelong traveler who has had other journeys and understands already the alternatives posed by Dante's and Tennyson's hero.[35] Cavafy has chosen to make his journey an adventure rather than an ordeal, a hedonic one, practiced in the art of luxurious lingering. Its setting is the wide Mediterranean, the inland sea that touches three continents, and the poem shows no interest in sailing beyond its rich and history-steeped littorals. One may imagine any number of potential identities for the "you" who is being addressed, but one of them may be Homer's Odysseus.[36]

"Ithaka"

1 As you set out for Ithaka
2 hope your road is a long one,
3 full of adventure, full of discovery.
4 Laistrygonians, Cyclops,
5 angry Poseidon—don't be afraid of them:
6 you'll never find things like that on your way

---

34. Cavafy, "The End of Odysseus," in *Selected Prose Works*, 103–11, quotation page 111. For the Greek, see "Τὸ Τέλος τοῦ Ὀδυσσέως," *Dokimasia* 5 (1974): 9–22, quotation page 16. The essay is reprinted in *Μικρὰ Καβαφικά Β*, 169–97.

35. See Michael Pieris, "Η πολιτικὴ ενδοχώρα της φιλοσοφικής 'Ιθάκης,'" *Η Σημερινή* (Nicosia, Cyprus), 11 December 1994; also his essay "The Theme of Second Odyssey in Cavafy and Sinopoulos," in *Ancient Greek Myth in Modern Greek Poetry*, ed. Peter Mackridge (London: Frank Cass, 1996), 96–108.

36. Cavafy, *Collected Poems*, trans. Keeley and Sherrard, 66–69.

7 as long as you keep your thoughts raised high,

8 as long as a rare excitement

9 stirs your spirit and your body.

10 Laistrygonians, Cyclops,

11 wild Poseidon—you won't encounter them

12 unless you bring them along inside your soul,

13 unless your soul sets them up in front of you.

14 Hope your road is a long one.

15 May there be many summer mornings when,

16 with what pleasure, what joy,

17 you enter harbors you're seeing for the first time;

18 may you stop at Phoenician trading stations

19 to buy fine things,

20 mother of pearl and coral, amber and ebony,

21 sensual perfume of every kind—

22 as many sensual perfumes as you can;

23 and may you visit many Egyptian cities

24 to learn and go on learning from their scholars.

25 Keep Ithaka always in your mind.

26 Arriving there is what you're destined for.

27 But don't hurry the journey at all.

28 Better if it lasts for years,

29 so you're old by the time you reach the island,

30 wealthy with all you've gained on the way,

31 not expecting Ithaka to make you rich.

32 Ithaka gave you the marvelous journey.

33 Without her you wouldn't have set out.

34 She has nothing left to give you now.

35 And if you find her poor, Ithaka won't have fooled you.

36 Wise as you will have become, so full of experience,

37 you'll have understood by then what these Ithakas mean.

1 Σὰ βγεῖς στὸν πηγαιμὸ γιὰ τὴν Ἰθάκη,

2 νὰ εὔχεσαι νἆναι μακρὺς ὁ δρόμος,

3 γεμάτος περιπέτειες, γεμάτος γνώσεις.

4 Τοὺς Λαιστρυγόνας καὶ τοὺς Κύκλωπας,

5 τὸν θυμωμένο Ποσειδῶνα μὴ φοβᾶσθαι,

6 τέτοια στὸν δρόμο σου ποτέ σου δὲν θὰ βρεῖς,

7 ἂν μέν' ἡ σκέψις σου ὑψηλή, ἂν ἐκλεκτὴ

8 συγκίνησις τὸ πνεῦμα καὶ τὸ σῶμα σου ἀγγίζει.

9 Τοὺς Λαιστρυγόνας καὶ τοὺς Κύκλωπας,

10 τὸν ἄγριο Ποσειδῶνα δὲν θὰ συναντήσεις,

11 ἂν δὲν τοὺς κουβανεῖς μὲς στὴν ψυχή σου,

12 ἂν ἡ ψυχή σου δὲν τοὺς στήνει ἐμπρός σου.

13 Νὰ εὔχεσαι νἆναι μακρὺς ὁ δρόμος.

14 Πολλὰ τὰ καλοκαιρινὰ πρωϊὰ νὰ εἶναι

15 ποὺ μὲ τί εὐχαρίστησι, μὲ τί χαρὰ

16 θὰ μπαίνεις σὲ λιμένας πρωτοειδωμένους·

17 νὰ σταματήσεις σ' ἐμπορεῖα Φοινικικά,

18 καὶ τὲς καλὲς πραγμάτειες ν' ἀποκτήσεις,

19 σεντέφια καὶ κοράλλια, κεχριμπάρια κ' ἔβενους,

20 καὶ ἡδονικὰ μυρωδικὰ κάθε λογῆς,

21 ὅσο μπορεῖς πιὸ ἄφθονα ἡδονικὰ μυρωδικά·

22 σὲ πόλεις Αἰγυπτιακὲς πολλὲς νὰ πᾶς,

23 νὰ μάθεις καὶ νὰ μάθεις ἀπ' τοὺς σπουδασμένους.

24 Πάντα στὸν νοῦ σου νἄχεις τὴν Ἰθάκη.

25 Τὸ φθάσιμον ἐκεῖ εἶν' ὁ προορισμός σου.

26 Ἀλλὰ μὴ βιάζεις τὸ ταξεῖδι διόλου.

27 Καλλίτερα χρόνια πολλὰ νὰ διαρκέσει·

28 καὶ γέρος πιὰ ν' ἀράξεις στὸ νησί,

29 πλούσιος μὲ ὅσα κέρδισες στὸν δρόμο,

30 μὴ προσδοκῶντας πλούτη νὰ σὲ δώσει ἡ Ἰθάκη.

31 Ἡ Ἰθάκη σ' ἔδωσε τ' ὡραῖο ταξεῖδι.

32 Χωρὶς αὐτὴν δὲν θἄβγαινες στὸν δρόμο.

33 Ἄλλα δὲν ἔχει νὰ σὲ δώσει πιά.

34 Κι ἂν πτωχικὴ τὴν βρεῖς, ἡ Ἰθάκη δὲν σὲ γέλασε.

35 Ἔτσι σοφὸς ποὺ ἔγινες, μὲ τόση πεῖρα,

36 ἤδη θὰ τὸ κατάλαβες ἡ Ἰθάκες τί σημαίνουν.

As in other poems already examined, Keeley and Sherrard retain a transliterated Greek spelling of the title, using "Ithaka" for "Ithaca," thus Helleniz-
ing the viewpoint through an orthographic device. The focus of the piece is
not the past, but hypothetical futures, pluralized via a mind that is skeptically
open to the ongoing search rather than intent upon arrival at a destination.

Significantly, Odysseus, the Homeric character, has been written right out of the poem and with him *nost-algia,* or longing for home: "When you set out on the journey to Ithaka, / pray that the road be long, / full of adventures, full of knowledge," 1–3). If the ear is pitched in a certain direction, one can hear an echo of Aristotle's reversal and recognition (*peripeteia* and *anagnorisis*) in these lines. In the *Poetics,* they are used to describe the tragic plot but also the plot of the *Odyssey.*[37] "Ithaka" glances at the great genres of Greek antiquity— epic and tragedy—and deflects them. It uses demotic Greek and thirty-six lines of poetry to do so.

With the marginalizing of Odysseus and *nostos* come other changes. The poem not only demystifies epic heroism but also remakes the notion of grandness by turning it into a subjective state—a condition of the soul—that inclines one toward experiences that broaden the range of everyday life. Reference to the two cannibalistic tribes that Homer's wanderer encounters, the Laistrygonians and the Cyclopes, arise only to be dismissed. If such monsters consume you, they are the monsters you breed, and angry Poseidon himself is a phantom of a phobic inner life. Consumption on this journey will have nothing to do with fear and everything to do with pleasure. In its play upon the senses of sight, touch, hearing, and smell, the lines are redolent of an orientalized Mediterranean of mixed tongues and cultural sophistication. The poem hinges upon two closely related phrases: "thoughts raised high" ("σκέψις ὑψηλή," 7) and "rare emotion" ("ἐκλεκτὴ συγκίνησις," 8), both evocative of the homoerotic desire and ephebic beauty that we have seen in other poems, notably, "Ionic" and "One of Their Gods." The adjective "rare" or "select" ("ἐκλεκτός") resonates with the phrase "sensual perfumes" ("ἡδονικὰ μυρωδικά," 20–21) several lines later, repeated twice for emphasis. Cavafy's self-commentary on the poem draws attention to this, the hedonic always carrying connotations of the deviant and the forbidden.[38]

These connotations need to be considered in light of the lofty thought— *skepsis*—that enables us to enjoy ports of call, Phoenician and Egyptian emporia rich not only with rare gems—"mother of pearl and coral, amber and ebony" (20)—but also with learned scholars (24). *Skepsis* resonates in these lines because the nondemotic, classical meaning stirs up the ancient notion of reflection, critical thought, and prolongation of the search. On the other hand, the "beautiful journey" ("ὡραῖο ταξεῖδι," 31) pulls in the other direction, bringing us back to worlds of pleasure that we could not have foreseen in setting out, certainly not with the Homeric epic as a point of reference. It is

---

37. See Aristotle, *Poetics,* ed. with rev. trans., Michelle Zerba and David Gorman (New York: W.W. Norton, 2018), chs. 6, 13, 14.

38. Cavafy, *Καβαφικά Αυτοσχόλια,* ed. Lechonitis, 26–27.

worth observing that the adjective translated as "lofty" ("ὑψηλή") is derived
from the ancient Greek word for "sublime," a poetic concept, from Longinus
to Kant, that is bound up with the idea of cognitive breaches and transgression
of limits. In the journey that the poem extols, there is always a space beyond.
It is the poverty and smallness of home—formulated as such in the mind of a
seasoned traveler—that provides the impetus to set out. Among other possible
interpretations, this is "what Ithakas mean" ("ἡ Ἰθάκες τὶ σημαίνουν," 36). The
plural form of the place name reorients the ancient text and generalizes the
experience of plural odysseys.

"Ithaka" provides an illuminating backdrop for one of Cavafy's early
unpublished prose poems, "Ships," composed around 1895, on how poetry
is made and circulated under a regime that monitors sexuality and related
content. The language of the piece, however, maintains a generalizing register and refrains from naming details. While Cavafy does not call it "suggéstif," the allegory aligns it with poems that are more clearly written in that
mode. The date of the piece places it within the same time frame as "Second
Odyssey" and "The End of Odysseus," when Cavafy was using Homeric texts
and odyssean metaphors of wandering, exile, and return to explore the possibilities of poetic expression. In fact, the final line of "Ships" cites the *Iliad*,
and the piece as a whole bears resemblance to the *Odyssey*'s use of seafaring
imagery in connection with epic song.[39] A poetics of weak links and oblique
relations, which this study has pursued in part through the concepts of multiformity and alternative tales, finds a provocative analogue in Cavafy's poetics
of indirection. The prosaic simplicity of the title sets off the artfulness of the
sustained metaphor that carries the piece: trading voyages that bear goods
(poems) to foreign markets where they are delivered (published) after suffering damage (censorship or another form of loss). *Nostos*, in the sense of safe
passage to a destination, is the chief preoccupation of the poem, though the
ancient Greek term never appears in the poem.

Composed mostly in demotic, "Ships" conceives of the creative process in
terms of commercial travel to foreign ports. Because Cavafy's own method of
publishing was decidedly noncommercial, the piece has an ironic edge that
calls attention to the incongruities of treating poems like merchandise. But
the imagery of market forces also captures, in an unironic way, the degree to
which poetic design is itself interwoven with contingency—with a force field
of material and economic circumstances that constantly interact with imagination and craft.[40]

---

39. See Dougherty, *Raft of Odysseus*, for a fuller discussion of these associations.

40. English translation of the poem is by the author; for the Greek, see *Κρυμμένα Ποιήματα,
1877; -1923*, ed. George Savidis (Athens: Ikaros, 1993), 115–17.

From Imagination to paper. It's a difficult passage, a dangerous sea. The distance is short at first glance, and yet how long a journey it is and how damaging to those ships that attempt it.

Ἀπὸ τὴν Φαντασίαν ἕως εἰς τὸ Χαρτί. Εἶναι δύσκολον πέρασμα, εἶναι ἐπικίνδυνος θάλασσα. Ἡ ἀπόστασις φαίνεται μικρὰ κατὰ πρώτην ὄψιν, καὶ ἐν τοσούτῳ πόσον μακρὸν ταξίδι εἶναι, καὶ πόσον ἐπιζήμιον ἐνίοτε διὰ τὰ πλοῖα τὰ ὁποῖα τὸ ἐπιχειροῦν.

Uncertainty is sounded immediately in these words.[41] They not only introduce a sense of urgency into the description of the poetic voyage "from Imagination onto Paper," but in juxtaposition with "Ithaka," they make us ponder how risk-laden the journey shaping *that* journey must have been. What was lost at sea in the venture that is this poem? Beginning in an expository, almost journalistic tone, the speaker rivets attention on the importance of the imaginary passage that it is describing. The scaled back, incomplete sentences that open the piece command attention, the hesitations expressing the difficulty of rendering the loss that the piece aims to articulate obliquely. If there is no formulaic language available for this poetic enterprise, recourse to an ancient imagery of the Mediterranean can at least provide a set of loose and ready prompts.

The poem is divided into four major parts: 1) a description of the imagination at work; 2) the effects of its transference to the blank page; 3) an expression of sadness for what is lost in transmission; and 4) rare moments in which imagination appears, miraculously, not to have been severely diminished by its transport into language and the public sphere. Throughout, there is an emphasis upon "damage" ("ζημία").

The first kind of damage comes from the highly fragile nature of the merchandise that the ships carry. In the marketplaces of the Imagination, the greatest number and most beautiful of the objects are crafted from delicate glass and translucent pottery and even with all the care in the world many things break on the route, and many break when they reach dry land. All such harm is irreparable because it's out of the question to turn back and to collect similarly formed objects. It's impossible to discover the same shop that sold them. The marketplaces of the Imagination have large and luxurious shops, but not of long duration. Their exchanges are brief, and the merchandise sells quickly. It is very rare to go back again and discover the same exporters with the same goods.

---

41. See Jusdanis, *Poetics of Cavafy*, 15–21.

Ἡ πρώτη ζημία προέρχεται ἐκ τῆς λίαν εὐθραύστου φύσεως τῶν ἐμπορευ-
μάτων τὰ ὁποῖα μεταφέρουν τὰ πλοῖα. Εἰς τὰς ἀγορὰς τῆς Φαντασίας, τὰ
πλεῖστα καὶ τὰ καλύτερα πράγματα εἶναι κατασκευασμένα ἀπὸ λεπτὰς
ὑάλους καὶ κεράμους διαφανεῖς, καὶ με ὅλην τὴν προσοχὴν τοῦ κόσμου
πολλὰ σπάνουν εἰς τὸν δρόμον, καὶ πολλὰ σπάνουν ὅταν τὰ ἀποβιβάζουν
εἰς τὴν ξηράν. Πᾶσα δὲ τοιαύτη ζημία εἶναι ἀνεπανόρθωτος, διότι εἶναι ἔξω
λόγου νὰ γυρίσῃ ὀπίσω τὸ πλοῖον καὶ νὰ παραλάβῃ πράγματα ὁμοιόμορφα.
Δὲν ὑπάρχει πιθανότης νὰ εὑρεθῇ τὸ ἴδιον κατάστημα τὸ ὁποῖον τὰ ἐπώλει.
Αἱ ἀγοραὶ τῆς Φαντασίας ἔχουν καταστήματα μεγάλα καὶ πολυτελῆ, ἀλλ᾽
ὄχι μακροχρονίου διαρκείας. Αἱ συναλλαγαί των εἶναι βραχεῖαι, ἐκποιοῦν
τὰ ἐμπορεύματά των ταχέως, καὶ διαλύουν ἀμέσως. Εἶναι πολὺ σπάνιον ἓν
πλοῖον ἐπανερχόμενον νὰ εὕρῃ τοὺς αὐτοὺς ἐξαγωγεῖς μὲ τὰ αὐτὰ εἴδη.

Imagination is a busy place. The Greek word for it, *phantasia,* derives from a
verb of vision, *phainetai,* which means "to seem" or "to appear," and in Cavafy
it is closely connected with an aesthetic sense that can create beauty in the
gap between art and life. It is the quasi-Kantian image-making faculty (*Einbil-
dungskraft*), which generates from physical perception the visual forms available for poetic fashioning. It includes shops, transactions between parties that
negotiate within shops, and delivery systems in the form of ships that export
goods. In short, imagination does not precede the worldly economic system
of exchange that puts poems into circulation among consumers. It is itself part
of a highly differentiated economy that actively trades within and across the
limits of the internal and the external, the private and the public, the mind
and the world. The most salient features of the objects that circulate in this
economy are their beauty, fragility, and evanescence. Readers of Cavafy will
detect in these qualities some of the preeminent attributes of his homoerotic
aesthetic—the allure of the elusive ephebic male, the stir of mysterious spiritual forces at work in ordinary affairs, and the crafted quality of memory that
turns temporal distance into a tenuous poetic present.

The loss on which the poem first focuses is related to the constitution of
the objects of the imagination; they are "delicate glass and translucent pottery," and they make their way into large and luxurious shops that are highly
transient. In short, they bear the marks of refinement and artificiality that
are typically associated in Cavafy with decadence and the erotic. Copious as
these products are in the market setting, they are also easily breakable, and
the harm they sustain is said to be "irreparable." Once they shatter, they are
forever gone. Delicate and transient as they are, the products of the imagination are not fungible, and this introduces a sense of precarity into the market
where they circulate. *Phantasia* has only a loose grip on the things it trades.

Moreover, this merchandise is for sale only briefly, and its transience is part of its allure. Again, the poem invites us to consider the damage it is itself sustaining in the very act of creation. This damage now extends to the storage space available on the vessels that transport the breakable contents.

The ships embark from the harbors of prosperous mainlands heavily laden, and then when they find themselves on the open sea, they are forced to jettison part of their cargo in order to save the whole. So hardly any ship succeeds in carrying to safety all the treasures that it took away. The things thrown overboard are, to be sure, the less valuable goods, but sometimes sailors in their haste happen to make mistakes and toss into the sea highly valuable objects.

Ἀναχωροῦν ἀπὸ τοὺς λιμένας τῶν εὐμαρῶν ἠπείρων καταφορτωμένα, καὶ ἔπειτα ὅταν εὑρεθοῦν εἰς τὴν ἀνοικτὴν θάλασσαν ἀναγκάζονται νὰ ῥίψουν ἓν μέρος ἐκ τοῦ φορτίου διὰ νὰ σώσουν τὸ ὅλον. Οὕτως ὥστε οὐδὲν σχεδὸν πλοῖον κατορθώνει νὰ φέρῃ ἀκεραίους τοὺς θησαυροὺς ὅσους παρέλαβε. Τὰ ἀπορριπτόμενα εἶναι βεβαίως τὰ ὀλιγοτέρας ἀξίας εἴδη, ἀλλὰ κάποτε συμβαίνει οἱ ναῦται, ἐν τῇ μεγάλῃ των βίᾳ, νὰ κάμνουν λάθη καὶ νὰ ῥίπτουν εἰς τὴν θάλασσαν πολύτιμα ἀντικείμενα.

As the objects of imagination move from the teeming marketplaces of prosperous mainlands, they partially lose their preciousness and become revalued as "cargo." Their sheer abundance, despite initial breakage, introduces complications. The act of aesthetic creation cannot retain or use everything that the image-making faculty supplies. It must sometimes jettison valuable goods—ones whose worth may be not be recognized in the swiftness of disposal. In order to prevent the wholesale loss of what it manages to bring to harbor, the poet is compelled to lighten and adjust his own freight. With the evocative image of sailors throwing things overboard, we are invited to think of the many interactive forces that might reduce content within the shifting bounds of imagination itself: chance, the onset of strong emotion in the writing process, the vagaries of memory, the limitations of craft, the poet's own judgment about past creative efforts. Cavafy's own organization of his poems reflects this allegorical process since he rewrote many works, chose to keep some hidden, never finished others, and completely dispensed with yet others. He would have us see his poetic corpus as a body of goods that have suffered loss and damage, but perhaps also a beneficial sorting out.

Only with the arrival of the ships at their destinations do we reach the point in the poem when imagination makes its way to the "white harbor of paper" ("τὸν λευκὸν χάρτινον λιμένα"). Now the values of place and time come into play, and they appear in the form of "customs officials" ("οἱ ἀξιοματούχοι τοῦ τελωνείου") who decide whether and how much of the cargo on the ships may be unloaded. Instead of repeating the word "damage" ("ζημία"), the poem now turns to "sacrifice" ("θυσία") to describe loss: literary standards (they recall Woolf's "spirit of the age") require "more sacrifices" when the ships reach land. Now it is a question of having to give up things that one venerates or holds valuable in order to come into public circulation, and different lands have different restrictions. Beginning as luxurious "merchandise" ("ἐμπορεύματα") and moving on to being "cargo" ("φορτίο"), what comes to shore among the objects of imagination is potential "contraband" ("λαθρεμπόριον"). If it is identified as such, it is either confiscated or refused entry into harbor—in other words, censored.

The glass vessels and pottery identified in the first lines now turn into the intoxicating substances they contain—wines and spirits, which are forbidden in many ports of call. Too heady to be admitted, they sometimes make their way into prohibition zones, traveling in "deceptive containers" ("ἀπατηλῶν κιβωτίων"), for which one does not have to go far in Cavafy to find examples. His poetry depends upon half-hidden things—things like the fine wines smuggled into policed zones "for select drinking parties." The combination of contingency, good fortune intermingled with bad, and a kind of cunning exercised in the circumvention of border controls contribute to the odyssean tonalities of "Ships." They suggest that imagination, while it suffers in arriving on the blank page, can manipulate the forbidden through coding—a kind of *metis* that enables at least a partial *nostos*.

With the loosening of constraints, "Ships" moves toward an end in two paragraphs whose emotional send-off captures what Cavafy often does in his final lines of verse: complex emotion distilled through memory. Although "we should be happy" about compromised victories, "there is something else that is more distressing, more distressing yet" ("Θλιβερόν, θλιβερὸν εἶναι ἄλλο πρᾶγμα").

> Sometimes certain large ships pass by with coral jewelry and masts of ebony, with large red and white flags flying, laden with treasures, and they don't even near the harbor, either because all the goods they carry are forbidden or because the harbor isn't sufficiently deep to receive them. And so they follow along their route. A tail wind blows their silky sails, the sun glazes the brilliance of their prows of gold, and they move away calmly and magnificently, move away forever from us and from our narrow harbor.

Εἶναι ὅταν περνοῦν κάτι πελώρια πλοῖα, μὲ κοράλλινα κοσμήματα καὶ
ἱστοὺς ἐξ ἐβένου, μὲ ἀναπεπταμένας μεγάλας σημαίας λευκὰς καὶ ἐρυθράς,
γεμάτα μὲ θησαυρούς, τὰ ὁποῖα οὔτε πλησιάζουν κἂν εἰς τὸν λιμένα εἴτε
διότι ὅλα τὰ εἴδη τὰ ὁποῖα φέρουν εἶναι ἀπηγορευμένα, εἴτε διότι δὲν ἔχει
ὁ λιμὴν ἀρκετὸν βάθος διὰ νὰ τὰ δεχθῇ. Καὶ ἐξακολουθοῦν τὸν δρόμον
των. Οὔριος ἄνεμος πνέει ἐπὶ τῶν μεταξωτῶν των ἱστίων, ὁ ἥλιος ὑαλίζει
τὴν δόξαν τῆς χρυσῆς των πρώρας, καὶ ἀπομακρύνονται ἠρέμως καὶ μεγα-
λοπρεπῶς, ἀπομακρύνονται διὰ παντὸς ἀπὸ ἡμᾶς καὶ ἀπὸ τὸν στενόχωρον
λιμένα μας.

Reminiscent of ancient seagoing vessels laden with goods drawn from several
continents, these Mediterranean ships of the imagination also recall "Ithaca"
with its rich emporia filled with "mother-of-pearl and coral, amber and ebony,
/ and sensuous perfumes of every kind" (19–21). But in that poem the marketplaces are open and accessible, offering more for travelers than they bring on
their journey, and thus enriching rather than diminishing them. In "Ships,"
the vessels that transport such wealth are beyond reach. They have a ghostli-
ness about them, a haunting sense of mystery on the high seas, of treasure that
has been lost.

It is difficult to say anything about these ghost ships because their contents lie beyond the power words; they are ephemeral and glimpsed rather
than known.

As luminous as the sight of them was, the forgetting of them is just as swift.
And when several years have passed, if perhaps one day—as we sit motionless gazing at the light or listening to the silence—there by chance come back
to our minds certain inspired verses, we don't recognize them at first, and
we wrack our memory to remember where we heard them before. After a
lot of effort, an ancient recollection awakens, and we remember that those
verses are from the song the sailors sang, the beautiful heroes of the *Iliad*
when their great, exquisite ships passed by and made their way along—who
knows where.

Εὐτυχῶς εἶναι πολὺ σπάνια αὐτὰ τὰ πλοῖα. Μόλις δύο, τρία βλέπομεν
καθ' ὅλον μας τὸν βίον. Τὰ λησμονῶμεν δὲ ὀγρήγορα. Ὅσῳ λαμπρὰ ἦτο
ἡ ὀπτασία, τόσῳ ταχεῖα εἶναι ἡ λήθη της. Καὶ ἀφοῦ περάσουν μερικὰ ἔτη,
ἐὰν καμίαν ἡμέραν—ἐνῶ καθήμεθα ἀδρανῶς βλέποντες τὸ φῶς ἢ ἀκούο-
ντες τὴν σιωπὴν—τυχαίως ἐπανέλθουν εἰς τὴν νοεράν μας ἀκοὴν στροφαί
τινες ἐνθουσιώδεις, δὲν τὰς ἀναγνωρίζομεν κατ' ἀρχὰς καὶ τυραννῶμεν τὴν

μνήμην μας διὰ νὰ ἐνθυμηθῶμεν ποῦ ἠκούσαμεν αὐτὰς πρίν. Μετὰ πολ-
λοῦ κόπου ἐξυπνᾶται ἡ παλαιὰ ἀνάμνησις καὶ ἐνθυμώμεθα ὅτι αἱ στροφαὶ
αὗται εἶναι ἀπὸ τὸ ἆσμα τὸ ὁποῖον ἔψαλλον οἱ ναῦται, ὡραῖοι ὡς ἥρωες τῆς
Ἰλιάδος, ὅταν ἐπερνοῦσαν τὰ μεγάλα, τὰ θεσπέσια πλοῖα καὶ ἐπροχώρουν
πηγαίνοντα—τίς ἠξεύρει ποῦ.

In a synaesthesia of sight and sound, the speaker suggests that the audi-
tory faculty may occasionally be aroused by a stir of notes in the air that are
vaguely familiar, trace-like, but hard to recognize (Cavafy's operative verb is
anagnorizō, the noun *anagnorisis*). The ear can tell that they compose "verses"
or "musical sounds ("στροφαί"), but where did they come from? Intent upon
trying to remember, the listener gradually realizes that the sounds emanate
from a rare ship once seen, which never came to harbor, but on whose decks
the sailors chanted, their song as alluring as the vessel they propelled was
luxurious. Bits and snatches reach shore. They are like the song "the heroes
of the *Iliad*" once sang, not on the return voyage, but on a journey while they
were still young and beautiful, before the war would ruin them. The simile
omits mention of Troy and the violence of battle, touching only subtly upon
the physical attractiveness of a male collective, bound harmoniously by song
and created for pleasure, not toil. Evocations of the sensuous ephebe enter the
poem discreetly, in an oblique manner, smuggled in like fine wines for select
drinking parties. The remainder is gone.

While "Ships" should not be taken as a definitive statement about Cavafy's
poetic craft, it offers an especially insightful view of the complex ways in
which he handles the relationship between poetry, imagination, and the half-
hidden homoerotic desires he often writes about. The piece not only innova-
tively synthesizes the tropes of diffusion, isolation, passage, and return, it also
moves at a slant toward its contraband subject matter, developing weak links
between its own poetics and Homer's, mingling the ancient and the modern
with the poignancy of irrecuperable loss. In the form of fictional biography
and a style that combines granite and rainbow, *Orlando* is not an allegory like
"Ships," but Woolf shapes it as a bittersweet return tale on several levels. There
are losses in the sex change; the transport across embodiments comes with
damage, especially to legal and social rights. But marriage is transformed into
an institution that can bend to accommodate errant forms of gender and sexuality, and social demands may be mitigated by a subject's use of clothing as
costume. Woolf's *Orlando* is less burdened by fragility than is Cavafy's "Ships,"
and the mystical vision of the cosmos that the protagonist experiences in the
last pages where "everything [is] partly something else, and each [gains] an
odd moving power from this union of itself and something not itself" (237) is

more integrative than the Iliadic ghost ship whose trace-like sounds haunt the soul. Both, however, are caught up in a spiral of deep emotion that keeps the ending open enough to continue the search for articulated meaning.

Cahier builds up to its own ecstatic and ambiguous end. After the lustral ship stages an appearance in the trans-Atlantic voyage, the poem sweeps the audience up into an ascent whose figure is the white dove. Unlike Woolf's goose, Césaire's dove is not a comically imagined creature, but another image of vexed whiteness that exposes how embedded in language the pigmentation crisis is. The dove recalls the albatross that appears earlier in the poem. But instead of suggesting abjectness—the clumsiness of an animal that can't walk on land without looking ridiculous—the dove ascends, "a licker of the sky" ("*monte lécheur de ciel*," 174), in an image of lustration once again. It disappears, however, into "the great black hole" ("*le grand trou noir*"), perhaps a signifier of an elevated negritude, where the speaker goes in search of a "tongue," a language ("*langue*"), that can transform the maleficence of night and darkness. The radical dynamism of this movement is enigmatic. Instead of a conclusion, the audience of *Cahier* is left with the puzzling image of ingress into a "motionless sweeping," or "*immobile véerition*."[42] Another of Césaire's concatenated words from Latin (*verro*=sweep), *véerition* suggests rapid movement. Combined with an adjective that means unmoving, it forms an oxymoron. What exactly is this kinetic stasis? An integration into the absolute? A mystical homecoming? An act of paralyzing the power of evil? The audience is left to wonder.

---

42. Césaire, *Journal of a Homecoming*, trans. Davis, xiii–xiv.

Toward an End

Tell all the truth but tell it slant—
Success in Circuit lies
Too bright for our infirm Delight
The Truth's superb surprise

As Lightning to the Children eased
With explanation kind
The Truth must dazzle gradually
Or every man be blind—

—EMILY DICKINSON

I T MAY SEEM counterintuitive to turn to a nineteenth-century American poet famous for her self-imposed seclusion and apparent disengagement from politics in approaching an end to this study of modern odysseys. Yet Emily Dickinson wrote compellingly of poetry, travel, and the uses of indirection at a time when the Civil War, the abolitionist movement, and activist groups in support of women's suffrage were fomenting around her. The human depths these events plumbed are also plumbed in the depths of the poetry she wrote, even if historical reference is rare in her verse. When one of her personas exhorts us to "Tell all the truth but tell it slant—," she indicates the reason, pointing to how our capacity for "Delight," feeble as it is ("infirm"), cannot measure up to Truth's "superb surprise," which "must dazzle gradually" to avoid blinding the receiver.

Initially, the poem seems to subscribe to an absolute notion of Truth, the capital "T" rendering it a metaphysical form and the light imagery ("bright," "lightning," "dazzle") associating it with a religious experience of ascent and discovery. But the word "all" sits ambiguously in the first line; it may mean "everyone," or it may mean "the whole"—tell everyone the "truth" and/or tell the "truth" completely, all of it. It's an admonition cast when there is doubt—when truth telling is a pragmatic act in the lower case. No sooner do we hear it than the poem moves into ellipsis, punning, and oxymoron. "Success" implies effort and attainment via the roundabout way, the detour. Yet in directing us to take such a route, the poem flags the possibility that "Success in Circuit lies" may mean "Success resides in Circuit" or that "Success in the form of Circuit tells falsehoods." Ambiguity gives way to equivocation. The pun leads us past the oxymoron of "infirm Delight" to the key word, which now appears in the upper case—not the "truth" of line 1 but the "Truth" of line 4. Who knows what "lies" in that "superb surprise," ambush or rapture. As the poem moves into similitude, restating what it means to tell it slant, it delivers another oxymoron. Truth is like "Lightning," but if so, can it really be "eased" to "Children," or anyone else for that matter? Lightning strikes, suddenly and unpredictably. The idea of it can perhaps be eased through explanation, but the phenomenon itself jolts. Similarly, can something brilliant "dazzle gradually"? The reader may be able to imagine a path toward increasingly radiant Truth, but like easing the Lightning, graduating the brilliance is, if not contradictory, then informed by a profound tension. Through its own slant telling, the poem enacts what it apparently describes—an enigmatic notion of truth that conceals while it reveals, recalling Cavafy's "half-hidden things," Woolf's "phosphorescent flare in the darkness," and Césaire's "immobile veerition."

Dickinson's sly eight-liner speaks to the imaginatively crafted journeys explored in *Modern Odysseys* where the body and the psyche appear at the margins of social order, ontologically precarious, poorly understood, and straining against the impoverishment of language. Bringing polymorphous gender identities, vagrant sexualities, and racial difference into consciousness at a time when they were still minimally articulated required the kind of poetic resourcefulness that Homer calls *metis* and that Dickinson connects with artful slantness. Despite its oral-formulaic poetry, the *Odyssey*'s use of sophisticated narrative structures, its awareness of its own diachronic depth, and its maneuvering around alternative tales take us into the fictional world of a character who travels the margins of the earth, encountering the unknown and living to tell his tale. In telling it, he also marks his own modernity in the paths of epic song, understanding that the bards internal to the epic depend upon him for what will one day be a *nostos* tale in their own repertoire. How this aligns with the ultimate justice of Zeus and a *deus ex machina* that hinges on collective forgetting remains puzzling. Among the many features of Homer's epic that make it a story for our time is the self-reflexive quality of the narrative, which questions the ground on which its own story stands and explores the surprise lurking in apparent closure. A poetics of indirection not only embraces these dimensions of odysseys; it enables us to shape methods of critical appreciation that give them their due.

In attenuating the relationship between Homer, Cavafy, Woolf, and Césaire, my project may raise the question of why retain the epic at all. The approaches I have adopted may strain the limits of comparison, making the texts I have assembled seem unlikely combinations joined by rather abstract tropes. But the activity of comparison must often confront such well-directed skepticism, and what seems less far-fetched to us now has only become so by virtue of being naturalized over time. Working with rather than against tenuity, this book has attempted to demonstrate how literary interpretation may move along byways that are neither positivistically available for discovery nor randomly invented in hermeneutic free association, but instead creatively generated in acts of reading between texts that have never been juxtaposed. We sometimes forget that imagination extends beyond the artist and the poem to the work of criticism, where new connections must be envisioned as the world around us grows multidirectionally, transnationally, and with increasing access to the foreign. *Modern Odysseys* has tried to contribute to this dialogue by exercising the meanings of telling it slant and by tracing some of the possibilities available to a poetics of indirection whose inspiration is drawn from the pioneering work of the writers it has tried to bring to new and wider audiences.

BIBLIOGRAPHY

Abate-Çelebi, Barbara Dell. *Penelope's Daughters*. Berkeley: University of California Press, 2010.

Abel, Elizabeth. *Virginia Woolf and the Fictions of Psychoanalysis*. Chicago: University of Chicago Press, 1989.

Alcock, Susan, John Cherry, and Jas Elsner, eds. *Pausanias: Travel and Memory in Roman Greece*. New York: Oxford University Press, 2003.

Aleksiuk, Natasha. "'A Thousand Angles': Photographic Irony in the Work of Julia Margaret Cameron and Virginia Woolf." *Mosaic* 33.2 (2000): 125–42.

Alexandre, Alfred. *Aimé Césaire: la part intime*. Montreal: Memoire d'Encrier, 2014.

Alexiou, Margaret. "C. P. Cavafy's 'Dangerous' Drugs: Poetry, Eros and the Dissemination of Images." In *The Text and Its Margins: Post-Structuralist Approaches to Twentieth-Century Greek Literature*, edited by Margaret Alexiou and Vassilis Lambropoulos, 157–96. New York: Pella, 1985.

Allan, Rutger. *The Middle Voice in Ancient Greek: A Study in Polysemy*. Amsterdam: Brill, 2003.

Anderson, Ryan. *When Harry Became Sally: Responding to the Transgender Moment*. New York: Encounter Books, 2018.

Apter, Emily. *Against World Literature: On the Politics of Untranslatability*. New York: Verso, 2013.

Aristotle. *Poetics*, edited with revised translation by Michelle Zerba and David Gorman. New York: W. W. Norton, 2018.

Aristoxenus. *Aristoxenus: Elementa Rhythmica: The Fragment of Book II and the Additional Evidence for Aristoxenean Rhythmic Theory*, edited by Lionel Pearson. New York: Oxford, 1990.

Armstrong, Richard. *A Compulsion for Antiquity: Freud and the Ancient World*. Ithaca, NY: Cornell University Press, 2005.

Arnold, A. James. "Beyond Postcolonial Césaire: Reading *Cahier d'un retour au pays natal* Historically." *Forum for Modern Language Studies* 44.3 (2008): 258–75.

———. *Modernism and Negritude: The Poetry and Poetics of Aimé Césaire*. Cambridge, MA: Harvard University Press, 1981.

Athenaeus. *The Deipnosophists*. Translated by Charles Gulick. Vol. 3. Cambridge, MA: Harvard University Press, 1929.

Atwood, Margaret. *The Penelopiad*. Edinburgh: Canongate, 2005.

Auerbach, Erich. *Mimesis: The Representation of Reality in Western Literature*. Translated by Willard Trask. 1946; Princeton: Princeton University, 2003.

Austin, Norman. *Archery at the Dark of the Moon: Poetic Problems in Homer's* Odyssey. Berkeley: University of California Press, 1975.

Ba, Mamadou. "S'orienter dans l'histoire: Césaire entre mémoire et promesse." In *Aimé Césaire: oeuvre et héritage*, edited by Lapoussinière, 188–95.

Bader, Bettina. "Egypt and the Mediterranean in the Bronze Age: The Archaeological Evidence." In *Oxford Handbooks Online* (2015). Accessed 5 May 2019. doi:10.1093/oxfordhb/9780199935413.013.35.

Bahun, Sanja. "Woolf and Psychoanalytic Theory." In *Virginia Woolf in Context*, edited by Randall and Goldman, 92–109.

Bakker, Egbert. "The Greek *Gilgamesh* or the Immortality of Return." *Eranos: The Proceedings of the 9th International Symposium on the* Odyssey (2000): 331–52.

———. *The Meaning of Meat and the Structure of the* Odyssey. New York: Cambridge University Press, 2013.

———. *Pointing at the Past: From Formula to Performance in Homeric Poetics*. Cambridge, MA: Harvard University Press, 2006.

———. "Rhapsodes, Bards, and Bricoleurs: Homerizing Literary Theory." *Classics @: Issue 3*. Accessed 5 May 2019. www.chs.harvard.edu/publications.sec/classics.ssp.

Banfield, Ann. "Time Passes: Virginia Woolf, Post-Impressionism, and Cambridge Time." *Poetics Today* 24.3 (2003): 471–516.

Beaton, Roderick. "C. P. Cavafy: Irony and Hellenism." *Slavonic and East European Review* 59.4 (1981): 516–28.

Beaulieu, Marie-Claire. *The Sea in the Greek Imagination*. Philadelphia: University of Pennsylvania Press, 2015.

Bell, Quentin. *Virginia Woolf: A Biography*. New York: Harcourt Brace Jovanovich, 1972.

Benítez-Rojo, Antonio. *The Repeating Island: The Caribbean and the Postmodern Perspective*. Translated by James Maraniss. 2nd ed. Durham, NC: Duke University Press, 1996.

Benveniste, Émile. *Problèmes de linguistique générale 1*. Paris: Gallimard, 1966.

Benzel, Kathryn. "Reading Readers in Virginia Woolf's *Orlando: A Biography*." *Style* 28.2 (1994): 169–82.

Bergren, Ann. *Weaving Truth: Essays on Language and the Female in Greek Thought*. Washington, DC: Center for Hellenic Studies, 2008.

Bernier, Celeste-Marie. *Characters of Blood: Black Heroism in the Transatlantic Imagination*. Charlottesville: University of Virginia Press, 2012.

Berman, Jessica, ed. *A Companion to Virginia Woolf*. London: John Wiley. 2016.

———. "Is the Trans in Transnational the Trans in Transgender." *Modernism/Modernity* 2.2 (2017). Accessed 5 May 2019. https://modernismmodernity.org/articles/trans-transnational.

———. *Modernist Commitments: Ethics, Politics, and Transnational Modernism*. New York: Columbia University Press, 2012.

Berman, Jessica, and Jane Goldman, eds. *Virginia Woolf Out of Bounds.* New York: Pace University, 2001.

Besslich, S. *Schweigen—Verschweigen—Übergehen: Die Darstellung des Unausgesprochenen in der Odyssee.* Heidelberg: C. Winter, 1966.

Boitani, Piero. *The Shadow of Ulysses: Figures of a Myth.* Translated by Anita Weston. Oxford: Clarendon, 1994.

Boittin, Jennifer Ann. *Colonial Metropolis: The Urban Grounds of Anti-Imperialism and Feminism in Interwar Paris.* Lincoln: University of Nebraska Press, 2015.

Bonifazi, Anna. "Inquiring into *Nostos* and Its Cognates." *American Journal of Philology* 130.4 (2009): 481–510.

Booth, Alison. "The Lives of Houses: Woolf and Biography." In *A Companion to Virginia Woolf,* edited by Berman, 13–26.

Boyiopoulos, Kostas. "The Darkening of the Mirror: Cavafy's Variations on *The Picture of Dorian Gray.*" *Journal of Modern Greek Studies* 30.1 (2012): 21–43.

Brathwaite, Edward Kamau. "Caribbean Man in Space and Time." *Savacou,* Pamphlet 2 (1974).

Braund, David, and John Wilkins, eds. *Athenaeus and His World: Reading Greek Culture in the Roman Empire.* Exeter: University of Exeter, 2000.

Breton, André. *Manifestes du surréalisme,* Paris: Gallimard, 1967.

——. Preface of *Cahier d'un retour au pays natal / Return to my Native Land: Bilingual Edition.* New York: Brentano, 1947.

Briggs, Julia. *Reading Virginia Woolf.* Edinburgh: Edinburgh University Press, 2006.

——. *Virginia Woolf: An Inner Life.* New York: Harcourt, 2005.

——."Virginia Woolf and the 'Proper Writing of Lives.'" In *The Art of Literary Biography,* edited by John Batchelor, 245–65. Oxford: Clarendon Press, 1995.

Burgess, Jonathan. "The Death of Odysseus in the *Odyssey* and the *Telegony.*" *Antiqua* 7 (2014): 111–22.

——. *The Tradition of the Trojan War in Homer and the Epic Cycle.* Baltimore: Johns Hopkins University Press, 2004.

Burkert, Walter. *The Orientalizing Revolution: Near Eastern Influence on Greek Culture in the Early Archaic Age.* Translated by Margaret Pinder. Cambridge, MA: Harvard University Press, 1992.

——. *Structure and History in Greek Mythology and Ritual.* Rev. ed. Berkeley: University of California Press, 1982.

Butler, Shane. "On the Origin of 'Deep Classics.'" In *Deep Classics: Rethinking Classical Reception,* edited by Shane Butler, 1–19. London: Bloomsbury, 2016.

Carr, Helen. "Virginia Woolf, Empire, and Race." In *The Cambridge Companion to Virginia Woolf.* 2nd ed. Susan Sellers and Sue Roe, 197–213. New York: Cambridge University Press, 2010.

Caughie, Pamela. "The Temporality of Modernist Life Writing in the Era of Transsexualism: Virginia Woolf's *Orlando* and Einar Wegener's *Man into Woman.*" *Modern Fiction Studies* 59.3 (2013): 501–25.

Cavafy, C. P. *Καβαφικά Αυτοσχόλια,* edited by George Lechonitis. Alexandria: N. P., 1942.

——. *Ποιήματα,* edited by George Savidis, 2 vols. Athens: Ikaros, 1963.

——. *Τα Ποιήματα Α (1897–1918),* edited by George Savidis. Athens: Ikaros, 1991.

——. *Τα Ποιήματα Β (1919–1933),* edited by George Savidis. Athens: Ikaros, 1991.

——. *Μικρά Καβαφικά Α,* edited by George Savidis. Athens: Hermes, 1985.

———. *Μικρά Καβαφικά Β,* edited by George Savidis. Athens: Hermes, 1987.

———. *Κρυμμένα ποιήματα (1877; –1923),* edited by George Savidis. Athens: Ikaros, 1993.

———. *Ατελή ποιήματα (1918–1932),* edited by Renata Lavagnini. Athens: Ikaros, 1994.

———. *Τα Πεζά (1882; –1931),* edited by Michael Pieris. Athens: Ikaros, 2003.

———. *Αποκηρυγμένα: Ποιήματα και μεταφράσεις (1886–1898),* edited by George Savidis. 2nd ed. Athens: Ikaros, 2013.

———. *Clearing the Ground: Poetry and Prose: 1902–1911,* edited and translated by Martin McKinsey. Chapel Hill, NC: Laertes, 2015.

———. *Collected Poems: Bilingual Edition,* edited by George Savidis. Translated by Edmund Keeley and Philip Sherrard. Rev. ed. Princeton: Princeton University Press, 2009.

———. *Collected Poems: Bilingual Edition,* edited by Anthony Hirst. Translated by Evangelos Sachperoglou. New York: Oxford University Press, 2007.

———. *Complete Poems.* Translated by Daniel Mendelsohn. New York: Knopf, 2012.

———. *The Forster-Cavafy Letters: Friends at a Slight Angle,* edited by Peter Jeffreys. Cairo: University Press of Cairo, 2009.

———. "Notes on Poetics and Ethics." Translated by Martin McKinsey. *Ploughshares* 11.4 (1985): 20–26.

———. "Our Museum." In *Selected Prose Works,* 42. For the Greek, see http://www.kavafis.gr/prose/content.asp?id=317&cat=6. Accessed 5 May 2019.

———. *Selected Prose Works,* edited and translated by Peter Jeffreys. Ann Arbor: University of Michigan Press, 2010.

Césaire, Aimé. *Cahier d'un retour au pays natal. Volontés* (Journal) 1939.

———. *Cahier d'un retour au pays natal.* Paris: Bordas, 1947.

———. *Cahier d'un retour au pays natal,* edited by Dominique Combe. Paris: Presses Universitaires de France, 1993.

———. *Complete Poetry of Aimé Césaire: Bilingual Edition.* Translated by A. James Arnold and Clayton Eshleman. Middleton, CT: Wesleyan University Press, 2017.

———. "Culture and Civilisation." *First International Conference of Negro Writers and Artists,* (Paris, Sorbonne, 19–22 September 1956). *Présence Africaine,* 8–10 (1956): 203–5.

———. *Discours sur le colonialisme.* Paris: Éditions Reclame, 1950; Paris: Présence Africaine, 1955. *Discourse on Colonialism.* Translated by Joan Pinkham. New York: Monthly Review Press, 1972.

———. *Journal of a Homecoming: Bilingual Edition.* Translated by N. Gregson Davis with Commentary by Abiola Irele. Durham, NC: Duke University Press, 2017.

———. "*Lettre au Maurice Thorez du 24 Octobre 1956.*" Translated by Chike Jeffers. *Social Text* 28.2 (2010): 145–52.

———. *Notebook of a Return to the Native Land.* Translated by Clayton Eshleman and Annette Smith. Middleton, CT: Wesleyan University Press, 2001.

———. "Poetry and Knowledge." In *Lyric and Dramatic Poetry, 1946–1982.* Translated by Clayton Eshleman and Annette Smith, xlii–lvi. Charlottesville: University of Virginia Press, 1990. In French, "*La poésie et la connaissance.*" *Tropiques* 12 (1945): 157–70.

———. *Toussaint Louverture: la révolution française et le problème colonial.* Paris: Présence Africaine, 2000.

———. *Une tempête.* Paris: Seuil, 1969.

Césaire, Aimé, René Ménil, and Suzanne Césaire, eds. *Tropiques: Revue Culturelle, 1941–1945.* Paris: Jean-Michel Place, 1978.

Césaire, Suzanne. "Le grand camouflage." *Tropiques* 13–14 (1945): 267–73; *The Great Camouflage: Writings of Dissent, 1941–1945*, edited by Daniel Maximin. Translated by Keith Walker. Middleton, CT: Wesleyan Press, 2012.

———. "*Misère de la poésie: John Antoine Nau*," *Tropiques* 4 (1942): 48–50.

———. "*Léo Frobenius et le problème des civilisations*," *Tropiques* 1 (1941): 27–36.

Chambers, Iain. *Mediterranean Crossings: The Politics of an Interrupted Modernity*. Durham, NC: Duke University Press, 2008.

Christensen, Joel. "The Clinical *Odyssey*: Odysseus' *Apologoi* and Narrative Therapy." *Arethusa* 51.1 (2018): 1–31.

Clackson, James. *Language and Society in the Greek and Roman Worlds*. New York: Cambridge University Press, 2015.

Clay, Diskin. "The Silence of Hermippos: Greece in the Poetry of Cavafy." *Greek, Roman, and Byzantine Studies* 3 (1977): 95–116.

Clay, Jenny Strauss. *The Wrath of Athena: Gods and Men in the* Odyssey. Princeton: Princeton University Press, 1983.

Clayton, Barbara. *A Penelopean Poetics: Reweaving the Feminine in Homer's* Odyssey. Lanham, MD: Lexington, 2004.

Clifford, James. *The Predicament of Culture: Twentieth-Century Ethnography, Literature, and Art*. Cambridge, MA: Harvard University Press, 1988.

Condé, Maryse. *Histoire de la femme cannibale*. Paris: Mercure de France, 2005. Translated by Richard Philcox. *The Cannibal Woman*. New York: Washington Square Press, 2007.

———. "*Négritude césairienne, négritude senghorienne*." *Revue de Littérature Comparée* 3–4 (1974): 409–19.

Condé, Maryse, and Richard Philcox. "Intimate Enemies: Conversation Between an Author and Her Translator." In *Intimate Enemies: Translations in Francophone Contexts*, edited by Kathryn Batchelor and Claire Bisdorff, 89–97. Liverpool: Liverpool University Press, 2013.

Constantakopoulou, Christy. *The Dance of the Islands: Insularity, Networks, the Athenian Empire, and the Aegean World*. New York: Oxford University Press, 2007.

Cook, Erwin. "Active and Passive Heroics in the *Odyssey*." *Classical World* 93.2 (1999): 149–67.

Crawford, Michael. "From Poseidonia to Paestum via the Lucanians." In *Greek and Roman Colonization: Origins, Ideologies, and Interactions*, edited by Guy Jolyon Bradley and John-Paul Wilson, 59–72. Cardiff: Classical Press of Wales, 2006.

Curtius, Anny Dominique. "Cannibalizing *Doudouisme*, Conceptualizing the Morne: Suzanne Césaire's Caribbean Ecopoetics." *South Atlantic Quarterly* 115.3 (2016): 513–34.

Daileader, Celia. "Othello's Sister: Racial Hermaphroditism and Appropriation in Virginia Woolf's *Orlando*." *Studies in the Novel* 45.1 (2013): 56–79.

Dalgarno, Emily. *Virginia Woolf and the Migrations of Language*. New York: Cambridge University Press, 2011.

Damrosch, David. *What Is World Literature?* Princeton: Princeton University Press, 2003.

Dante. *Inferno*. Translated by John Ciardi. New York: Signet, 1996.

Dash, J. Michael. *The Other America: Caribbean Literature in a New World Context*. Charlottesville: University of Virginia Press, 1998.

Davies, Malcolm. *The Greek Epic Cycle*. 2nd ed. London: Bristol Press, 2001.

Davis, N. Gregson. *Aimé Césaire*. New York: Cambridge University Press, 1997.

———. "Forging a Caribbean Literary Style: 'Vulgar Eloquence' and the Language of Césaire's *Cahier d'un retour au pays natal*." *South Atlantic Quarterly* 115.3 (2016): 457–67.

———. "'Homecomings without Home': Representations of (Post) Colonial *Nostos* (Homecoming) in the Lyric of Aimé Césaire and Derek Walcott." In *Homer in the Twentieth Century: Between World Literature and the Western Canon,* edited by Barbara Graziosi and Emily Greenwood, 191–209. New York: Oxford University Press, 2007.

———. "Negritude as Performance: The Interplay of Efficacious and Inefficacious Speech Acts in *Cahier d'un retour au pays natal.*" *Research in African Literatures* 41.1 (2010): 142–54.

de Gay, Jane. *Virginia Woolf's Novels and the Literary Past.* Edinburgh: Edinburgh University Press, 2007.

de Jong, Irene. *A Narratological Commentary on the* Odyssey. New York: Cambridge University Press, 2001.

Delas, Daniel. *"Césaire et le sacré: poésie et sacrifice."* In *L'écriture et le sacré: Senghor, Césaire, Glissant, Chamoiseau.* Montpellier: Presses Universitaires de la Méditerannée, 2002.

Dell, Marion. *Virginia Woolf's Influential Forebears: Julia Margaret Cameron, Anny Thackeray Ritchie, Julia Prinsep Stephen.* London: Palgrave Macmillan, 2016.

Desormeaux, Daniel. "The First of the (Black) Memorialists: Toussaint Louverture." Translated by Deborah Jenson and Molly Krueger Enz. *Yale French Studies* 107 (2005): 131–45.

Detloff, Madelyn, and Brenda Helt, eds. *Queer Bloomsbu*ry. Edinburgh: Edinburgh University Press, 2016.

Diagnostic and Statistical Manual of Mental Illness. 5th ed. Washington, DC: American Psychiatric Association, 2013.

DiBattista, Maria. *Imagining Virginia Woolf: An Experiment in Critical Biography.* Princeton: Princeton University Press, 2009.

Dick, Susan. "Literary Realism in *Mrs. Dalloway, To the Lighthouse, Orlando* and *The Waves.*" In *The Cambridge Companion to Virginia Woolf,* edited by Susan Sellers and Sue Roe, 50–71. 2nd ed. New York: Cambridge University Press, 2010.

Dickey, Colin. "Virginia Woolf and Photography." In *Edinburgh Companion to Virginia Woolf and the Arts,* edited by Humm, 375–91.

Dimock, G. E. "The Name of Odysseus." *Hudson Review* 9.1 (1956): 52–70.

———. *The Unity of the* Odyssey. Amherst: University of Massachusetts Press, 1989.

Diop, Cheikh M. S. *"Labilité et resilience: contours des notions."* In *Aimé Césaire: oeuvre et héritage,* edited by Lapoussinière, 326–44.

Dougherty, Carol. *The Raft of Odysseus: The Ethnographic Imagination of Homer's* Odyssey. New York: Oxford University Press, 2001.

Doyle, Laura, and Laura Winkiel, eds. *Geomodernisms: Race, Modernism, Modernity.* Bloomington: University of Indiana Press, 2005.

Dué, Casey. *Achilles Unbound: Multiformity and Tradition in the Homeric Epics.* Washington, DC: Center for Hellenic Studies, 2018. Accessed 8 September 2019. http://nrs.harvard.edu/urn-3:hul.ebook:CHS_Due.Achilles_Unbound.2018.

Dué, Casey, and Mary Ebbott. Homer Multitext Project. Introduction. Accessed 8 September 2019. https://chs.harvard.edu/CHS/article/display/1169.

———. Iliad *10 and the Poetics of Ambush, A Multitext Edition with Essays and Commentary.* Washington, DC: Center for Hellenic Studies, 2010. Accessed 9 September 2019. http://nrs.harvard.edu/urn-3:hul.ebook:CHS_Due_Ebbott.Iliad_10_and_the_Poetics_of_Ambush.2010.

Edmunds, Lowell. "Epic and Myth." In *A Companion to Ancient Epic,* edited by John Foley, 31–44. Hoboken, NJ: Wiley-Blackwell, 2005.

Edwards, Brent Hayes. "Aimé Césaire and the Syntax of Influence." *Research in African Literatures* 36.2 (2005): 1–18.

———. "The Ethnics of Surrealism." *Transition* 78 (1999): 132–34.

———. *The Practice of Diaspora: Literature, Transnationalism, and the Rise of Black Internationalism.* Cambridge, MA: Harvard University Press, 2003.

Edwards, Sarah. "'Permanent Preservation for the Benefit of the Nation': The Country House, Preservation, and Nostalgia in Vita Sackville-West's *The Edwardians* and Virginia Woolf's *Orlando.*" In *Modernism and Nostalgia: Bodies, Locations, Aesthetics,* edited by Tammy Clewett, 93–110. New York: Palgrave Macmillan, 2013.

Ekdawi, Sarah. "Cavafy's Byzantium." *Byzantine and Modern Greek Studies* 20 (1996): 17–34.

———. "Cavafy's Mythical Ephebes." In *Ancient Greek Myth in Modern Greek Poetry: Essays in Memory of C. A. Trypanis,* edited by Constantine Athanasius and Peter Mackridge, 33–44. London: Frank Cass, 1996.

———. "Days of 1895, '96, and '97: The Parallel Prisons of C. P. Cavafy and Oscar Wilde." *Modern Greek Studies Yearbook* 9 (1993): 297–305.

———. "'Missing Dates': the 'Μέρες' Poems of C. P. Cavafy." *Byzantine and Modern Greek Studies* 35.1 (2011): 73–75.

Ekdawi, Sarah, and Anthony Hirst. "Hidden Things: Cavafy's Thematic Catalogues." *Modern Greek Studies, Australia and New Zealand* 4 (1996): 1–34.

Eliot, T. S. "Ulysses, Order, and Myth." *Dial* 75 (1923): 480–83.

Elkins, Amy. "Old Pages and New Readings in Virginia Woolf's *Orlando.*" *Tulsa Studies in Women's Literature* 29.1 (2010): 131–36.

Emlyn-Jones, Chris. "True and Lying Tales in the *Odyssey.*" *Greece and Rome* 33.1 (1986): 1–10.

Entralgo, Pedro Laín. *The Therapy of the Word in Classical Antiquity.* Translated by L. J. Rather and John Sharp. New Haven: Yale University Press, 1970.

Eribon, Didier. *Insult and the Making of the Gay Self.* Translated by Michael Lucey. Durham, NC: Duke University Press, 2004.

Falconer, Rachel. *Hell in Contemporary Literature: Western Descent Narratives Since 1945.* Edinburgh: Edinburgh University Press, 2007.

Fanon, Franz. *Les damnés de la terre.* Paris: Maspero, 1961.

———. *Peau noire, masques blancs.* Paris: Seuil, 1952. Translated by Charles Markmann. *Black Skin, White Masks.* London: Pluto, 1986.

Fantuzzi, Marco, and Christos Tsagalis, eds. *The Greek Epic Cycle and Its Ancient Reception: A Companion.* New York: Cambridge University Press, 2015.

Fardin, Liliane. "*Volcan: épouvante ou espérance: mythe et réalité.*" In *Aimé Césaire, oeuvre et héritage,* ed. Lapoussinière, 309–16.

Faubion, James. "Cavafy: Toward the Principles of a Transcultural Sociology of Minor Literature." *Modern Greek Studies, Australia and New Zealand* (2003): 19–39.

Felski, Rita, and Susan Stanford Friedman. "Comparison." *New Literary History* 40.3 (2009): v–ix.

Fenik, Bernard. *Studies in the* Odyssey. *Hermes Einzelschriften 30.* Wiesbaden: Steiner, 1974.

Flack, Leah. *Modernism and Homer: The Odysseys of H. D., James Joyce, Osip Mandelstam, and Ezra Pound.* New York: Cambridge University Press, 2015.

Flesher, Erika. "Picturing the Truth in Fiction: Re-visionary Biography and the Illustrative Portraits for *Orlando.*" In *Virginia Woolf and the Arts,* edited by Diane Gillespie and Leslie Hankins, 39–47. New York: Pace University, 1997.

Foley, John. *Homer's Traditional Art.* University Park: Pennsylvania State University Park, 1999.

Foley, John, and Justin Arft. "The Epic Cycle and Oral Tradition." In *The Greek Epic Cycle,* edited by Fantuzzi and Tsagalis, 78–95.

Fonkoua, Romuald. *Aimé Césaire*. Paris: Perrin, 2010.

Ford, Andrew. *Homer and the Poetry of the Past*. Ithaca, NY: Cornell University Press, 1992.

Forsdick, Charles, and Christian Høgsbjerg. *Toussaint Louverture: A Black Jacobin in an Age of Revolutions*. London: Pluto, 2017.

Forster, E. M. *Pharos and Pharillon*. 2nd ed. London: Hogarth Press, 1923.

Foucault, Michel. *The History of Sexuality: An Introduction*. Translated by Robert Hurley. Vol. 1. New York: Pantheon, 1978.

Fowler, Robert, ed. *The Cambridge Companion to Homer*. New York: Cambridge University Press, 2004.

Frame, Donald. *The Myth of Return in Early Greek Epic*. New Haven: Yale University Press, 1978.

Friedman, Joel, and Sylia Gassel. "Odysseus: The Return of the Primal Father." *Psychoanalytic Quarterly* 21 (1952): 215–23.

Friedman, Susan Stanford. *Planetary Modernisms: Provocations on Modernity across Time*. New York: Columbia University Press, 2015.

———. "World Modernisms, World Literature, and Comparativity." In *The Oxford Handbook of Global Modernisms,* edited by Mark Wollaeger and Matt Eatough, 499–525. New York: Oxford University Press, 2012.

Frier, Bruce. "Making History Personal: Constantine Cavafy and the Rise of Rome." *Cavafy Forum* (2010). Accessed 5 May 2019. https://lsa.umich.edu/content/dam/modgreek-assets/modgreek-docs/CPC_Frier_Makinghistorypersonal.pdf.

Frobenius, Leo. *Kulturgeschichte Afrikas: Prolegomena zu einer Historischen Gestaltlehre*. Zurich: Phaidon, 1933.

Froula, Christine. *Virginia Woolf and the Bloomsbury Avant-Garde: War, Civilization, and Modernity*. New York: Columbia University Press, 2007.

Fulton, Dawn. *Signs of Dissent: Maryse Condé and Postcolonial Criticism*. Charlottesville: University of Virginia Press, 2008.

Gadamer, Hans-Georg. *Truth and Method*. Translated by Joel Weinsheimer and Donald Marshall. 2nd ed. New York: Crossroad, 1992; German edition, *Wahrheit und Methode*. Tübingen: Mohr Siebeck, 1960.

Garland, Robert. *Wandering Greeks: The Ancient Greek Diaspora from the Age of Homer to the Death of Alexander the Great*. Princeton: Princeton University Press, 2014.

Garraway, Doris. "'What Is Mine': Césairean Negritude between the Particular and the Universal." *Research in African Literatures* 41.1 (2010): 71–86.

Gates, Henry Louis, and Kwame Anthony Appiah. *Africana: The Encyclopedia of the African and African-American Experience*. 5 Vols. 2nd ed. New York: Oxford University Press, 2005.

Gilroy, Paul. *The Black Atlantic: Modernity and Double Consciousness*. Cambridge, MA: Harvard University Press, 1993.

Girard, Philippe. *Toussaint Louverture: A Revolutionary Life*. New York: Basic Books, 2016.

Glissant, Édouard. *Le discours antillais*. Paris: Seuil, 1981; Paris: Gallimard, 1997. Translated and edited by J. Michael Dash as *Caribbean Discourse: Selected Essays*. Charlottesville: University of Virginia Press, 1989.

———. *Poétique de la relation*. Paris: Gallimard, 1990. *Poetics of Relation*. Translated by Betsy Wing. Ann Arbor: University of Michigan Press, 1997.

Goff, Barbara, ed. *Classics and Colonialism*. London: Duckworth, 2005.

Goff, Barbara, and Michael Simpson. *Crossroads in the Black Aegean: Oedipus, Antigone, and Dramas of the African Diaspora*. Oxford: Oxford University Press, 2007.

Gordon, Lewis, Tracy Denean Sharpely-Whiting, and Renee White, eds. *Fanon: A Critical Reader.* Malden, MA: Wiley-Blackwell, 1996.

Graziosi, Barbara, and Emily Greenwood, eds. *Homer in the Twentieth Century: Between World Literature and the Western Canon.* New York: Oxford University Press, 2007.

Graziosi, Barbara, and Johannes Haubold. "The Homeric Text," *Ramus* 44 (2015): 5–28.

Greenwood, Emily. *Afro-Greeks: Dialogues Between Anglophone Caribbean Literature and Classics in the Twentieth Century.* New York: Oxford University Press, 2010.

———. "Dislocating Black Classicism: Classics and the Black Diaspora in the Poetry of Aimé Césaire and Kamau Brathwaite." In *African Athena: New Agendas,* edited by Daniel Orrells, Gurminder Bhambra, and Tessa Roynon, 362–72. New York: Oxford University Press, 2011.

———. "Re-rooting the Classical Tradition: New Directions in Black Classicism." *Classical Receptions Journal* 1.1 (2009): 87–103.

Greimas, Algirdas. *"La déscription de la signification et la mythologie comparée." L'Homme* 3.3 (1963): 51–66.

Gualtieri, Elena. "The Impossible Art: Virginia Woolf on Modern Biography." *Cambridge Quarterly* 29 (2000): 349–61.

Gualtieri, Maurizio. "Greeks, Lucanians, and Romans at Poseidonia/Paestum (South Italy)." In *A Companion to the Archaeology of the Roman Republic,* edited by Jane Evans, 369–86. New York: Wiley-Blackwell, 2013.

Haas, Diana. "Around the Revisions of Cavafy's 'Σ'ένα βιβλίο παληό—('In an Old Book–'), 1922–1929." In *Imagination and Logos: Essays on C. P. Cavafy,* edited by Panagiotis Roilos, 245–62. Cambridge, MA: Harvard University Press, 2010.

———. "Cavafy's Reading Notes on Gibbon's *Decline and Fall.*" *Folia Neohellenica* 4 (1982): 25–96.

———. "Early Cavafy and the European 'Esoteric' Movement." *Journal of Modern Greek Studies* 2.2 (1984): 209–24.

———. *Le problème religieux dans l'oeuvre de Cavafy: Les années de formation, 1882–1905.* Paris: Université de Lille III, 1987.

———. Νόμος και Έγκλημα στην ερωτική ποίηση του Καβάφη." *Μόλυβδο—Κόνδυλο—Πελεκητής* 7 (2000): 146–56.

Hacking, Ian. *Mad Travelers: Reflections on the Reality of Transient Mental Illness.* Charlottesville: University of Virginia, 1998.

Halberstam, Jack. *Trans*: A Quick and Quirky Account of Gender Variability.* Berkeley: University of California Press, 2018.

Hale, Thomas. *Les écrits d'Aimée Cesaire, bibliographie commentée.* Montreal: Les Presses de l'Université de Montreal, 1978.

Halim, Hala. *Alexandrian Cosmopolitanism: An Archive.* New York: Fordham University Press, 2013.

Hall, Edith. *The Return of Ulysses: A Cultural History of Homer's Odyssey.* Baltimore: Johns Hopkins University Press, 2008.

———. "Survival of Culture." In *Survival: The Survival of the Human Race,* edited by Emily Shuckburgh, 53–79. New York: Cambridge University Press, 2008.

Hall, Karen. *Things of Darkness: Economies of Race and Gender in Early Modern England.* Ithaca, NY: Cornell University Press, 1995.

Hall, Stuart. "Negotiating Caribbean Identities." *New Left Review* 1.209 (1995): 3–14.

Haller, Dieter. "The Cosmopolitan Mediterranean: Myth and Reality." *Zeitschrift für Ethnologie* 129 (2004): 29–47.

Hansen, William. "Homer and the Folktale." In *A New Companion to Homer,* edited by Ian Morris and Barry Powell, 444–45. Leiden: Brill, 1996.

———. "Odysseus and the Oar: A Comparative Approach to a Greek Legend." In *Approaches to Greek Myth,* edited by Lowell Edmunds, 247–79. 2nd ed. Baltimore: Johns Hopkins University Press, 2014.

Hardwick, Lorna, and Christopher Stray, eds. *A Companion to Classical Receptions.* Oxford: Blackwell, 2008.

Hart, Matthew. *Nations of Nothing but Poetry: Modernism, Transnationalism, and Synthetic Vernacular Poetry.* New York: Oxford University Press, 2012.

Hartog, François. *Memories of Odysseus: Frontier Tales from Ancient Greece.* Translated by Janet Lloyd. Chicago: University of Chicago Press, 2001.

Haubold, Johannes. *Greece and Mesopotamia: Dialogues in Literature.* New York: Cambridge University Press, 2013.

———. "Beyond Auerbach: Homeric Narrative and the Epic of Gilgamesh." In *Defining Greek Narrative,* edited by Douglas Cairns and Ruth Scodel, 13–28. Edinburgh: Edinburgh University Press, 2014.

Hénane, René. *Glossaire des termes rares dans l'oeuvre d'Aimé Césaire.* Paris: Jean-Michel Place, 2004.

Heubeck, Alfred, Stephanie West, J. B. Hainsworth, Arie Hoekstra, Joseph Russo, Manuel Fernandez-Galiano, eds. *Commentary on Homer's* Odyssey. 3 Vols. Oxford: Clarendon, 1988–92.

Hirsh, Elizabeth. "Virginia Woolf and Portraiture." In *Edinburgh Companion to Virginia Woolf and the Arts,* edited by Humm, 171–75.

Holmes, Brooke. *The Symptom and the Subject: The Emergence of the Physical Body in Ancient Greece.* Princeton: Princeton University Press, 2014.

Holroyd, Michael. *Lytton Strachey: A Critical Biography.* New York: Norton, 1995.

Homer. *Hesiod, the Homeric Hymns, and Homerica.* Translated by H. G. Evelyn-White. Rev. ed. Cambridge, MA: Harvard University Press, 1970.

———. Homer Multitext Project. Accessed 5 May 2019. https://www.homermultitext.org.

———. *Odyssey.* Edited by Helmut van Thiel. Hildesheim: Georg Olms, 1991.

———. *Odyssey.* Translated by Robert Fagles. New York: Penguin, 1996.

Horden, Peregrine, and Nicholas Purcell. *The Corrupting Sea: A Study of Mediterranean History.* Oxford: Wiley-Blackwell, 2000.

Hovey, Jaime. "'Kissing a Negress in the Dark': Englishness as a Masquerade in Woolf's *Orlando.* *PMLA* 112.3 (1997): 393–404.

Humm, Maggie, ed. *Edinburgh Companion to Virginia Woolf and the Arts.* Edinburgh: Edinburgh University Press, 2010.

Irele, Abiola. "A Defence of Negritude: À Propos of 'Black Orpheus' by Jean-Paul Sartre." *Transition* 50 (1975/76): 39–41.

———. "The Poetic Legacy of Aimé Césaire." *French Politics, Culture & Society* 27.3 (2009): 81–97.

James, C. L. R. *The Black Jacobins: Toussaint Louverture and the San Domingo Revolution.* 2nd rev. ed. New York: Vintage, 1989.

Janko, Richard. *Homer, Hesiod, and the Hymns.* Cambridge, MA: Cambridge University Press, 1982.

Jansen, Laura. "Borges and the Disclosure of Antiquity." In *Deep Classics: Rethinking Classical Reception,* ed. Shane Butler, 291–307. London: Bloomsbury.

Jay, Paul. *Global Matters: The Transnational Turn in Literary Studies.* Ithaca, NY: Cornell University Press, 2010.

Jeffreys, Peter. "Cavafy, Forster, and the Eastern Question." *Journal of Modern Greek Studies* 19.1 (2001): 61–87.

———. *Eastern Questions: Hellenism & Orientalism in the Writings of E. M. Forster & C. P. Cavafy.* Greensboro, NC: ELT Press, 2005.

———. *Reframing Decadence: C. P. Cavafy's Imaginary Portraits.* Ithaca, NY: Cornell University Press, 2015.

Jouve, Nicole. "Virginia Woolf and Psychoanalysis." In *The Cambridge Companion to Virginia Woolf,* edited by Sellers and Roe, 245–72.

Jusdanis, Gregory. *Belated Modernity and Aesthetic Culture: Inventing National Literature.* Minneapolis: University of Minnesota Press, 1991.

———. "Farewell to the Classical: Excavations in Modernism." *Modernism/Modernity* 11.1 (2004): 37–53.

———. *The Necessary Nation.* Princeton: Princeton University Press, 2001.

———. *The Poetics of Cavafy: Textuality, Eroticism, History.* Princeton: Princeton University Press, 1987.

———. "Why Cavafy Is So Popular." *Studies in the Literary Imagination* 48.2 (2015): 111–21.

Kaan, Heinrich. *Psychopathia Sexualis: A Classic in the History of Sexuality.* 1884. Edited by Benjamin Kahan. Translated by Melissa Haynes. Ithaca, NY: Cornell University Press, 2017.

Kaivola, Karen. "Revisiting Woolf's Representations of Androgyny: Gender, Race, Sexuality, and Nation." *Tulsa Studies in Women's Literature* 18.2 (1999): 235–61.

Kalikoff, Hedy. "Gender, Genre, and Geography in Aimé Césaire's *Cahier d'un retour au pays natal.*" *Callaloo* 18.2 (1995): 492–505.

Kaplan, Cora. "Black Heroes/White Writers: Toussaint L'Ouverture and the Literary Imagination." *History Workshop Journal* 46 (1998): 33–62.

Katz, Marilyn. *Penelope's Renown: Meaning and Indeterminacy in the* Odyssey. Princeton: Princeton University Press, 1991.

Keeley, Edmund. *Cavafy's Alexandria: Study of a Myth in Progress.* Cambridge, MA: Harvard University Press, 1976.

———. "Cavafy's Voice and Context." *Grand Street* 2.3 (1983): 157–77.

Kefala, Eleni. "Hybrid Modernisms in Greece and Argentina: The Case of Cavafy, Borges, Kalokyris, and Kyriakides." *Comparative Literature* 58.2 (2006): 113–27.

Kelley, Robin. "A Poetics of Anticolonialism." *Monthly Review* 51.6 (1999). Accessed 5 May 2019. http://monthlyreview.org/1999/11/01/a-poetics-of-anticolonialism.

Kennard, Jean. "Power and Sexual Ambiguity: The 'Dreadnought' Hoax, *The Voyage Out, Mrs. Dalloway,* and *Orlando.*" *Journal of Modern Literature* 20.2 (1996): 149–64.

Knowles, James. "The Joke About the Elgin Marbles." *Nineteenth Century* 29 (1891): 495–506.

Kohn, Robert. "Erotic Daydreams in Virginia Woolf's *Orlando.*" *Explicator* 68.3 (2010): 185–88.

Köhnken, Adolf. "Odysseus' Scar: An Essay on Homeric Epic Narrative Technique." In *Homer's Odyssey: Oxford Readings in Classical Studies,* edited by Lillian Doherty, 44–61. New York: Oxford University Press, 2009.

Koulouris, Theodore. *Hellenism and Loss in the Work of Virginia Woolf.* Farnham: Ashgate, 2011.

———. "Virginia Woolf's Greek Notebook (VS Greek and Latin Studies): An Annotated Transcription." *Woolf Studies Annual* 25 (2019): 1–197.

Lambropoulos, Vassilis. "The Greeks of Art and the Greeks of History." *Modern Greek Studies, Australia and New Zealand* 11 (2003): 66–74.

———. "Syncretism as Mixture and Method," *Journal of Modern Greek Studies* 19.2 (2001): 221–35.

Lapoussinière, Christian, ed. *Aimé Césaire: oeuvre et héritage: colloque du centenaire*. Paris: Jean-Michel Place, 2017.

Lawrence, Karen. "Orlando's Voyage Out." *Modern Fiction Studies* 38.1 (1992): 253–77.

———. *Penelope Voyages: Women and Travel in the British Literary Tradition*. Ithaca, NY: Cornell University Press, 1994.

Lee, Hermione. *Virginia Woolf.* New York: Vintage, 1996.

Leontis, Artemis. *Topographies of Hellenism: Mapping the Homeland*. Ithaca, NY: Cornell University Press, 1995.

Lesher, L. H. "Perceiving and Knowing in the *Odyssey.*" *Phronesis* 26.1 (1981): 2–24.

Levaniouk, Olga. "*Aithôn, Aithon,* and Odysseus." *Harvard Studies in Classical Philology* 100 (2000): 25–51.

———. *Eve of the Festival: Mythmaking in* Odyssey 19. Washington DC: Center for Hellenic Studies, 2011.

Levi, John. *Empire of Ruin: Black Classicism and American Imperial Culture*. New York: Oxford University Press, 2017.

Lévi-Strauss, Claude. "The Structural Study of Myth." *Journal of American Folklore* 68 (1955): 428–44.

Liddell, Robert. *Cavafy: A Biography.* London: Duckworth, 1974.

Lionnet, Françoise, and Shu-Mei Shi, eds. *The Creolization of Theory*. Durham, NC: Duke University Press, 2011.

Loichot, Valerie. *The Tropics Bite Back: Culinary Coups in Caribbean Literature*. Minneapolis: University of Minnesota Press, 2013.

Loney, Alexander. *The Ethics of Revenge and the Meanings of the* Odyssey. New York: Oxford University Press, 2019.

Lord, Albert. *The Singer of Tales.* Cambridge, MA: Harvard University Press, 1960.

Louden, Bruce. *Homer's* Odyssey *and the Near East*. New York: Cambridge University Press, 2011.

———. "Is There Early Recognition Between Penelope and Odysseus? Book 19 in the Larger Context of the *Odyssey.*" *College Literature* 38.2 (2011): 76–100.

———. *The* Odyssey: *Structure, Narration, and Meaning*. Baltimore: Johns Hopkins University Press, 1999.

Louverture, Toussaint. *Mémoires du Général Toussaint Louverture écrits par lui-même*. Paris: Pagnerre, 1853. First translated by J. R. Beard. *Toussaint L'ouverture: A Biography and Autobiography,* 1863. Accessed 5 May 2019. https://www.marxists.org/reference/archive/toussaint-louverture/memoir/index.htm

Lowe, Lisa. *Critical Terrains: French and British Orientalisms*. Ithaca, NY: Cornell University Press, 1992.

Lowenstam, Steven. "Talking Vases: The Relationship between the Homeric Poems and Archaic Representations of Epic Myth." *Transactions of the American Philological Association* 127 (1997): 21–76.

———. "The Uses of Vase-Descriptions in Homeric Studies." *Transactions of the American Philological Association* 122 (1992): 165–98.

Mactoux, Marie-Madeleine. *Pénélope: légende et mythe*. Paris: Les Belles Lettres, 1975.

Malanos, Timos. Περί Καβάφη. Alexandria, 1935.

Malkin, Irad. *The Returns of Odysseus: Colonization and Ethnicity*. Berkeley: University of California Press, 1998.

Marchand, Suzanne. "Leo Frobenius and the Revolt against the West." *Journal of Contemporary History* 32.2 (1997): 153–70.

Marks, J. "Alternative Odysseys: The Case of Thoas and Odysseus." *Transactions of the American Philological Association* 133 (2003): 209–26.

———. *Zeus in the* Odyssey. Washington, DC: Center for Hellenic Studies, 2008.

Marriott, David. "*En moi*: Franz Fanon and René Maran." In *Franz Fanon's Black Skin, White Masks: New Interdisciplinary Essays*," edited by Max Silverman, 146–78. Manchester: Manchester University Press, 2005.

Martin, Richard. "Cretan Homers: Tradition, Politics, Fieldwork," *Classics@ 3, The Homerizon: Conceptual Interrogations in Homeric Studies* (2005). Accessed 5 May 2019. https://chs.harvard.edu/CHS/article/display/1827.

Martindale, Charles, and Richard Thomas, eds. *Classics and the Uses of Reception*. Oxford: Wiley-Blackwell, 2006.

Maximin, Daniel. "*La poésie, parole essentielle*." *Présence Africaine* 126.2 (1983): 7–23.

Mbom, Clément. "*Toussaint Louverture, Martin Luther King Jr., Léopold Senghor, Nelson Mandela, et Aimé Césaire: cinq mondes, un même idéal*." In *Aimé Césaire: oeuvre et héritage*, ed. Lapoussinière, 50–61.

McConnell, Justine. *Black Odysseys: The Homeric* Odyssey *in the African Diaspora since 1939*. Oxford: Oxford University Press, 2013.

McKinsey, Martin. *Hellenism and the Postcolonial Imagination: Yeats, Cavafy, Walcott*. Madison, NJ: Fairleigh Dickinson University Press, 2010.

———. "Where Are the Greeks: Revisiting Cavafy's 'Philhellene.'" *Cavafy Forum* (2010). Accessed 5 May 2019. https://lsa.umich.edu/content/dam/modgreek-assets/modgreek docs/CPC_Mckinsey_Philhellene_wherearethegreeks.pdf.

Meineck, Peter, and David Konstan, eds. *Combat Trauma and the Ancient Greeks*. New York: Palgrave Macmillan, 2014.

Melas, Natalie. *All the Difference in the World: Postcoloniality and the Ends of Comparison*. Redwood City, CA: Stanford University Press, 2006.

———. "Poetry's Circumstance and Racial Time: Aimé Césaire, 1935–1945." *South Atlantic Quarterly* 115.3 (2016): 469–71.

———. "Untimeliness, or *Négritude* and the Poetics of Contramodernity." *South Atlantic Quarterly* 108.3 (2009): 563–80.

Miller, Christopher. "Editing and Editorializing: The New Genetic *Cahier* of Aimé Césaire." *South Atlantic Quarterly* 115.3 (2016): 441–55.

———. "The Revised Birth of Negritude: Communist Revolution and the 'Immanent Negro.'" *PMLA* 125.3 (2010): 743–49.

Miller, Madeline. *Circe*. New York: Little, Brown and Company, 2018.

Mills, Jane. *Virginia Woolf, Jane Ellen Harrison, and the Spirit of Modernist Classicism*. Columbus: The Ohio State University Press, 2014.

Minchin, Elisabeth. *Homer and the Resources of Memory: Some Applications of Cognitive Theory to the* Iliad *and the* Odyssey. New York: Oxford University Press, 2001.

Monk, Ray. "This Fictitious Life: Virginia Woolf on Biography, Reality, and Character." *Philosophy and Literature* 31.1 (2007): 1–40.

Montaigne, Michel de. *The Complete Essays.* Translated by M. A. Screech. London: Penguin, 1987. In French, *Essais,* edited by Emmanuel Naya, Delphine Reguig, and Alexandre Tarrête. 3 Vols. Paris: Gallimard, 2009.

Montanari, Franco, Antonio Rengakos, and Christos Tsagalis, eds. *Homeric Contexts: Neoanalysis and the Interpretation of Oral Poetry.* Berlin: de Gruyter, 2012.

Montiglio, Silvia. *From Villain to Hero: Odysseus in Ancient Gree*ce. Ann Arbor: University of Michigan Press, 2011.

———. *Wandering in Ancient Greek Culture.* Chicago: University of Chicago Press, 2005.

Moore, Madeline. "*Orlando:* An Edition of the Manuscript." *Twentieth Century Literature* 25.3/4 (1979): 303–55.

Morgan, Peter. "Literary Transnationalism: A Europeanist's Perspective." *Journal of European Studies* 47.1 (2017): 3–20.

Morris, Ian, and Barry Powell, eds. *A New Companion to Homer.* Leiden: Brill, 1996.

Mueller, Melissa. "Helen's Hands: Weaving for *Kleos* in the *Odyssey.*" *Helios* 37.1 (2010): 1–21.

Murnaghan, Sheila. *Disguise and Recognition in the* Odyssey. 2nd ed. Lanham, MD: Lexington, 2011.

———. "The Misadventure of Staying Home: Thwarted *Nostos* in De Chirico and Rebecca West." In *Odyssean Identities,* ed. Gardner and Murnaghan, 112–32.

Murnaghan, Sheila, and Hunter Gardner, eds. *Odyssean Identities in Modern Cultures.* Columbus: The Ohio State University Press, 2014.

Nagler, Michael. "Odysseus: The Proem and the Problem." *Classical Antiquity* 9.2 (1990): 335–56.

Nagy, Gregory. *The Ancient Greek Hero in 24 Hours.* Cambridge, MA: Belknap Press, 2013.

———. "A Cretan Odyssey, Part 1." *Classical Inquiries* (2015). Accessed 8 September 2019, https://classical-inquiries.chs.harvard.edu/a-cretan-odyssey-part-1/

———. "A Cretan Odyssey, Part 2." *Classical Inquiries* (2015). Accessed 8 September 2019. https://classical-inquiries.chs.harvard.edu/a-cretan-odyssey-part-2.

———. "Diachronic Homer and a Cretan Odyssey." *Oral Tradition* 31.1 (2017): 3–50.

———. The Homer Multitext Project. http://nrs.harvard.edu/urn-3:hlnc.essay:Nagy.The_Homer_Multitext_Project.2010

———. *Homer: The Preclassic.* Berkeley: University of California Press, 2017.

———. Homeric Poetry and the Problems of Multiformity: The 'Panathenaic Bottleneck.'" *Classical Philology* 96.2 (2001): 109–19.

———. *Homeric Questions.* Austin: University of Texas Press, 1996.

———. "Oral Traditions, Written Texts, and Questions of Authorship." In *The Greek Epic Cycle,* edited by Fantuzzi and Tsagalis, 9–77.

———. *Poetry as Performance: Homer and Beyond.* New York: Cambridge University Press, 1996.

———. "Signs of Hero Cult in Homeric Poetry." In *Homeric Contexts,* edited by Montanari, Rengakos, and Tsagalis, 7–72.

Nesbitt, Nick. *Caribbean Critique: Antillean Critical Theory from Toussaint to Glissant.* Liverpool: Liverpool University Press, 2013.

Ngal, Georges. *Aimé Césaire: Un homme à la recherche d'une patrie.* 2nd rev. ed. Paris: Présence Africaine, 2000.

Nicolson, Nigel. *Portrait of a Marriage.* New York: Atheneum, 1973.

———, ed. *Vita and Harold: The Letters of Vita Sackville-West and Harold Nicolson.* New York: Putnam, 1992.

Nobus, Dany. "*Polymetis* Freud: Some Reflections on the Psychoanalytic Significance of Homer's *Odyssey.*" *Comparative Literature Studies* 43.3 (2006): 252–68.

Noland, Carrie. "Translating Césaire." *Modernism/Modernity*, 26.2 (2019): 419–25.

Nwankwo, Ifeoma. *Black Cosmopolitanism: Racial Consciousness and Transnational Identity in the Nineteenth-Century Americas.* Philadelphia: University of Pennsylvania Press, 2005.

O'Meally, Robert. *Romare Bearden: A Black Odyssey.* New York: Moore Gallery, 2007.

Olson, Douglas. *Blood and Iron: Stories and Storytelling in Homer's* Odyssey. Leiden: Brill, 1995.

Orrells, Daniel, Gurminder Bhambra, and Tessa Roynon, eds. *African Athena: New Agendas.* New York: Oxford University Press, 2011.

Ozkan, Hediye. "The Spirit of Carnival: Virginia Woolf's *Orlando* and Constantinople," *Interactions* (2017). *HighBeam Research.* 30 September 2018. Accessed 5 May 2019. https://www.highbeam.com.

Pache, Corinne. "Women after War: Weaving *Nostos* in Homeric Epic and in the Twenty-First Century." In *Combat Trauma and the Ancient Greeks,* edited by Meineck and Konstan, 67–86.

Page, Denys. *Folktales in Homer's* Odyssey. Cambridge, MA: Harvard University Press, 1973.

Palcy, Euzhan, and Annick Thébia-Melsan. *Aimé Césaire: une voix pour l'histoire,* Film. London: Saligna and So On, 1994.

Pantelia, Maria. "Spinning and Weaving: Ideas of Domestic Order in Homer." *American Journal of Philology* 114.4 (1993): 493–501.

Papanikolaou, Dimitris. "Days of Those Made Like Me: Retrospective Pleasure, Sexual Knowledge, and C. P. Cavafy's Homobiographics." *Byzantine and Modern Greek Studies* 37.2 (2013): 261–77.

———. "'Words That Tell and Hide': Revisiting C. P. Cavafy's Closets." *Journal of Modern Greek Studies* 23 (2005): 235–60.

Parker, Robert. *Miasma: Pollution and Purification in Early Greek Religion.* Oxford: Clarendon, 1996.

Paschalis, Michael. "Cavafy's 'Iliadic' Poems." In *Imagination and Logos: Essays on C. P. Cavafy,* edited by Panagiotis Roilos, 153–72. Cambridge, MA: Harvard University Press, 2010.

Pausanias. *Description of Greece.* Vol 3. Translated by W. H. S. Jones. Cambridge, MA: Harvard University Press, 1933.

Peradotto, John. *Man in the Middle: Name and Narration in the* Odyssey. Princeton: Princeton University Press, 1990.

Perides, Michael. Ο βίος και το έργο του Κωνσταντίνου Καβάφη. Athens: Ikaros, 1948.

Pieris, Michael. "Η πολιτική ενδοχώρα της φιλοσοφικής 'Ιθάκης.'" *Η Σημερινή* (Nicosia, Cyprus), 11 December 1994.

———. "The Theme of Second Odyssey in Cavafy and Sinopoulos." In *Ancient Greek Myth in Modern Greek Poetry,* edited by Peter Mackridge, 96–108. London: Frank Cass, 1996.

Pindar. *The Odes of Pindar.* Translated by C. M. Bowra. Oxford: Oxford University Press, 1935.

Porter, James. "Erich Auerbach and the Judaizing of Philology." *Critical Inquiry* 35.1 (2008): 115–47.

———. "Homer: The History of an Idea." In *The Cambridge Companion to Homer,* edited by Robert Fowler, 324–43. New York: Cambridge University Press, 2004.

———. "Ideals and Ruins: Pausanias, Longinus, and the Second Sophistic." In *Pausanias: Travel and Memory in Roman Greece,* edited by Susan Alcock, John Cherry, and Jas Elsner, 63–92. New York: Oxford University Press, 2003.

Prins, Yopie. *Ladies' Greek: Victorian Translations of Tragedy.* Princeton: Princeton University Press, 2017.

Proclus. *Chrestomachy.* In *Hesiod, the Homeric Hymns, Epic Cycle, and Homerica.* Translated by Hugh G. Evelyn-White. Rev. ed. Cambridge, MA: Harvard University, 1970.

Propp, Vladimir. *Morphology of the Folktale.* Translated by Laurence Scott. 2nd ed. Austin: University of Texas Press, 1968.

Pucci, Pietro. *Odysseus Polytropos.* Ithaca, NY: Cornell University Press, 1987.

———. "The Proem of the *Odyssey,*" *Arethusa* 15.1–2 (1982): 39–62.

Purves, Alex. "Unmarked Space: Odysseus and the Inland Journey," *Arethusa* 39 (2006): 1–20.

Putzel, Steven. "Virginia Woolf and British 'Orientalism.'" In *Virginia Woolf Out of Bounds,* edited by Jessica Berman and Jane Goldman, 105–12. New York: Pace University, 2001.

Raaflaub, Kurt. "War and the City: The Brutality of War and Its Impact on the Community." In *Combat Trauma and the Ancient Greeks,* edited by Meineck and Konstan, 15–46.

Rabaka, Reiland. *The Negritude Movement: W. E. B. Du Bois, Léon Damas, Aimé Césaire, Léopold Senghor, Frantz Fanon, and the Evolution of an Insurgent Idea.* Lanham, MD: Lexington, 2015.

Rabbitt, Kara. "In Search of the Missing Mother: Suzanne Césaire, *Martiniquaise.*" *Research in African Literatures* 44.1 (2013): 36–54.

Race, William. "Phaeacian Therapy in Homer's *Odyssey.*" In *Combat Trauma and the Ancient Greeks,* edited by Meineck and Konstan, 47–66.

Rado, Lisa. *The Modern Androgyne Imagination: A Failed Sublime.* Charlottesville: University of Virginia Press, 2000.

Raitt, Suzanne. *Vita and Virginia: The Work and Friendship of V. Sackville-West and Virginia Woolf.* Oxford: Clarendon, 1993.

Ramsay, Jason. "Mad Travelers: Book Review." *Journal of Mind and Behavior* 21.4 (2000): 261–65.

Randall, Bryony, and Jane Goldman, eds. *Virginia Woolf in Context.* New York: Cambridge University Press, 2012.

Rankine, Patrice. *Ulysses in Black: Ralph Ellison, Classicism, and African American Literature.* Madison: University of Wisconsin Press, 2006.

Reece, Steve. "The Cretan Odyssey: A Lie Truer Than Truth." *American Journal of Philology* 115.2 (1994): 157–73.

Reinhold, Natalya, ed. *Woolf Across Cultures.* New York: Pace University Press, 2004.

Reuter, Victoria. "A Penelopean Return: Desire, Recognition, and *Nostos* in the Poems of Yannis Ritsos and Gail Holst-Warhaft." In *Odyssean Identities in Modern Culture: The Journey Home,* edited by Hunter Gardner and Sheila Murnaghan, 89–111. Columbus: The Ohio State University Press, 2014.

Rexer, Raisa. "Black and White and Re(a)d All Over: *L'étudiant noir,* Communism, and the Birth of Négritude." *Research in African Literatures* 44.4 (2013): 1–14.

Richardson, Michael, ed. *Refusal of the Shadow: Surrealism and the Caribbean.* Translated by Krzysztof Fijałkowski. New York: Verso Books, 1996.

Ricks, David. "How It Strikes a Contemporary: Cavafy as a Reviser of Browning." *Kambos: Cambridge Papers in Modern Greek* (2003): 131–52.

Riesz, János. "Senghor and the Germans." *Research in African Literatures* 33.4 (2002): 25–37.

Rimbaud, Arthur. *A Season in Hell / Une Saison en Enfer: Bilingual Edition.* Translated by Louise Varèse. New York: New Directions, 2011.

Robinson, Michael. *The Lives and Works of the Pre-Raphaelites.* London: Hermes House, 2012.

Roessel, David. "The Significance of Constantinople in *Orlando.*" *Papers on Language & Literature* 28.4 (1992): 398–416.

Rohdenberg, Rebecca, and J. Marks. "Taphians and Thesprotians within and beyond the *Odyssey*," *Kyklos* 1 (2012). Accessed 5 May 2019. https://chs.harvard.edu/CHS/article/display/5194.

Roilos, Panagiotis. *C. P. Cavafy: The Economics of Metonymy*. Urbana: University of Illinois Press, 2009.

Romm, James. *The Edges of the Earth in Ancient Thought: Geography, Exploration, and Fiction*. Princeton: Princeton University Press, 1992.

Ronchetti, Anne. *The Artist, Society, and Sexuality in Virginia Woolf's Novels*. London: Routledge, 2004.

Ronnick, Michele Valerie. *The Autobiography of William Sander Scarborough: An American Journey from Slavery to Scholarship*. Detroit, MI: Wayne State University Press, 2004.

Rufz de Lavison, Étienne. *Mémoire sur la Maison des Aliénés de Saint Pierre*. Paris: J.-B. Baillière, 1856.

Russo, Joseph. "Re-Thinking Homeric Psychology: Snell, Dodds, and Their Critics," *Quaderni Urbinati de Cultura Classical* 101.2 (2012): 11–28.

Sackville-West, Vita. *Letters of Vita Sackville-West to Virginia Woolf*, edited by Louise DeSalvo and Mitchell Leaska. New York: William Morrow, 1985.

———. *Passenger to Teheran*. London: Hogarth, 1926; London: Taurus Parke, 2007.

Sarker, Sonita. "Woolf and Theories of Postcolonialism." In *Virginia Woolf in Context*, edited by Randall and Goldman, 110–28.

Sartre, Jean-Paul. "Black Orpheus." Translated by John MacCombie. *Massachusetts Review* 6.1 (1965): 13–52. Originally published in French, "Orphée Noir." In *Anthologie de la nouvelle poésie nègre et malgache de la langue française*, edited by Léopold Senghor. Paris: Presses Universitaires de France, 1948.

Satia, Pryia. *Spies in Arabia: The Great War and the Cultural Foundations of Britain's Covert Empire in the Middle East*. New York: Oxford University Press, 2009.

Saunders, Max. *Self Impression: Life-Writing, Autobiografiction, Literature, and the Forms of Modern Literature*. New York: Oxford University Press, 2013.

Saussy, Haun, ed. *Comparative Literature in an Age of an Age of Globalization*. Baltimore: Johns Hopkins University Press, 2006.

Savidis, George. *Οι Καβαφικές Εκδόσεις, 1891–1932: Περιγράφη και Σχόλιο* [The Cavafian Publications]. Athens: Tachydromou, 1966.

Savidis, Manuel. "Cavafy: Biographical Note." Accessed 5 May 2019. http://www.cavafy.com/companion/bio.asp.

Scarth, Alwyn. *La Catastrophe: The Eruption of Mount Pelée: The Worst Volcanic Disaster of the 20th Century*. New York: Oxford University Press, 2002.

Scharfman, Ronnie. "Aimé Césaire: Poetry Is/and Knowledge." *Research in African Literatures* 41.1 (2010): 109–20.

Schnapp, Jeffrey, Michael Shanks, and Matthew Tiews. "Archaeology, Modernism, Modernity." *Modernism/Modernity* 11.1 (2004): 1–16.

Scott, Alison. "'Tantalising Fragments': The Proofs of Virginia Woolf's *Orlando*." *Papers of the Bibliographical Society of America* 88.3 (1994): 279–351.

Seaford, Richard. "The *Psuchē* from Homer to Plato: A Historical Sketch." In *Selfhood and the Soul: Essays on Ancient Thought and Literature in Honour of Christopher Gill*, edited by Richard Seaford, John Wilkins, and Matthew Wright, 11–32. New York: Oxford University Press, 2017.

———. *Reciprocity and Ritual: Homer and Tragedy in the Developing City-State*. Oxford: Clarendon, 1992.

Sedgwick, Eve. *The Epistemology of the Closet*. Berkeley: University of California Press, 1990.

Seferis, George. *On the Greek Style: Selected Essays in Poetry and Hellenism*. Translated by Th. D. Frangopoulos. Athens: Denise Harvey, 1992.

Segal, Charles. *Singers, Heroes, and Gods in the* Odyssey. Ithaca, NY: Cornell University Press, 1994.

Sellers, Susan, and Sue Roe, eds. *The Cambridge Companion to Virginia Woolf*. 2nd ed. New York: Cambridge University Press, 2010.

Semley, Lorelle. "When Blacks Broke the Chains in 'The Little Paris of the Antilles.'" In *To Be Free and French: Citizenship in France's Atlantic Empire*. 115–59. New York: Cambridge University Press, 2017.

Seneca. *Moral Letters to Lucilius*. New York: CreateSpace Independent Publishing, 2016.

Senghor, Léopold, ed. *Anthologie de la nouvelle poésie nègre et malgache de la langue française*. Paris: Presses Universitaires de France, 1948.

———. "The Spirit of Civilisation or the Laws of African Negro Culture." *First International Conference of Negro Writers and Artists. Présence Africaine*, 8–10 (1956), n.p.

Seshagiri, Urmila. *Race and the Modernist Imagination*. Ithaca, NY: Cornell University Press, 2010.

Sharpely-Whiting, Tracy Denean. "Anti-Black Femininity and Mixed-Race Identity: Engaging Fanon to Reread Capécia." In *Fanon: A Critical Reader*, edited by Gordon, Sharpley-Whiting, and White, 155–62.

———, ed. *Franz Fanon: Conflicts and Feminisms*. Lanham, MD: Rowman and Littlefield, 1997.

———. *Negritude Women*. Minneapolis: University of Minnesota Press, 2002.

Shay, Jonathan. *Odysseus in America: Combat Trauma and the Trials of Homecoming*. New York: Scribner, 2003.

Sifaki, Evgenia. "Self-Fashioning in C. P. Cavafy's 'Going Back Home from Greece.'" *Synthesis* 5 (2013): 29–48.

Silverman, Max, ed. *Franz Fanon's Black Skin, White Masks: New Interdisciplinary Essays*. Manchester: Manchester University Press, 2005.

Snodgrass, Anthony. *Homer and the Artists: Text and Picture in Early Greek Art*. New York: Cambridge University Press, 1998.

Solovyova, Natalia. "The National and 'the Other' as a Biography of the Creative Mind: *Orlando* by Virginia Woolf." In *Woolf Across Cultures*, edited by Reinhold, 215–25.

Somé, Patrice. "The Anatomy of a Cosmogony: Ritual and Anaphora in Aimé Césaire's *Cahier d'un retour au pays natal*." *Journal of Ritual Studies* 7.2 (1993): 33–52.

Sourieau, Marie-Agnès. "*Suzanne Césaire et* Tropiques: *de la poésie cannibale à une poétique créole*," *French Review* 68.1 (1994): 69–78.

Spengler, Oswald. *Der Untergang des Abendlandes*. Vienna: Verlag Braumüller, 1918. *The Decline of the West*, edited by Arthur Helps and Helmut Werner. Translated by Charles Atkinson. New York: Oxford University Press, 1991.

Stanford, W. B. "The Homeric Etymology of the Name Odysseus." *Classical Philology* 47.4 (1952): 209–13.

———. *The Ulysses Theme: A Study in the Adaptability of a Traditional Hero*. 2nd ed. Oxford: Blackwell, 1968.

Stephen, Leslie. "A New 'Biographia Brittanica.'" *Athenaeum* 23 (1882): 85–52.

Strabo. *Geography*. Translated Horace Jones. Cambridge, MA: Harvard University Press, 1923.

Stryker, Susan, Paisley Currah, and Lisa Jean Moore, "Introduction: Trans-, Trans, or Trangender?" *Women's Studies Quarterly* 36.3/4 (2008): 11–22.

Swinford, Elise. "Transforming Nature: *Orlando* as Elegy." In *Virginia Woolf and the Natural World*, edited by Kristin Czarnecki and Carrie Rohman, 196–201. Liverpool: Liverpool University Press, 2011.

Symonds, John Addington. *Sketches and Studies in Italy and Greece*. Third Series. London: Smith, Elder, and Company, 1879.

Thomas, Julian. "Archaeology's Place in Modernity." *Modernism/Modernity* 11.1 (2004): 17–34.

Thomas, Richard. "Cretan Homers: Tradition, Politics, Fieldwork." *Classics @3*, Colloquium at Center for Hellenic Studies. Accessed 5 May 2019. https://www.chs.harvard.edu/CHS/article/display/1307.

Thurston, Michael. *The Underworld in Twentieth-Century Poetry: From Pound and Eliot to Heaney and Walcott*. New York: Palgrave Macmillan, 2010.

Tombrou, Maria. "Καβάφης και Μπραουνινγκ." *Νέα Ἑστία* 153 (2003): 787–809.

Tsagalis, Christos. "*Odyssey* 24.191–202: A Reconsideration." *Wiener Studien* 116 (2003): 43–56.

———. *The Oral Palimpsest: Exploring Intertextuality in the Homeric Epics*. Washington, DC: Center for Hellenic Studies, 2008.

Tziovas, Dimitris. "Beyond the Acropolis: Rethinking Neohellenism." *Journal of Modern Greek Studies* 19 (2001): 189–220.

van Nortwick, Thomas. *The Unknown Odysseus: Alternate Worlds in Homer's* Odyssey. Ann Arbor: University of Michigan Press, 2008.

Vergeron, Jules. "*La Maison Coloniale de la Santé de Saint Pierre.*" *Revue Maritime et Coloniale* 4 (1844): 34–50.

Vinci, Felice. "The Nordic Origins of the *Iliad* and the *Odyssey*: An Up-to-Date Survey of the Theory." *Athens Journal of Mediterranean Studies* 3.2 (2017): 163–86.

Walcott, Derek. *What the Twilight Says: Essays*. New York: Farrar, Strauss, and Giroux, 1999.

Walker, Keith. "The Transformational and Enduring Vision of Aimé Césaire." *PMLA* 125.3 (2010): 756–63.

Walters, Tracy. *African American Literature and the Classicist Tradition: Black Women Writers from Wheatley to Morrison*. New York: Palgrave Macmillan, 2007.

West, Martin. *The East Face of Helicon: West Asiatic Elements in Greek Poetry and Myth*. Oxford: Clarendon, 1999.

———. *The Epic Cycle: A Commentary on the Lost Troy Epics*. New York: Oxford University Press, 2013.

———. *The Making of the* Odyssey. New York: Oxford University Press, 2014.

Wilde. Oscar. Criminal Trial Transcript, Accessed 5 May 2019. http://law2.umkc.edu/faculty/projects/ftrials/wilde/Crimwilde.html.

Wilder, Gary. *Freedom Time: Negritude, Decolonization, and the Future of the World*. Durham, NC: Duke University Press, 2015.

Wollaeger, Mark, and Matt Eatough, eds. *The Oxford Handbook of Global Modernisms*. New York: Oxford University Press, 2012.

Woolf, Virginia. "A Dialogue on Mount Pentelicus." In *The Complete Shorter Fiction of Virginia Woolf*, edited by Susan Dick, 63–68. San Diego: Harcourt Brace Jovanovich, 1989.

———. *The Diary of Virginia Woolf*, edited by Anne Oliver Bell and Quentin Bell. 5 Vols. London: Hogarth, 1977–85.

———. *The Essays of Virginia Woolf*, edited by Andrew McNellie. 4 Vols. London: Hogarth; New York: Harcourt; San Diego: Houghton Mifflin Harcourt, 1986–2008.

———. *Granite and Rainbow: Essays.* New York: Houghton Mifflin, 1975.

———. "Julia Margaret Cameron." In *The Essays of Virginia Woolf, 1925–1928,* edited by Andrew McNellie. Vol. 4, 375–86. London: Hogarth, 1994.

———. *The Letters of Virginia Woolf,* edited by Nigel Nicolson and Joann Trautmann. 6 Vols. New York: Harcourt Brace Jovanovich, 1975–1982.

———. *Moments of Being: A Collection of Autobiographical Writings,* edited by Jeanne Schulkind. 2nd ed. New York: Harcourt, 1985.

———. *Orlando: A Biography,* annotated by Maria DiBattista. New York: Harcourt, Inc., 2006.

———. "The New Biography." In *The Essays of Virginia Woolf,* ed. Andrew McNeillie. Vol. 4, 473–80. London: Hogarth.

———. *A Room of One's Own.* New York: Harcourt Brace, 1929.

———. *Virginia Woolf's Travel and Literary Notebook, 1906–1909.* Accessed 5 May 2019. https://www.bl.uk/collection-items/virginia-woolfs-travel-and-literary-notebook-1906–09.

Wormhoudt, Arthur. *The Muse at Length: A Psychoanalytic Study of the* Odyssey. Boston: Christopher Publishing House, 1953.

Wynter, Sylvia. "'A Different Kind of Creature': Caribbean Literature, the Cyclops Factor and the Second Poetics of the *Propter Nos.*" In *Sisyphus and Eldorado: Magical and Other Realisms in Caribbean Literature,* edited by Timothy Reiss, 143–67. 2nd ed. Trenton, NJ: Africa World Press, 2002.

Young, Philip. *The Printed Homer: A 3000-Year Publishing History of the* Iliad *and the* Odyssey. Jefferson, NC: McFarland, 2008.

Zeitlin, Froma. "Figuring Fidelity in Homer's *Odyssey.*" In *The Distaff Side: Representing the Female in Homer's* Odyssey, edited by Beth Cohen, 117–54. New York: Oxford University Press, 1995.

Zerba, Michelle. *Doubt and Skepticism in Antiquity and the Renaissance.* New York: Cambridge University Press, 2012.

———. "Renaissance Homer and Wedding Chests: The *Odyssey* at the Crossroads of Humanist Learning, the Visual Vernacular, and the Socialization of Bodies." *Renaissance Quarterly* 70.3 (2017): 831–61.

INDEX

Achilles, 170–71

Addison, Joseph, 176

Aeneid (Virgil), 2

Aeschylus, 194

Africa, in Césaire's *Cahier*, 127, 130–34, 184, 188, 192

alaomai (to wander), 118

"Albatross, The" (Baudelaire), 112, 207–08

Alexander the Great, 47, 48

Alexandria: Cavafy on, 18–19; Cavafy's life and visitors in, 21–22, 146–47; "like a homeland" and as insular city, 82–83; Museum of Alexandria, 38–39; as sensual city, 91

American School of Classical Studies at Athens, 8

androgyny, 92, 143

Antikythera Odysseus (statue), 9

Antillanité, 6

Antilles. See *Cahier d'un retour au pays natal* (Césaire); Césaire, Aimé; Martinique

apoikiai (homes away from home), 37

archipelagoes: Cavafy and, 51; Césaire and, 60–64, 105–6; interconnectedness of,

75; Walcott on, 52. *See also* islands and isolation

Aristarchus of Samothrace, 163

Aristophanes of Byzantium, 163

Aristotle, 199

Aristoxenus, 44–45

Athenaeus of Naucratis, 41–45

Atwood, Margaret, 161

Auerbach, Erich, 123

Bambara, 193

Baudelaire, Charles: "The Albatross," 112, 207; *Les Fleurs du Mal*, 86

Bell, Vanessa, 24

biography genre, Woolf's *Orlando* and, 12, 66–69, 96, 136, 141–42, 146

Black Atlantic, 7, 11, 51–52, 62, 117. *See also* slave trade

black classicism, 5

Bloomsbury group, 24, 92

boats and ships: Black Atlantic, Césaire's *Cahier,* and, 51–52; Césaire's proud pirogue, 52, 162, 191–92; Odysseus's raft, 52, 80, 192; slave ships in Césaire's *Cahier*, 134–35, 192–93

Brathwaite, Edward Kamau, 52

Breton, André, 25, 53–54, 129

Brosses, Charles de, 63

Browning, Robert, 150

Cabrera, Lydia, 53

Cahier d'un retour au pays natal (Césaire): Africa as detour, 127, 130–34; Antillean foundation tales and, 52–53; Antillean French in, 53; Antilles geography and "my spilt blood" in, 60–62; Black Atlantic, boat images, and, 51–52; as Black odyssey, 10–11; Breton introduction "A Great Black Poet," 54; Breton on, 25; cannibalism, literary, 132–33; commencement of writing, 51; diffusion and mixture in, 51–64; islands and isolation in, 101–13; "*j'accepte*," 189–90; *katabasis* in, 56–57, 102, 113; "leaving" Europe, 127–28, 133; naming and *le mot juste* in, 55; *négritude* in, 55–56, 60–64; orality and, 106, 194; passage and detour in, 126–35; *pays natal*, 12, 51, 127, 129, 131, 135, 145; pirogue, proud, 52, 162, 191–92; the pongo as figure of racial abjection, 103, 108–13, 133; prayer, 186–89; publication history, 53–54; return and split endings in, 184–95; sexual imagery and gender in, 58–59, 61, 130; slave ships, 134–35, 192–93; taxonomy in, compared to Woolf, 176; totem in, 128–29; Toussaint Louverture as heroic figure, 103–8, 192; tree, incised, 184–87, 189; trial by ordeal, lustration, and uses of ritual, 192–94; white dove, 207

Calypso, 76, 78–81, 118–19, 163, 169–70

Cameron, Julia Margaret, 23

cannibalism, literary, 132–33, 145, 176

Cantos (Pound), 11, 12

carnivalesque, in Woolf's *Orlando*, 138–41

cartographies: archipelagoes and, 75; in Césaire's *Cahier*, 56, 60, 62; manifolds and, 27; of slave trade, 60

Case, Janet, 23, 46

Catalina, Victoria Josefs Dolores, 142

Cavafy, C. P.: archaeology and, 38–39; biographical sketch, 21–22; Browning and, 150; compositional method and revi-

sion, 40–41; cosmopolitan Alexandria and, 37–38, 146–47; diffusion and mixture, 37–51; ephebe as distinctive figure for, 155–58, 206; family wealth and, 37; Forster and, 9, 22, 147; hedonism and, 37, 48, 195; Hellenism of, 38–40, 46, 147; homosexuality as public secret, 46; indirection and, 12; invertism and, 92; islands and isolation, 82–94; "Odysseys" exhibition and, 9; passage and detour, 146–59; poetic strategies of diaspora and Hellenism, 4, 39, 45, 73, 151, 195; return and split endings, 195–207 stationary life after itinerant youth, 146–47; themes of, 4; trans* studies and, 7

—works: "The City," 83–87, 93–94, 114 "Days of 1896," 88–94, 114, 158; "The End of Odysseus," 195–96, 200; "The Funeral of Sarpedon," 49; "The Glory of the Ptolemies," 46–48, 50; "Going Back Home from Greece," 148–53, 159; "Hidden Things," 87–88, 94, 114; "In a Town of Osroini," 48–50, 71, 148; "Ionic," 153–55; "Ithaca," 25, 195, 196–200; "Notes on Poetics and Ethics," 22, 82–83, 93; "One of Their Gods," 155–59, 175, 199; *Poems (1905–1915)*, 41, 83; *Poems (1916–1918)*, 41; *Poems (1919–1930)* (or –*1931* or –*1932*), 41; "Poseidonians," 41–46, 50, 71, 148; "Second Odysseus," 195, 200; "Ships," 195, 200–207

Cervantes, Miguel de, 2

Césaire, Aimé: biographical sketch, 24–26; on "descent into oneself," 101–2; on finding the sacred again, 107, 191; French Communist Party and, 25, 54; indirection and, 12; interviews, 54, 101–2, 191; Maison de Santé and, 115–17; as part of Martinique landscape, 10, 26; quoted on Congress of Black Writers poster, 188; revision and, 54–55; self-abasement strategies, 111–12, 135; themes of, 4; tripartite Caribbean soul in, 51, 64, 127, 134, 145, 159, 191

—works: "*Depuis Akkad depuis Elam depuis Sumer*," 51–52; *Discours sur le colonialisme*, 25, 111; "lagunal calendar," 190–91; "*La poésie et la connaissance*," 103–4, 129; "Preliminary Question," 190; "Word," 62–63. See also *Cahier d'un retour au pays natal* (Césaire)

Césaire, Suzanne Roussi: *"Le grand camouflage,"* 56, 111; *"Léo Frobenius et le problème des civilisations,"* 129, 131; marriage
and divorce, 26; *"Misère de la poésie,"*
132–33; in Paris, 25

Charmides, 49–50

"Charmides" (Wilde), 50

Chrestomathy (Proclus), 15

clothing and identity, in Woolf's *Orlando*,
145–46, 174–75

colonialism and decolonization: "cannibalism" and, 132 –33; of Caribbean soul, in
Césaire, 51, 63–64, 191; Cavafy's "Going
Back Home from Greece" and, 150;
Césaire's *Discours sur le colonialisme*,
25, 111; Césaire's pongo figure and, 103,
108–13, 133, 135; First Congress of Black
Writers (Paris, 1956) and, 188; Louverture and, 103–8; Maison de Santé (Martinique) and, 115–17; shifting personas
and masks in Césaire and, 19, 71, 105,
113, 126–27, 159; taxonomy and, 176,
190; trivialization of female-as-colonial,
131–32; Woolf's *Orlando* and, 69, 138,
140–41; wounds of, in Césaire's *Cahier*,
185. See also *Cahier d'un retour au pays
natal* (Césaire); race and racialization

concealment. See hiddenness and
concealment

Condé, Maryse, 133, 135

Congress of Black Writers, First (Paris, 1956),
188

Constantinople: Cavafy and, 21, 146; in
Woolf's *Orlando*, 67, 68, 137–40, 173,
174

Coronio, Aglaia (born Ionides), 21

Crete: as diffusion and mixture, 29–32; Odysseus's Cretan tales, 28–37, 73, 123–25,
126

Cyclops, 108, 112–13, 125, 133, 135

Dahomey kingdom, 133–34

Damas, Léon, 25, 53, 55

Dante, 2, 57, 195–96

Darwish, Mahmoud, 75, 76

Davies, Margaret Llewelyn, 97–98

"Days of 1896" (Cavafy), 88–94, 114, 158

decolonization. See colonialism and
decolonization

Deipnosophists, or *Dinner Table Philosophers*
(Athenaeus), 44

de la Mare, Walter, 115

"Depuis Akkad depuis Elam depuis Sumer"
(A. Césaire), 51–52

descent. See *katabasis*

detour. See passage and detour

deus ex machina, 183, 194, 210

"Dialogue on Mount Pentelicus, A" (Woolf),
10, 23

Dickinson, Emily, 209–10

diffusion and mixture: about, 18, 27–28;
Cavafy's Hellenism and, 37–40; in
Cavafy's "In a Town of Osroini," 48–50;
in Cavafy's "Poseidonians," 41–46; in
Cavafy's "The Glory of the Ptolemies,"
46–48; in Césaire's *Cahier*, 51–64;
Crete, diversity and syncretism of,
31–32; in Homer's *Odyssey*, 28–37; in
Woolf's *Orlando*, 64–73

Discours sur le colonialisme (A. Césaire), 25,
111

Divine Comedy (Dante), 2

Don Quixote (Cervantes), 2

Douglas, Alfred, 46, 93

Eliot, T. S., 11, 22

Ellis, Havelock, 92

endings. See return and split endings

"End of Odysseus, The" (Cavafy), 195–96, 200

ephebes, 153–59, 175, 199, 206

epic cycle, 14–16, 17, 162, 169, 196

epic genre vs. folktale, 120–21

Ethiopians, Homeric, 33–34

Etruscans, 44

Eugammon of Cyrene, 15–16

Europe: as continent of war atrocities, 128;
"leaving," in Césaire's *Cahier*, 127–28, 133

Fanon, Franz, 26, 113

Fleurs du Mal, Les (Baudelaire), 86

folktale genre, 120–21, 125–26

forgetting: Césaire's *Cahier* and, 190; end of
Homer's *Odyssey* and, 172, 194, 210;
Lotus Eaters and, 119–20; Woolf's
Orlando and, 96–97

Forster, E. M., 9, 21–22, 147

Frobenius, Leo, 6, 129, 131

fugue state, 116–17

"Funeral of Sarpedon, The" (Cavafy), 49

gender: in Cavafy's "Days of 1896," 91; in Césaire's *Cahier*, 58–59, 105, 113, 132; gender
consciousness in Woolf's *Orlando*, 65,
70, 73, 140–43, 173–75, 177, 182, 184;
negritude and, 105; as performative, in
Woolf's *Orlando*, 145–46; transgender,
transsexuality, and trans* movements
in Woolf, 7, 12, 136, 142, 159; trivialization of female-as-colonial, 131–32; Victorian, in Woolf's *Orlando*, 175–77. See
also *Orlando* (Woolf)

genealogy, 3, 28–29, 32–33, 35, 105, 121–22, 144

Ghana Empire, 133–34

Gibbon, Edward, 147

Glissant, Édouard, 6, 26, 52

"Glory of the Ptolemies, The" (Cavafy),
46–48, 50

"Going Back Home from Greece" (Cavafy),
148–53, 159

"*Grand camouflage, Le*" (S. Césaire), 56, 111

"Great Black Poet, A" (Breton), 54

Guberina, Petar, 51, 54

gypsies, 68, 139, 141–45

Harrison, Jane Ellen, 23

Harvard Center for Hellenic Studies, 8

H. D., 11

hedonism: Cavafy and, 37, 41; Cavafy's
"Ithaca" and, 195–200; Cavafy's "Ships"
and, 195; Cavafy's "The Glory of the
Ptolemies" and, 47–48; *nostos* and
homoeroticism in Cavafy and, 195

Helen in Egypt (H. D.), 11

hell and descent. See *katabasis*

Hellenism: alternative sexualities linked
to, 38–40, 50, 147, 152, 195; of Cavafy,
38–40, 46; in Cavafy's "Going Back
Home from Greece," 150–53; in Cavafy's
"In a Town of Osroini," 50; in Cavafy's
"Poseidonians," 41–46; in Cavafy's "The
Glory of the Ptolemies," 46–48; of For-
ster, 147

Herman, Judith Lewis, 75

hiddenness and concealment: *kalypso* (to
hide), 81, 119, 123–24; Odysseus,
Calypso, and, 78–81; Odysseus facing
Penelope and, 167; Odysseus's wound,
the Phaeacian episode, and, 123–25;
the olive-tree bed as secret in Homer's
Odyssey, 169–70. See also islands and
isolation

"Hidden Things" (Cavafy), 87–88, 94, 114

homecoming. See *nostos*; return and split
endings

homeland, 12, 82–83

Homer. See *Iliad*; *Odyssey*

Homeric Hymn to Hermes, 154

Homeric Question, the, 15

Homer Multitext Project (Harvard Center for
Hellenic Studies), 8

homoeroticism and same-sex desire: Cavafy's
"Going Back Home from Greece,"
148; Cavafy's "Hidden Things," 87–88;
Cavafy's homosexuality as public
secret, 46; Cavafy's "In a Town of Osroini" and, 49–50; Cavafy's "Ithaca," 199;
Cavafy's "One of Their Gods," 155–59;
Cavafy's "Poseidonians" and, 44–46;
Cavafy's "Ships," 202; diaspora and, 4,
19–20, 40, 44, 94, 195; ephebic imagery,
153–59, 175, 199, 202; Forster, Cavafy,
and, 147; shame and the closet in
Cavafy's "Days of 1896," 88–94; Wilde
trials, 93; in Woolf contrasted with
Cavafy, 148; Woolf's *Orlando*, racialized
same-sex desire in, 72–73, 179. See also
gender; sexual identity and ambiguity

Hottentots, 131–32

Iliad (Homer): Cavafy and, 195, 200; genealogy in, 32; *kleos* in, 36; pillaging in, 119;
trickery in, 80

imagination (*phantasia*), in Cavafy's "Ships,"
200–204

"In a Town of Osroini" (Cavafy), 48–50, 71,
148

indirection, poetics of: about, 11–13, 18, 20,
86, 93, 161, 195, 210–11; biographer's
view in Woolf's *Orlando* and, 101;
Cavafy and, 40, 41, 83; in Cavafy's
"Days of 1896," 93; in Cavafy's "Ships,"
195, 200; in Cavafy's "The City," 86;

Dickinson and, 209; Homeric studies and approaches to, 13–16; the *Odyssey*, indirection of, 36–37; odysseys and, 210–11; slant and oblique tellings, 2–3, 8, 12, 50, 161, 206; works inspired by Homer's *Odyssey* and, 11, 12–13. *See also* diffusion and mixture; islands and isolation; passage and detour; return and split endings

Inferno (Dante), 57

insularity. *See* islands and isolation

invertism, 92

"Ionic" (Cavafy), 153–55, 199

islands and isolation: about, 17–19, 30–31, 51, 75–76; Cavafy's Alexandria as insular city, 82–83; in Cavafy's "Days of 1896," 88–94; in Cavafy's "Hidden Things," 87–88; in Cavafy's "The City," 83–87; in Césaire's *Cahier*, 101–14; in Homer's *Odyssey*, 76–82; Pont Pelée eruption and, 115–16; in Woolf's *Orlando*, 94–101. *See also* archipelagoes

"Ithaca" (Cavafy), 195, 196–200

Jackson, Julia, 23

James, C. L. R., 104

Journal of a Return to the Native Land (Césaire). See *Cahier d'un retour au pays natal* (Césaire)

Joyce, James, 2, 11

Kaan, Heinrich, 92

kalypso (to hide), 81, 119, 123–24

katabasis (descent to underworld): in Cavafy's "The City," 86; Césaire on "descent into oneself" and Pelée eruption, 101–2; in Césaire's *Cahier*, 56–57, 113; comeback and, 1; Rimbaud's *Saison en Enfer* and Dante's *Inferno*, 57; the sexually deviant as divine in Cavafy's "One of Their Gods," 158; sleep as, 95–96; in Woolf's *Orlando*, 95–97, 174–75

katharsis, 92

Keeley, Edmund, 47, 49, 85, 90, 158, 198

kleos (reports that circulate by word of mouth): Cavafy's "Poseidonians" and, 46; definition of, 18, 35–36; itinerancy in *Odyssey* and, 35–36; as literary fame, 100–101; Penelope, Odysseus, and,

77–79; "publication" of the *Odyssey* and, 183; wandering at sea and, 119–20; in Woolf's *Orlando*, 100–101, 183

Krafft-Ebbing, Richard von, 92

"lagunal calendar" (A. Césaire), 190–91

Lam, Wifredo, 53

Land, The (Sackville-West), 99

language: Antillean French in Césaire's *Cahier*, 53; in Cavafy's "Poseidonians," 44; feminine adjectives in Cavafy's "Days of 1896," 91; force of poetic language, 128–30, 143, 184; French broken by Césaire and English ransacked by Woolf, 186; *le mot* in Césaire's *Cahier*, 55, 190; representing the foreign, in Woolf's *Orlando*, 72, 143; taxonomical, 175–76, 190

Lawrence, D. H., 22

Lotus Eaters, 119–20

Louverture, Toussaint, 103–8, 192

lustration, 192–94

lying and deceit: in Césaire's *Cahier*, 58–59; Odysseus and, 34–36, 121, 126. See also *metis*; trickery and tricksterism

Magna Graecia, 33, 39, 43, 73

Maison de Santé, Martinique, 115–17

mapping. *See* cartographies

Martinique: as diseased landscape, 184; Maison de Santé, 115–17; Mont Pelée eruption, 55–56, 102, 115

Ménil, René, 25

mental illness: Maison de Santé (Martinique) and, 115–17; travel madness and fugue state, 116–17; Woolf and, 24, 94, 97–98

metis (cunning intelligence): about, 3, 27; Cavafy's "Poseidonians" and, 44; Cavafy's "Ships" and, 204; Dickinson and, 210; Odysseus and, 34, 36, 44; Penelope and, 166, 170; *polytropos* and, 2–3, 27; self-abasement and, 135; Woolf's *Orlando* and, 136, 177. See also lying and deceit; trickery and tricksterism

Milton, John, 59

"*Misère de la poésie*" (S. Césaire), 132–33

mixture. *See* diffusion and mixture

"Modern Fiction" (Woolf), 181

Montaigne, Michel de, 27, 86

Mont Pelée, Martinique, 55–56, 102, 115

Mrs. Dalloway (Woolf), 136

multiformity, 8, 14, 16, 17, 200

Museum of Alexandria, 38–39

naming. *See* taxonomy and naming

Nardal, Jane and Paulette, 25

négritude: in Césaire's *Cahier*, 55–56, 60–64, 105, 110–12, 146, 192, 207; concept of, 6, 53, 188; gender and, 105; Sartre on, 102

Nicolson, Harold, 24, 141

noos (mind; perception), 124–25, 166

nostos (homecoming): Cavafy and, 151, 195, 200, 204; as diffusion and mixture, in the *Odyssey*, 19, 35–36; as journey of the soul, 36; marginalized in Cavafy's "Ithaca," 199; *metis* and, 135; naming of Odysseus and boar-hunt wounding, 121–25; Odysseus's shipwreck, 157–58; Odysseus's slaughter of the suitors and, 171; *Odyssey* split endings and disruption of, 161, 164, 168, 169, 171, 210; as passage, 19; Phaeacia anticipating Ithaca, 125; Phemius singing about, in the *Odyssey*, 77–78; psychic dimension of, in the *Odyssey*, 118, 126; Woolf's mental illness and, 96; in Woolf's *Orlando*, 94, 100

"Notes on Poetics and Ethics" (Cavafy), 22, 82–83, 93

Odysseus: as Achillean, 170–71; as Aethon, 29, 33–34; Autolycus, 121–22, 124; boar hunt, wound, and scar, 122–24; Calypso, Ogygia, and concealment, 78–82; as folk avatar vs. epic hero, 120–21, 125–26; marginalized in Cavafy's "Ithaca," 199; *metis* and lying of, 34–36, 121, 126; "much suffering" epithet, 125; naming of, 121–22; postponed recognition, 123–24. *See also* lying and deceit; trickery and tricksterism

Odyssey (Homer): *alaomai* and *planomai* (wandering) and *pontos* (sea), 118–19; boar hunt, 122–23; Cretan tales, 16, 19, 28–37, 73, 99, 123–26; Cyclops, 108, 112–13, 133, 135; Demodocus, 100, 125, 183; diffusion and mixture in, 28–37; drop-

ping off the map, the Lotus Eaters, and Circe, 119–20; external agency from above connected with hero self-sabotage, 116; folktale vs. epic and, 120–21, 125–26; Homeric similes in Nausicaa episode, 157–58; islands and isolation in, 76–82; modernity and, 210; the oar and the olive-tree bed as signs, 165, 168–70; Odysseus on Ogygia, Calypso, and concealment, 76, 78–82, 118–19, 124, 163, 169–70; passage and detour in, 118–26; as performance composition and not *Ur*-text, 13–14; Phaeacian episode, 95, 99, 100, 124–25; plurality, historical sedimentation, the epic cycle, and, 14–16; *polytropos, metis*, and, 2–3, 27, 34, 36; prophecy of Teiresias, 164–65, 168–69; "publication" of, 183; slaughter of the suitors, 163, 167–68, 170–72; split endings (romantic and apocalyptic), 162–72; trial by ordeal, lustration, and foundational violence, 194; works inspired by, 2, 11. *See also* Odysseus

odysseys: concept of, 1–2, 17–20; indirection and telling it slant, 2–3; multiplicity and plurality of, 13–16, 27. *See also* indirection, poetics of

"Odysseys" exhibition (National Archaeological Museum, Athens, 2017–18), 9–10

Ogygia, 18–19, 76–81

Omeros (Walcott), 2, 11, 52

"One of Their Gods" (Cavafy), 155–59, 175, 199

"On Not Knowing Greek" (Woolf), 10

Oresteia (Aeschylus), 194

orientalism: British, in Woolf's *Orlando*, 71, 137–45; Cavafy and, 20, 147–48

Orlando (Woolf): aristocratic grounding of, 65; as biography, 12, 66–69, 96, 136, 141–42, 146; the carnivalesque in, 138–41; clash with 20th century, 180–82; clothing-identity relationship, 145–46; the crypt, 97; diffusion and mixture in, 64–73; erotic descent into nocturnal streets of London, 174–75; gypsies and questions of nature and culture, 143–45; house in, 69–70, 94, 144; islands and isolation in, 94–101; *katabasis* in, 95–97; literary misogyny and, 176–77; marriage to Rosina Pepita, 141–42; marriage to Shelmerdine, 173; mythical sleep in, 95–96; Nicholas Greene, 100–101, 180, 182; "The Oak Tree," 99, 137, 144, 173–74, 180–83, 186; orientalism in, 136–45; passage and detour in, 136–46; phantasmagoria of the mind, 12, 19, 136, 146; portraits and photographs, 97–99; pregnancy, 177–78; publication history, 65–66; racism in, 69, 72, 179; return and split ending in, 172–84; Sasha, 72, 94–95, 181; sex change, 137–46; transgender, transsexuality, trans* studies, and, 7, 12, 136, 142, 159; Victorian gender roles and, 177; wild goose, 182; writer, Orlando as, 99–101

"Orphée noir" (Sartre), 102

Osroini, 48–50

Othello (Shakespeare), 72–73

paideuma, 129, 131

Paradise Lost (Milton), 59

passage and detour: about, 19; Cavafy in Alexandria and, 146–47; in Cavafy's "Going Back Home from Greece," 148–53; in Cavafy's "Ionic," 153–55; in Cavafy's "One of Their Gods," 155–59; in Césaire's Cahier, 126–35; in Homer's Odyssey, 118–26; Maison de Santé (Martinique), mental illness, and mad traveler disease, 115–17; narrative as passage, 19; in Woolf's Orlando, 136–46

Passenger to Teheran (Sackville-West), 137–38

Pausanias, 16, 78

Penelope: alternative stories about, 78; indirection, obliquity, and, 36; metis and, 166, 170; Odysseus's Cretan tales to, 28–37; as person left behind, 76–77; split endings and, 163–70; weaving of, 36, 77

Pepita, Rosina, 139, 141–42, 146, 174

phantasmagoria: Cavafy and, 147; of the mind, in Woolf's Orlando, 12, 19, 136, 146, 173

Picasso, Pablo, 188

Picture of Dorian Gray, The (Wilde), 86

Pindar, 78

planomai (to wander), 118

Poems (1905–1915) (Cavafy), 41

Poems (1916–1918) (Cavafy), 41

Poems (1919–1930) (or –1931 or –1932) (Cavafy), 41

"Poésie et la connaissance, La" (A. Césaire), 103–4, 129

Poetics (Aristotle), 199

poetry as vatic knowledge, 129–30

polymechania (resourcefulness), 27, 36, 192

polymetis (crafty), 27, 36

polytropos (many-skilled), 2–3, 27, 36

pongo figure, 103, 108–13, 133, 135

pontos (sea), 118–19

Pope, Alexander, 176

"Poseidonians" (Cavafy), 41–46, 50, 71, 148

Pound, Ezra, 11, 12

"Preliminary Question" (A. Césaire), 190

Pre-Raphaelite circles, 21, 23

Proclus, 15

Ptolemies, 47–48

race and racialization: Black Atlantic, 7, 11, 51–52, 62, 117; Césaire's pongo as figure of racial abjection, 103, 108–13, 133; Fanon's female negrophobia, 112–13; of same-sex desire, in Woolf's Orlando, 72–73, 179; Toussaint Louverture as heroic figure, 103–8; Western color symbolism, reversal of, 106. See also Cahier d'un retour au pays natal (Césaire); Orlando (Woolf); slave trade

recognition scenes: in Homer's Odyssey, 29–30, 123–24, 163–64, 166; in Woolf's Orlando, 72, 142, 178–79

return and split endings: about, 19–20, 161–62; in Cavafy's "Ithaca," 196–200; in Cavafy's "Ships," 200–207; in Césaire's Cahier, 184–95; in Homer's Odyssey, 162–72; in Woolf's Orlando, 172–84

Rimbaud, Arthur, 57, 86

ring composition, 163

Room of One's Own, A (Woolf), 65, 143, 175

Roussi, Suzanne. See Césaire, Suzanne Roussi

Sachperoglou, Evangelos, 90

Sackville-West, Lionel, 142

Sackville-West, Vita: about, 24; affairs with other women, 141; entailment litigation, 180; The Land, 99, 183; language fluency of, 140; Passenger to Teheran, 137–38; photographs of, for Orlando,

98–99; in relation to Woolf's *Orlando*, 66–68, 180, 183

Saison en Enfer, Une (Rimbaud), 57, 86

Sarpedon, 49

Sartre, Jean-Paul, 102

"Second Odyssey" (Cavafy), 195, 200

Seferis, George, 40

Seleucia and Seleucids, 47–48, 155

Seneca, 86

Senghor, Léopold, 25, 53, 55, 188

sexual identity and ambiguity: Africa as *terre maternelle* in Césaire, 130–31; androgyny, 143; clothing and identity, in Woolf's *Orlando*, 145–46; crafted language of sexuality in Cavafy and Woolf's *Orlando*, 91, 93, 137, 142–43; Hellenisms and, 50, 147, 152–53, 195; sex change in Woolf's *Orlando*, 138–46; in Woolf's *Orlando*, 72, 138. *See also* gender; homoeroticism and same-sex desire; *Orlando* (Woolf)

sexuality, homoerotic. *See* homoeroticism and same-sex desire

Shakespeare, William, 72–73

Sherrard, Philip, 47, 85, 90, 158, 198

ships. *See* boats and ships

"Ships" (Cavafy), 195, 200–207

similes, Homeric, 87, 157–58

skepsis and skepticism, 83, 166, 199–200

Sketches and Studies in Italy and Greece (Symonds), 45

Sketch of the Past, A (Woolf), 24, 96

slant tellings. *See under* indirection, poetics of

slavery, Antillean. See *Cahier d'un retour au pays natal* (Césaire)

slave trade: cartographies of, 60; Middle Passage, 19, 52, 192; slave ships in Césaire's *Cahier*, 134–35, 192–93; as zone of opacity, 12

sleeps, mythical: in Homer's *Odyssey*, 95; in Woolf's *Orlando*, 95–96, 139, 142

soul, tripartite Caribbean, in Césaire, 51, 64, 127, 134, 145, 159, 191

Spartali, Marie, 21

Spengler, Oswald, 6

"Spirit of Civilisation, The" (Senghor), 188

split ending. *See* return and split ending

Stephen, Leslie, 23, 67, 136

Stesichorus, 11

Strabo, 42

Swift, Jonathan, 176

Sybaris, 42

Sybarites, 44–46

Symonds, John Addington, 45–46

taxonomy and naming: Césaire's *Cahier* and, 55, 184, 190; Odysseus, naming of, 121–22; Woolf and, 175–76

Telegony, 15–16, 162, 165–66, 169–70, 196

"Tell all the truth but tell it slant" (Dickinson), 209–10

Tennyson, Alfred, Lord, 195–96

"The City" (Cavafy), 83–87, 93–94

"thingification" ("*chosification*"), 111, 135, 183

Three Guineas (Woolf), 65

Timbuktu, 133–34

totem, 128–29, 137

To the Lighthouse (Woolf), 136

transgender, transsexuality, and trans* movements. *See* gender; *Orlando* (Woolf); sexual identity and ambiguity

travel madness, 116–17

trees: incised tree in Césaire's *Cahier*, 184–86, 189; olive-tree bed as sign in Homer's *Odyssey*, 169–70, 186; Orlando's "The Oak Tree," 71, 99, 137, 144, 173–74, 180–83

trial by ordeal, 192–94

trickery and tricksterism: in Césaire's *Cahier*, 56, 58–59, 133; folklore and, 125; in the *Iliad*, 80; layered border crossings and, 146; Odysseus as trickster, 82, 125–26; in the *Odyssey*, 2–3

tropes: defined, 17; diffusion, island, passage, and homecoming as, 18–20; multiforms vs., 17

Ulysses (Joyce), 2, 11, 12

"Ulysses" (Tennyson), 195–96

Vaughan, Margaret "Madge" Symonds, 46

Virgil, 2

Voyage Out, The (Woolf), 25

Walcott, Derek: Antillean foundation tales and, 53; *Omeros*, 2, 11, 52

wandering. *See* passage and detour

weaving: of Calypso, 79; of Helen, 36; of Penelope, 28, 36, 77

Wilde, Oscar: "Charmides," 50; *The Picture of Dorian Gray*, 86; trials, 93

Woolf, Leonard, 22, 24, 137

Woolf, Virginia: biographical sketch, 22–24; on Freud and taxonomizing, 175–76; invertism and, 92; mental illness, episodes of, 24, 96–97; photographs, significance of, 97–98; reflected in Athens cityscape, 9–10; themes of, 4; trans* studies and, 7; Vita Sackville-West and, 24, 67–68, 98–99, 180, 183; on writing as "shock-receiving capacity," 96

—works: "A Dialogue on Mount Pentelicus," 10, 23; "Modern Fiction," 181; *Mrs. Dalloway*, 136; "On Not Knowing Greek," 10; *A Room of One's Own*, 65, 143, 175; *A Sketch of the Past*, 24, 96; *Three Guineas*, 65; *To the Lighthouse*, 136; *The Voyage Out*, 25. See also *Orlando* (Woolf)

"Word" (A. Césaire), 62–63

Wordsworth, William, 104

writing: literary cannibalism in Césaire's *Cahier*, 132–33; orality and, 194–95, 210; Orlando's inkblot, 100, 178, 180; Orlando's "The Oak Tree," 71, 99, 137, 144, 173–74, 180–84; as passage, 19; Victorian literary misogyny in Woolf's *Orlando*, 176–77

Zambaco, Maria (born Ionides), 21

CLASSICAL MEMORIES/MODERN IDENTITIES

Paul Allen Miller and Richard H. Armstrong, Series Editors

Classical antiquity has bequeathed a body of values and a "cultural koine" that later Western cultures have appropriated and adapted as their own. However, the transmission of ancient culture was and remains a malleable and contested process. This series explores how the classical world has been variously interpreted, transformed, and appropriated to forge a usable past and a livable present. Books published in this series detail both the positive and negative aspects of classical reception and take an expansive view of the topic. Thus it includes works that examine the function of translations, adaptations, invocations, and classical scholarship in the formation of personal, cultural, national, sexual, and racial formations.

Modern Odysseys: Cavafy, Woolf, Césaire, and a Poetics of Indirection
MICHELLE ZERBA

Archive Feelings: A Theory of Greek Tragedy
MARIO TELÒ

The Ethics of Persuasion: Derrida's Rhetorical Legacies
BROOKE ROLLINS

Arms and the Woman: Classical Tradition and Women Writers in the Venetian Renaissance
FRANCESCA D'ALESSANDRO BEHR

Hip Sublime: Beat Writers and the Classical Tradition
EDITED BY SHEILA MURNAGHAN AND RALPH M. ROSEN

Ancient Sex: New Essays
EDITED BY RUBY BLONDELL AND KIRK ORMAND

Odyssean Identities in Modern Cultures: The Journey Home
EDITED BY HUNTER GARDNER AND SHEILA MURNAGHAN

Virginia Woolf, Jane Ellen Harrison, and the Spirit of Modernist Classicism
JEAN MILLS

Humanism and Classical Crisis: Anxiety, Intertexts, and the Miltonic Memory
JACOB BLEVINS

Tragic Effects: Ethics and Tragedy in the Age of Translation
THERESE AUGST

Reflections of Romanity: Discourses of Subjectivity in Imperial Rome
RICHARD ALSTON AND EFROSSINI SPENTZOU

Philology and Its Histories
EDITED BY SEAN GURD

Postmodern Spiritual Practices: The Construction of the Subject and the Reception of Plato in Lacan, Derrida, and Foucault
PAUL ALLEN MILLER